To: Mike
You have been and will always be one of our favorites. I'll be insulted if you don't come visit

Ed Dillard
2/28/94

BEHIND THE TIMES

BEHIND THE TIMES

INSIDE THE NEW *NEW YORK TIMES*

EDWIN DIAMOND

VILLARD BOOKS / NEW YORK / 1994

Villard Books is a registered trademark of Random House, Inc.

Library of Congress Cataloging-in-Publication Data

Diamond, Edwin.
Behind the Times : inside the new *New York Times* / by Edwin
Diamond.
p.   cm.
Includes index.
ISBN 0-679-41877-6
1. New York Times.   I. Title.
PN4844.N42N375   1994
071'.471—dc20   93-14744

Manufactured in the United States of America on acid-free paper

9 8 7 6 5 4 3 2 1

First Edition

Book design by JoAnne Metsch

To Justine, Jared, Leah, Chloe, Sasha, and Ethan,
who take us into the twenty-first century

CONTENTS

BEHIND THE TIMES

INTRODUCTION:
A LITTLE WILD STREAK

WEEKNIGHTS AT TEN, a driver leaves the New York Times Building on West 43rd Street and carries two copies of the first edition of the next day's paper to the West 67th Street residence of Max Frankel, the paper's executive editor. If Frankel is at a business dinner or social engagement, he may excuse himself to be home soon after the driver arrives. For the next two and a half hours, he reads the paper from front to back: news, features, reviews. Some nights, he pushes himself to look at the food recipes in the Living section, at the wedding notices, at the copy in the department stores' advertising. As Frankel explains it, he is trying to see the *Times* as its readers do, in finished form. He asks himself the traditional *Times* questions about whether the reader is reading a "*Times* kind of story" handled in a "*Times* way." But shortly after he took over the top editing job in late 1986, he added a fresh requirement: The *Times*, he concluded, must be made "user friendly" and inviting to read. Frankel keeps a memo pad beside him for writing notes to one or another of the nine hundred men and women who report, write, illustrate, edit, and lay out the paper. While some of his notes praise or criticize what he's just read, Frankel comments to his editors mostly on the overall product: Were there too many long pieces, or writing that was too wooden? Did the pictures and headlines invite readers into stories? The *Times*, he explains, reaching for an analogy, "is like a supermarket of news." The paper has to "keep all its shelves richly stocked." As readers hurry down the aisles, "We've got to tell them what's there." Frankel's exercise each night with newspaper and memo pad is designed to offer "systemic comments"—manager to staff—so that customers keep patronizing the supermarket. Ever the wordsmith, he's also likened the *Times* to a symphony orchestra, and himself to its conductor.

Frankel was fifty-six years old when he became the eleventh editor of the *New York Times*. Given the normal retirement age of sixty-five for news department executives, he can expect to run the *Times* until 1995. Just halfway through his tenure, however, he found that the *Times* all too often ran him.

The most public breakdown in the system occurred in the early spring of 1991. The news staff was coming down from the high of the Gulf war. The paper's extensive coverage of Operations Desert Shield and Desert Storm was an affirmation of the way the *Times* really saw itself: not a folksy marketplace but the world's greatest news-gathering organization—the institutional *Times*, balanced, thorough, authoritative, a colossus astride the globe. The allies' one-hundred-hour ground campaign over, George Bush riding high in the polls, Saddam Hussein beaten if not bowed, the *Times* took stock of its own performance. *Winners & Sinners*, an in-house bulletin used at the time by Frankel and his top editors to pass on comments about the staff's work, noted that it wanted to call an honor roll for the paper's coverage of the Gulf war—but it didn't have the space. "The men and women who have yet again made the paper mandatory reading for the country and the world at a time of crisis could not possibly be listed here without glaring omissions and distortion through truncation," the bulletin declared. "Just a list of those who have worked six- and seven-day weeks since the gulf crisis began would fill these pages and spill over. Our correspondents in the Middle East have been magnificent, their work supplemented splendidly by reporters in Washington, around the country and New York." Once again, the editors concluded, "to work at our newspaper is to experience awe."

Within a matter of weeks, the air of self-congratulation evaporated. Frankel's talk about "a *Times* kind of story" told in "a *Times* kind of way" took on new meaning. In the editions of Wednesday, April 17, 1991, the *Times* ran a profile of the woman who said she was raped by William Kennedy Smith at the Kennedy family estate in Palm Beach,

Florida, during the Easter holiday two weeks before. The story carried the double byline of Fox Butterfield and Mary B. W. Tabor. It disclosed that the woman's name was Patricia Bowman and offered, in numbing detail, particulars of her life, beginning with her birth date, August 11, 1961, in Akron, Ohio. Noting that she had a "poor academic record" at Tallmadge High School, the article went on to quote a school acquaintance who said Bowman was popular socially and "had a little wild streak." The *Times* helpfully explained that meant she "liked to drive fast cars, go to parties and skip classes." The profile reported that Bowman had been seriously hurt in a car crash, had attended a number of small colleges without graduating, and that she had a daughter born out of wedlock ("She had a brief affair with Johnny Butler . . . the father of her child, friends say. It is unclear why the couple did not marry"). Two paragraphs were devoted to her adult driving record, and the information that she received seventeen tickets for speeding, careless driving, and being involved in an accident between 1982 and 1990. An account of Bowman's barhopping nights on the Palm Beach "club scene" required another four paragraphs. A chef, interviewed by the *Times*, described how Bowman came by the restaurant where he worked late one night, ate a special meal he cooked for her, accompanied him to a bar, and then fell into a conversation with some other men—leaving him, the story said, "disappointed." The profile also took up the fast times and marital history of Bowman's mother. Jean Bowman, it seems, worked her way up from the secretarial pool of an Akron machinery company to a corporate position, divorced Bowman's father, and eventually married Michael G. O'Neil, the chairman of the General Tire and Rubber Company—"one of her company's largest customers," the *Times* noted. (In case anyone missed that point, the article included the information that Jean Bowman was named as the "other woman" in O'Neil's divorce.) In 1989, the *Times* reported, Patricia Bowman's stepfather O'Neil bought her a house near his retirement home, paying $161,800 for a "new contemporary three bedroom with pale peach walls." O'Neil was "successful," "blunt spoken," and "used to getting his way," the *Times* said, hinting at the theme that the two principals in the forthcoming rape trial were actually surrogates: the real story "pitted" one powerful, wealthy Irish Catholic against another powerful, wealthy Irish Catholic family, perhaps the most prominent in the country. The *Times* version presented Bowman as an unstable barfly looking for something more than a one-night stand, while the oafish Kennedy-Smith wanted only a little consensual fun. She was used and discarded, and Michael G. O'Neil didn't intend to take that lying down. (A *Times*man later told me O'Neil was a conservative who "hated" the Kennedys since the days of John and Robert Kennedy, but that the *Times* chose not to develop "the political angle" in the story.)

The *Times* ran the woman's profile on page 17. The story immediately became page-one news—in a dozen other papers. Frankel and the *Times* were excoriated for breaking with past practices and publishing the name of a woman involved in a rape case. The overall tone of the story was mocked in low and high places. The editor of the checkout-counter sheet, *National Enquirer*, piously noted that he chose not to print the woman's name: "I think we took a more ethical standard than the *Times* did." The president of the United States slyly announced at a Washington correspondents' dinner that while he no longer had the freedom to slip out of the White House and pick up one of the supermarket tabloids, "I can still read the *New York Times*." The loudest cries of pain came from the *Times* staff. A petition of protest expressing "disgust" at the story collected over one hundred names. Frankel, assistant managing editor Allan M. Siegal, and national editor Soma Golden appeared at an extraordinary staff meeting to explain to three hundred upset people the editors' handling of the story. "Hold your applause to the end," Frankel began lightly, in an attempt to lower the level of anger.

From the start, Frankel sought to frame the discussion at the meeting around the ethics of using rape victims' names and whether or not secrecy adds to the shame—a legitimate exercise of the kind that keeps graduate journalism classes going for a week or so. Several of his questioners, offended by the *Times*' attention to the nudge-wink details of Bowman's—and her mother's—life, tried to refocus on less philosophic matters. In its salacious tone and in the selected frissons of Bowman's life—leading on the chef for dinner, for example, then not giving him the gratuity he expected—the *Times* narrative came across as the journalistic equivalent of the men's locker-room verdict, "she's a tease who's asking for it." The *Times* rape story, from conception through final editing, in point of fact was largely a male enterprise, and a young *Times*woman, a recent hire from a smaller paper, rose at the meeting to express her bewilderment at some of the article's assumptions. "This isn't the *Times* I thought I was joining," she told Frankel.

The seminar-room discussions about ethical standards and sexist modes of thought missed the more immediate, practical lesson: specifically, the changed news standards at the *Times*. The headline over *Time* magazine's account of the *Times'* coverage went directly, if nastily, to this point: "Tarting Up the Gray Lady of 43rd Street," it read. In his analysis, *Time* writer Richard Lacayo suggested that the Bowman story was part of Frankel's effort to give the *Times* "a more with-it image."

Lacayo was on to one part of the story. The "paper of mandatory reading" during the Gulf war and other global crises had, on the side, developed its own little wild streak. The Florida rape story appeared only a few days after the *Times* ran, on page one, Washington bureau reporter Maureen Dowd's uncritical preview of *Nancy Reagan: The Unauthorized Biography*. Among the book's more sensational "revelations," author Kitty Kelley insinuated, and the *Times* passed on, the hot news that Mrs. First Lady dallied with Frank Sinatra in the White House when Mr. President was away. During the spring of 1991, too, the *Times* ran prominent articles on polygamy in Utah, the popularity of do-it-yourself sex videos, and, on the front page of the Home section, the trend among teenagers to have their friends sleep over (in the same bed). "Each of these features worked on its merits," remembered Josh Mills, a Business Day editor who participated in the news conferences at which some of these stories were pitched by the national desk. "But they added up to more of the frequent departures from, shall we say, 'our conservative voice.' " A *Times* metro reporter said she and other reporters found themselves wondering "if the markers were shifted in the middle of the night, and the rules changed."

Times journalists make their living in part by trying to connect the dots and visualize the Big Picture. A number of outwardly disparate elements appeared to come together in the spring of 1991: the Kennedys . . . and sex, the Reagans . . . and sex, Mormons . . . and sex, home videos . . . and sex, teenagers . . . and sex. Some reporters continued to resist the inference, preferring to believe that the dots did not connect. "I would warn you away from grand theories about downshifts at the *Times*," said Alan Finder, a metro-desk reporter. "When you run one hundred stories a day, there are going to be screwups." Other reporters believed there was no single Big Picture plan but rather Frankel's more modest goal of making parts of the news report lighter and more inviting: the read-young, with-it, "user friendly" *Times.* "Reporters kept hearing from their desk editors the phrase, 'Let's liven up this story,' " said E. R. Shipp, another metro reporter.

When the new publisher Arthur Sulzberger, Jr., and Frankel were asked about the wild streak of stories involving Bowman, Reagan, sex videos, and sleepover friends, they maintained that the "ideas" were usually right but that at times the "execution" was off. Sulzberger was particularly animated: "While we made mistakes in the way we handled the rape story, a lot of people did do the right thing. Fox Butterfield did right in the information he collected. The national desk did right in its editing and Al Siegal did right in his editing. But somehow, when it all came together, it wasn't right." Sulzberger's editors offered a number of little-picture explanations for their failures of "execution": misconstrued instructions, deadline pressures, fumbled responsibilities among desks ("I thought you were watching it . . .", "Well, I thought *you* were watching it . . ."). At most, the official *Times* conceded certain vague "deficiencies in editing." As an "Editors' Note" in the editions of April 26 explained, while the Florida rape story was presented in such a way that *Times* readers might "infer" the woman's account was being challenged by the *Times,* "no such challenge was intended, and the *Times* regrets that some parts of the article reinforced such inferences." "Editors' Note" boxes appear from time to time in the same space near the bottom left-hand side of page two; they are the top editors' way of publicly apportioning responsibility for individual or institutional errors of judgment. In the Bowman case, however, the Note clumsily tried to shift part of the blame to the readers—for responding to the article's cues and making mean-spirited "inferences." Similarly, at the staff meeting, when a questioner remarked that a lot of people thought the story was punitive and sexist, Soma Golden, the *Times'* national editor, replied that she couldn't be held accountable for the conclusions drawn by "every weird mind that reads the *New York Times.*"

The Bowman story was no aberration existing in the overactive imaginations of readers. The markers at the *Times* began to be moved and the Gray Lady hustled toward retirement almost two decades before, during the regime of Frankel's predecessor, A. M. Rosenthal. Abe Rosenthal was an advocate of more aggressive news coverage—when the subject didn't brush up against one or another of his prejudices. He was initially disparaged for introducing the soft, life-style sections of the 1970s but they helped win new upmarket readers and improved the *Times'* advertising revenues at a time when New York City had just avoided municipal bankruptcy and was still losing manufacturing jobs. His successor, Frankel, was under pressure as well in the summer of 1991. The *Times'* circulation had reached an all-time high, daily (1.1 million) and Sunday (1.7 million); but the long recession throughout the New York region and the Northeast cut deeply into advertising revenues and made circulation sales all the more important for the financial health of the paper. This truism led outsiders, as well as some *Times*people, to a Big Picture conclusion: In pursuit of circulation, the Frankel *Times* was willing to get down and scratch for the kind of dirt that, in the past, it left to the city's rude tabloids.

The notion that the *Times* was trying to muscle in on its crosstown competition had a certain surface plausibility. The city's tabs looked extremely vulnerable in the summer of 1991. The *Daily News* had just emerged from a costly strike, only to fall into the dubious embrace of a new owner, the highly leveraged British press magnate Robert Maxwell (within seven months Maxwell was dead and the *News* headed for bankruptcy court). The *New York Post's* finances were shaky (in a matter of months, too, owner Peter Kalikow filed for personal bankruptcy). New York *Newsday*, while journalistically respectable and bankrolled in part by earnings from the older, established *Newsday*, still had not achieved sustained profitability. From the *Times'* vantage point, why not show a little streak of sex and sensation to attract people hurrying past newsstands or street boxes? Decades before, Adolph Ochs figured out a way to get stories of crime and New York lowlife into his proper pages; he treated them as "sociology."

In fact, the marketing-conscious *Times* disdained one-shot impulse buys. That was the tabs' desperate tactic. The *Times* of the 1990s didn't need raw circulation numbers; it needed specific subscribers in order to sell a carefully tuned demographic profile to advertisers. When the *Times* had the chance to pick up tab readership during the *News'* 1990–91 strike, the Sulzbergers deliberately chose not to do so. The *News'* circulation dropped by almost two-thirds from its prestrike levels of 1.09 million, largely because the *News* management couldn't get the papers delivered (the striking unions' legal picketing—and their extralegal acts of intimidation—insured that result). Opportunity knocking, the *Times* made no effort to open the door to let in any of the hundreds of thousands of *News* readers bereft of their morning paper. From the upmarket vantage point of the *Times*, these readers deserved to be kept outside; they were the great unwashed. No one said any of this, of course; but the *Times'* *in*action spoke louder than any words: Arthur Sulzberger ordered no more than 35,000 extra copies printed daily during the strike. That way, a *Times*man explained, *Times* readers who bought the paper at newsstands were assured of getting "their" copies even if an uninvited *News* reader had, earlier, bought a newsstand *Times*. The *Times'* desired demographic mix was saved from contamination. "We are never going to be the *Daily News*," Arthur Sulzberger said cheerfully. More cheerfully still, he added: "Why would we ever want to be?"

In the summer of 1991, however, the *Times* did worry about some rivals farther from home. A significant amount of its circulation growth in recent years came from well beyond New York, from sales in the Northeast corridor running from Boston to Washington, and from the *Times* national edition, which reached a circulation of 250,000 in 1991. To some extent, the *Times* competed for readers' and advertisers' attention with the two national dailies, the *Wall Street Journal* and *USA Today*; with strong regional papers like the *Washington Post* and the *Chicago Tribune*, and with the newsweeklies. Yet this competition didn't sufficiently explain the *Times'* jumpiness, either. A totally different kind of "competition" was making the *Times* nervous: Arthur Sulzberger worried less about the *Times* losing readers to another newspaper than he did about readers losing the *Times*-newspaper habit. The extensive market research commissioned by the publisher's office was full of warnings about the enemy of inattention. According to these surveys, endlessly quoted around the building, Americans under forty like to spend their time "omnidirectionally"—stretching and watching morning television, or listening to the radio while driving to work. The act of reading a newspaper is, sadly, unidirectional: It requires some single-minded engagement. Such fears about the end of newspapers were not confined to the proprietors of the *Times*. The same month that the Reagan and Bowman stories appeared, *presstime*, the publication of the American Newspaper Publishers Association, commended to members a report on how newspapers are changing "to entice readers." (Shortly thereafter, the ANPA changed too, renaming itself the Newspaper Association of America.)

Editors accustomed to looking at their handiwork with feelings of reverence weren't likely to be put off by the challenge of enticing omnidirectional thirtysomethings: the awe-inspiring *New York Times* can handle it. But enticement journalism turned out to be trickier than expected for Frankel and his editors.

The news desk was, as usual, slow off the mark in handling Palm Beach with tab-type stories. The first accounts of Bowman's charges and the pretrial police investigation were played far back in the paper, under a sedate, one-column headline (an A head, in *Times* talk). The national competition, such as the *Miami Herald* and the *Washington Post*, was consistently ahead during the first week of the story. In the city, the *New York Post*—financially hobbled, its depleted reporting staff restricted to four-day work weeks—beat the *Times* to the "news" that there was a second woman at the Kennedy mansion the night of the alleged rape. Better yet for newsstand purposes, the woman claimed she spotted Senator Edward M. Kennedy without his pants on. The *Post* teased the headline "Teddy's Sexy Romp" out of this scooplet— and sold 20,000 extra copies on the streets of New York that afternoon. The *Times* remained immobile until the Bowman narrative began to create that critical mass of sexual titillation, celebrity voyeurism, and TV frenzy that makes certain stories "hot news." Others took the lead with the sensational details. Slowly, the *Times* committed its resources; Soma Golden later remarked that, personally, she found the whole case "a bit unsavory . . . but competitively you've got a story that everyone's on."

Frankel's *Times* may weigh in late on hot news, but once it does so, the results must be authoritative, with the most diligent reporting, magazine-quality presentation, and the resonant "sociology" of it all. The pattern was set the year before, in the *Times'* treatment of the Tawana Brawley rape case and the Father Bruce Ritter scandal. In each case, Frankel and his editors let weeks go by while other news organizations reported on the day to day developments. Then they assigned teams of four or more experienced reporters to the stories and gave them all the resources they needed, with no firm deadlines to report back. The teams produced fresh, exhaustively sourced information, and the articles based on their researches ran well over two thousand words each, the length of a magazine cover story. These were "blockbusters" that "settled" the cases, at least to the *Times'* satisfaction. The Brawley story concluded that the black teenager invented her tale of rape by a gang of whites. The Ritter story decided that the

Catholic priest, the revered founder of Covenant House for troubled young runaways, had extracted homosexual favors from two of the teenage residents. Other news organizations had earlier come to the same conclusions in each case, but their reports lacked the force of the *Times'*. Ritter, for example, denied the charges against him when they initially appeared in the *New York Post*, and continued with his ministry. Several weeks went by, the *Times* story was published—and, literally in a matter of hours, Ritter left New York for "study and prayer" under instructions from his order. End of the Father Ritter story.

Fox Butterfield, the senior writer of the "Wild Streak" article, had been a *Times* foreign correspondent as well as author of a superb book about China, *Alive in the Bitter Sea*. He was a star reporter for the metro desk when the *Times'* investigative team discredited Tawana Brawley's story (it was Butterfield who later explained to me the strategy of the *Times'* blockbuster approach). In April 1991, when Patricia Bowman made her charges of rape, Butterfield was chief of the Boston bureau, doubling as a "swing reporter" available to the national desk for big stories. Butterfield was well connected socially (the industrialist Cyrus Eaton was his grandfather) and he knew the various Kennedys of Massachusetts and Washington. Soma Golden assigned the team of Butterfield and Mary Tabor, a news assistant in the Boston bureau, to Palm Beach a week after Bowman made her accusations. Golden later told the staff meeting that Butterfield and Tabor received the assignment because the *Times'* Miami bureau man, Roberto Suro, "was away for the week." A *Times*woman who heard the explanation thought it incredibly lame. She wanted to ask Golden: "What week was that?" Another *Times*woman did confront Golden, asking about the wisdom of giving the Palm Beach assignment to a "well-known friend of the Kennedy family." Golden said she knew of no such connection.

Other staff members wanted to know if Butterfield and Tabor had lifted the smarmier scenes from the life of Bowman out of the files of Kennedy staff investigators. The official reply, that "all the reporting was the *Times'*," was an exquisitely Talmudic answer. Conceivably, all the information could have come from shoe-leather reporting and from computer data bases accessed from Palm Beach: the woman's grades from her high school in Ohio; her driver's record from the Florida department of highway safety; her mother's sexual history from divorce court proceedings; the barhopping stories from other barflies; the sales price of the three-bedroom house from deeds registered in county files. Palm Beach is a small resort community, where gossip is the second major occupation, after good living. But Butterfield and Tabor, for all their presumed skills, joined the story in progress, well after a blockbuster team of lawyers and private investigators hired by the Kennedy family was on the case. Narrowly, it was possible that "all the reporting" was the *Times'*—developed from knowledgeable leads and photocopied materials proffered by good sources.

The *Times'* strategy of revealing the name of the woman was less artfully explained. Frankel said that he had been wrestling for some time with the question of the *Times'* "obligation" to print what it finds out in stories of wide public interest. The case of the jogger raped in Central Park just a year before had bothered him: the biographical details of her life laid bare, her name spoken in court and printed in the *Amsterdam News*, a small-circulation weekly intended for black New Yorkers, but not carried in the *Times*. Frankel formed a committee of editors to think about the policies the *Times* ought to follow. While the committee pondered, as committees do, reality intruded. Tuesday afternoon, April 16, Al Siegal, the custodian of *Times* style and correct usage, was doing a final edit on the Butterfield-Tabor copy. Siegal made extensive changes, with Golden at his side; later she told the staff meeting that almost a third of the story—"the racier copy"— was cut. Shortly after 6:30 P.M. "NBC Nightly News" broadcast Bowman's name as part of an NBC report on whether news organizations should broadcast (!) the name of rape victims. Siegal and Golden inserted Bowman's name in the story; a seven-paragraph explanatory "policy sidebar," to run next to the main article, was quickly written under their supervision. "The *New York Times* ordinarily shields the identities of complainants in sex crimes, while awaiting the courts' judgment about the truth of their accusations," the sidebar said. Then, shifting into a third-person voice, Siegal-Golden quoted themselves: "The *Times* has withheld Ms. Bowman's name until now, but editors said yesterday that NBC's nationwide broadcast took the matter of her privacy out of their hands."

The chain of helplessness didn't begin there. NBC offered for *its* excuse the fact that *The Globe*, a supermarket tabloid, ran Bowman's name and a grainy photo of her the day before. And *The Globe*, in its prim turn, pointed to the *London Sunday Mirror*, which had identified

Bowman and published her picture the week before. Several *Times*-people found the Siegal-Golden citation of television laughable: "When have we ever given a shit what NBC said before," I was told by a reporter who attended the staff meeting. Michael Gartner, the president of NBC News and a law school graduate, at least stood on half-firm ground when he made his decision. A First Amendment absolutist, Gartner had for years made the argument that press accounts ought to treat rape victims like other victims of violent crime, "to take the stigma out of being raped." After the rape-beating of the Central Park jogger, Gartner argued both publicly and within NBC News for the use of her name on principle ("specifics add credibility to the story"). There was also the matter of fairness, pending a jury's verdict: during the Central Park arraignments and trial, the accused rapists, blacks and Hispanics from the projects, were named. The jogger, white, Wellesley- and Yale-educated, an investment banker, was not.

The *Times'* editors could make no such claims of consistency. During the jogger case, the editors withheld her name. Then, Al Siegal pushed off responsibility onto the *Times'* readers, as Golden later did in the Bowman case. "News organizations don't function in a vacuum," Siegal said in April 1990. "Society would find it repugnant to add to her obloquy. If we faced a similar degree of revulsion from our readers at revealing defendants, we'd consider it."

What changed for the *Times* when the scene of the alleged rapes moved from Central Park to Palm Beach? Some of the protesters detected class bias at work: the community college drop-out accorded less consideration than the Yale MBA and Wall Street banker (the perfect *Times* reader, demographically). *Times* columnist Anna Quindlen made just such a charge in her Sunday Op-Ed page space two days after the staff meeting; as far as the editors of the *Times* were concerned, Quindlen wrote, women who have prestigious jobs will be treated more fairly than "women who have 'below average' high school grades [and] are well known at bars and dance clubs." Others wanted to know why the *Times* hadn't produced a similar investigative profile of the well-connected man in the case, William Kennedy Smith. They were told, "one is in the works." (When it eventually appeared, there were new outcries. A *Washington Post* profile of Kennedy Smith quoted several women, most of them anonymously, who described his loutish and sometimes violent sexual behavior; the *Times'* Kennedy

Smith article, produced by the Washington bureau, didn't include these alleged episodes. Bureau people later said they were unable to confirm the accounts to the editors' "satisfaction.")

If not social standing as a determinant of *Times* treatment, then perhaps some cultural gap separated the buttoned-down, over-fifty senior *Times*men from the barhopping Palm Beach woman, and from some of their own junior reporters. The heaviest applause during the staff meeting came when a *Times*woman, age thirty, told Frankel and Siegal: "I go places at night with people you might find questionable, and God forbid anything should happen to me, because I'm sure you could find someone that I went to high school with who'd be willing to say anonymously that I had a 'wild streak.' " There was considerable intellectualizing about why the male editors "didn't get it," or seemed punitive about a woman involved in date rape (Palm Beach) as opposed to stranger rape (Central Park). More than anything, though, the staff overlooked a practical explanation for the Bowman story: the editors had already made an investment of the *Times'* prestige in the Palm Beach story. A team of investigative reporters and supervising editors had produced a "competitive" story over several days of high-profile effort, and the editors wanted it out. NBC provided the opening to detonate the blockbuster, and permit the *Times* to settle the case that "everyone was on." The use of Bowman's name made it possible for the *Times* to introduce the stepfather's name and complete the social drama: the House of O'Neil against the House of Kennedy.

All the talk of "deadline pressures" made it sound as if the Butterfield-Tabor story somehow slipped through the system, when actually everyone involved knew what was expected from them. The "little wild streak" quote was so attractive that the copy editor repeated it in the subhead. Moreover, the story appeared in the editions of April 17 together with an article on Edward M. Kennedy filed by correspondent Robin Toner from Washington. The Toner story reported on the commencement address Senator Kennedy had given at American University the day before; it went on to describe how Kennedy was the senate's "most visible standard bearer for liberal causes," despite all the tab headlines and, seemingly, a persistent drinking habit. The Toner story began on page one and continued on page 17, allowing the *Times* to present the narratives of Bowman and Kennedy as a package. At the top of page 17, the headline informed readers: "Woman in Florida Rape Inquiry Fought Adversity and Sought Acceptance." Below, readers learned: "Torn by His Roles on Life's Stage, Kennedy Can't Avoid Dark Cloud." It was a neat twinning of the traditional public-policy *Times* and the contemporary enticement *Times*, the old Journal of Record and the new homage to *People* magazine.

When Patricia Bowman testified during the Kennedy Smith trial, the TV networks used electronics to project a blue dot over her face, to keep up the pretense of anonymity. After the Florida jury returned a not-guilty verdict on the rape charge, Bowman decided to defend her version of the encounter. She appeared, sans dot, on national television with Diane Sawyer of ABC News. One year later, Frankel was asked to reconstruct the *Times'* handling of the Bowman story—to remove the dot, so to speak, obscuring the *Times'* processes. He agreed. "There were several days of great tension because of two *Times* policies," Frankel recalled. "First, the policy of protecting the anonymity of victims of sex assault. Second, a similar policy of not naming the accused until there are official charges. The accused being a Kennedy Smith, the whole thing got out of control." Frankel remembered that he grew increasingly upset. "We were doing something very unfair to the accused, and we did not have the slightest suggestion in print as to who the accuser was: a Palm Beach socialite? A whore? Or what? So I pressed very hard for every biographical detail that we could get, even if we weren't going to name her. The reader was entitled to know who was making these accusations. Then we ran into trouble: the stepfather and his wealth, and his hiring of fancy lawyers. If we couldn't name her, we couldn't name him. His company was one of the Fortune 500. We were absolutely bound up in a mess. We had no way to tell the true story of who was attacking Kennedy Smith as long as we stuck to the policy of anonymity. I said, 'OK. So we can't name her and we can't name her stepfather. Let's do the best we can.' That very night, we're working on the biographical sketch, and NBC pushed the name out. I said, 'That solves our problem.' It never occurred to me that after twelve million people knew the name, the press would still pretend that anonymity existed. NBC not only solved our problem, but it forced us to rush our biography into print that night, when we might have wanted to work on it another day or two. In the rush, that story was not as deftly done as it should have been." Frankel concluded: "We got it in the neck both ways. The rest of the world still pretending that the name was private and the press attacking us—with some cause—about aspects of the story we printed."

I asked Frankel his reactions to the Anna Quindlen column criticizing his decisions, and whether the *Times'* policy on the anonymity of rape victims had changed. "If she wants to debate our policy, fine," he replied. "I think she's wrong. I still don't think it was a mistake to name the victim, under the circumstances. I think the story could have been written better. What I resented was that Quindlen didn't come to me first to find out what she was disagreeing about. But that's her business."

The uncritical handling of Kitty Kelley's *Nancy Reagan: The Unauthorized Biography* resulted from another conjunction of old *Times* and new *Times*. Normally, major publishing houses send review copies of new books to newspapers and magazines well in advance of publication date. No one worries much about reviews that "break" the news-release date because 999 out of one thousand new books contain no stop-press news worth breaking. Not so with the oeuvre of Kelley, "America's premier slash biographer." Simon & Schuster had a major investment in the Nancy Reagan book, paying Kelley a reported $3.5 million advance against royalties. Together, author and publisher devised a clever promotion plan to insure that everyone would get a big payday. To build early suspense, the publishers tightly controlled the book's galleys and held back all review copies—except two. The week before the official Monday, April 8, publication date, one of these copies was, in the press's patois, "made available" to the *Times*. The second advance copy went to Garry Trudeau, the creator of "Doonesbury," which at the time was syndicated to seven hundred newspapers around the world. The pairing was exquisite. Kelley and her publishers stood to get a *Times* news story over the weekend, which meant high-road exposure for the book. The next week, when Simon & Schuster shipped books to the stores, millions of "Doonesbury" readers could check out a series of Trudeau's strips based on materials in the book. It was the kind of masterly manipulation of the media that Michael Deaver, Ronald Reagan's publicity specialist, would have appreciated.

The scheme generated the expected attention, and more. Frankel and his editors decided to messenger the book to Maureen Dowd of the Washington bureau. "I got the book at midnight," Dowd later told the journalist Jeffrey Goodell. "I stayed up all night and read it." According to Dowd, her editors told her to "write it out straight"—no analysis or interpretation. Her story was placed on page one of the *Sunday Times* of April 7. The idea, once again, was fine in the abstract: A Kitty Kelley unauthorized biography was guaranteed to be an enticement-news event. No matter how familiar and trashed-over the celebrities that Kelley chooses for her subjects, she usually manages to scrape up a few malignant specimens of scandal in the private recesses of their lives. In *Jackie Oh!* Kelley "disclosed" that Jacqueline Kennedy Onassis received electroshock treatments for depression. And in *His Way: The Unauthorized Biography of Frank Sinatra*, Kelley replayed the old legends of the singer's friendship with organized crime figures, while adding the indispensable "news" from yellowed newspaper clips that his mother, Dolly, was the neighborhood abortionist back home in Hoboken, New Jersey, a half century before.

Maureen Dowd seemed like the right person to handle the Kelley book. In the spring of 1991 Dowd was one of the *Times'* White House correspondents. She was a thirty-one-year-old reporter for *Time* magazine when the *Times* hired her as a metro desk reporter in 1983; three years later she joined the Washington bureau in time to cover the last years of the Reagan presidency. While working for the *Times*, she kept her hand in magazine work, contributing a satirical advice column to the monthly *Mademoiselle* (Dowd used the pen name "Rebecca Sharp," after the plucky, scheming character in Thackeray's *Vanity Fair*). Dowd was a rising star of the Frankel era, much praised by the New York editors for what they regarded as her "stylish" writing and distinct "voice." The editors encouraged her to do lively features; she didn't disappoint with her Kelley article.

Frankel later told associates that he thought he had signed off on an article about the Kelley book that would stress the public policy angle—how the unelected Nancy Reagan tyrannized the White House staff and generally directed her actor-husband in the role of his lifetime, the President of the United States. The Dowd story started out high-mindedly, then jumped to innuendo. Kelley's book described Nancy Reagan's and Sinatra's long, closed-door "lunches" in the White House private quarters, with quote marks around the word to imply what Kelley—and the publishers' lawyers—weren't willing to say directly: that Nancy Reagan and Sinatra were having an affair in the White House. Dowd's article brushed by Kelley's previous publishing history, as well as her habit of conflating rumor and fact. Mike Wallace, the CBS newsman (and Nancy Reagan friend), complained to the *Boston Globe* about Dowd's complaisant treatment of the Kelley methodology. "If you're going to be used the way the *Times* was, then you check your facts . . . or you take the five most scandalous stories and check them out. You do not print the gory details in uncritical fashion." Wallace thought that, at a minimum, the *Times* should have run a companion piece, exploring "Who's Kitty Kelley and what's her track record." Wallace also said that he talked to Nancy Reagan and that she felt bruised by the book and "ticked off at the *Times.*"

Frankel appeared to side with Wallace and the other critics of the Dowd article. At the staff meeting protesting the Bowman story, Frankel said that the Dowd piece was "not up to *Times* standards." Once again, good idea, bad execution. Some of Frankel's auditors thought he was laying off responsibility too far down the line, to the writer who produced the lively copy expected of her and to the Washington desk editors who flagged the "New York Special" through, without slowing it down. Dowd certainly thought she was being unfairly treated. The protest meeting was relayed via speakerphone to Washington, where several bureau people, including Dowd, were listening. When Frankel's comments came over the line, Dowd, flushed and angered, rushed out of the room. She had to be persuaded not to resign. She had done what she was asked to do—turned the story around in two days, in a lively manner, and for her efforts she was put down.

The argument that the editors didn't know the contents of the Kelley story impressed no one. *Times* reporters contend daily with a huge, hierarchical, multilayered editing system: copy desks, department desks, "backfield" editors who oversee the work of the news desks, and behind them, the North Wall, or simply, The Wall, the collective of senior editors—and their deputies and assistants—sitting along the 44th Street side of the newsroom. "I can't buy the story that 'they bought it sight unseen,' " E. R. Shipp later said. A second reporter who spoke out at the staff meeting said flatly: "They wanted the titillation." Even if Dowd didn't finish her story until Saturday morning, she still had to run it by several editors. Frankel himself had created a news department structure to insure total control of what appeared on page one; star stylists were not excepted. There were special procedures for the Sunday edition, in part because the Sunday report sold 50 percent more copies than the daily and was something of a showcase for the *Times'* most enticing efforts, and in part because of the usual weekend slowdown in hard news. With fewer "yesterday" and "today" stories of Congress, government agencies, and City Hall, desk editors felt added pressure to find the trend stories Frankel wanted in the paper. Consequently, each week on Wednesday, department desks circulated a list of the proposed Sunday page-one lineup to the senior editors. On Thursdays, the senior editors met to go over the list with the weekend editor, whose principal functions were to track trend stories already being developed and to commission new ideas. On Fridays, the weekend editor brought the lineup to the managing editor, Joseph Lelyveld, and to Frankel. On Saturdays, Frankel made it a point to call in and check the lineup with the weekend editor—several times during the day, if necessary.

All the layers, meetings, phone calls, and backup systems made the *Times* the *Times*. It was—had been for decades—an editors' paper. Frankel talked up good writing, and introduced *more* supervisors. In hundreds of hours of interviews, I never encountered a *Times* reporter or writer who complained about the *under*editing of stories. How then did the experienced editors handling the Bowman case and the Reagan book manage to trip on their own cleverness? A *Times*woman with twenty-plus years at the paper offered one explanation. "The *Times* is an elitist paper, and our editors have elegant, elitist minds," she said. "When such minds try to think in popular nonelitist terms, they miss badly. We get 'wild streaks.' "

No one editor, obviously, can control all the words and images that pour into the *Times*, daily and on Sunday. Frankel's initial efforts with his midnight notepad were directed at "process" and "systems." He gradually remade the centralized structure he had inherited from his predecessor Abe Rosenthal and worked toward a more collegial newsroom. The Sulzbergers didn't want radical change on the third floor when they appointed Frankel. His assignment was to preserve the *Times*' position as a world-class newspaper and as a successful business enterprise—"to ensure the continuum," in Frankel's words. The paper's image of respected authority, and its capacity for making money, had to be maintained. But the overly aggressive displays of power of the immediate past needed reigning in: The family, befitting the tradition of Our Crowd, wanted the news department to go about its business less noisily. Frankel more or less succeeded; he created the impression of collegiality. Frankel adopted the practice of beginning his regular memos to the staff with the salutation: "Friends." He converted part of the spacious third-floor office he inherited from Rosenthal into a conference area for North Wall meetings. Frankel appointed Soma

Golden national editor, and promoted other women to positions of responsibility. The daily page-one meetings changed; "Frankel listened, and asked 'ordinary guy' questions, instead of hostile putdowns," a participant reported. The shift in atmospherics reached the arts and culture desks far from The Wall. "We sensed a flexibility and the chance for more cultural stories out front," the film critic Janet Maslin said. "Page one was suddenly up for grabs." Frankel ended the copy desk practice of not permitting a reporter to have more than one byline per edition (by the old reasoning, two bylines in the paper might cause people to conclude that "the stories were not reported carefully enough"—as if *Times* readers kept score). Frankel also encouraged the desks to be generous in crediting other publications when a *Times* story picked up materials that first appeared somewhere else. Thus, in the *Times* of August 4, 1992, the lead campaign story credited a *Washington Post* article for its account of the Clinton camp's plans to deal with "bimbo eruptions." Across the page, political reporter Richard Berke had two bylines for separate stories on George Bush's sputtering reelection effort. Frankel's "staff friendly" administration was an improvement on the Rosenthal years: The newsroom remained vast and impersonal, but the discord level was lowered.

Frankel's efforts to make the *Times'* news pages more user friendly were less successful. Or rather, they sometimes succeeded too well. The bizarre behavior—the little wild streaks—of the Frankel years tended to break out when the *Times* strained to be less *Times*-like. Long before the Patricia Bowman and Nancy Reagan episodes, Frankel's *Times* experimented with enticement journalism. It started tentatively enough, with a remarkable article by reporter Jane Gross. "There is a single woman in New York, bright and accomplished, who dreads nightfall, when darkness hugs the city and lights go on in warm kitchens," Gross's article began. From page one onto the jump, or continuation, of the story, Gross required almost 2,400 words to tell a tale intended to touch thousands of *Times* readers. The "bright and accomplished" woman wasn't homeless and sleeping in the dark streets; she could fill her refrigerator easily. Still, she suffered; she was unmarried, Gross explained, and nearing forty, and there were only so many straight, single men out there. In short, yuppie angst.

Frankel signaled that he wanted to run more such impressionistic, magazine-length articles, but the ideas came easier than the execution.

As far back as the 1988 presidential race, the *Times* decided to plumb the candidates' personal habits and private life. Presidential "character" had become a legitimate focus of press attention in Lyndon Johnson's Vietnam years and during the disgrace of Watergate in Richard Nixon's second term. Every four years since, the *Times* and other news organizations took their Eagle Scout oath to offer coverage that was more thorough, more analytical, more comprehensive. In his turn, Frankel decided on a fresh way to get at character. The Washington bureau sent out a questionnaire to the active presidential candidates. Bureau chief Craig Whitney asked each man (no women were running) to waive his rights of privacy for any government or medical files that may exist on him, and to make this material available to the *Times*. The questionnaire also asked for birth certificates, marriage and drivers' licenses, employment records, lists of friends and advisers, and financial and tax documents showing net worth. The prospect of a *Times* search of raw FBI files, with their pages of unsubstantiated, often malicious rumor and gossip, angered several of the candidates. Senator Paul Simon tartly reminded Whitney that "we are all candidates for the presidency, not for sainthood." A candidate agitated by the questionnaire leaked it to the *Times'* competitors. They quickly pounced.

The ensuing uproar played out as a preview of the wild times of 1991. The Quindlen part of angry columnist was taken by A. M. Rosenthal, newly transferred to the *Times* Op-Ed page from the news department. Rosenthal noted the press's new appetite for sexual candor. He suggested, though not by name, that Frankel, Whitney, and the other character police disclose more about themselves; "Correspondents and editors, have you ever committed adultery?" Rosenthal asked. "Homosexual experiences, any? Names, please." Frankel played the Frankel part, avuncularly explicating the *Times'* case for the "valid pursuit" of character in a staff memo intended to allay concerns about the snooping *Times*. "Friends," he began. "There's been some lively debate about the extent of our interest in the personal lives and backgrounds of presidential aspirants." Frankel acknowledged that "we have put some questions to candidates that reach a bit too far." The *Times* would no longer seek FBI or CIA files, or those medical records that "do not bear on a person's fitness for the Presidency." Nevertheless the *Times* would continue to press for relevant medical records, such as information about diseases requiring heavy medication, as well as financial and personal data. Frankel then brought up "the further question of social and sexual conduct." Such conduct would continue to be relevant for the *Times*, he said, "mostly because the candidates themselves have paraded their wives and families and fidelity to family values before the public by way of claiming certain character and personality traits. Where these claims turn out to be fraudulent, they are as noteworthy as any other serious misrepresentation to the electorate. Reports on family life, or the lack of it, are not normally the stuff of front-page headlines, but they can have their place in rounded portraits of a politician's character."

As usual, Frankel had produced a cogent argument, making the intellectual case for the campaign-press's coverage of sexual fidelity —or more precisely, infidelity. By 1992, however, during Bill Clinton's race for the presidency, Frankel argued against his own principles. *Star*, a weekly tabloid sold at newsstands and supermarket checkout counters, publicized the claim of Gennifer Flowers, a former television actress and aspiring country-and-western singer, that she had a twelve-year-long affair with Clinton. In fact, *Star* did in 1992 a cut-rate version of what Frankel had proposed to do in 1988; *Star* reporters talked to people who knew the candidate and examined relevant court documents in Little Rock (Flowers's name was initially made public the year before in connection with a law suit brought against Clinton by a dismissed Arkansas state employee). True, *Star* did some things that the *Times* would never do. It staged a news conference to present Flowers to the world; it produced an audiotape of steamy conversations, apparently between the singer and the governor. The weekly also paid a reported $100,000 for Flowers's story— cash for trash—and then boasted that it would earn back the money, and more, by distributing a larger press run of the issue featuring Flowers.

Frankel's *Times* was slow to pick up *Star*'s tale of infidelity. When the *Times'* first story appeared, it was well back in the paper. Just as the prominence that the *Times* gave Patricia Bowman and Nancy Reagan became big news in other newspapers and magazines, so too did the *Times'* burial of Flowers's story excite wide comment. When Howard Kurtz of the *Washington Post* called to ask about the *Times'* studied disinterest in the *Star* story, Frankel announced: "I'm quite ashamed for my profession." What really bothered him was the execution, not the idea. "We don't want to take our news report [on the candidates' sex lives] from the likes of the *Star*, or from someone whose ultimate veracity we can't vouch for." *The* Times *hadn't done the reporting.* Logically, if Flowers had come forward first to the *Times*, not asked for money, talked to the editors, played her tapes, and given the names of corroborating sources (the ones she supplied to *Star*), then her story would have been *"Times* news."

Police-blotter stories bedeviled Frankel's *Times* as much as presidential politics. In *Outrage: The Story Behind the Tawana Brawley Hoax,* a team of *Times* reporters described another adventure of the new enticement *Times.* Together, authors Robert D. McFadden, Ralph Blumenthal, M. A. Farber, E. R. Shipp, Charles Strum, and Craig Wolff represented over one hundred years of *Times* experience. McFadden et al. attempt to explain why the *Times'* first account of the Brawley case amounted to no more than "a shallow dip" in a complex story, why no follow-up story appeared for six weeks, and why the editors didn't pursue the case vigorously for nearly another eleven weeks. "If the *Times* was sometimes slow to react," the Brawley team explained, "it was generally because its editors knew that sensational events often proved chimerical. Moreover, they knew all too well how the *Times,* by its unique weight in the news business, could catapult obscure events to the forefront of the nation's consciousness, setting the news agenda each morning for the networks, local television and radio stations, and hundreds of newspapers and magazines. A misstep by the *Times* was more than embarrassing; it could skew the nation's perception of what was really 'news.'" No wonder the attempts to be young and hip often looked awkward: the Frankel *Times* carried the weight of the entire country on its back when it tried to get down.

And so the *Times* moved unsteadily through both its worlds—uneasy doing enticement news and losing a step in its older role of agenda setter. On May 19, 1992, Vice President Dan Quayle delivered a speech in San Francisco two weeks after the devastating "Rodney King riots" down the California coast in south central Los Angeles. In the course of his remarks attributing the riots to a "poverty of values"— fostered by Democrats, Hollywood, the media, and other enemies of the Republic—Quayle complained about the television sitcom character Murphy Brown. The script writers had given Candice Bergen, who played the Brown character, a baby in the final, ratings-wise sequence of the 1991–92 season, without marrying her to the child's father. According to Quayle, this was an example of how liberals mocked "the importance of fathers." *USA Today* played the "Murphy

Brown" comments, together with photographs of the vice president and Bergen, on the front page ("Quayle: Murphy No Role Model"). The *New York Daily News* did the same ("Quayle to Murphy Brown: You Tramp"), so did the *New York Post* ("Dan Rips Murphy Brown"). The *Times* ran its account of Quayle's speech on the front page, with the headline: "Quayle Says Riots Arose from Burst of Social Anarchy." In the jump of the story on page 20, the *Times* mentioned the Brown reference. On May 20, the television newscasts followed the Low Press's lead. The next day, the editors of the *Times* hurried to catch up to the parade they used to lead. The *Times* ran a page-one story, plus three pictures, and the headline: "Appeal of Brown Now Clear at the White House." Belatedly too, the light bulbs went on in *Times* editors' heads.

Even when playing catch-up, the *Times* presented itself as a serious-minded collective: self-effacing technicians, dressed in the white coats of the laboratory, diligently pursuing the news. The paper was intended throughout to convey institutional authority. The news pages and opinion columns were set in a dignified typeface, dating from 1967, called—appropriately—8½ point Imperial. Front-page headlines employed far older type styles, such as Latin condensed, a design going back to the *Times* of the early 1900s. The *Times*' sober, "objective" mien was, at best, misleading. The *Times* of May 20, 1992, for example, was a far different paper from the *Times* of twenty-five years before, when the Imperial type was adopted. The modern *Times* was edited with the aid of computers and read by far more people outside New York than in the city. But the new technology and broader distribution systems were perhaps the least of the changes. As we will see, over the past two decades, the *Times* redefined the meaning of news. Led by its editor, A. M. Rosenthal, the *Times* in the 1970s broadened coverage of "soft news" topics and introduced the daily feature sections revolving around upscale consumerism: the so-called sectional revolution. The "new" *New York Times*, the paper's promotional slogan boasted. Some critics viewed the changes as frivolous, a violation of the *Times*' traditional mission. But the new sections attracted younger readers and vastly improved the *Times*' advertising revenues at a time when both the New York economy and the Times Company were financially strapped.

In the 1990s, a second shift was under way as Max Frankel, who succeeded Rosenthal in late 1986, made the *Times* more "reader friendly." As in the 1970s on Rosenthal's watch, economic pressures were squeezing the *Times'* profit margins. Worse, a generation of Americans had come of age seemingly with little interest in reading a serious newspaper on a regular basis; according to the *Times'* market surveys, this younger audience preferred to get its news from less-demanding television or such "Lite news" products as the national, all-color daily, *USA Today*. Frankel responded by loosening up writing styles at the *Times* and further broadening news coverage.

Together, these two changes fundamentally transformed the *Times*. They helped create a new *Times*, one no longer tied to its home city, or to its original serious-news franchise: a publication that might be called (though not likely by the *Times'* promotion department) *Not the New York, Not the Times*. This new *Times* was a paper at once softer, quirkier, more individual, more subjective, and untidier than the traditional *Times*. The story of the *Times'* own transition makes for a narrative more compelling than what the *Times* usually reports about other American institutions.

A DAY IN THE LIFE
6:31 a.m. — 9:30 a.m.

The sun rose at 6:31 A.M. and temperatures were in the thirties in New York City on February 28, 1989, according to the editions of the *New York Times* on sale the next day. The news coverage that Tuesday was typical of the new *Times*.

The weather report, for example, was the only local news on the front page of that edition. The rest of the page was given over to events occurring elsewhere. In Washington on Tuesday, the *Times* reported, George Bush held a series of meetings with uncommitted Democratic senators in an effort to win votes for John Tower, the president's nominee for Secretary of Defense; Oliver North's lawyers stalled the trial of the former Reagan aide on a technicality; the FBI announced it wanted to improve its affirmative action record; the Supreme Court ruled unanimously that a city is liable for injuries suffered by inadequately trained workers, and the State Department warned the Palestine Liberation Organization to refrain from attacks on Israel. From Albany, the *Times* reported that Governor Mario Cuomo and the Long Island Lighting Company had signed an agreement to shut the Shoreham nuclear power plant, while in Chicago, Richard M.

Daley won the Democratic primary in a vote that split along racial lines, according to exit polls conducted by the *Times*. Abroad, a special dispatch to the *Times* datelined Caracas reported that dozens of Venezuelans were killed and hundreds wounded in two days of rioting over the government's new economic measures.

Inside the paper, *Times* stories had a similar generic cast. Marian Burros' "De Gustibus" column noted that Americans were marking the centennial year of the "lowly" hamburger; on the lead business page, James Hirsch reported that the R. J. Reynolds Tobacco company's effort to test-market a "smokeless" cigarette had ended in failure, and the Living section carried an article about the rise of personal trainers across the country, some of them charging as much as $200 for a half-hour workout. On the first sports page, the main story dealt with the return to Texas of Jimmy Johnson, to become head coach of the Dallas Cowboys. The Yankees also made news from Spring training in Florida, following reports of drinking aboard the team's charter flights during the past season. Only two local New York teams were in action that Tuesday; on page B-10, well inside the second section, hockey writer Alex Yannis reported that the Devils tied the Bruins, and from Uniondale on Long Island, Robin Finn described another loss by what she called the "amorphous" Islanders, a struggling club with new players at every position. On the editorial page and the Op-Ed page, three separate *Times* commentaries assessed the month-old administration of George Bush, using the president's first trip to Asia as their starting point. The three pieces—the lead editorial (unsigned), the "Editorial Notebook" by Robert Semple, and an Op-Ed article by John B. Oakes—rendered three separate verdicts. The editorial admonished Bush because he had "failed to speak out" against repression in China, while Semple thought "Bush had done himself credit" in China. Oakes found the administration "floundering" on all fronts.

February 28 was a routine day at the *Times*. Editors assigned stories, reporters covered events, printers produced a press run of just over one million copies, trucks and route men (and women) delivered the papers to homes, apartments, hotels, newsstands, coffee shops, convenience stores, and street vending boxes in every state in the union. There was nothing in the news columns to suggest anything about these ten thousand men and women who helped put out the paper that Tuesday, beyond the bylines on the stories. The *Times*, for all its thoroughness—

and pride of product—hardly ever dwelled on its own processes. Of course, the entity known as "The *Times*" did speak on the editorial page (sometimes in several voices, as in the case of the president's Asian trip). A diligent reader could also find a small window into the institutional ways of the *Times* by looking for two discreet boxes placed just above the Macy's and Saks Fifth Avenue ads on page three. There, under the standing head "Corrections," the *Times* redressed its errors. Thus, in the paper of March 1, readers learned that a picture caption in the *Times* the day before had misidentified the people shown celebrating the opening of the new Presbyterian Hospital building. The *Times* then gave the correct order of appearance. While the names were of little use without the picture, the paper nevertheless was telling its readers that accuracy counts at the *New York Times*, right down to the identifications of partygoers in group photos.

The *Times'* "Corrections" tended to run daily. A second box, called "Editors' Note," appeared less frequently. In the editions dated March 1, next to the box correcting the hospital caption, the *Times* undertook a more elaborate critique of its journalism. In the *Times* of January 10, the Note reminded any readers who didn't keep the information at their fingertips, the paper had reported that Eduard Nakhamkin, an art dealer, was trying to "monopolize" the representation of Soviet artists in the United States. According to the "Editors' Note," "the article should have reported Mr. Nakhamkin's view . . . that Soviet artists are still free to choose other representatives." Again, an instruction about the paper: Fairness and balance—getting quotes from the story's subjects—are required in *Times* journalism.

The *Times* seldom had anything more to say about its own processes. If readers were somehow allowed inside the paper on a typical workday, this is what they would have learned, behind the front page.

9:00 A.M.

This Tuesday, Arthur Ochs Sulzberger, publisher and chairman of the *Times,* had more immediate concerns than Tower's drinking habits, the rioting in Caracas, and the fate of dissidents in China. Sulzberger was worried about what was happening outside his own door in a city exhibiting many signs of civic collapse. The Times Building occupied the middle of the block of West 43rd Street, approximately halfway between Broadway—the now seedy "crossroads of the world"—and Eighth Avenue, with its twenty-five-cent peep show parlors and hole-in-the-wall theaters offering live sex performances. Sulzberger's father and his grandfather had worked from the same fourteenth-floor offices at the *Times*. But the owner's suite was hardly insulated from the increasing street sleaze below. Sulzberger had on his desk the final draft of a letter he was sending to Edward I. Koch, the then mayor of New York, expressing "gave concern" over a series of "twenty-three robberies and/or assaults" on *Times* employees in the most recent fourteen-month period. "The situation worsened last week when one of our electricians was seriously injured in a robbery that took place at the Port Authority Bus Terminal while going home," the Sulzberger letter declared. The publisher detailed the steps the *Times* had taken to increase the safety of its employees, including the hiring of more *Times* private security guards. In addition, Sulzberger told the mayor, "representatives of the *Times* have met with the highest-ranking police officer in the midtown area about protection, and despite their most diligent efforts, the problem appears only to have worsened." Sulzberger concluded: "any assistance from your office would be greatly appreciated."

The letter went out over Sulzberger's signature, and Koch immediately set up the requested meeting—although not a word about the series of assaults, the publisher's actions, or the mayor's response ever appeared in the *Times*.

9:15 A.M.

That same Tuesday morning, Sam Roberts, the urban affairs columnist of the *Times,* was also arranging to talk to Koch. Roberts' column appeared on Thursdays on the front page of the B section (the second of the four sections of the paper), and he normally spent Tuesdays reporting his topic for that week, and Wednesdays writing the column. Roberts wanted Koch's reaction to a proposal of Governor Cuomo's for a state commission on New York City. Roberts was also trying to arrange to interview the governor for the Thursday column. As a backup in case the interviews fell through, Roberts set up a meeting with officials and residents of the Senate Hotel on upper Broadway. The Senate, sponsored by Goddard-Riverside, a private social agency, had just reopened as a residence for the elderly and the formerly homeless, particularly those with emotional problems. The Goddard-Riverside visit was set for 10:00 A.M. and Roberts left his Upper West Side apartment early enough to have breakfast with Samuel Freedman, a former *Times* reporter. Every year, two or three promising young *Times*men and women leave for other publications, or try free-lancing or book writing. Freedman was finishing his book, on the New York City school system—explored mainly through the experiences of one dedicated, overworked teacher at one decaying, Lower East Side high school. Freedman wanted Roberts to read the manuscript and give him some feedback. After Roberts looked through the Freedman manuscript, he walked to the Senate Hotel to begin the research for his backup column. Freedman, Roberts thought, had written a moving narrative of dedication and despair, the kind of gritty New York story that belonged in the *Times*.

9:20 A.M.

Anthony Lewis, whose column appeared twice a week on the Op-Ed page, also got an early start. Two decades ago, Lewis was the chief of the *Times* bureau in London. As part of the perks of office, a chauffeur drove him to the bureau each morning in the company's Jaguar; his office boasted a view of the dome of St. Paul's Cathedral and the Thames in the distance. Lewis supervised twenty-seven employees and the London wire room was a key relay point for cable traffic from the foreign desk in New York to the *Times* bureau in Saigon (cables were charged at so-called Empire rates). After his London tour, Lewis chose to live, and write his column, in Boston. These days he traveled by the "T"—the Boston subway—to his *Times* office. He had been out of town the day before, and a large pile of mail awaited him. His secretary helped him answer two dozen letters. Then Lewis read the *Times,* the *Boston Globe,* the *Financial Times* of London, and the *Wall Street Journal*—and began thinking about a topic for his next column.

9:25 A.M.

The pace on the Times Building's pressroom floor, below street level, was leisurely early Tuesday morning. Pressmen's Union men Dave Davies, Jimmy Reilly, John Stapleton, and Bobby Reynolds, adjusted and changed the rollers inside the presses, cleaning the reels where the newsprint feeds in, tidying up under the large folding machines that put the pages together. The pressmen's overnight shift, supervised by Rudy Rella, assistant general foreman for production at 43rd Street, usually ended around 4 A.M., depending on the size of the print order. Rella normally came in late in the afternoon and stayed just past midnight to check the quality of the press run, making sure that the mixture of ink and water was correct and the type readable. The right mix was a matter of concern for the *Times*; one of the readers' long-standing complaints was that the ink came off on their hands. Sulzberger had made a smear-proof *Times* a top business-side priority over the next three years.

9:30 A.M.

In Honolulu, Robert Reinhold of the *Times'* Los Angeles bureau was finishing up what he judged one of his more frantic assignments in twenty years as a *Times* reporter. At 6:30 A.M. Los Angeles time on the Friday before, the *Times'* national desk in New York had awakened him with the news that the cargo door of a United Airlines flight had explosively detached from the airframe of a Boeing 747 shortly after the jumbo jet departed from Honolulu on its way to New Zealand. The plane was flying at 23,000 feet at the time, and the resulting decompression sucked out the passengers sitting near the door; nine people died in the nightmarish accident, and the crippled jet returned to Honolulu. The desk wanted Reinhold, whose Los Angeles bureau responsibilities extended from as far east as Denver all the way west to the Hawaiian Islands, to cover the story. Reinhold stuffed a few shirts in a carry-on bag and managed to make the next Los Angeles–to–Honolulu flight, at 9:00 A.M. L.A. time. He arrived in the Islands at 1:00 P.M. Hawaiian time—thirty minutes past the normal deadline for filing copy to New York, because of the five-hour time difference. He quickly grasped his competitive position: four people from the *Los Angeles Times* were on scene, putting together a chronology of the flight based on interviews with passengers. Reinhold realized he was encountering something of a first in his career: a rival paper able to deploy *greater* resources than the *New York Times.* The Los Angeles paper's new presence, he noted, was not confined to "one shots"—such as its blanket coverage of the United flight. It was evident generally, throughout the Pacific Rim.

Reinhold didn't leave Honolulu Airport to check into his hotel until late that night. The *Times'* deadline was stretched to accommodate his page-one story, and he was able to match a part of the *Los Angeles Times* story, interviewing survivors of the accident as they waited in the terminal to depart Honolulu on other flights. The next morning, Reinhold woke by 5:00 A.M., knowing that the *Sunday Times'* deadline was 9:30 A.M. local time. As soon as he finished telephoning in his Sunday story, he was back at the airport to do more reporting, and to attend a briefing by the National Transportation Safety Board, the federal agency investigating the accident. Sunday, he repeated his routine, reporting and filing for the Monday paper. Later, the *Times* gave him a Publisher's Award for February: a $500 check as well as official recognition of his reporting work.

By Tuesday, February 28, the federal investigation was shifting to Washington, and Reinhold decided that as long as he was in Honolulu, he would look into a story about the Islands that had long intrigued him. First, however, he went for a jog under Diamond Head in the gray and drizzly early morning.

1

—

PUNCH AND HIS TIMES

ARTHUR OCHS SULZBERGER began coming to a desk at the *Times* in 1954, when he was twenty-eight years old. From the day he walked into the building, he had to contend with the impression that he was an intellectual lightweight, and undeserving of his position at the paper. This early judgment, based as much on hearsay as any firsthand evidence, was never wholly erased. In the Punch Sulzberger years, the *Times* became the centerpiece of a billion-dollar company; the paper burnished its reputation as a world-class publication, while surviving the rough passage to the new post-print era of television—and still Sulzberger's associates and employees debated his precise contributions. One man, who was as close as anyone professionally to Punch Sulzberger—and so asked for anonymity—believes to this day that Sulzberger succeeded in large part by *not* getting too involved. This executive tells a story of the time when Punch Sulzberger and a friend were being driven by the publisher's chauffeur on one of the parkways leading from New York to the family's country estate. The car gets a flat; the passengers and the chauffeur emerge and Sulzberger moves toward the trunk to find the tire jack and spare. The friend pulls Sulzberger aside, whispering that the best way to help is to stand aside, and let the chauffeur fix it. "Staying out of the way of the hired hands," says the executive. "That was Punch's contribution."

The story may be apocryphal; Sulzberger has no recollection of it. Certainly, it represents a harsh verdict. The butler didn't do it, not all of it by any means. Punch Sulzberger's managerial style, while unusual, was not passive. If the hired hands were overly dismissive of his role at the *Times*, it was in part because his family initially held a similar low judgment of his abilities.

Arthur Ochs Sulzberger was born in 1926, the youngest of the four children of Arthur Hays Sulzberger and Iphigene Ochs Sulzberger; his mother was the only child of Adolph S. Ochs, who bought the *Times* in 1896. Because Arthur Ochs Sulzberger came after his sister Judith in birth order, the family gave him the name "Punch" (the part he played to her "Judy"). The name seemed to suit his sunny disposition and indifferent academic performance as a child. The Sulzbergers then lived on East 80th Street in Manhattan, and the young boy went to a succession of expensive private schools, including St. Bernard's in New York; there, in the manner of the day, left-handed children were forced by their first teachers to write with their right hand. In Sulzberger's case, the resulting reversed-letters script convinced his parents that he had dyslexia.

His grades were further confirmation of their worries. The young prince, the sole male heir, should by all natural rights one day run the *Times*, as his grandfather and father had. Yet he was judged not very bright by his own parents. In later years, he would joke to interviewers about the schools he had quit "right before they were going to throw me out." His laid-back recollections masked deeper feelings. He had a long memory; his *Times* holdings made him one of the wealthiest men in America, yet he never contributed to the schools where he had been judged a "slow student" in his youth, though they rattled the tin cups of the annual alumni-fund drives in his direction.

The war provided a way to escape both family and school; in 1943, at age seventeen, he left the Loomis School in Connecticut to join the Marines, with his father's written permission. He did well enough, serving in the South Pacific toward the end of the war as a radio man and driver in rear echelons. "Before I entered the Marines, I was a lazy good-for-nothing. The Marines woke me up," Punch would later say. After his discharge he attended Columbia University, enrolling in a general studies program (his father was a trustee, and that helped with the admissions office). In 1951, a year after the start of the Korean war,

Sulzberger was recalled to active duty, to be a public information officer in Japan and Korea.

There was never any doubt about what he had to do after the Marines. His father arranged a job for him at the *Milwaukee Journal*, a prosperous and well-run paper known for its serious journalism; like the *Times*, the *Journal* of that era invariably won a place on the lists of "ten best" newspapers in the country. It was 1953; at the age of twenty-seven, with a wife and young child, Punch Sulzberger had at last begun his newspaper career.

Punch Sulzberger joined the *Times* itself the next year, and in a matter of months was sent abroad, to Europe, for further "seasoning." He was stationed for a time in the *Times'* Paris bureau, and did nothing to dispell his reputation as an amiable nonentity. One weekend he was in Le Mans for the auto races when one of the cars swerved off the roadway, plowed into the crowd, and killed eighty-three people. Eyewitness Sulzberger relayed not one word of the horrific accident to the bureau, not even an alerting phone call. Perhaps he wasn't really a news hound; perhaps he was too distracted by personal matters. His marriage, to the former Barbara Grant of the Bendel's department store family, fell apart in his Paris days, despite the efforts of the couple's parents to act as mediators. His wife won custody of their only son, Arthur Jr. Eventually, Punch married again, to the former Carol Fox Fuhrman. The first Mrs. Sulzberger also remarried, and divorced and remarried again. She settled in Topeka, Kansas, with her new husband, who worked at the Karl E. Menninger clinic.

Punch Sulzberger was marking time in Paris. Punch's father, Arthur Hays Sulzberger, had succeeded his father-in-law as publisher of the *Times* when Adolph Ochs died in 1935. Ochs had kept the title of publisher until his last days, well into his seventy-seventh year. The elder Sulzberger had resolved not to make his designated successor twist slowly in the wind while waiting for the publisher's chair to vacate. But the son was not the family's choice for the job in 1961 when AHS, as he signed his *Times* memos, was incapacitated by a stroke. Punch Sulzberger would be publisher, someday. He and his three sisters were to share equally the controlling Ochs trust upon the death of their mother, but until then Iphigene Ochs Sulzberger had the decisive vote. In the early 1960s, a woman with an independent turn of mind still was not likely to consider a woman for the job of publisher of the *Times*, even one of her own daughters.

Still, that didn't guarantee the job to Punch Sulzberger. He was thirty-five when AHS was stricken, and his family judged him too young to be put in charge of the paper. (In 1960, one year before, the *Times* had supported John F. Kennedy for president; at forty-three, Kennedy was not considered too young to run the country.) Instead the publisher's post went to Sulzberger's brother-in-law, his senior by thirteen years, Orvil Dryfoos, who was married to Punch's oldest sister, Marian. Once again Sulzberger had been defined by birth order. The family plan called for Dryfoos to run the paper for a decade or so, until his sixties. Then, sometime in the 1970s perhaps, it would be his brother-in-law's turn. Outwardly, Punch Sulzberger seemed to shrug off the decision; he remained a person of pleasant disposition, as well as a good son and brother. He was given the title of deputy publisher.

Turner Catledge, the paper's executive editor at the time, remembered Sulzberger then as a good-natured colleague who spent his time "wandering around the building inspecting things"—peering, for example, at the building pipes as if studying the ventilation system. He was a hobbyist and a tinkerer, happy when playing fix-it on the family's estate in Stamford, Connecticut. Sulzberger later said that at the *Times* he was "the executive in charge of nothing. . . . Nobody wanted to give me anything to do—no honest-to-God job." When Dryfoos died of a heart attack in 1963, Sulzberger became publisher, in effect, by default. His parents—his father was by then confined to a wheelchair—deliberated what to do for three weeks, scanning what was for all practical purposes a nonexistent field of candidates. For a time the Sulzbergers had thought of asking James Reston to take the job, but Reston cherished his Washington insider's role. A politic man, he also had the good sense to be an advocate of Punch, the dynastic choice. There was one other possibility from outside the family. Amory Bradford, a Yale graduate and former Wall Street lawyer, was the general manager of the *Times* in 1963. But realistically Bradford could only be a candidate in his own mind. He was widely known as an arrogant administrator, and had alienated just about everyone who had to work with him. Bradford was also a highly troubled man, and after he left the *Times* he went through three marriages, as well as a long struggle with alcoholism and depression. By the mid-1970s, the former Skull and Bones man and Century Association member had embraced New Age thinking. He startled his fellow Centurions by appearing one day in the Club dining room with a full beard and shoulder-length hair.

Today, after three decades of consciousness-raising, one of the daughters, Ruth Sulzberger Golden, might have been considered a possibility to head the *Times*. In 1963, she was publisher of the other family paper, the *Chattanooga Times*. But Golden also had some personal distractions, namely, a shaky marriage that eventually ended in divorce. And, in any event, a woman's place in the early 1960s was still a step to the rear and to the side. Ruth Golden may have been considered capable of running one of Tennessee's leading newspapers, but the *Times* of Chattanooga was not the *Times* of New York.

Finally, there was another family member, John Bertram Oakes, the editor of the *Times*' editorial page and a nephew of Adolph Ochs. John Oakes's father, George Washington Ochs, had anglicized the family name during World War I, as a form of protest against Germany's militaristic behavior, according to the son. Johnny Oakes was thirteen years older than Punch Sulzberger and unlike his cousin in a number of ways. Oakes was a Phi Beta Kappa graduate of Princeton, voted "most likely to succeed" by his classmates in 1934. He had been a Rhodes scholar at Oxford, worked as a newspaper reporter in Trenton, New Jersey, and Washington, and risen from private to major in the U.S. Army during World War II. After the war, he joined the *Times* as editor of the Sunday Review of the Week. In 1949 he became a member of the editorial board. Arthur Hays Sulzberger appointed him editor of the editorial page in 1961. While cousin Punch wandered around looking at heating systems, Oakes toured Africa, to write about the former colonial nations and their "ordeal of independence" for the *Times Magazine*.

On the editorial page, Oakes staked out generally centrist positions for the *Times*. He was an early conservationist and advocate for the national parks. He favored lowering the voting age from twenty-one to eighteen. Over time, he became a supporter of reform of New York state's abortion laws. At first, he argued that proposals to remove all restrictions to abortions except the concurrence of the woman's physician were "quite extreme"; eventually, he said he was persuaded to change by the arguments put forward by his editorial board colleagues. To complete the picture of intelligence and grace, Oakes was a handsome, dignified-looking man, with a firm gaze and a full head of gray hair, brushed back straight from his forehead, military fashion. He also enjoyed a happy marriage, living with his family in a spacious upper Fifth Avenue apartment, spending his weekends horseback riding and bicycling with his three daughters in Central Park.

For all his admirable qualities and proven abilities, Oakes now says he was an unlikely candidate to be publisher of the *Times*. "I had no business experience at all," he explained. "I wasn't inclined that way and I still am not." While there were doubts about his cousin Punch, he added, "I was never in doubt about the outcome or that it would go to the Sulzberger side of the family."

With no real choice except their son, Iphigene and AHS nevertheless needed the encouragement of Scotty Reston in order to do the right family thing. Tom Wicker, then a young, sharp-eyed reporter in the Washington bureau, now says, emphatically, "Reston swung it." Almost twenty years later, in her memoirs, Iphigene Sulzberger characterized the decision as "something of a gamble." Punch, she remembered, was "still learning the newspaper business."

The paper that Punch Sulzberger took over in 1963 seemed set in stone, the repository of centuries-long traditions. Actually Adolph S. Ochs acquired the paper in 1896: Ochs's *Times* only acted as if it were an institution two hundred years old. Just eight years after he bought the *Times*, Ochs commissioned a grand structure for his paper, a Times Tower to rise twenty-four floors above the ground, the second highest building in the city. On the afternoon of January 18, 1904, Iphigene B. Ochs, Adolph Ochs's eleven-year-old daughter, helped her father dedicate the building. The temperature hovered at three degrees above zero, and Iphigene's mother, Mrs. Effie Ochs, insisted that her daughter wear bulky black tights over her high-button shoes. The child protested, but her mother won out. The ceremonies proceeded with just one slight hitch; Iphigene was to pat the cornerstone with an ivory-handled trowel and say, "I declare this stone to be laid plumb, level and square." She said "plump" instead.

The editor of the *Times*, Charles R. Miller, also spoke at the ceremonies. He noted the height of the Tower; "We affront physical nature and defy her laws," Miller declared. Most of all, Ochs's *Times* defied the natural newspaper order. On January 18, 1904, there were twelve dailies besides the *Times* being published in New York City. Copies of their editions for that day were sealed in a copper box, and the box placed inside the cornerstone troweled by Iphigene Ochs. (More than half a century later, the Allied Chemical Corporation bought Times Tower; by then, the *Times'* operations had been consolidated in a large Beaux Arts building a half block down the street). In March 1964, the cornerstone was removed and the copper box opened. Standing by was

Arthur Ochs Sulzberger, Sr., Iphigene's only son and the new publisher of the *Times*. The old newspapers from January 18, 1904, were examined by Sulzberger and his sister, Marian. Ten of the thirteen papers had ceased publication or had been merged, and no longer existed in their turn-of-the-century form. The eleventh paper, the *New York Post*, had changed from a broadsheet to tabloid size in the interim. A twelfth paper, the *Morning Telegraph*, had been reconstituted as a thoroughbred-racing paper carrying entries and results from the major tracks. The thirteenth paper in the copper box was the *Times*, the only publication still publishing the news of the day under its own name and original format. Within two years of the unsealing of the box, the merged papers—including the *World-Telegram and Sun*, and the *Journal-American*—would also be gone, awkward titles and all.

Some of the departed papers were victims of changing economic conditions and shifts in popular tastes. Others died of self-inflicted wounds—their own myopia, outmoded business plans, or plain bad leadership. Their closings left New York City at the beginning of the 1970s with only three general-interest dailies: the *Times*, the afternoon *Post*, and the *News*, a morning tabloid that began publication in 1919 as the *Illustrated Daily News*. In the early years of the 1990s, the *Post* and *News* were money losers, and there was compelling evidence that one or both of them might go under.

A number of factors help explain why the *Times* managed to avoid the death march of American newspapers and survive as one of daily journalism's great successes. Some of the reasons for success are directly traceable to decisions made by Adolph Ochs, by his son-in-law Arthur Hays Sulzberger, and by his grandson Arthur Ochs Sulzberger. Other factors contributing to the *Times'* success had relatively little to do with the actions of either the family or the paper's executives.

Adolph S. Ochs was the son of Julius Ochs, a German-born Jew who had emigrated from Bavaria to Tennessee in 1845. Julius Ochs first made his way in America as a peddler. His son Adolph entered journalism through a side door, as a printer's devil, emptying the hellboxes—the receptacles of used type—for the compositors on Tennessee country newspapers in the early 1870s. In 1878, just out of his teens, Adolph Ochs started the *Chattanooga Times* with $37.50 in borrowed funds. By the 1890s he believed he had sufficient experience, if not the necessary capital, to expand his newspaper holdings. In the summer of

1896, he set out to acquire the *Times* of New York, a well-regarded daily then facing bankruptcy. His daughter Iphigene later wrote that the *Times* was controlled at the time by a group of Wall Street bankers "who very much wanted a New York paper that backed gold." The presidential elections were less than six months away, and the Democratic party candidate, the populist William Jennings Bryan, was running on the radical (in the bankers' eyes) platform of free silver. Though he was, like most propertied Southerners, a Democrat, Ochs decided that his Chattanooga paper would back William McKinley, the Republican candidate. McKinley, along with Wall Street and the rest of the banking interests, stood firm on the gold standard.

Ochs may have been an untested quantity in New York, but he was reliable on the currency issue. He was able to borrow $75,000 to purchase controlling interest in the *Times*; then he set about persuading the remaining stockholders of the old *Times* company to reinvest in his new company. Ochs later told his daughter how his knees were knocking when he arrived to make his stock-transfer appeal to the fierce, formidable J. P. Morgan. After the two men exchanged greetings, banker Morgan quickly asked: "Where do I sign?" Ochs had his deal in less than five minutes.

Ochs didn't acquire ownership of the *Times* outright; he had to show a profit for three straight years before formally becoming the controlling stockholder. It was an uphill struggle. The paper's daily circulation stood at about nine thousand on the August day in 1896 when Ochs became publisher. His first move was inspired; he cut the newsstand price from three cents to a penny. The newspaper-reading public responded, and the *Times* was born again. Within four decades, by the time Ochs died in 1935, the *Times'* daily circulation had passed 400,000. Meanwhile, the competing dailies, Joseph Pulitzer's *World* and William Randolph Hearst's *Journal-American*, were entering their long swoon toward extinction. Some of the *Times'* rivals screamed the news from their front pages. It was said of Hearst that he wanted *New York American* readers to look at page one and say "Gee whiz," to turn to page two and exclaim "Holy Moses," and then at page three, shout "God Almighty!"

Ochs had a different vision. The day after he took over the *Times*, an editorial page announcement informed readers of the new management's intention to "give the news impartially without fear or favor, regardless of party, sect, or interest involved. . . ." Ochs's *Times* had an air of sobriety. Its credo, "All the News That's Fit to Print," carried the clear message that certain kinds of news were not considered *Times* news. Hearst might boast that he started a war with Spain to help his papers' circulation; Pulitzer may have contributed to the birth of yellow journalism (along with Frank Munsey, James Gordon Bennett, and Charles Dana). Ochs chose to make the *Times* the serious paper: no comics, no cartoons, no shouting headlines. Today his approach would be called market positioning—shrewdly claiming the niche of respectability in a field crowded with noisemakers. But Ochs was also smart enough to know that even serious newspapers required enticing "reader" pieces: stories about crime, sex, and violence—sensationalism in other papers, sociology in the *Times*.

He also made another managerial decision, to reinvest *Times* profits—after adequate provision for his family, and his share holders—in the *Times'* news-gathering operations.

Ochs's approach was bold in its day. There were other serious papers in New York, such as the *Sun* and the *Herald*, although none quite matched the gravamen of the *Times*. Given the antic habits of most of the competition, the position of reliable, objective recorder of the news would not seem that hard to claim. But almost all popular journalism in America at the turn of the century was somewhat suspect. The *Times* was no exception: Ochs's first business ties to the financial establishment of New York were never a well-kept secret.

The years before the United States entered the Great War of 1914–18 were not an easy time to publish a paper with such ties. Ochs didn't want the *Times* to be considered either pro-British or pro-German. It had been accused of both positions, the former because of its ties to big banking, the latter because of the Ochs family's origins. The war years also put a great strain on Ochs's professed nonpartisanship. When the *Times* gave sympathetic coverage to an apparent peace overture by Austria, Ochs became the target of "almost universal execration," according to the historian, and Ochs family friend, Barbara Tuchman. During the Great War, too, some of the *Times'* editorial stands helped start other rumors that the paper was British owned. (The story had no factual basis, though Ochs was an admirer of the *Times* of London and its publisher, Lord Northcliffe.)

Ochs's desire to lower the *Times'* voice was founded on something more than good marketing strategy. While his New York of the

1890s—like the city of the 1990s—was open to entrepreneurs and self-made men, there were nevertheless certain unspoken limits to the meritocracy. Ochs was able to parry the charges that J. P. Morgan, or the British, owned the *Times*; but he had to deal with the undeniable fact that the *Times was* owned by Jews. The *Times'* identity as a "Jewish paper" caused Ochs as much anxiety as the labels "Morgan paper" or "British paper." The paper's successes made him, by definition, a prominent Jewish New Yorker. Moreover, his wife, Effie, was the daughter of Rabbi Isaac M. Wise of Cincinnati, one of the paramount figures of Reform Judaism in America. Reform Jews believed in assimilation. When Adolph Ochs attended a dinner at Delmonico's during his first months as owner of the *Times*, he took pleasure in the fact that "the party was made up of the crème de la crème of New York Jewish culture and refinement . . . not a coarse joke, nothing boisterous, not too much drinking—nothing that would not have taken place in the very best society."

Reform Judaism also opposed a Zionist state in Palestine; Ochs wanted it known that he believed Judaism was a religion, rather than a national identity. On one occasion, Ochs explicitly instructed his city editor not to give "too much space" to the efforts of the American Jewish Committee to aid European Jews caught in the war zone. The AJC campaigners, Ochs explained to the editor, "work to preserve the characteristics and traditions of the Jew, making him a man apart from other men. I am interested in the Jewish religion—I want that preserved—but that's as far as I want to go." The passage of time did nothing to soften his position. "Religion is all I stand for as a Jew," Ochs declared in 1925. Over the years, Jewish groups faulted Ochs's *Times* over its policies on the immigration of Eastern European Jews to America. "No paper was more anxious to exclude these 'undesirables,' " one academic critic concluded.

The rise of Hitler in the 1930s subsequently produced a number of studies aimed at showing the paper's alleged inattention to the Nazi noose closing on German Jews; in fact, the coverage was no more criminal than any other news organization's over the same period. Jewish critics of the *Times* were on firmer ground in the Middle East. Long after Ochs's death, in the years when Arthur Hays Sulzberger was publisher, the *Times* continued to oppose the idea of a Zionist homeland. In AHS's time, if anything, the paper went through ever greater contortions over the "Jewish question." The top editorships were occupied as if by custom by men with unmistakably Anglo-Saxon names—Edwin James, Turner Catledge, and, in the Washington bureau, Arthur Krock (a Jewish convert to the Episcopal Church) and James Reston. As late as the 1950s, Catledge remembered, AHS cautioned that he didn't want people to think of the *Times* as a "Jewish newspaper." In the 1970s Punch Sulzberger repeated almost the same words to Leonard Silk, the *Times* economics writer, and his son, Mark Silk. The *Times* did not have a Jewish chief editor until the late 1960s, when Abe Rosenthal became managing editor. Even then, his name appeared on the masthead as A. M. Rosenthal—the same form used in his byline when he was a correspondent—and not as Abraham Michael Rosenthal, or Abraham M. Rosenthal. Other bylines were similarly deracinated; the *Times*' exceptional labor reporter Abraham Henry Raskin appeared as A. H. Raskin, the metro desk reporter Myron Abba Farber became M. A. Farber.

Such stories have been told and retold by *Times*people, usually with a knowing shake of the head. In the early 1960s, Ben Franklin, then a young reporter in the Washington bureau, claimed that he witnessed an example of what he called the "Jewish craziness." The newly hired Franklin was on his first orientation trip to the home office in New York. "As soon as the city edition came up on hand trucks from the pressroom," Franklin remembered, "I saw two copy boys begin to do their 'Jew-Arab count.' Using string measures, one would scan the paragraphs of Middle East or Israeli news stories, if there were any, and break down the coverage in column inches, and then read off the numbers for the other copy boy to record on a sheet of paper: 'Jew . . . Arab . . . Arab . . . Jew . . . Jew . . . Jew . . . Arab . . .'" The editors, Franklin said, concluding his incredible tale, "wanted to have equal inches at the end of week, or else a bell would go off, like a smoke alarm."

Under Punch Sulzberger some of these unwritten rules gradually were bent and, in some cases, broken. Unfolding news events in the 1960s, more than the new publisher's dictates, pushed the *Times* forward. According to E. Clifton Daniel, who was the paper's managing editor at the time, the *Times*' final rejection of—in Daniel's words— "Ochs's antizionism" was forced by the Six-Day War of 1967, when Israel moved on three fronts against the Egyptians, Syrians, and Jordanians. "The war came at a critical point in Punch's thinking," Daniel says. "Here was Jewish nationalism on the rise; there was a need for the *Times* to change and it did."

The changes occurred gradually. Initially, the most visible sign of movement was signaled by Punch Sulzberger's choices for senior editors of the paper. Abe Rosenthal, the son of Russian Jewish immigrants, rose to the top of the editorial masthead in 1970. He served for almost two decades as Punch Sulzberger's editor. Rosenthal was replaced by Max Frankel, a refugee from Nazi Germany. By 1990 Sulzberger had effectively designated Joe Lelyveld, the son of a rabbi from Cincinnati, to be Frankel's successor. Many *Times*people were convinced that, as one executive put it, "there would never be a non-Jewish editor of the *Times* again in our lifetimes." This man did not intend to imply there was anything sinister or cabalistic in such a development. In New York, a city with one of the largest Jewish communities in the world, and in journalism, an industry where Jews are overrepresented in terms of their numbers relative to the general population, it was altogether natural that the *Times* newsroom contained a large group of Jews—and that some of them would be promoted to senior editorships.

(On January 1, 1993, Howell Raines, the Washington bureau chief, and a Southerner in the Turner Catledge mold, became editorial page editor, a position that put him in line to succeed Joe Lelyveld and break the "Jewish succession" string.)

The paper's post-1967 coverage of Jewish affairs in general and of Israel in particular was another, more complex matter. As the Middle East became one of the seemingly permanent flashpoints in the world, the *Times* foreign desk regularly had to deal with stories that rolled off the news wires like live grenades, ready to detonate. The editors tried elaborate countermeasures aimed at protecting the paper's reputation. According to Thomas Friedman, one of the *Times*' foreign correspondents, the *Times* as late as the 1980s had an unwritten rule of "never allowing a Jew to report from Jerusalem." Friedman was born in 1952 and grew up in Minneapolis— "a Jew who was raised on all the stories, all the folk songs, and all the myths about Israel," he would later remember. In 1984, Abe Rosenthal appointed Friedman chief of the *Times* bureau in Jerusalem, making him the first Jew to hold the job. Rosenthal thought he had broken the Jewish "barrier" five years earlier when he designated David K. Shipler as the *Times*' Jerusalem man. But when Rosenthal boasted about the move at an editors' meeting, one of his colleagues corrected him: The bearded, sad-faced Shipler was a Protestant ("He just looked like a rabbi").

Friedman served in the Middle East for almost a decade, and then took a leave of absence from the *Times* to write about his experiences. In his journals he examined how the weight of his Jewish past, as well as the *Times'* past, affected his work—an introspective analysis the *Times'* "objective" format barred from its news pages. Before his assignment in Jerusalem, Friedman covered the Israeli invasion of Lebanon in 1982 for the *Times*. He entered the Shatila refugee camp in Beirut on Saturday morning, September 18, 1982, soon after Lebanese Phalangists, operating within Israeli Army jurisdiction, had conducted a three-day "mop-up" of Shatila and nearby Sabra. The operation, supposedly aimed at rooting out Palestinian "terrorists," instead resulted in the massacre of civilian noncombatants, perhaps as many as eight hundred to one thousand men, women, and children. Shatila-Sabra became "a personal crisis" for Friedman, convinced as he was of Israeli knowledge—and probably, approval—of what happened inside the camp. Sitting at his typewriter, trying to reconstruct the massacre, he felt driven by "two conflicting impulses," the truth-telling role of a *Times* journalist and his private Jewish sympathies. "One part of me wanted to nail [Israeli Prime Minister] Begin and [Defense Minister] Sharon. . . . Yet another part of me was also looking for alibis—something that would prove Begin and Sharon innocent, something that would prove the Israelis couldn't have known what was happening." Friedman's reporting convinced him of official Israeli complicity. He angrily banged on the table during an interview with the Israeli senior army commander and raged at the general: "How could you do this?" Friedman realized that he was really saying, "How could you do this to me. . . . I always thought *we* were different. . . . What do I tell people now?"

The encounter left Friedman "literally sick to my stomach." He telephoned *Times* foreign editor Craig Whitney back in New York and told him, "I really don't want to shovel this shit anymore. Let somebody else write the story." Whitney reminded him that he was the *Times* correspondent on scene. Duty won out: Friedman's reconstruction of the Shatila-Sabra massacre appeared in the *Times* of September 26, 1982. The article stirred near unanimous condemnation of Israel, and helped Friedman win a Pulitzer Prize in international reporting. It also reaffirmed the conviction of some American Jews that the *Times* was "anti-Israel." The contradictory twin notions that the *Times* was a "Jewish paper" and that the *Times* was "anti-Zionist" endured through the decades. Subscribers to the first notion had to reconsider their position when Arthur O. Sulzberger, Jr., succeeded his father in 1992. Young Arthur had been confirmed at St. Thomas Episcopal Church on the Upper East Side of New York City, in the religion of his mother and her second husband.

Whatever other burdens Arthur inherited when he took charge of the *Times*, one aspect of "the Jewish paper" issue had at last been put to rest. The *Times* of the 1990s was being run by an Episcopalian. Perhaps the *Times*, starting at the top with the family and moving down through the reporting ranks, had been overly sensitive. But Adolph Ochs, his son-in-law AHS, and his grandson Punch were hardly guilty of reflexively imagining the worst, or of sensing slights where none existed (another supposed "Jewish trait"). The family, try as it might to be private and low profile, occupied a prominent position in a keenly competitive field. The *Times* attracted attention; as it grew and flourished, the scrutiny of its "Jewish roots" also increased, sometimes for purely commercial reasons.

The *Times*' major rival as the quality morning paper in the middle third of the century was the *New York Herald Tribune*. The *Herald Tribune* had a noble history—Horace Greeley was a cofounder, and by tradition it was the paper of the Republican upper classes in the city. Its owners in the years between the wars were the Reids, a family that seemingly wandered out of the Social Register and into a daytime soap opera. The scion, the handsome Ogden Reid, became an alcoholic; his ambitious wife, Helen Reid, was a former secretary who married the boss's son; in her later years, she balanced running the paper, caring for her ailing husband, and raising their two sons to succeed their father. After Ogden Reid's death in 1947, the brothers, Whitelaw and Ogden (known respectively to *Herald Trib* people as the White Prince and the Dark Prince), engaged in a fratricidal struggle for control of the paper, only to see a third party supplant them both.

These private dramas didn't stop Helen Reid from patronizing the family that owned the *Times*. She tried to hire away Turner Catledge, the *Times*' editor, by promising him a chance to move "in a different social circle . . . from those Jews on Forty-third Street." (The genial Catledge later suggested her words might have been just "a slip of the tongue.")

It wasn't hard to figure out what Helen Reid thought of that "social circle." Ochs's *Times* ran a regular column listing the arrival of all out-of-town buyers in the city clothing industry, a practice that continued for two decades after his death. The *Herald Tribune* disdained the "rag trade." William Robinson, the Reids' business manager in the late 1940s, once explained that almost half of the *Times*' readership (around 500,000 at the time) consisted of what he called "transient" readers. As Robinson broke down the figures, 75,000 readers bought the *Times* solely for its classified ads; a second group of about the same size bought the *Times* for its "business service in the apparel trades," and a third group of some 50,000 Jews read the *Times* obituary columns "to be sure they will know of the passing of relatives and friends." Pulled out of thin air, the figures supported Robinson's preordained conclusion: 200,000 copies were bought for "a reason other than the news and editorial content of the *Times*." Because the *Herald Tribune*'s own circulation was around 300,000 at the time, Robinson's fanciful arithmetic made it seem that, qualitatively speaking, the audiences for the two papers was roughly the same size. The whole sniffish exercise was made worse by Robinson's patronizing judgment that the *Times*' Jewish readers were mostly garment workers, and narrow-minded as well, interested only in the deaths of "their own kind."

Robinson was soon gone from the newspaper business; the Reids eventually followed, first selling a share of the *Herald Tribune* in 1958 to another member of the WASP Republican establishment, John Hay "Jock" Whitney, sportsman, horse breeder and Eisenhower's ambassador to Great Britain (as well as a man of personal dignity and good character). After returning to New York in 1961, Whitney pumped millions of his own money into the paper, but the *Herald Tribune* continued to slip behind the *Times*. By 1964 the *Herald Tribune*'s losses had reached an estimated $15 million. While Whitney's *Herald Trib* faltered, Sulzberger's *Times* flourished.

In retrospective accounts, the *Times* unfailingly attributed its success to the superiority of its news coverage in the years during and right after the war—a claim that has largely gone unchallenged. The official story requires considerable qualification.

Through the 1930s and early 1940s, the two papers were in a rough kind of equilibrium. By the end of World War II, however, the *Times* began to gain steadily relative to the *Herald Tribune* in both the number of its readers and its advertising revenues. The record of those years judged so critical to the fortunes of the two papers was analyzed by the

Times in a special report published in 1945. The document was not strictly speaking a communication to shareholders in the contemporary fashion: the Times Company stock was held in private hands, almost all in the name of the Ochs trust. But the 1945 document had the same public relations thrust of an annual report, reviewing as it did "what the *New York Times* accomplished" in the war years. The War Production Board, the report noted, had taken 1941, the year America went to war, as its base line for the rationing of newsprint. In that year, the *Times* had a weekday circulation of 455,000 and consumed 100,000 tons of newsprint (in 1990, with a daily circulation of over 1 million and a Sunday circulation of 1.6 million, the *Times* consumed 100,000 tons of newsprint every three months). The Board reduced this ration allotment each successive year; at the war's end in 1945, the *Times* was receiving 75,000 tons of newsprint. "Alone among major New York newspapers," the *Times* 1945 report noted, the *Times* never requested or received any supply above its quota.

Yet, good soldier that it was, the *Times* pointed out, it published 8,800 columns of war coverage and other news stories—more than any other American newspaper. Translating those news columns into advertising lineage, the paper calculated that it had passed up the chance to earn over $2 million in additional income. Nor did it stop soldiering on in the service of its readers after the war ended. In the three-month period following the Japanese surrender in August 1945, the *Times* boasted, readers could rely on their paper for such important documents as the "Army and Navy Pearl Harbor Reports," a document running over 117 columns; General George C. Marshall's Biennial Report (92 columns), and the verbatim texts of the indictments of major Nazi war criminals (32 columns).

The theme of the wartime paper devoted to expanded news—coverage so thorough that the competition was left behind, in the dust of history—has been taken up regularly in the years since 1945 by historians of the *Times*. For example, Gay Talese, in his tribute to the power and glory of the *Times*, concluded that the decision to increase the size of the paper's staff and "spare no expense covering the war" may have been the wisest move Arthur Hays Sulzberger ever made as publisher. Talese argues, plausibly enough, that the *Times* produced a superior newspaper as a result of that decision and began luring readers away from the *Herald Tribune*; these readers stayed with the *Times* after the war and into the 1950s and 1960s, while the *Herald Tribune* continued to lose circulation. In this accounting, the *Times'* farsightedness extended to the paper's relations with advertisers: The paper rationed advertising space so that its customers among the smaller stores would not be crowded out of the tighter papers, while the *Herald Tribune* "fattened up" on the big retail-store ads that couldn't be accommodated in the *Times.*

Such tales of the *Times'* selfless wartime service were neatly debunked by Richard Kluger, in his memoir of the *Herald Tribune.* Kluger showed that the *Herald Tribune* never carried a higher proportion of advertising than the *Times* during the war. Nor did the *Herald Tribune* profit from opportunistic policies; during those years its earnings remained less than half of the *Times'* earnings. Most important of all, the evidence of the defection of *Herald Tribune* readers to the *Times* during and after the war seems, at best, ambiguous. The papers' relative fortunes did shift, in 1947, well after the war and the end of newsprint rationing. In the immediate postwar period, the *Herald Tribune's* daily and Sunday circulation was about two-thirds that of the *Times.* The numbers were: for the daily papers, *Herald Tribune,* 348,000, *Times,* 538,000; for Sunday, *Herald Tribune* 708,000, *Times,* 1 million.

These figures did change, and dramatically, but for a much more mundane reason than the rewards and punishments of wartime duty. At the end of 1946, the *Herald Tribune* raised its newsstand price from three cents to five cents. The *Times,* with more ads and more news, stayed at three cents for three more years. The *Herald Tribune* suffered a 30,000 loss in circulation immediately after the price hike. The price rise was a "major blunder" on the part of the Reids, Kluger concluded; at three cents, the bigger, newsier *Times* was a better bargain.

The decision to raise its prices was only one of the many business mistakes the *Herald Tribune* made. The paper's moderate Republicanism and thoughtful news coverage between the wars found a natural constituency in the leafy, upper-middle-class towns outside New York. But when the great postwar migration from the city began to swell, the paper failed to move fast enough to engage the new residents of tract-house suburbia. When the *Herald Tribune* dropped its practice of including free introductory copies of the paper in the Welcome Wagons that greeted families newly arrived in Roslyn or Englewood or White Plains, the *Times* took its rival's place on the Wagon. The *Times'* circulation department also grasped the idea that home delivery was the most efficient long-term way to build readership: Regular subscribers took much of the guesswork out of determining the size of nightly press runs (and helped avoid costly returns from dealers).

No one contributed more to this postwar strategy than Nathan W. Goldstein, the *Times'* circulation manager from 1948 to 1974. Nat Goldstein knew the city and suburban delivery routes as well as the back of his hand. He developed close working relations with the forces that controlled the nighttime streets: the police, wherein nominal legal authority resided, and the newspaper drivers and deliverers union (its unsavory leadership tied to organized crime, usually just one step ahead of the antiracketeering laws).

Goldstein's connections benefited the *Times* in a number of ways. Papers delivered at 3:00 A.M. to still-shut newsstands did not "disappear" the way the deliveries of the other papers sometimes did, especially in those periods when managements were not on the best of terms with their union drivers. Friendly police officials shared helpful information with Goldstein. In 1968, when New York City police were about to descend on Columbia student-demonstrators occupying university buildings, the police commissioner, Howard Leary, called his good friend Goldstein to tip off the *Times* that the police bust was set for 1:00 A.M. (Goldstein asked Leary to move up the action to 11:00 P.M., so the *Times* could make its second edition with the story; Leary turned him down.)

Meanwhile, the *Times* advertising department was learning how to keep its best customers happy. The paper hit upon a way to give sizable advertising discounts to the big retail department stores—by getting the manufacturers of the advertised goods to contribute part or all of the cost of the ads. One architect of this cooperative arrangement, known as vendor-paid advertising, was Monroe Green, a University of Pennsylvania graduate (Wharton, class of 1927). Green also pushed the *Times* to make the *Times Magazine* a major display space for fashion coverage—and the full-page apparel advertising that accompanied such news coverage. Green began his career at Macy's; in 1935 he joined the *Herald Tribune* as an advertising space salesman. He did well; but when Helen Reid turned aside his request for a raise—"Oh, Mr. Green, you're just too impatient," she told him—he left the paper after just six months. Green spent the next six years in the advertising department at Hearst's *Journal-American*, and then went to work for Arthur Hays Sulzberger at the *Times*. Green said he later learned, from "friends whose credibility I could not doubt," that Helen Reid had vowed, "I will not hire another Jew as long as I live."

Thus, the familiar description of the high-minded, principled *Times* put forward by friendly critics covered only half the story. That *Times* did exist, presided over by courtly Southern editors and quiet, Reform proprietors. But so did the other *Times*, of aggressive salesmen and street-wise circulation people. While the owners and editors were visible Upstairs, among the crème de la crème, the proles sweated anonymously Downstairs. The clichéd "good gray *Times*" must be, at the very least, colored with touches of Green and Goldstein.

By the 1950s, at the zenith of AHS's rule, the *Times*' reputation as one of the leading American newspapers was secure. Few readers turned to the *Times* expecting fine writing or pleasing graphics. The paper was known mainly for its thorough reporting, and its aura of serious purpose. *Times* reporters and editors were among the best-paid newspaper people in America. There were layers of editors, a deliberate work pace, a sense of tasteful superiority: The reporters from the papers and the gentleman from the *Times* are here, madam! In 1954, a young journalist from Baltimore named Russell Baker joined the *Times*. Later, he remembered the place as being "comically overstaffed." Baker was in his late twenties; he had been hired away from the *Baltimore Sun* by Scotty Reston to work in the *Times*' Washington bureau. Reston informed Baker that before joining the bureau, he would have to spend three months in New York in order to know "his way around the home office."

Baker arrived on a Sunday in November; no one gave him anything to do on his first day, and he passed the time writing a letter to his wife back in Baltimore. He described for Mimi Baker the "vast" and "bleak" newsroom, stretching from 43rd to 44th streets, where desks were "aligned in rows as neatly as stones in a military graveyard." Halfway down the block shirtsleeved men were playing bridge, while others were working on crossword puzzles or browsing through newspapers. At the *Sun* a half dozen reporters had covered the whole of Baltimore for the night desk; at the *Times* swarms of people in the newsroom had nothing to do for days at a time—a "sea of tedium," Baker remembered. He eventually came upon an explanation for the paper's leisurely ways. Meyer Berger, the revered city side reporter who later wrote an official history of the *Times*, traced the *Times*' work habits to an earlier era: "Mr. Ochs always liked to have enough people around to cover the story when the *Titanic* sinks."

There was something to be said for overstaffing. In the AHS years, Sulzberger's editor Turner Catledge set up a permanent *Times* presence in the South. The *Times'* reporter, a Tidewater, Virginia, native and ex-marine named John H. Popham, was based in Chattanooga, Adolph Ochs's old hometown. Beginning in the late 1940s, Popham traveled through the South, putting fifty thousand miles a year on his car (before the federal interstates existed). He covered the civil rights story before it had a name. "Popham roamed the South, developing contacts, learning the territory, meeting the players, black and white," his friend and former *Times* colleague, John Herbers, later remembered. Popham knew he would be left alone by his editors as long as he did a good job. "That was Turner Catledge's style," Herbers says. "Hire good people, cheer them on, give them an incentive to produce." Because Popham was a white Southerner, he moved with relative ease on the Main streets of the South, among the small-town mayors, deputy sheriffs, and store owners. And because he was from the *Times*, he was able to move as well through the other South—from an African Methodist Episcopal church in Mississippi to a Negro weekly newspaper in North Carolina to a black ministers' meeting in Atlanta.

While Popham worked on his own, creating an enduring newsroom legend, there were other legacies of the AHS years that the paper would rather forget. Within the paper three news entities, each claiming to be "the *Times*," jostled for position. The newsroom staff, numbering around 800, put out the daily Monday through Saturday paper. These *Times*people worked for the managing editor, Catledge. In addition, a smaller group of around one hundred belonged to the Sunday staff, reporting to Lester Markel. Markel joined the *Times* in 1923, and by the 1950s was running the Sunday paper as a separate principality. The Sunday paper employed its own styles of punctuation and grammar, which differed from the daily's. The Review of the Week section frequently ran articles written as if on the assumption that subscribers had not read any newspapers during the previous six days. Markel also was in charge of the *Book Review* and the *Times Magazine*, which also sometimes acted as if no daily *Times* existed. Markel cared about the big public issues, and he made the *Magazine* a journal of national and international affairs. Yet as late as the 1960s, the *Magazine* paid contributors a penurious $250 for articles of three thousand words or more—and expected the writers to endure multiple rewrites from the demanding Markel, at no added pay. One of his Sunday favorites was the British writer Lady Barbara Ward, whose specialty was economics and politics. When Markel once was reproached about her long-winded essays, he was said to have exclaimed, "I made her rewrite it three times." The riposte was, "Yes, and you ran all three versions back to back."

Scotty Reston's Washington bureau represented another entity. The bureau's independence was first established in the 1930s by Arthur Krock, the converted Episcopalian and consummate Washington insider (in 1940 Krock helped a well-connected Harvard student named John F. Kennedy write his senior thesis about British politics during Hitler's rise to power; the thesis was later published as a book, entitled *Why England Slept*). Russell Baker in his day quickly learned that the world of the *Times* was divided into Reston men and New York men, each group with its own fealties. This helped explain Baker's inactive period of duty while at the home office: He was behind enemy lines. A fourth *Times* "nation" was based overseas; AHS's nephew Cyrus O. Sulzberger held the title of chief correspondent, and often appeared to preside over his own foreign-news service. Cy Sulzberger and other overseas correspondents were known to travel from one country to another without notifying the foreign desk in New York. When Cy Sulzberger obtained a private interview with General of the Army Douglas MacArthur, the correspondent stretched his notes into a six-part series for the *Times*. In New York, the editors wanted to cut the material to one article; Cy Sulzberger took his case to his uncle. The interview ran in six parts, beginning on page one.

For all the institutionalized redundancy, there were nevertheless telling holes in the *Times'* news coverage. Through the AHS years, the paper ran a regular column devoted to news and personalities of official Washington, but nothing similar for New York City. The *Times'* best local reporter, the storied Meyer Berger, was writing mood-of-the-city pieces and publishing them—in *The New Yorker*. Catledge in time persuaded AHS to start a Berger column called "About New York," and it became a great success with many readers. AHS wasn't among its fans; he fretted that Berger's subjects were "light" and "un-*Times*-like." The topics that fascinated Berger—in Catledge's words, "working people, ethnic subcultures, and neighborhood bars and customs"—held minimal appeal for Sulzberger. "The *Times* had never written about that level of New York, and he wasn't sure it should," Catledge remembered. After Berger's death in 1959, Catledge pushed as a replacement a young reporter named Gay Talese, who had caught his editors' eyes with his graceful writing for the sports department. AHS refused to resume the column; he wanted a no-frills paper. The gritty "little people" stories didn't fit the *Times*' self-image.

AHS's beau ideal of a newspaper appealed to a number of people—readers, advertisers and talented young men who wanted to work for the *Times* in part because it was the serious paper of record. James Goodale, a graduate of the University of Chicago Law School, joined the *Times*' outside counsel, Lord, Day and Lord, in 1959. As an undergraduate at Yale, Goodale had thought about a career as a political journalist. At Lord, Day, he enjoyed his arm's-length involvement with the *Times*, and jumped at the chance to become general attorney of the company in 1963. The *Times* of the postwar era, he believed, wanted to shape public opinion of national and international affairs—"That's what excited me when I joined the company; that was the Ochs spirit." The best instruments of the *Times*' potential influence, in Goodale's view, were the *Times Magazine* and the editorial pages. But when Goodale exchanged his outsider's perspective for a participant's role, he was taken aback by what he found at the top managerial levels of the paper.

The place was a big factory, he thought, and a badly run one at that. "Management was concerned solely with getting out the paper each day, and never looked beyond the nightly deadlines," he recalls. "No one had the time, or interest, to sit back and think about next week, or next year." Budget projections and forward planning were unheard of; union negotiations sought only "labor peace," and so generous contracts were signed. The *Times*' management styles affronted the former Lord, Day lawyer: "Millions of dollars were coming in and millions were going out. No one knew where, or why. No one knew how to make the money stay." Unlike a factory that made, say, widgets, the *Times* couldn't store its inventory, the news, toward the day when production might be interrupted by strikes or other unforeseen work stoppages.

All the aspects of the old Ochs rule that had seemed so admirable to outsiders looked different on the inside. The desire to be independent severely limited capital expenditures, for the family didn't want to borrow and be indebted to the financial markets (as Ochs had been at the very start). New acquisitions and diversification were seen not as opportunities but as threats: They would dilute the "purity" of the company. The idea of realizing more than 1 or 2 percent net return on revenues was somehow inappropriate, as if too boisterous and coarse for this particular family business. Arthur Hays Sulzberger, like Ochs before him, put his physical and intellectual energies into the daily tasks of the *Times*. He was content to remain a private company, pay out modest dividends, stay out of the red, and retain family control. The *Times*, obviously, wasn't ready for America's go-go years. It was an unfashionable one-product company. "All he wanted to do was publish a good newspaper," John May, a businessman and member of the *Times'* board of directors in the post-AHS years recalled, as if talking about a man who has chosen to study Latin or Greek when all his friends were becoming MBAs.

AHS had made some tentative efforts to get the company involved in related communications businesses. The *Times* acquired a radio station, WQXR, in 1944. In the postwar years, too, the *Times* experimented with new technologies and attempted to grow beyond the New York area. It stumbled badly, and its attempts were taken as proof of the quaint old ways.

In the last decade, facsimile transmission has become a familiar part of business communications and the means for producing nationally distributed publications, such as the *Wall Street Journal*, *USA Today* and—belatedly—the National editions of the *New York Times*. The fax has become an American household word, just as Japanese-made fax machines are now household appliances. Few *Times*people are aware that their own company, decades before the Japanese, was a major force in the facsimile business, holding more than fifty patents and commanding the services of the preeminent researcher in the field, Austin G. Cooley. An MIT electrical engineer, Cooley first began testing the transmission of graphic materials by wire in the years after World War I. By 1922 he was working for the *Times*, and the paper was using the facsimile technology in its news bureaus throughout the United States and Europe. For almost twenty years, the bureaus supplied stories and photographs both for the *Times'* pages and for other newspapers who had signed on as clients of the service.

In the 1940s the *Times* got out of distribution, selling the fax service to its competitor, the Associated Press, while retaining the fax equipment business. A few *Times*people continued to talk up the potential of facsimile transmission. In September 1953, for example, a *Times* executive named C. Raymond Hulsart attempted to create interest in the product with Donald B. Macurda, a banker at the First Boston Corporation, on lower Broadway. "An acknowledged need for facsimile exists in the banking business," Hulsart wrote, and added, presciently: "Detailed and statistical communications between departments or units of multiple-plant industrial operations present a problem readily solved by facsimile." In 1956 the *Times* enterprisingly published an experimental electronic paper using fax technology during the Republican National Convention in San Francisco. News pages made up in New York were transmitted to San Francisco via phone line, and then printed for distribution around the convention hall and at the delegates' hotels. Today orbiting satellites have supplanted phone lines for long-distance publishing: the much-heralded communications revolution. The principle involved is no different from the *Times'* 1956 experiment.

Having helped start the revolution, however, the *Times* walked away from its first benefits. In 1959, just as other publishers were beginning to realize the potential of electronic publishing, AHS decided to get *out* of the fax business. The Times Facsimile Company was sold to Litton Industries for $1,250,000. The *Times* also transferred to Litton most of the patents, trademarks, and contracts—and the services of the estimable Cooley. About this time a Chicago newspaper publisher named Bruce Sagan kept turning over in his mind the implications of the 1956 *Times* convention venture. Sagan was just 27 years old and already published a string of weeklies in the Chicago area. The *Times*, he reasoned, was producing a valued daily paper, strong in national and international coverage, and one that Sagan had read when he was growing up in Manhattan, and later used to buy as a college student at the University of Chicago bookstore (it was delivered by air mail, three days late).

Sagan understood that other, less successful papers in Chicago and around the country were in the process of consolidating or disappearing; the New York papers memorialized in the Times Tower copper box were testimony to that reality. Sagan reasoned that the *Times'* fax technology—plus his own printing presses—could together create a successful new product for these regional markets. On July 29, 1959, he mailed off his proposal to Arthur Hays Sulzberger. "Your company has developed a process for sending over wire composed pages and receiving at the other end the information on an offset negative," Sagan wrote. "We have recently installed a 16-page Vanguard offset newspaper press which we are using in the experimental printing of one of our weeklies." Sagan then made his pitch: "It is perhaps time for someone to try a national daily newspaper. . . . Do we have anything to discuss?" On August 4, Sulzberger replied, in full: "As I understand your letter of July 29th, your question is whether or not we would be interested in using the facsimile method of reproduction to make the *New York Times* available in other communities. The only answer I can give you at the present time is no."

The *Times* did start a limited national edition three years later, after Arthur Hays Sulzberger's illness and the appointment of his son-in-law, Orvil Dryfoos, as publisher. It was not a well-thought-out venture. Instead of facsimile, the *Times* used the old linotype technology; type was set in New York and transmitted to presses in Los Angeles for printing and distribution. The project, called "Westward Ho" within the paper, soon faltered. Some Westerners may have wanted a pocket version of the New York paper, but the *Times'* choice of a centralized printing plant meant that the company was dependent on small aircraft—and the vagaries of weather—to get the paper delivered to areas beyond Los Angeles.

Punch Sulzberger killed "Westward Ho" within a year of succeeding Dryfoos. The *Times* didn't revive the idea of a nationally distributed edition until the late 1970s, well after the *Wall Street Journal* had demonstrated how to reach a national market with the technologies of facsimile and space satellite. Following the *Journal* model, the *Times* used a satellite to link a network of printing plants (some owned by the *Times*, some under contract) through facsimile technology. In the Chicago area, the Southtown Economist, Inc., Bruce Sagan's company, won the contract to become the *Times'* printer. On April 24, 1980, after the *Times* signed its facsimile-transmission agreement with Community Newspapers, Sagan sent Punch Sulzberger a bantering note, attaching photocopies of the letters Sagan had exchanged two decades before with Arthur Sulzberger. Punch Sulzberger replied as his father had, by return mail. He thanked Sagan for the "wonderful" correspondence, and made a little joke about the *Times'* deliberate ways: "Dad put a committee together 21 years ago, and they just reported out."

That was Dad, and that was Punch: the father uninterested in seizing opportunities to take the *Times* beyond its "one product" and indeed beyond its base in New York, the son willing to expand and diversify. While AHS spurned a column on New York by Gay Talese because it was too soft, the son started the daily magazine sections (and rode out the sneering remarks about the *Times'* pasta desk, and its hard-hitting investigations of the best marinara in town). If AHS tolerated the separate fiefdoms of strong-willed editors, the son didn't exactly crack heads; but he got everyone's attention, consolidating the daily and Sunday papers and ending the autonomy of the Washington bureau.

Above all, the son was credited with transforming the *Times* into a public corporation. The "historic" *Times* had been content to earn a modest profit for the family; the modern *Times* made no apologies about wanting returns of 18 to 20 percent earnings on revenues (the media industry "standard" for well-run corporations). The needs of *Times* readers had to be served, but so did the needs of the newer Wall Street audience of stockholders and security analysts. The *Times'* first obligation, Punch Sulzberger told *Times* economics writer Leonard Silk in 1980, "is to be profitable." Sulzberger quickly added, as if in deference to Dad, "Isn't that a terrible way to put it? But if we're not profitable, we can't have any other mission." (The second mission was "to cover the news—to call the shots as we see them.")

The too-neat contrast between then and now, father and son, requires scrutiny, and qualification. AHS's *Times* held facsimile technology in its hands, and let it get away, but Punch Sulzberger's *Times* was a leader in data-base publishing, and in its turn walked away from that lucrative field. Sulzberger's *Times* also abandoned its interests in cable television and made no significant investments in the new technologies that began to change the media business in the 1980s. Instead it opted for small Sunbelt newspapers and special-interest magazines— with marginal success.

True, in the summer of 1993, in his sixty-seventh year and nearing the end of his formal career, Punch Sulzberger made a climactic Big Picture acquisition, presiding over the agreement to bring the *Boston Globe* under the control of the Times Company. The agreement was described as a $1.1 billion deal; actually, little cash was involved: the

Times offered to pay by issuing millions of new shares of its common stock, thereby diluting their earnings per share (the deal carefully left untouched the class of stocks held by the Sulzberger family). A *Times* news story in the editions of June 13, 1993, gave a—predictably—upbeat analysis of the agreement linking "two newspaper giants." Outsiders, however, were puzzled by the acquisition. While the *Globe* was the dominant paper in its corner of the Northeast, Boston, like New York, had been slow to recover from the early 1990s recession. In 1992 the net income of the *Globe's* parent company, Affiliated Publications, totaled a respectable $14.1 million. Of course, the *Globe* was not a glamorous business acquisition when measured against all the brave new tomorrowland talk about 500-channel cable TV systems and interactive media services. But it fit the Sulzberger temperament: an economically centrist move, progressive but not radical, with grand ego satisfactions to be derived from his fellow newspaper publishers. Some Wall Street analysts reacted sourly; they had no appreciation of how the *Globe* purchase played among the peers of the Sulzbergers.

For the rest, Punch Sulzberger's custodial record when he passed control of the *Times* on to his son was mixed, particularly as it affected the content of the paper. The consolidation of editorial power in one man, the volcanic Abe Rosenthal, created the predictable Actonian corruption, while the celebration of consumption in the new upscale sections inevitably weakened coverage of the unbeautiful city. The strategy of moving the *Times* out of the New York market also produced equivocal results. Punch Sulzberger's 1990s version of a national-satellite edition of the *Times* may not work any better than the *Times'* effort in the early 1960s. By the time the national *Times* reached the markets beyond the Hudson, the *Wall Street Journal* and *USA Today* were there, in place. The *Journal* had become a "second read" of a business-minded audience (its first read was the hometown paper, the *Cleveland Plain Dealer,* or the *Chicago Tribune,* for local news and sports). In smaller cities, for less demanding readers, the folksy *USA Today,* with its short stories and TV-like color graphics, became a second read.

In one managerial area, though, Punch Sulzberger achieved absolute success. With tenacity, and the help of good lawyers, he guaranteed his family's control of the *Times* well into the middle of the twenty-first century.

A DAY IN THE LIFE
9:45 A.M.—10:05 A.M.

9:45 A.M.

Half the world away from 43rd Street in the other direction, Bill Keller, the *Times'* bureau chief in Moscow, had a clock that worked to his advantage. Keller could put in a full day of reporting in Moscow, organize his notes, and write his story—and it was still early in the day in New York. He also had an easy commute to work: His apartment at one end of the fortress-like building at 12/24 Sadova Samotechnaya was fifty feet from the second-floor flat that had been converted into the *Times'* offices. Sadova Samotechnaya is one of the ring roads in Moscow, and number 12/24 is part of the foreign journalists' ghetto in the capital. Several other American newspeople, as well as Japanese and British journalists, lived in the same building. Five minutes away was the U.S. Embassy. Keller, compact and clear-eyed, was born in California in 1949. At Pomona College, he edited the student paper and spent weekends as a backpacker. When a big earthquake cut off Moscow's communications with Soviet Armenia, Keller alternately hitchhiked and walked along the 160-mile perimeter of the earthquake zone, from the Armenian capital of Yerevan to the hardest-hit towns of Leninakan and Spitak. The morning of Tuesday, February 28, he strolled to his office knowing that the *Times* had just nominated him for a Pulitzer Prize for his earthquake coverage (one month later, on March 30, Keller won his Pulitzer in the international reporting category).

9:50 A.M.

On 43rd Street in front of the *Times* building, two twenty-wheel trucks, numbers 49 and 08, pulled up to the pressroom bays just east of the lobby entrance, toward Broadway. The two trucks, both thirty-three-foot-long trailers pulled by ten-foot cabs, were from the Baldwin Transportation Company, 108 Leggitt Avenue in the Bronx near the Hunts Point railhead, where the trucks off-loaded the newsprint rolls the night before. The shipment had come by rail over the weekend from the Spruce Falls Power and Paper Company Limited, Spruce Falls, Canada. The driver of the first truck, Mike Casanova of the Teamsters Union, was delivering order number 73; it consisted of ten newsprint rolls, each weighing one ton and as big around as a kitchen table. The *Times'* two printing plants, one at 43rd Street, the other in Carlstadt, New Jersey, received over eight thousand such rolls that week; in all, some 400,000 tons of newsprint was budgeted to publish the *Times* of the late 1980s and early 1990s.

In Boston, his pile of newspapers read, Tony Lewis had his idea for his column for the edition of March 2. The Congressional opponents of the John Tower nomination, Lewis thought, were using dangerous tactics in relying on untested charges from an FBI report.

10:00 A.M.

The editors and reporters who worked on the twenty-odd departmental desks responsible for the *Times'* daily news report arrived in the New York newsroom and offices: the main dayshift of 450 men and women. In Washington, Michael Oreskes was among the first of the thirty-five men and women who worked in the bureau to appear at the *Times'* offices on I Street. The offices, located in the former Army-Navy Building, were elegantly appointed, with modern work stations, ergonomically designed—as the more sardonic *Times* bureau people told it—to maximize the computer-human interface. Only the rolltop desk of James Reston, the longtime bureau chief and columnist, broke with the cool modern design. But Reston's old-fashioned "country editor's desk" was an artful replica; upon closer inspection, a visitor saw that Reston's desk had a built-in LED display clock and other electronic features.

The bureau was in a prestige location, with two floors connected by an interior staircase, the Washington mark of high-powered law firms, well-connected public relations counselors, and other Capital rainmakers. Oreskes, an emerging star of the *Times* for his work during the past presidential campaign, had returned that morning from New York, where he participated in a conference on "the Sound Bite Election." One of his fellow panelists was Roger Ailes, George Bush's media adviser and the creator of some of the Bush "attack" commercials (Dukakis riding in a tank, polluted Boston Harbor). Back in Washington, Oreskes prepared, in his words, "to wade through the mud of the Tower story." The appointment was being held up while the Senate debated Tower's "fitness" to be secretary of defense. There were reports of drinking, womanizing, and too-cozy relationships with military contractors. It was trial by leak, Senator William Cohen, Republican of Maine, had complained in a brief conversation with Oreskes. The reporter considered Cohen a smart, decent senator; Oreskes arranged a longer interview.

In the office pantry, Barbara Gamarekian, a member of the

bureau for three decades, poured a cup of coffee, checked the message center for calls, and sat down to read an office copy of the *Times*. She had already read the *Washington Post* at home, turning to its Style section for a story she expected to be there. All day Monday, the bureau had heard rumors about the possible defection of Steven Roberts to *U.S. News & World Report*. Roberts, forty-six years old and a twenty-five-year *Times* veteran, was considered by his colleagues "the classic *Times* career reporter": productive, ambitious, and with a network of excellent Washington sources willing to help, and be helped by, the *Times*. "His work was never less than a 8.7 on a journalistic scale of 10," in one *Times*man's assessment. Roberts was married to Cokie Roberts of National Public Radio; he often appeared on public television's "Washington Week in Review." The editors of the *Post* judged Roberts' departure from the *Times* newsworthy enough to be put on the first page of Style Tuesday morning.

The *Post* described Roberts's desire to write "on a broader canvas than the *Times* was offering" and said that he wished to "get away from the grind of the daily beat." The *Post* hinted also that Roberts was unhappy about the *Times* rule limiting the amount of outside work, including regular TV appearances, that staff members were permitted. Post writer Eleanor Randolph quoted Max Frankel, who explained that the *Times* didn't want "our people to be regulars on TV shows." In Frankel's view, a TV producer who wanted to build up an on-air staff "shouldn't do so on the back of the *New York Times*."

The *Post* had managed to needle its rival—the references to the *Times'* clampdown on free-lance work, to the fact that other places were now offering competitive salaries. But the article stopped short of the rest of the story, the part *Times* bureau people were talking about. Roberts had begun his career at the *Times* in elite company, as one in the series of news clerks that James Reston hired, usually right after graduation from Harvard. Roberts began much like all of Reston's clerks, opening mail for the columnist, arranging appointments, tracking down information. It was the gentleman's way for *Times* mentorship: Reston's news clerks were, almost without exception, young, white, Ivy league males. A clerkship typically insured smooth passage to permanent staff assignment. With Reston's approaching retirement the news clerk's job had been abolished, along with some of the older gentlemanly agreements.

Steve Roberts had just finished his tour of duty as a *Times* correspondent in the Reagan White House. The *Times*, by way of reward, offered him a next step forward in his career—the job of supervising the "Washington Talk" page. Roberts upset the script, and turned down the promotion. He preferred the high-profile exposure of television punditry to bureau-desk work that was both anonymous and subservient to other, anonymous editors in New York. Frankel and his associates—collectively known in the bureau as "New York"—were angered. When Roberts went to his bureau chief, Howell Raines, to plead for a waiver of the free-lance rule, to continue his TV work, it was the turn of New York to say no. Then, in the manner of the military—"request permission to speak to the Captain, sir!"—Roberts sought Raines's permission to talk to Frankel. He was told that "New York" had nothing to say to him. A quarter-century career at the *Times* ended. A few months later, the "Washington Talk" page was discontinued by Frankel. Some bureau people thought the feature was a casualty of the continuing low-intensity warfare between Washington and New York. Others concluded that the cutback on Washington political news was part of Frankel's efforts to make the *Times* livelier, and more reader friendly.

10:05 A.M.

Karl Meyer took the elevator to the tenth floor of the Times Building, where the editorial board and the columnists work in a university-like setting. The ceiling-high book stacks and card files of the *Times'* library form a central core; around it are the modest private offices of the "faculty" of writers and editors. Meyer, a member of the editorial board, was preoccupied. He had been involved intermittently with a book project since 1984—an anthology of the American newspaper column starting with Benjamin Franklin. Oxford University Press had scheduled it for publication in the fall, and Meyer was late with his manuscript. He closed the office door, spread out manila folders, and worked on the end notes for his free-lance project.

2

OUR CROWD, OUR PAPER

LIFE AT THE *TIMES* has exacted a toll on the family owners. Each of the four men who preceded Arthur O. Sulzberger, Jr., as publishers became seriously ill on the job. In the years between 1921 and 1933, the patriarch Adolph S. Ochs suffered two incapacitating "nervous breakdowns," as they were described. Ochs's son-in-law and successor, Arthur Hays Sulzberger, suffered a series of strokes beginning in the late 1950s and was an invalid for the last eleven years of his life. Orvil Dryfoos, AHS's son-in-law and successor, suffered a fatal heart attack two months after the settlement of the devastating New York City newspaper strike of 1962–63. The dispute closed down the *Times* for 114 days as Dryfoos took the lead in *Times* management's negotiations with its unions; he was fifty and had been the *Times* publisher for just two years at the time of his death. Barbara Tuchman, the historian and a family friend, offered a diagnosis of "professional stress."

The fourth man, Arthur's father, Punch Sulzberger, in middle age became a convert to an exercise and diet program in midtown Manhattan (the Cardio-Fitness Center, which promised in full-page ads in the *Times*: "Now you can lose your flab and save your heart in a personalized program"). Sulzberger's regular sessions of aerobics and stretches, which he usually scheduled at 6:30 in the morning, before arriving at his *Times* office, helped trim him down. In 1988 an abscess in his jaw under a wisdom tooth put him in the hospital. Two years later, the condition returned, so severely that he was unable for a time to speak or to eat solid foods. A year after that, he experienced an excruciating inflammation of the hip joints, the pain so intense that the act of putting on or taking off his suit jacket became a test of stamina. Fortunately, the condition was treatable with medication. He was still recovering when his son, Arthur Jr., became publisher in January 1992.

The wrenching demands of keeping the *Times* the *Times* was to some extent a self-imposed burden. The *Times* existed in a special category, and not just in the minds of the owner-family. The worker ranks also saw themselves as part of a great institution. "We have a commitment to excellence that trickles down to the lowest levels of the newsroom," Warren Hoge, an assistant managing editor of the *Times*, declared grandly. "It's quite heady." Hoge was explaining to an interviewer why some of the *Times*' best journalists spurn the "lure of more money" from other publications. "They don't get the sense elsewhere of being driven to perform, of being among the most admired journalists. It's our professional atmosphere, the feeling that we are the best." According to Hoge, "those who do leave wish to come back after a year away because they miss that spirit." Hoge's grasp of the facts may be somewhat shaky: The number of departees from the *Times* over the years suggests that not everyone found the *Times* newsroom atmosphere so bracing. But the mind-set is authentic; many *Times*people do regard the paper as an enterprise on another plane, far beyond the daily journalistic calling.

The burden of ownership wasn't a topic the family wanted aired in the news columns of the paper. A group of midlevel *Times* editors learned this at first hand. In 1979 Iphigene Ochs Sulzberger completed her memoirs, a 296-page book, written with the help of her granddaughter, Susan Dryfoos, Orvil Dryfoos's daughter. Iphigene, Ochs's only child, the eleven-year-old in high-button shoes and bulky tights who helped lay the cornerstone of the Times Building in 1904, embodied the history of the modern *Times*. She was an eyewitness to all the changes at the paper, and Susan Dryfoos had shaped her grandmother's informal recollections into an endearing story. Their publisher, Dodd, Mead & Co., was sure the *Times Magazine* would be interested in running an excerpt. Galleys were sent over to the *Times*; the magazine's top editors, knowing the procedure when the family was involved, passed on the proposal to the publisher's office. The protocols observed, the magazine staff expected automatic clearance. The fourteenth-floor startled the editors by vetoing publication, with no explanation. One editor belatedly concluded that "the memoir brought up too much about the medical history of the family," and that Punch Sulzberger didn't want "to give any unnecessary attention to his own mother's book."

The *Times Magazine* missed out on an intimate narrative of the *Times'* ruling family. It turned out, for example, that Adolph Ochs's first breakdown was in part the consequence of the stresses created by the labyrinthine financial dealings which finally insured his control of the *Times*. Ochs didn't own the *Times* outright until 1916, twenty years after his initial "purchase." That appears to be the case, at any rate; the record is murky, in part because of Ochs's breakdown. Iphigene Sulzberger told Harrison Salisbury that her father destroyed the accounting books detailing the relevant loans, interest payments, and stock investments during the severe "fit of depression" that gripped him through the years 1921 and 1922. Similarly, Ochs's second collapse in 1933 grew out of anxieties about the *Times'* business. The country was in the depths of the Great Depression and, according to Iphigene Sulzberger, her father "agonized" over the potentially shattering threat the economy posed to his newspaper properties. Ochs also became obsessed with the Lindbergh baby kidnapping and worried for the safety of his own grandchildren. To assuage her father, Iphigene took her children to Europe in the summer of 1934, to get them out of harm's way. Punch Sulzberger was eight years old at the time of the trip.

When Ochs died in 1935, his son-in-law, Arthur Hays Sulzberger, inherited another potential threat to continued family control. Ochs held all the shares of the *New York Times* and the *Chattanooga Times* in his own name, even though his lawyers had urged him, for estate tax purposes, to put some share of these holdings in his wife's or daughter's name. He stubbornly refused ("He was a self-made man, proud of being the family provider," Iphigene Sulzberger explained). He did, however, provide that the estate, upon his death, would go to the Ochs Trust. In that way, the normally large inheritance taxes levied on private fortunes could be avoided, and the estate passed on, tax free, to the children of Iphigene and Arthur. The children's children would eventually have to pay taxes on their inheritance, but as Iphigene

Sulzberger pointed out, with the estate split thirteen ways, their tax bracket would not be as high.

There were still the taxes that would be due at the time of Ochs's death, a sum amounting to $6 million including the lawyers' fees, according to Iphigene Sulzberger. Arthur Hays Sulzberger conceived of an ingenious way to deal with these taxes. Upon the death of Adolph Ochs, the son-in-law arranged for the New York Times Company, with its strong cash flow, to purchase from the Ochs Trust a bloc of its preferred stock amounting to $6 million. In that way, the Trust could pay off the taxes due. The alternative would have been to raise the cash by selling off shares of the family's *Times* stock or by borrowing from the banks. Either of these alternatives, Arthur Hays Sulzberger later said, would have compromised the family's control of the *Times*, and "we were prepared to make any sacrifice to avoid that."

The plan was perfectly legal and prudent—except for one rather large miscalculation. The president of the United States, Franklin D. Roosevelt, had campaigned against the "malefactors of great wealth" in 1932 and 1936 (in both elections, with the endorsement of the *Times*). One of FDR's proposed New Deals involved using the federal tax code to prevent the inheritance of large fortunes. Roosevelt eventually pushed through legislation forbidding managements from selling stock back to their own companies, but not before the Ochs deal was completed. Arthur Sulzberger later heard from several sources he regarded as reliable that Roosevelt had privately characterized the Ochs stock-purchase plan as "a dirty Jewish trick" to avoid taxes. When Roosevelt invited Arthur Sulzberger to lunch at the White House on December 28, 1939, the "dirty trick" allegation didn't come up directly; Sulzberger was perhaps too polite. But the conversation did touch on the episode in general. According to minutes of the meeting prepared by Sulzberger and placed in the *Times*' archives, the president told the publisher that while "the Ochs settlement was too large," it was perfectly legal. Furthermore, "I would have done the same thing myself."

The news columns of the *Times* eventually treated the family's protracted, multigenerational efforts to insure continued control of the *Times*' properties. In the days after Iphigene Ochs Sulzberger's death on February 26, 1990, at the age of ninety-seven, the paper gave meticulous coverage to the terms of the Ochs Trust. A page-one story on February 27 concentrated on the biographical details of Mrs. Sulzberger's life, noting that she had passed on to her family "the traditions of the *Times* and its dedication to serious journalism, to good taste and to progressive values," while a related story on the obituary page dealt with the stock shares her father had left her. The Adolph Ochs Trust, the paper reported, held 83.7 percent of the Times' controlling class-B stock. The class-A stock, publicly traded on the American Stock Exchange, was effectively nonvoting stock. The arrangement was intended to insure that outsider holders of Times stock could not gain control of the paper. It had been developed by the family's lawyers when the *Times* became a public company in the 1960s, and the arrangement was widely imitated since by other newspaper families, including—Punch Sulzberger likes to point out—the Grahams of the *Washington Post*. "They copied us," he says. "We call the voting shares the class-B stock, they call it the class-A stock. Otherwise it's identical."

Upon Iphigene Sulzberger's death, the Ochs Trust was dissolved and reconstituted in the form of four new trusts, one for each of her children—Punch and his sisters Marian, Judith, and Ruth. The four were designated as trustees for each trust, to be held in their names for their thirteen children and twenty-four grandchildren who were alive on August 5, 1986. According to the new terms, the trusts are to last twenty-one years beyond the lifetime of the last surviving grandchild. The new agreement also strictly prevents any family member from selling any part of the class-B stock to outsiders.

There were good reasons the Sulzbergers put their lawyers to work on the new trust arrangements in 1986. Iphigene Sulzberger was in her nineties, but an updated agreement with detailed provisions about the resale of class-B stock had little to do with the actuarial tables. The specific form of the new trust arrangement was framed with the experience of another publishing dynasty in mind, the Barry Bingham family of Louisville, Kentucky. The travails of Barry Bingham, Sr., his wife, Mary, and their three adult children were chronicled in the pages of the *Times* all through 1985. No one followed the story more closely than the Sulzberger family.

The Binghams of Louisville, like the Reids of New York, were another one of those storybook "aristocratic" families in the newspaper business. The Sulzbergers had known the Binghams for decades, through the publishers' association and other newspaper-industry committees. The Binghams owned the *Louisville Courier-Journal*, the leading newspaper in the mid-South and one of the best dailies in the country; the company also included broadcasting properties and a gravure facility. As the retired patriarch Barry Bingham, Sr., neared his eightieth birthday, his children sharply split over the direction of the company, and about their own roles in its future. Their disagreements turned father against son, sister against brother. For almost two years, the Binghams remained divided over a plan that would have permitted two of the children to share the properties while providing for the buy-out of a third. In the end, a difference over a relatively modest sum of money hardened the family split. One sister, Sallie Bingham, had asked $32 million for her shares; her brother, Barry Bingham, Jr., acting in the name of the company, was willing to offer her only $26.3 million. But something more than dollars was involved. Behind the $5.7 million difference were several emotional intangibles, such as Sallie Bingham's feminist views and her feelings of parental neglect, Barry Jr.'s lifetime in others' shadows, and his efforts to force his sisters off the company's board of directors. The father, convinced he could not break the impasse, put the paper up for sale. In 1986 the *Louisville Courier-Journal* properties were sold for $434 million to the Gannett Company, the media corporation that owned *USA Today*, among other papers.

The Bingham story was a cautionary tale for the Sulzberger family. Two of the longest news stories ever published in the *Times* scrupulously chronicled first "The Fall of the House of Bingham" (January 19, 1986) and then revisited the family and its misfortunes later in the year to report on "The Binghams: After the Fall" (December 21, 1986). The two articles ran well over ten thousand words, and won a Pulitzer Prize for *Times* reporter Alex S. Jones. The overtones of Greek tragedy in the *Times* headlines were deliberate, and the lessons of family hubris explicit. One passage read like an internal memo for consumption in the *Times*' boardroom. "For large families struggling with the problems of multigenerational ownership of a business, the saga of the Binghams and their failure to hold together was particularly poignant," Jones wrote. "And for the dwindling number of families still operating their own newspapers, the news from Louisville was chilling."

Jones, with his wife, Susan Tifft, expanded the articles into a book. They allowed Arthur Sulzberger, Jr., an advance look at the manuscript. He returned it with the one word comment, "horrifying." Punch Sulzberger, Arthur's father, remembered that he read "every word of the Bingham stories." Afterward, "I told my sisters, 'I'll be nice to you!' " Then, turning serious, he said: "We all get along very well as a family, my sisters and I. There's no way it can all go down the drain here." If some of the Sulzbergers' children or grandchildren have no interest in the company, he explained, "they can always sell into the pool, and go away and buy IBM or become hot dog vendors or whatever." The family interest comes first, before all else: Richard N. Cohen, a stockbroker and the husband of Judith Sulzberger Cohen—the Judy to Punch—was on the board of directors of the Times Company. When the Cohens' marriage ended in divorce, the wife resumed using her maiden name—and Cohen was removed from the board, after twelve years of service.

The Times' new family–stock "pool" was formalized in the months after the Bingham split became the talk of the newspaper business. The four Sulzberger children—and their children—announced in June 1986 that they had agreed on a recapitalization plan for the Times Company's class-B stock, essentially the family trust set up by Ochs. Holders of class-B stock elect 70 percent of the company's board of directors. The 1986 agreement keeps all class-B stock within the family. If a family member wishes to sell the Times Company stock—taking the money and running, as did Sallie Bingham—he or she cannot sell to outsiders until the stock is first offered to the other family members, and then to the company. Even in the all-but-inconceivable event that neither the family nor the company offered to buy the stock, the shares can be sold to nonfamily members only after being converted to the class-A noncontrolling stock available to the public. The agreement, signed August 5, 1986, would remain in effect twenty-one years beyond the lifetime of the last surviving family member who was alive on that date. In this way, the Sulzbergers insured family control well into the twenty-first century. Whatever conceivable dissension arises among the Sulzbergers, the *Times* stays in the family "until way out there," in Punch Sulzberger's words.

The emotional attachment of the various Sulzberger family members to the *Times* is a private matter. The value of their financial connection is relatively easy to calculate. The same editions of the *Times* that reported the news of Iphigene Ochs Sulzberger's death and the terms of the new trusts also carried the information that the Times Company's revenues reached $1.8 billion in 1989. The company does not break out specific earnings figures, but operating profits from the

Times newspaper alone were estimated to be $200 million that same year. A general formula used in the media business places the value of a newspaper property at $1,000 per reader. The circulation of the daily *Times* reached 1.1 million in 1990, while the Sunday circulation climbed toward 1.7 million in the same period.

This wealth places the Sulzbergers among "the owners of the Great Republic," in the phrase of Gore Vidal. The family belongs to the American ruling class, which since the depression of the 1930s has chosen, in Vidal's words, "not to be known to the public at large." While the deeds of Wall Street raiders, leveraged-buy-out kings, show-business personalities, and other nouveaux riches helped fill the pages of newspapers—including the *Times'*—during the Reagan era, the enduring rich were seldom heard or seen. Shunning celebrity, they kept to what Vidal calls their "private islands." Within this orbit, the personal styles of Punch Sulzberger and his son, Arthur Jr., simultaneously suggest self-deprecation *and* entitlement—as if they want you to believe they are not among the nobles who own America, but know that you understand that they are. In early 1988, at the start of the presidential election primaries, the Reverend Jesse Jackson visited the *Times'* editorial board. Like other presidential candidates who have been invited to the publisher's executive suite through the years, Jackson was there to make himself known to the *Times'* senior executives and editorial board. If the *Times'* endorsement of the Jackson candidacy in the April primary in New York was unlikely, given the Sulzbergers' cautious politics, then at least some favorable notice in the paper's editorial page would be helpful, preferably before primary day. The two Sulzbergers—Arthur O. Sulzberger, Jr., was then assistant publisher—sought to explain to Jackson the collegial nature of the *Times.* Jackson believed the Sulzbergers were free to endorse whomever they chose in the campaign. The Sulzbergers demurred: "Mr. Jackson, we don't own this place. The stockholders own the *New York Times.*" Jackson would have none of it. Come on, he chided in the tone of someone who wasn't born yesterday, "You control the voting stock."

The Reverend Jackson had grasped the meaning of "the power of the press" more readily than some of the paper's reporters, who when they went out on stories, sometimes fell into the habit of thinking they were "the *Times.*"

The *Times* belongs to the Sulzbergers, whatever the formal listing on the American Stock Exchange. They seldom venture from their private island. Although Punch Sulzberger ran the *Times* for a third of a century, he confined his public life to a minimum of formal appearances—presiding at the *Times'* annual stockholders' meetings and fulfilling his obligations for the American Newspaper Publishers Association. In late middle age, too, he took on the duties of board chairman of the Metropolitan Museum of Art in New York. Ronald Reagan, a master of the calculatedly "modest" gesture, once remarked that one of the best things about the presidency was living in the White House "over the store." Similarly, Punch Sulzberger joked that he became chairman of the Met because "I live right across the street."

The Met chairman's post might well have been tailored for Sulzberger as he neared his sixty-fifth birthday. The assumption of his employees was that at some time around his birth date the father would pass on the publisher's title to his son, Arthur, the only male heir of Punch Sulzberger from his two marriages. "The age of sixty-five, or sixty-six, is a pretty good time to move on," he reflected as the date approached. "You've done what you could do in that kind of job; someone else should pick up on it." Sulzberger didn't want to suggest that he was "burned out," but only that "it was a good time for a change." The passing of power was partial: The father relinquished his formal role at the newspaper, but remained as chairman of the Times Company. Along with the title of publisher, the son inherited a fresh set of anxieties about the *New York Times*.

Arthur O. Sulzberger, Jr., the fifth man to become publisher of the family paper, was born in 1951, long after the death of the founder of the dynasty, his great grandfather Adolph H. Ochs. Arthur Jr.'s recollections of his grandfather, Arthur Hays Sulzberger, and of his uncle Orvil Dryfoos, his predecessors as publisher, were hazy. For a time, it seemed that he might not get to know his own father much better.

His parents had divorced in 1956, when he was five. His mother, Barbara, remarried, and for the next eight years, young Arthur traveled back and forth between his two natural parents. Some weekends he spent with his father at "Granny's house," Iphigene Ochs Sulzberger's gracious 262-acre estate, Hillandale, near Stamford, Connecticut. There, through the late 1950s and early 1960s, young Arthur played with his cousins, enjoying the estate's olympic-size pool, its all-weather tennis court, and its private five-acre lake. From their ranks some thirty years hence, the next publisher of the *Times* would come, if the paper still belonged to the family.

Children barely in their teens may not ordinarily dwell on such matters of power and primogeniture, and young Arthur certainly was a normal young boy. Handsome, smallish, outgoing, he was an active student at the Browning preparatory school on East 62nd Street in New York. The 1970 Browning yearbook credits him with three years on the Debating Club and two years of junior varsity football. He also spent three years on the school newspaper, the *Browning Grytte*, rising to assistant editor in his final year.

In the middle of this ordinary prep school routine, however, he decided to leave his mother and live permanently with his father. Edward Klein, a former *Times* senior editor who came to know both Sulzberger men during an eleven-year tenure at the paper, theorized that "a sense of dispossession" may have overwhelmed the boy. His father and Punch's second wife, young Arthur's stepmother, already had two children, both girls, the older one from the new Mrs. Sulzberger's first marriage. There was always a possibility of another child—this time, a male, who would bear the Sulzberger name, and might then become the next head of the dynasty. Between his thirteenth and fourteenth birthdays, young Arthur left his mother's apartment on East 74th Street and moved into his father's home on Fifth Avenue.

From Browning, Sulzberger went on to Tufts University, where he majored in political science. As his grandfather had done for Punch, so, too, did Punch arrange for his son the chance to accumulate on-the-ground experience at a good regional newspaper. Arthur worked as a reporter for the *Raleigh* (North Carolina) *Times* and then in the London bureau of the Associated Press. His mother had again divorced and remarried, and was living with her third husband in Topeka. Visiting her in Kansas, young Arthur met, literally, the girl next door, Gail Gregg. They began seeing each other and were married in 1975 in the backyard of the Greggs' Victorian house in Topeka. According to Edward Klein, their wedding was a scene from a modern marriage; the groom's side of the family was represented by three fathers, two mothers, one stepsister, three sisters, (half, step-, and full), a half brother, and an "assortment of long-haired cousins." Gregg kept her maiden name. When Arthur was working for the AP in London, she was at the rival United Press International.

In recent years, Arthur began gathering a group of *Times*people his own age around him to be his new "team" at the paper. After hours, in social settings, he sometimes regaled them with the same kind of self-deprecating stories his father used to tell his associates. In London, Arthur recalled at one such dinner party, he and Gail directly competed against each other. During a minor British cabinet crisis, reporters on the sidewalk outside Number 10 Downing Street were being restrained by police; as AP man Sulzberger tried to press closer to find out what was going on, he recounted, he spotted UPI reporter Gregg inside the police cordon, getting a clean beat on the story. If it wasn't quite like his father's debacle at the Le Mans auto race, it nevertheless produced appreciative chuckles among the guests.

His non-*Times* seasoning considered complete, Arthur joined the family paper in 1978. He worked first on the news side, as a general assignment reporter in the Washington bureau and then for the metropolitan desk in New York. In Washington, Sulzberger played his part of the prince in waiting, fraternizing, drinking, and staying out late with the Falstaffs of the bureau. In New York, his metro training included half a year covering City Hall during the second term of Edward I. Koch. His business-side apprenticeship at the *Times* began in 1982, in the advertising department. He went out on sales calls, and then worked as a strategic planner. By 1987 he was working in operations, overseeing the production of the paper, and joking about his assignment: "I'm a journalist who just got off on the wrong floor."

Arthur Sulzberger's bantering humor was deceptive: He always knew what was expected of him, on whatever floor he worked. Ten years after Sulzberger's Washington tour, in the early winter of 1988, Ben Franklin, a *Times*man since 1959 and at sixty-one one of the older members of the Washington bureau, was being forced into early retirement. Officially, Franklin was informed that his retirement was part of an economy drive. Franklin went up to New York, as he puts it, to get "embalmed"—that is, complete the details of his severance package, including the terms of his pension and health-care benefits. He remembered dreading the walk through the third-floor newsroom. On impulse, Franklin decided to go up to the executive floor and unburden himself to Arthur Sulzberger, his old fellow bureauman, at the time the newly appointed assistant publisher of the *Times*.

Franklin found no Prince Hal. Sulzberger was very much part of the management loop; far from being ignorant of Franklin's situation, the assistant publisher had signed off on the economy drive. He looked

Franklin in the eye and told him that the bureau was bloated; costs had to be cut and a message sent to the whole staff. "The paper must have the right to put people where they are needed and away from where they're not needed." Franklin closed out his *Times* career feeling anger and bitterness. He had given his best years to the paper; now "the bean counters had taken over, to team up with the careerists, who were always there." Franklin eventually found work he could enjoy at *Nucleonics*, a McGraw-Hill company magazine. Franklin held on to his shares of Times stock, and complained when it stalled in the low twenties through the early years of the 1990s. The economy drive that cost him his job had not helped the stock price.

The title "assistant publisher" had been created for Arthur. His apprenticeship seemed to stretch on and on through the 1980s. His father held on to the two titles of publisher of the *Times* and chairman-CEO of the Times Company. Careful readers could spot signs of the newsroom's sly "Arthur watch" in the pages of the paper. A short news story in the *Times* of February 18, 1989, noted that England's Prince Charles was visiting Washington, D. C. The forty-year-old heir to the British throne dined with some noble Americans his own age, including Arthur O. Sulzberger, Jr., by then deputy publisher of the *Times*, and Donald Graham, the publisher of the *Washington Post*. Donald Graham's mother, Katharine Graham, then seventy-two, still held the title of chairman of the parent Washington Post Company. The story said Prince Charles talked with his dinner companions about the travails of being a king in waiting, and having "to invent one's job as one went along."

The *Times*' publisher in waiting took on a select few social obligations as he marked time in the company hierarchy. He became interested in the Outward Bound program and eventually became one of its trustees. The Outward Bound "experience" is a kind of sleepaway camp for adults. Participants are usually thirtysomething men on the way up the corporate or public ladder. They undertake rugged outdoor challenges, such as mountain climbing, rafting, or wilderness backpacking, in order to learn the arts of cooperation, self-reliance, male bonding, and survival away from the boardroom. Normally, the younger Sulzberger got his exercise, and the experience of urban survival, in morning jogs through Central Park across from the West Side apartment he and Gail Gregg shared with their two young children. Some non-*Times* people tried to hang the name Pinch on him, as much to play off the family succession as to signify the son's slim runner's build. It wouldn't stick: "You can call me that, once," he informed an acquaintance, with barely a smile breaking across his broad, pleasant features.

The son was no knockoff version of the father. Quite the contrary, the younger Sulzberger was in some ways in competition with the senior Sulzberger. The family had agreed to the passing of authority: Arthur's status was not in doubt. Although he had older sisters, no woman was seriously considered a candidate to run the paper (in that respect nothing had changed from 1963 to 1991). True, there were the male children of Punch's three older sisters, and, as it happened, three cousins of Arthur Sulzberger were also working their way up the Times Company hierarchy at the same time: Michael and Stephen Golden, the sons of Ruth Sulzberger Holmberg, and Daniel Cohen, the son of Dr. Judith Sulzberger (who had resumed the use of her maiden name). The newsroom noted Michael Golden's promotion to the job of publisher of *McCall's*, part of the Times Magazine Group; it observed Daniel Cohen's progress in the *Times'* advertising department. Cohen went through Tufts together with Arthur Sulzberger and they were friends as well as cousins and colleagues. A knowledge of *Times* history added to the pleasures of Sulzberger family-watching. In 1919 two other family members had been put on parallel tracks to the top. They were Arthur Hays Sulzberger, Iphigene's husband, and Julius Ochs Adler, the son of Adolph Ochs's sister Ada. Both men had joined the paper after being mustered out of the army. Ochs assigned his son-in-law Sulzberger to duties primarily on the editorial side of the *Times*; Adler was given duties on the business side. Ochs also gave each man—and Iphigene—a single vote to select the successor on his death. As long as Iphigene was happily married to Arthur Hays Sulzberger, Gay Talese wrote in his history of the *Times*, "the odds would be with Sulzberger 2 to 1."

There was no suggestion of a vote this time. The only real family rivalry seemed to be between the two Arthurs. The date of Prince Charles's ascension to the British throne depended solely on the longevity of his mother, the queen. Arthur O. Sulzberger, Jr., had to wait on the intentions of his father. The son had to consider, for example, whether his father really intended to give himself over full-time to the activities of ceremonial elder of the New York social establishment. The elder Sulzberger's term as head of the publishers' association had expired in 1989, although he stayed on the committee of the leading publisher-owners charged with lobbying the Congress for stricter regulation of the telephone companies and their plans to get into the data-transmission business. Electronic information services could rob newspapers of the classified advertising so essential to their continued existence.

Punch Sulzberger's duties at the Met also took up work time each week. Refreshingly, he stayed outside the showy orbit of "the new collectors" who bought art the way they acquired Southhampton houses or trophy wives. He had joined the Met's board in 1968 as much because of a prudent businessman's belief that the *Times* should be involved in the culture of the city as from any abiding interest in the museum's holdings. He had no collection of his own to speak of at the time, and did not accumulate any major artworks in the years since, although he did like to buy antique maps, mainly seventeenth- and eighteenth-century cartographers' conceptions of the North American continent. He hung them on the paneled wall of the fourteenth-floor reception room outside his office. His favorite depicted the northeast U.S. coast, with illustrations along the margins of beavers at work, building dams. The European cartographer had never encountered beavers before, Sulzberger explained to a visitor, and had to imagine how the beavers built their dams across streams. The engraving shows the beavers walking upright, carrying stones and other materials on their broad tails. A parable of the *Times*' newsroom, perhaps? "Oh yes, though here they carry the stones on their heads," Sulzberger replied.

At the Met, he had felt most comfortable serving on the museum's arms and armor committee: The military hardware appealed to the gadgeteer in him. But there were certain other intangibles. His wife, Carol Sulzberger, a lively, gregarious woman, enjoyed the New York social scene. She had sources and telephone mates—friends would be too strong a word—among the *Times*' women reporters who covered the worlds of couture and society, thirty-year veterans like Enid Nemy. Carol Sulzberger particularly relished the stage-center role occupied by the wife of the publisher of the *Times*. Both Sulzbergers understood that he was tapped as chairman of the board not because of his tastes in art, or because he lived in the neighborhood. While the Met directors serve on one of the two or three most socially prestigious boards in America, they know their true role is simple, even banal: Donate one's own money for the Museum building funds and acquisitions programs, or prevail upon friends and acquaintances to donate their money. "Give it, or get it," one board member summed up for me. It didn't hurt that the museum had a friend at the *Times*, although

Sulzberger characteristically framed the relationship in terms of the *Times* reviewers' authority to write critically about the Met's exhibits, rather than his power over their notices. "I sit here and cross my fingers every time a show opens," he says. "You know, it's difficult for me to say, 'Charlie, give me a couple of million dollars for a show,' and then to see it kicked in the head by the *Times*."

The arts critics at the *Times* did not treat the Met's shows as harshly as Sulzberger suggests. On the contrary, he was a great success as chairman. Between 1987 and 1990, in the first three years of his tenure, $125 million in contributions flowed in from other owners of the Republic. Under Sulzberger, too, foreign capitalists were afforded the opportunity to meet the publisher of the *Times*, and support the good works of the museum. He was part of a museum delegation to Japan; there, in his words, he had to "gently rattle the tin cup" for contributions from Tokyo industrialists and business leaders—the noble owners of Japan (and the heads of companies that the *Times* covered in its business-news pages).

Yet these missions to Japan appeared more dignified than his greeter's role at the corporate receptions and private parties held at the museum. In the 1980s, the Met board permitted companies that donated $30,000 or more in any calendar year to rent space in the museum's Temple of Dendur and Great Hall, for black-tie dinners and cocktail receptions. Individual nouveaux riches were also allowed to hold affairs at the Met, usually under the same terms that applied to companies. The Texas financier Sid Bass and his bride-to-be, Mercedes Kellogg, held their pre-wedding party in the Charles Engelhard Court; Bloomingdale's chairman, Marvin Traub, was the host of a reception for Robert Campeau (before Campeau's highly leveraged Federated Department Stores tottered into bankruptcy); the LBO king Henry Kravis, and his fashion designer wife, Carolyne Roehm, held a sit-down dinner for 140. All of these affairs were eclipsed when the daughter of the greenmail specialist Saul Steinberg married a son of the Tisch family (CBS, Loews). The Steinberg-Tisch wedding reception at the Met, according to the gossip columns in the *Times*' tabloid competitors, cost $3 million, a sum that included a $17,000 cake and floral arrangements consisting of fifty thousand French roses and gold-dipped magnolia leaves. Club Met, the tab columnists took to calling the museum during Sulzberger's tenure.

Sulzberger had reasoned that because the building at night was "going to be dark anyway," and because companies were willing to pay handsomely for the privilege of having their parties at the Met, "Why not open it up?" It had been a businessman's matter-of-fact assessment. But Sulzberger didn't need all the sniping about New York's "rent-a-palace" and its "parvenue party venue." There were other, more rewarding, ways to spend one's energies. And so the early 1990s at the *Times* became something of a replay of the early 1980s: Punch Sulzberger was no more willing to surrender his *Times* power and glory than Abe Rosenthal had been. Sulzberger didn't really want to spend his settled days making small talk with Brooke Astor at the Fashion Designers of America awards dinner.

Punch Sulzberger had carried out his patriarchal role well. Family fears about loss of control of the *Times* had at last been exorcised. No one had to grow sick with worry about creditors, or other outsiders, wresting away the newspaper. The Sulzbergers, father and son, however, needed all their resiliency to deal with the onset of a fresh set of anxieties about the *Times*. It was no longer sufficient that Punch Sulzberger had preserved the dynastic ownership. The future shape of the *Times* as a journalistic enterprise had to be determined as well. The *Times* he had taken over in 1963 went about its business recording the official news of the day—from Europe, Washington, City Hall, the financial markets—for a serious-minded readership composed, in the main, of the business and professional classes in New York. These readers knew what to expect: the old, gray—but good—*New York Times*. The *Times* he was turning over to his son no longer considered itself the newspaper of record. It actively avoided that title. "The record is boring for most people," Warren Hoge declared. "We don't record the news, we find the news." The modern *Times* sought a national audience; it aimed to be friendly to a new audience that—the market research claimed—was uninterested in traditional newspapers.

The research said that this new generation had to be lured into the habit of reading a daily paper, and no one was a more avid disciple of the new thinking than Arthur O. Sulzberger, Jr.

As the younger Sulzberger exerted his influence, the concerns about being attractive to younger readers began to make the *Times* sound like a stuck whistle. In the Sunday edition of January 6, 1991, the *Times* ran three separate articles about the "decline of reading." The lead article in the business section, by Alex Jones, filled most of the first page and another page inside. It carried the headline "Rethinking Newspapers," and referred in its subhead to "a nagging long-term problem: Fewer people are reading newspapers." An accompanying one-column graphic, with the head "Fewer Readers," depicted the number of U.S. households (an upward curve) and the total daily circulation of U.S. newspapers (a flat line). Deeper in the Business section that same Sunday, the "Forum" feature offered "The Upheavals in the Media," by a guest expert, Professor Jib Fowles of the University of Houston. According to Fowles, the nation's "baby boomers"—more obsessive concern with the under-forty generation—were "hitting their stride in their careers and at home . . . [and] simply have less time to devote to reading. . . ." Finally in *Education Life,* a quarterly supplement of the *Times,* staff reporter Roger Cohen described "aliterate" Americans: people who know how to read but don't. Cohen wrote of a University of Pennsylvania graduate who "sees nothing strange in not reading because 'half my friends don't read either.' With television, sports, and movies occupying his leisure time, he says reading 'just never interested me that much.' "

The younger Sulzberger, then, had strong views about the paper that was his inheritance. The *Times*people who spoke derisively about "Junior's paper" did so out of the belief that his *Times* would be overly attuned to the demands of readers and advertisers. They feared it would be a "product" that was "market-driven," and not the traditional, "serious" *Times.* The critics' memories were short. The drive to be user friendly had begun fifteen years before, when Arthur was still learning the business at the AP.

A DAY IN THE LIFE
10:10 A.M.—11:05 A.M.

10:10 A.M.

Anthony Lewis vaguely remembered that Eisenhower once said people should be able to face their accusers, and not "get shot down from the back." The columnist telephoned Professor Fred Greenstein at Princeton, a specialist on the Eisenhower years. Greenstein didn't recall the quote. Lewis tried Stephen Ambrose, author of a two-volume biography of Eisenhower and a member of the University of New Orleans faculty. Ambrose was traveling in Mississippi. (He eventually returned Lewis's call, but didn't recognize the quotation either.) On the third call, to William Ewald, Jr., a former Eisenhower speech writer and author of

Who Killed Joe McCarthy?, Lewis got the lead he needed. The quote could be found in the public papers of Eisenhower.

11:00 A.M.

Karl Meyer put aside his folders and gathered with a dozen of his editorial board colleagues for the second of their three regular weekly meetings. The other two meetings were held Mondays and Thursdays. Editorial page editor Jack Rosenthal, a former official at the Justice Department during the Kennedy years, presided at one end of the large walnut table in the board's conference room on the tenth floor. His deputy, Leslie Gelb, who had been with the State Department in the Carter administration, sat at the other end. On the wall behind them hung framed copies of *Times* editorial pages over the decades— each one from a *Times* edition of May 1. Max Frankel picked the pages and had them mounted when he was editorial page editor a decade before. The May 1 date caused smiles among visitors, who appreciated the "uncharacteristic touch of the Jacobin at the *Times*," in Meyer's words. The meeting began, as usual, a few minutes late. Rosenthal went around the table; members spoke their minds. Once again the board took up the Tower nomination: Should the *Times* weigh in? No decision was made, or rather, it was decided a Tower commentary could await further developments in the Senate hearings. Meyer promised to do a short editorial on Iraq's human rights violations, based on an Amnesty International report carried as a small item in the news pages of the *Times*. Each board member wrote editorials on two or more specialties. Meyer concentrated on the Third World and human rights topics.

The board turned to the civil war in El Salvador, and an animated discussion of Central America. The discussion continued for fifteen minutes. Two visitors from the region were due to visit the *Times* later in the day.

11:05 A.M.

In a space near the southwest corner of the building, toward Eighth Avenue, a meeting of the Style-section editors began. The desks of the Women's Page at one time clustered in this corner. The page was long gone, replaced by the new feature sections in the great reorganization of the mid-1970s (and a casualty as well of the changing American social order, in which the category of "women's news" itself was judged patronizing). Editors were working on the redesign of the second section of the Sunday paper—to introduce a new "Styles of the *Times*" feature (it arrived in May 1992, after the usual bureaucratic battles of control and Talmudic discussions about content).

The old section—"Sunday Main Part 2"—had grown into an unattractive collection of news columns dominated by three pages of wedding announcements and by oversize ads for cameras and electronic equipment, set in line after line of unreadable agate type. The old section was also something of a dumping ground for features held over from the news pages during the week. Still, the section had a distinct flavor. With its leisurely stories datelined Baton Rouge, Louisiana, Cheyenne, Wyoming, or Bethlehem, Pennsylvania, it often read like the *National Geographic*: a slow-paced travelogue of Americana.

All that was changing under the direction of Claudia Payne, a talented editor with a mane of blond hair. Payne introduced new features to accompany the Macy's and Bloomingdale's ads for $495 suede bags and $1,900 designer dresses. Under the heading "Evening Hours," Manhattan society benefits and the chic parties of the week received a half page of candid photographs. The captions often consisted only of the subjects' names—so well known, the *Times'* arbiters of style were saying, that no further elaboration was needed ("Alexander von Auersperg greets Yasmin Aga Kahn Jeffries at Plaza," read the caption under two smiling faces, puckered lips aimed at proffered cheek). The latest creative talent, young men and women working in fashion and design, were photographed and profiled as "Style Makers." A full page was devoted to places to spend money on Sundays— "Sunday Outing," "Sunday Menu," "Sunday Dinner." "The accent is on youth," *Times Talk*, the in-house newsletter, reported.

Times Talk neglected to add that the new 'youth-oriented' section was the end product of a power struggle going back fourteen years. When the *Times'* daily feature sections were created, the news and business departments had worked well together on the initial four sections—Sports Monday, Home (Wednesday), Living (Thursday), and Weekend (the Friday arts and entertainment guide). But the editors and the sales staff could not agree on what the final section, for Tuesday, should cover. The business side wanted a fashion section, to sell space in the new pages to the department stores. The news department, after the perceived fluff of the first four sections, wanted to offer something more serious and "*Times*-like." Punch Sulzberger sided with the news department, and Science Times was born. A decade and a half later, the advertising sales staff at last was going to get the fashion showcase it desired. The *Times* would now have two prime positions to offer advertisers in the Sunday paper: Main Part 1 and Main Part 2. The accent was on selling space.

11:05 A.M.

In the Washington bureau, Barbara Gamarekian worked on a story about infidelity, drinking, and changing mores on Capitol Hill. The idea was inspired by the Tower fight and intended for the Washington Talk page. The wife of Congressman Ron Dellums of California returned Gamarekian's call, and they talked about a spouse's view of the subject for ten minutes. Gamarekian called lobbyists, Congressmen, and staff workers on the Hill; she interviewed William Proxmire, the recently retired senator from Wisconsin, and Kevin Phillips, the conservative writer.

3

THE CHANGES:
1. SOFT TIMES

"A FEW RANDOM THOUGHTS about possible articles for the Home section," began the note from Arthur O. Sulzberger to A. M. Rosenthal.

It was the summer of 1978. The *Times* was introducing its new sections covering such topics as food, furniture, and design. These daily magazines, one for each weekday, represented the *Times'* prime editorial initiative of the 1970s. They signaled a major investment of both money and staff, the centerpiece of the effort to attract new readers. Americans were spending an ever increasing amount of time in front of their television sets. They were getting the first hard reports of developments in Washington, Wall Street, or the Middle East from network news on the nights before their morning papers were delivered. Attracted by nightly television and the early morning shows like "Today" on NBC—and, later, by "new media" networks like the twenty-four-hour CNN—the traditional audiences for news seemed to be drifting away from their newspapers. Around the country, editors tried new formats to lure readers. The *Washington Post*, the *Los Angeles Times*, and the *Miami Herald* had all taken the lead in developing sections devoted to "life-style" features.

Change came harder at the *Times*, where past habits weighed heavily on decisions. Punch Sulzberger worried about the harm that might be done to "our traditional franchise"—the coverage of serious national and international news—as newsroom resources were shifted around. He had doubts about the paper's ability to deal with the new franchise. The *Times* was still feeling its way unsteadily among these softer topics; neither Sulzberger nor Rosenthal was fully satisfied with the new Home section. The execution was a bit off, the stories were judged not sufficiently "pertinent" to the lives of the audience desired by the *Times*. Rosenthal, for example, told Nancy Newhouse, the Home editor, that her section was "too architectural in tone." Newhouse should run more "interesting and useful" stories oriented toward consumers' needs, and fewer "columns on design." Both Rosenthal and Sulzberger kept their secretaries busy transcribing possible story ideas. Sulzberger, conscious of the chain of command, sent his memos to Rosenthal; the publisher counted on his executive editor to deal with the departmental editors.

The publisher's memo with his ideas for the Home section was dated July 6. Sulzberger noted that "awnings may be coming back, in that they are decorative and cut the heat. If so what's up?" He pointed out that "the home medicine cabinet is usually a mess—filled with old prescription drugs, half used bottles of cold remedies, etc. What should it contain—according to a doctor?" Sulzberger also had a suggestion for a story on city apartments with wood-burning fireplaces ("Where do you buy the wood and store it?"). He wondered about the hallways and other common areas in co-op apartments where the opinions of many tenants had to be taken into account—he expressed special interest in "the lobbies of the older houses along Fifth and Park Avenues." In a similar vein, he suggested a story on the decor of the offices of "working men and women . . . such as Joe Cullman [the Phillip Morris chairman] and Edgar Bronfman [of the Seagrams distillers family]." A week later, a second Sulzberger memo of story suggestions declared that "area rugs . . . seem to be coming back," asked if anyone had solved the problems of noisy home washing machines and messy laundry areas and raised some practical questions about the fire extinguishers "that every home should have." Sulzberger wanted the *Times* to answer such questions as "What kind? Where should it be stored? How long do they last? Are they better for an oven fire, or salt? . . ."

There were eighteen ideas in the first memo and eleven ideas in the second memo. Suggestion number 7 in the second memo revealed more about Sulzberger the trend spotter than he perhaps intended: "People all over are covering their homes with aluminum siding. How

about interviewing someone who did it and getting the entire economics from paint and fuel saved to cost, etc. Was it worth it?" The
advantages of aluminum siding are usually promoted in the spiels of
late-night television pitchmen; homeowners in Astoria, or Bensonhurst, might go the aluminum siding route. Was this really a trend
among the audience of suburbanites that the *Times* was trying to court?
The publisher assured his editor that aluminum siding was definitely
upscale. According to the memo, the "people all over" Sulzberger had
in mind were "Marian and Andrew [who] did their house in Darien."
Marian Sulzberger Dryfoos Heiskell was one of Punch's older sisters;
her husband, Andrew Heiskell, had been chairman of the board of
Time Inc. Darien, Connecticut, is one of the tonier suburban addresses in the greater New York area.

Editors often have a picture in their minds of the "dear reader" to
whom their work is addressed. When the *Times* was starting its new
sections, Rosenthal told me, he always tried to imagine how the stories
would be received by "people like Teddy White"—the author and
Rosenthal friend, the late Theodore H. White. When I reported this
recollection to Punch Sulzberger, his reaction was one of laughter.
"I've heard Abe say that," Sulzberger said. "I don't know why he
picked Teddy." Sulzberger himself had no such ideal reader in mind
for the sections. "I'm not trained in that way of perceiving things," he
explained. "I read the sections with my own eyes. I deal with the paper
every day and I have no problem expressing myself with a memo or
phone call." Again, he laughed: "What the hell, that's what ownership
means."

Sulzberger's story ideas for Home and Living had a certain fey
charm; they grew from his own experience, and that of his friends and
relatives. The suggestions about the Heiskells' siding, the halls of Park
Avenue co-ops, and the executive suites of "office workers" like Cullman and Bronfman all added up to something more than the sum of
the trivial parts. They helped set a tone at the *Times*. The paper always
had a singular readership in the family of Adolph S. Ochs. The sectional revolution at the *Times* left that tradition untouched.

Punch Sulzberger was an unlikely revolutionary in any case. Neat,
square-chinned, orderly, he dressed conservatively in bankers' gray or
dark blue suits, subdued shirts, quiet regimental ties, and polished
black shoes. In his fifties, his hairline began retreating, drawing atten-

tion to his high forehead and largish ears. The big head and the small body gave him an elf-like mien, a quality further enhanced by his reputation for what is known as an "impish" sense of humor. Before the new sections started, the *Times* was looking for a new title for the page it had designated for "Women's News." Sulzberger wrote one of his editors: "I have no objection to changing the name of Women's News to something, but I do not think the something is 'Living Styles.' That really sounds cornier than anything. Can't we think of some other names? We could even have a contest and come up with something fancy like Edsel!" A *Times* editor, in all seriousness, advised a friend seeking a favor from Sulzberger to put his request in limerick form, "because that will get his attention." His peers in the news business endured one of Sulzberger's more elaborate word plays at one of the annual meetings of the American Newspaper Publishers Association, the owners' trade and lobbying group. Presiding as the outgoing ANPA chairman, Sulzberger solemnly announced that he was passing on the gavel to the new chairman William H. Cowles III (pronounced Coles). Then he explained how much he regretted that the next ANPA meeting in 1990 would not be in Pennsylvania, "for then we could bring Cowles to Newcastle."

Thus, the witty Punch, the publisher as he wished to be seen in the world. In an era when egocentric, publicity-hungry billionaires constantly sought to out-Trump one other, Sulzberger came across as diffident, almost anachronistic. As head of the ANPA, he was expected to contribute a five-hundred-word chairman's letter to the readers of *presstime*, the association's monthly magazine. For the issue of February 1989, he apologized for beginning to repeat himself after just ten months of his assignment. "As with Christmas shopping, I have delayed to the last moment and now nothing very brilliant seems to be coming out of the typewriter." The contribution he produced was pure boilerplate, with the sleep-inducing headline, "The nation's diversity is reflected in its newspapers." With generous margins and ample white space, his homily managed to filled the column.

Artfully, Sulzberger made a show of his unshowiness. Every morning he came to the *Times* he produced the ID card formally required of *Times*people as they pass through the security checkpoint halfway between the revolving doors at the entrance and the elevator banks at the rear of the lobby. The guards naturally recognized him and used to try to wave him past. Gradually, they came to understand that

Sulzberger wanted to go through with the search for his billfold and the display of his ID. "There are rules and it's very important to me that I don't break them," he said when asked about the daily ritual.

This was the modest Punch, the same nice guy who helped out at the Met because he lived in the neighborhood. His sister Ruth Golden profiled him early in his *Times* career, for the company house organ, *Times Talk*. He likes to drink Scotch, she wrote, and loves puns and gadgets, habitually arrives early for trains and planes, never remembers names and wants "his own surroundings orderly and neat." Three decades later he still played the part of convivial fellow, coming unaccompanied to the reception room of the fourteenth-floor executive suites to meet an appointment. The puckish style didn't always endear him to every group. In the mid-1980s, a group of professional women in New York organized a Women's Forum to discuss major questions of the day with leading opinion makers. No market researcher could have put together a more representative group of desired *Times'* women readers. Sulzberger was invited to speak to the Forum. He began by joking, "You probably want to ask why the ink of our paper comes off on your hands"—an offhand remark intended to be amusing but having the effect of patronizing the "ladies" of the Forum. According to one of his auditors, a research professor at the City University of New York, "his comments went downhill from there."

Within the *Times* corporate family, he could also misjudge his audience. At the *Times* 1988 stockholders' meeting held in the Grace Rainey Rogers Auditorium of the Metropolitan Museum of Art, Sulzberger presided, his reading glasses slightly askew. The questions from the audience were good ones, with a sharp curve or two thrown in. Sulzberger handled them openly for the most part; only the angle of his head, which slumped into his chest as he looked through his notes to answer the tougher comments, betrayed any annoyance.

He greeted the stockholders with a few brief announcements, delivered in head-down fashion. William Scranton was leaving the *Times* board of directors, at the age of seventy-one; the former governor of Pennsylvania was, among other things, going to use his new free time to study Latin, and "we wish him good luck and good grades." Sulzberger introduced Scranton's replacement, George B. Monroe, for eighteen years the CEO of the Phelps Dodge company (mining and chemicals) and after college, for a time a professional basketball player with the Boston Celtics. Sulzberger reported that 1987 had been a year of strong performance for the *Times*, with revenues 12 percent higher than in 1986, and 1988 was expected to be a record year. In the previous twelve months too, a new weekly section for television-program listings had been introduced in the *Times* (Sulzberger neglected to mention that the *Times* was perhaps the last major newspaper in the country to recognize in this fashion the part television played in its readers' lives). Also, the *Times*' new $450-million production plant in Edison, New Jersey, was on schedule. The plant would enable the *Times* within three years to offer color graphics and photography in its news pages—"better than the best color reproduction in *USA Today*, the standard of the industry," Sulzberger said. More immediately, the *Times* had started publishing earlier that month a new three-section national edition. The first marketing tests of the paper, an edited compilation of news and features from the four-section New York edition, were being conducted in California, and "it looks as if it's going to be a winner." His words were mild enough, considering that the *Times* was investing $100 million in its latest effort to enlarge its base of readers beyond the New York area.

Then it was time for questions from the shareholders. Harry Korba, of Yonkers, rose to add to the chairman's report. "You should know," Korba began, "that George Monroe compiled a terrific record in the 1947–48 season for Boston." Sulzberger beamed as Korba reeled off Monroe's statistics, including his foul-shooting percentage. But then Korba had some questions about the *Times*' corporate aircraft and what it cost to maintain them. Sulzberger's smile froze. The *Times* owned two planes and one helicopter, which together required $1 million a year to operate, he answered, adding: "They are not for personal use."

Another shareholder wanted to know the amount of Sulzberger's personal expense account. About $80,000 a year, came the short reply. A woman said that the company's common stock was selling at 43 when the last annual meeting was held; now it was around 29¾. Her question, though, was a general one: What was Sulzberger's reaction to the big Wall Street market crash of the past October? "I'm aghast and confused," he answered.

Another shareholder wanted to know what the *Times* was paying for the services of its outside lawyers; he also had a follow-up question: "How many lawyers does the *Times* employ on staff?" Sulzberger rummaged for the figures: The outside lawyers' fees were $4.6 million in 1987 and $4.8 million in 1986, while the number of in-house lawyers had risen to eleven in 1987 from nine in 1986.

A middle-aged woman pointed out that the *Times* had "no females on its masthead" and only one female corporate executive—Katherine P. Darrow, the general counsel—"and she dates from 1980." "We try to keep a lean staff," said Sulzberger. The questioner persisted, noting that women need "mentors" and that "your own son was just moved up. . . ." Sulzberger shuffled his notes; "I assure you," he said, "the advance of women is high on my agenda." (Not long afterward, Carolyn Lee became an assistant managing editor, one of five AMEs in the news department at the *Times*, and Elise J. Ross was named a senior vice president, one of four on the business side of the paper.)

Another questioner, a younger woman, suggested the *Times* ought to have day care facilities for employees with young children; perhaps Mr. Sulzberger could appoint a committee to look into such an arrangement, "although 43rd Street is not the best neighborhood for children." Sulzberger managed a patient reply: "I am leery of committees, but my colleagues and I will look into it."

Two questions about whether the Sulzberger family was divesting itself of its stock and whether the *Times* was going to move from 43rd Street both received a short, emphatic "no." A middle-aged man asked, "How much influence do you need to get a wedding announcement in the *Times*?" "Not much," Sulzberger replied, "just send it to me." The laughter that followed was quickly dissipated by a series of questions about why copies of the *Times* were no longer available in coffee shops and corner stores in Sheepshead Bay and other locations in Brooklyn. The questioners were mostly elderly men, with broad Eastern European accents. Sulzberger looked genuinely surprised, as if he didn't know that the *Times* had in the last decade systematically scaled back its distribution in the older borough neighborhoods in favor of expanded suburban home delivery. "I'll look into it," he promised.

Finally, as if on cue, a stooped figure slowly got to his feet. His name was Jacob ("Jack") Besterman and he had been with the *Times* since 1951, working in the composing room, setting advertising copy. When the new computer technology arrived, Besterman and hundreds of other typesetters agreed to a buyout of their union contracts. Besterman had completed his thirty-first year with the *Times* in 1982, but continued to draw a weekly paycheck until his seventieth birthday in 1986. "I never attended a meeting like this before," he told Sulzberger. "I came to say that this is the greatest company in the world." It was a sweet note on which to end the day.

But before Sulzberger could bring down his gavel, a middle-aged woman jumped up to break the mood. She introduced herself as "Edith Siegel, stockholder, of Riverdale." "If everything is so cozy at our company," Edith Siegel asked, "then why isn't our stock being recommended by the security analysts?" Sulzberger seemed genuinely surprised again. "It's not true," he said. "Jack Reidy of Drexel Burnham recently had good things to say about our stock." Then he added, almost plaintively, "But it doesn't seem to do any good."

The *Times'* stockholders had not been overly contentious by the standards of many such company meetings. Sulzberger, however, opted for sites far from New York for the *Times'* next annual meetings. In 1989 Sulzberger convened the stockholders meeting at WNEP-TV, the *Times*-owned television station in Moosic, Pennsylvania, outside Scranton. In 1990 the traveling *Times* road company met in Duluth, Georgia, at the offices of the *Gwinnett Daily News*, the *Times*-owned daily in the largely white suburbs northeast of Atlanta. Ostensibly, the sites were being rotated to allow the participation of stockholders in cities where the *Times* operates outside New York. The explanation convinced no one. Away from New York, chairman Sulzberger was able to conduct annual meetings that were short and polite—tea dansants, without the discordant brass and woodwinds of Korba, Siegel, and the forsaken readers of Brooklyn. The tactic became so obvious that the *Times* decided it had to return to New York again for the 1991 meeting. (The hard times of the early 1990s, in any event, claimed the Gwinnett paper: the Sulzbergers shut it down in 1992.)

The soft-news sections were only the most visible sign of change at the *Times* during the three decades of Punch Sulzberger's tenure. The geography of the *Times* changed. The security analysts understood that Punch Sulzberger no longer operated a New York City business; he headed a national enterprise, with a chain of newspapers in the Sunbelt states as well as a magazine group and broadcast properties. Less obviously, though the *Times* newspaper still called itself the *New York Times*, it had ceased to be a New York paper. There were no longer enough of the kind of readers the *Times* wanted to attract within the city and near suburbs. The readers of Sheepshead Bay had been written off; the paper now looked beyond to the nation across the Hudson. Walter Mattson, Sulzberger's top business-side executive, put the situation most directly in a confidential memorandum in early 1976, when New York was still feeling the effects of the municipal fiscal crisis, the loss of manufacturing jobs, and "white flight" out of the city. "Some of our most loyal readers are sinking their roots deeper in the suburbs as they find their jobs as well as their homes are there," Mattson noted. "Our studies have shown that as a person's association with the city became more remote he is less likely to be a *Times* reader."

Subsequently, the special sections were credited with making the paper attractive to a new suburban and national audience, and thus "saving" the *Times*. In the early 1970s, the *Times* circulation and advertising revenues flattened; by the 1980s, they were both on the rise again. "The new sections certainly *reinvigorated* the *Times*, put it that way," Punch Sulzberger now says. "But 'save' it? What they did was give us a chance to practice a new kind of journalism, new for the *New York Times* anyway." In the past, he said, the *Times* had dealt with design, furnishings, homes, food, and fashion "on the edges." The decision "to do them in a new way and with all that space gave us a great boost, with our advertisers and readers." The greatest boost for the *Times*, however, came as much from the paper's physical availability as from the trumpeted editorial changes. Quite simply, the circulation department got the new paper into suburban driveways. The *Times*' campaign to increase home-delivery in the affluent counties of Westchester, Nassau, and Suffolk in New York, Fairfield in Connecticut, and Bergen in New Jersey wasn't the stuff of newsroom legend; but the paper's business managers understood the importance of suburban subscribers. Home delivery eliminated the uncertainties of newsstand and coffee shop sales, which could vary from day to day because of an Act of God like heavy rain or scorching heat. It made the size of daily press runs predictable and avoided costly returns from news dealers. Home delivery also meant that the *Times*' advertising-sales department could go to retailers with a detailed demographic picture of *Times* subscribers. Bloomingdale's could be reassured that its ads were reaching the desired audience. That explained why, in the late fall of 1990, when the *News* was struck by its unions, the *Times* decided *not* to increase its press run significantly or adjust its newsstand distribution routes to pick up *News*' readers. "Management didn't want that kind of blue-collar audience for our advertisers," a *Times* man recounted, smiling wickedly. Then he imitated an eater spitting out food: "Phoo! Not for us!"

*   *   *

No sooner had the suburban target audience been captured than the *Times* found it had to cast its net still wider. By the late 1980s, the desired pickings to be found in the city and in New York, New Jersey, and Connecticut had been thinned out. Television, cable channels, and special-interest magazines were attracting the younger, upmarket men and women who, in an earlier time, would have been regular newspaper readers. Six months after the chairman's optimistic report to the stockholders in the Grace Rainey Rogers auditorium, Sulzberger used his "chairman's corner" in the December 1988 issue of *presstime* to worry about newspapers' "readership and marketing problems." "Business was lousy," he wrote. Worse, "Too many future readers (if one listens to the portenders of doom) are either illiterate, lazy or both." The doom-sayers, several of them on the executive floor of the *Times*, were especially pessimistic about further circulation growth in New York and the Northeast. In early 1989, Sulzberger began addressing the *Times*' own "readership and marketing problems" by creating a new national *Times* intended to attract an audience beyond the city *and* its suburbs.

It helped that Sulzberger's homey concerns were like those of the upper-middle-class business and professional people who were a prime part of the national target audience. As the paper had progressively less to do with New York City, its new community of interests increasingly centered on social and economic identities. The *Times* reader could live in Manhattan, or Highland Park, Illinois, or Santa Monica, California—wherever educated, affluent people resided. Sulzberger expected the prototypical *Times* reader to worry about awnings, area rugs, and storage for the home fire extinguisher, and about how the president and the secretary of state were addressing the great issues of the day. These were his interests too.

Sulzberger's public manner masked the extent that the *Times* took its cues from him. Strong-willed owners often cast long shadows through their publications, for good or bad. But few people have bothered to group the "diffident" Punch Sulzberger with larger-than-life figures like Luce, Hearst, or McCormick. While Sulzberger claimed not to know about great art (or any other speciality), he knew what he liked. Perhaps it was just serendipity, but the interests he promoted through the decades were just the kind that *Times* readers might find congenial. In the 1960s, Sulzberger let Turner Catledge, his executive editor, know the publisher's likes and dislikes. One note protested a photographic spread in the *Times Magazine* showing what Sulzberger called "absolutely way-out crazy furniture." He suggested to Catledge that he replace the home furnishings editor with "someone who has more traditional taste. I would be happy to help with the selection."

Sulzberger sent similar complaints to Rosenthal, when he was the executive editor. At one point, the work of a *Times* music critic, Edward Rothstein, annoyed Sulzberger. Reviewing a recital of the mezzo D'Anna Fortunato, Rothstein wrote that the singer had a "sonorous power [that] was not intrinsically sensuous." Sulzberger pounced on that phrase, as well as a passage in which Rothstein reported that "each song had a distinct after-breath, extending into the silences." Sulzberger's memo to Rosenthal began, "I am not an expert, to say the least, on singing, but I think I do know something about the use of the English language. Mr. Rothstein, on the other hand, is, apparently, an expert on singing, but should go back to school to relearn the use of his mother tongue." Rothstein left the *Times* shortly afterward; he continued to write criticism for the *New Republic* and other magazines. Occasionally he contributed free-lance pieces to the *Times*, and in mid-1991, a decade later, he was rehired; the statute of limitations had run out.

Sulzberger's preferences in literature were no more highfalutin than the tastes he brought with him when he became chairman at the Met. He wasn't an art patron, and he didn't accumulate a lot of books, either. John Leonard, editor of the *Book Review* from 1971 to 1975, recalls that Sulzberger would drop by the *Review* offices just before his vacation trips to Europe or the Caribbean and ask for extra copies of the latest whodunits and spy novels—"the kind of books I can toss overboard." Leonard obliged, with regret. "Just once," Leonard says, "I wished he had asked for one of the books we had chosen for major treatment on page one of his own *Book Review*."

Sulzberger was especially vigilant about "sexual materials" in the pages of the *Times*. The *Book Review* assigned the free-lance writer Ellen Willis to review two newly published studies of pornography, both written from a feminist point of view. Sulzberger read the *Book Review* carefully enough that week, and bracketed one passage in the Willis review. He had it photocopied, and attached it to a note for Rosenthal. "Every once in a while I get absolutely fascinated at the incredible goobledegook that finds its way into the pages of the *New York Times*," the note began. "The attached review by Ellen Willis is a perfect example. I can only assume that the editor was awed by the selection of her words and felt stupid if he didn't know what on earth she was talking about." The bracketed passage read: "The pornographic image, which objectifies and degrades the (usually female) body, represents a ritual in which the (usually male) pornographer or user, playing both killer and victim, reenacts the murder of his bodily self; since the murder can never be truly accomplished, it must be compulsively repeated." (Willis's work appeared rarely in the *Times* from then on; she continued to publish her criticism in the *Village Voice* and in magazines, and in 1990 became an associate professor of journalism at New York University.)

If Sulzberger missed some offending materials in the *Times*, he often could count on like-minded readers to alert him. One Sunday, the Fashion section in the *Times Magazine* featured an article by Anne-Marie Schiro. An accompanying photograph showed a model standing to the side of a mirror, her back to the camera; she was wearing two skimpy pieces of lingerie, both on sale at Bloomingdale's. According to the copy, "The combing jacket gives a little cover to Zandra Rhodes' breast-baring version of the teddy." A reader from New Canaan, Connecticut, Isabel Byron of Field Crest Road, wrote Sulzberger to protest what she called "soft porn" in the *Times*. While Byron's definition of pornography might be debated, her eyesight was unquestionably excellent: When the photo is studied with extra care, it's possible to see a blurred suggestion of one of the model's nipples reflected in the mirror. Sulzberger sent a photocopy of the page and the Byron letter to Rosenthal, with his own note: "You put this bosom in the paper, so I think you should reply to Mrs. Byron. Was this the only picture that we had, and did we have to go so far?" This last phrase was underlined twice in ink; a handwritten sentence added more emphasis, "I don't like it in the *Times*."

Similarly, after a straightforward and rather bland feature article on unwed mothers appeared in the *Times*, Sulzberger sent off another memo to Rosenthal: "So far this morning (11:30 A.M.) my office has received four calls on the . . . story on the glorification of having illegitimate children. . . . Can't we be a little bit more discriminating about what we run on that page?" One of the women supposedly "glorified" in the article was the singer Lainie Kazan. And one of the readers objecting to the story, a businessman named Franklin Miller of Merrick, on Long Island, claimed that he had known Kazan when they both went to Hofstra University. As Miller put it, Sulzberger's memo read, "even then she sang better horizontally than she could vertically."

Sulzberger was hardly a "typical" *Times* reader. As desirable as their demographics were, the middle- and upper-class professionals in the *Times*' target audience were not all able to live on Fifth Avenue, maintain an apartment in London, winter quarters in Florida, a country estate, and pay themselves $900,000 a year in salary, bonuses, and long-term compensation. Presidential candidates, senators, governors, foreign heads of state, Fortune 500 CEOs and Wall Street financiers didn't come to lunch in the executive dining room of just any company. But Sulzberger knew his own comfort zone, and he didn't want the *Times* to venture too far from the middle register in its coverage. When the news department under Rosenthal proposed that one of the new daily-magazine sections be related to "coping with life," Sulzberger bridled. He told Rosenthal, "I've often been unhappy with the way we've tackled this generalized idea in the past. I'm left very cold, indeed, by the thought of a section of sociological problem-raising—the article we ran on lesbian mothers coping with raising children inevitably comes to mind." The proposed section never materialized.

The Living and Home sections were the closest Sulzberger's *Times* came to regular coverage of coping-with-life stories for most of the 1970s and 1980s. When Frankel became editor, and Arthur Sulzberger, Jr., began asserting himself, the number of "sociological problem-raising" stories gradually increased—the son differentiating himself from the father, while continuing to assert the power of the publisher to shape the "product." With both Sulzbergers, influence was exercised discreetly. It was not the style of either father or son to address lower-ranking editors or reporters directly, unless sorely provoked. One evening Punch Sulzberger picked up the phone shortly after the first edition of the *Times* arrived, called the copy desk and ordered the editor on duty to remove the word "crappy" from an article. The next day, he put his displeasure into writing in a memo addressed to his top editors. "About 99 percent of the time I've dealt with the senior editors," Sulzberger said. "But if I'm home at night and see something in the first edition that I don't like, I have no difficulty calling the desk and saying, 'Take that out.'"

While Home and Living occupied the attention of Punch Sulzberger, he made relatively fewer suggestions for Weekend, Sports

Monday, and Science Times, the three other daily magazines started in the late 1970s. To some extent, Sulzberger's attention to Home and Living grew out of personal reference points. He thought like a co-op owner or suburbanite, albeit again a well-connected one. Home particularly appealed to his gadgeteer's interests. He also, unapologetically, saw these sections in relation to the needs of the *Times'* advertisers. Retail stores, the fashion industry, architects, designers, and home furnishings companies were covered in Home. Food, nutrition, recipes, good eating, supermarket chains, restaurants, and gourmet shops were treated in Living; most of these subjects dealt with, or were of direct interest to, major *Times* advertisers.

Punch Sulzberger was alert to this relationship. "When the new [furnishings-display] rooms open in the major department stores, let's be sure to look at them and talk to the designer," one memo began. Another Sulzberger memo chided editors for being too New York City–oriented, noting that *Times'* furniture and design articles often listed the main Manhattan locations of department stores carrying the merchandise but omitted the addresses of the suburban branches. When Larry Lachman, then chairman of Bloomingdale's, announced he was retiring and going into the consulting business, Sulzberger brought the executive's "availability" to the attention of Rosenthal, not once but twice. "I think he could be helpful to us, particularly in our home furnishings area," Sulzberger wrote after his first memo received no response. "I would like to suggest that you invite him in to meet with a small group of the editors, to see if this couldn't be so. I would be happy to absorb the cost of this in my budget and not charge it to the news department, if that is a problem for you." Sulzberger added: "I am not trying to do him a favor, but ourselves a favor. Larry is an extremely bright retailer and he might be of assistance in helping us define our market place and serve its needs."

Rosenthal, to his credit, vigorously resisted. He argued that any such arrangement would be "a serious mistake," and make it look as if the *Times'* integrity were being compromised: There would be "all kinds of journalistic and ethical problems . . . [for] the Living and Home sections. . . . Stretching a point—but not too far—it would be almost as if we hired [former New York City mayor] Abe Beame to be a consultant on political affairs." With that, the Lachman matter was dropped. Unfortunately, Rosenthal would later undercut his principled stands in such matters.

*   *   *

The publisher constantly searched for ways to improve the *Times'* business affairs. Behind the front page, however, the *Times* seemed to stumble along unresolutely. James Goodale, who joined the *Times* as an in-house lawyer, ended his *Times* career in 1980 as vice chairman of the company, the number-two position after Sulzberger. Goodale, then thirty, arrived at the *Times* in 1963, the year Sulzberger became publisher. The pressures, and the infighting among Sulzberger's executives, were horrendous: "I gave my blood there," Goodale remembers. Goodale believes that his most important contribution was to help take the company public in 1967—"It was the only way to deal with the incredible screwups at the place. Let the world see how the *Times* was run, and then we would have to clean up all of it."

Naturally enough, Punch Sulzberger has a different recollection, maintaining now that he regarded public ownership as the single best way to insure continued family control of the paper. But Sulzberger acknowledges that he tried to make the *Times* a more efficient place throughout his tenure. In the manner of the gadgeteer, he tried the latest management tools, particularly those sharpened by graduate departments at leading research universities: executives' seminars, committees on the future, retreats for editors in contemplative settings away from staff and phones. The most elaborate of these efforts, and as it turned out, the one that caused Sulzberger and the *Times* the greatest public embarrassment, involved a management specialist named Chris Argyris. (Eerily, a generation later, in 1992, publisher Arthur Sulzberger, Jr., replicated the Argyris agony, in the son's case with the theories of a managerial guru named W. Edwards Deming.)

Argyris was the James Bryant Conant Professor of Education and Organizational Behavior at Harvard University. In 1969 Punch Sulzberger asked Professor Argyris to come to the *Times* and give a series of talks on management skills to the *Times'* senior executives. Sulzberger had just presided over a widely publicized disaster in the Washington bureau of the *Times*. He had agreed to appoint one of Rosenthal's chief assistants as the new bureau chief in Washington—and then had reversed his decision when the Washington bureau lobbied him against the choice of a "New York man" over one of their own. Sulzberger told his associates that there must be a better way to run the paper; the idea of "everyone sitting down" and listening to "rational discussion" appealed to him.

Argyris, however, disdained the seminar approach. He had a more elaborate plan. He persuaded Sulzberger to sponsor instead a multiyear "management study and executive development program" at the *Times*. The Argyris project would proceed in two stages. First Sulzberger granted Argyris and his assistants—and their tape recorders—unprecedented access within the *Times* building. Argyris was given his own office at the *Times*, and permitted to attend executives' meetings, budget sessions, and story conferences. In all, he tape-recorded more than fifty such meetings. Of the forty top executives at the paper, thirty-eight cooperated "enthusiastically," including Sulzberger. Argyris was not allowed to interview "lower level" *Times*-people. He was told that the top editors believed such interviews would "upset" the staff (despite the ban, Argyris managed to talk to twenty reporters and desk editors).

In the second stage of the project, Argyris conducted what he called interventions—a series of sessions with Sulzberger and other *Times* executives intended to convey to them what he had found, "to help them communicate better with each other, and with the publisher." The aim was to instruct everyone to improve their "interpersonal skills and listening abilities." Institutions like the *Times*, Argyris believed, were "living systems" that periodically required "self-examination and self-renewal." Before coming to the *Times*, Argyris had done interventions and prescribed for the living systems of IBM, Polaroid, General Electric, and the State and Defense Departments, among others. Midway through the intervention phase, however, Argyris abruptly ended the *Times* project.

There had been hostility from the first. Sulzberger and his executives, Argyris came to believe, were not really interested in change, openness, or candor. As he was told by one senior *Times*man: "You know you've become a full member of this organization when you genuinely believe that few changes are possible *and* that it is necessary to hold such a belief to remain sane."

It was relatively easy for Sulzberger's men to dismiss Arygris's work. While they were processing the great events of the day, he was scoring the tapes of his interviews on "thirty-six variables that enhance or detract from individual interpersonal competence, that facilitate or inhibit effective group dynamics or intergroup relationships, and that result in organizational norms that increase or impede effectiveness." It sounded like so much psychobabble. Yet Argyris had a point: The *Times* needed help. When Argyris began his interviews at the *Times*,

Sulzberger and his top associates were debating proposals to start a new feature department. It would appear daily; it would consist of a full page made up of materials from *Times* writers as well as contributions from outsiders. John B. Oakes, Sulzberger's cousin and the editorial-page editor, had first conceived of the idea a decade before. He had long wanted to accommodate outsiders' contributions that were, as he put it, "too long to be a letter to the editor and too short for a Sunday *Magazine* essay." Later, Scotty Reston lent his Washington presence to the idea. But the plan languished. While both Oakes and Sulzberger now remember that they wanted to accommodate divergent views in the *Times*, they also worried that such counterpoint might detract from the *Times'* own editorial voice. Mostly, though, the idea became immobilized in a tangle of conflicting interests because of the proposed location of the new feature. Physically, it was to be placed opposite the editorial page of the paper. That page was by tradition given over to obituaries. While Sulzberger and his associates agreed that the death notices did not require such prime display, different factions had different ideas for the space. The business department wanted to use the page to sell more advertising; Rosenthal wanted the space for more news. Oakes wanted the page for the new department—and he wanted it to be under his jurisdiction. Sulzberger chose not to decide among the competing claims.

For four years, committees convened, planners planned, editors jockeyed—and the impasse continued. Finally, in 1970, Oakes remembered, he made the beau geste. He withdrew as a claimant for the space, telling his cousin Sulzberger that if it was a choice between having a department under Oakes's control or no department at all, then Oakes would step aside. That enabled Argyris to settle the matter in one so-called intervention session, a meeting of the executives involved that lasted just thirty minutes. The result was the creation of a separate department, under the jurisdiction neither of the news staff nor of the editorial-page board: the Op-Ed page of the *Times*. In the Sunday paper of September 30, 1990, the *Times* marked the twentieth anniversary of the Op-Ed page with a commemorative section. The introductory history spoke of the "eloquent" advocacy of Reston. Nothing was said of interventionist Argyris's contribution, an unstartling omission. The glancing recognition accorded Oakes was a surprise. It turned out that when the editors planning the anniversary section met with Punch Sulzberger to see if he had any special "marching orders" for them, one of the men, Robert Semple, came away with the message: "Don't reopen old wounds."

There were other, perhaps justified, reasons for the editors' hostility toward Argyris. Sulzberger had given the researcher permission to publish a book or article about his experiences at the *Times*, provided the *Times*' identity was cloaked. There were guarantees that *Times* executives would have the right of manuscript review and that an elaborate system of coding would be used. In the final manuscript, the publisher Sulzberger became Mr. P; Mr. R was Rosenthal, and both Mr. Q and Mr. T stood in for Oakes (at his insistence, to throw off readers). The paper itself was called the *Daily Planet.* No one was fooled when the materials were published in 1974, with the title, *Behind the Front Page: Organizational Self-Renewal in a Metropolitan Paper.* To Sulzberger's chagrin, the rest of the publishing world, and the *Times* staff, enjoyed a few laughs at the expense of Mr. P.

Enough soiled laundry emerged from Argyris's tape-recorded meetings to hang out to dry for months afterward. Argyris's readers sit in as Rosenthal and Oakes each accuse the other of "unbalanced" journalism. Oakes thinks the news department is too soft and featurized—"magazine-like," he tells Rosenthal. Rosenthal counters that the editorial page is too "shrill." Both men worry that the *Times* is drifting "leftward." But the most startling discussions on the tapes center on Mr. P. Sulzberger laments that he "can't run this place like it used to be managed" in the lax old days under his father. Yet no one cares much for Mr. P's "undisciplined" style. Sulzberger, for example, set up an executive committee, but then bypassed it and dealt directly with his subordinates; he talks to some excomm people individually about the proposed new feature and then tells them, "Don't discuss this with the others." The executives willingly go along with such little deceptions; they don't want to be open in front of the others, who they regard as their rivals. They see everything in a you-win/I-lose framework.

Argyris's tape recorder is running during the big Op-Ed page debate. Playing interventionist, he moves the discussion to the reasons why, after four years, there is still no decision:

SULZBERGER: "Each of you tells me your views and then you leave and nothing happens."

EXECUTIVE A: "After four years of waiting I think [Sulzberger] should make a decision."

EXECUTIVE B: "Why do we have to focus on Sulzberger? Why can't we talk about the best decision-making structure? Why do we have to get into this behavioral science crap, if you'll forgive the expression?"

SULZBERGER: "But will we learn anything?"

ARGYRIS: "Perhaps this is another fear. If we talk about Sulzberger, then it makes it more legitimate for him and others to talk about us."

SULZBERGER: "Why is it necessary to look at how we operate as a group? Let's take an issue and discuss it."

ARGYRIS: "Once in a while, it's important to open up the hood of your car and see if the motor is working effectively."

SULZBERGER: "My father used to say if you had a car going fifty miles an hour, never open up the hood."

ARGYRIS: "This is a choice that we now have to make. Do we want to look at our behavior?"

SULZBERGER: "I think we have to. We can't go back to the old days. . . . My difficulty is that I try to involve everyone and I get no decision made. . . . I wanted to open up the big issues of the paper. Where are we going? Are we drifting, resting on our laurels? I wanted . . . a rational discussion that would lead somewhere. . . . I've never been able to succeed in doing it. And I've tried every format I know. Everyone starts to defend what he is doing and we end up with a one-to-one relationship. . . . Let me say this. I'm willing to start over again."

It is Argyris, however, who falters. The interventionist expresses frustration at his failure to get the group to vent their feelings about Sulzberger. Argyris vents his own feelings, telling Mr. P that he is the most "ambivalent" CEO Argyris ever met: "You want people to be open with you, and yet you don't want to get rid of historical legacies; you were open about your feelings toward others, yet, as I listened to the tape, I don't think you were as open about your own feelings toward yourself."

Rosenthal later wrote dismissively of the project—a vision of the *Times* filtered through Argyris's "own version of what a corporation should be." "Live and learn," Rosenthal concluded. But Sulzberger never lost faith in the magic bullets of the academy—a touching trait his son would inherit in his turn as publisher. His own Mr. Fix-It turn of mind made him receptive; and if he was ever beset by doubts, then the pressures of performance required of public corporations pushed him forward. And so, just a few years after the Argyris experiment, Sulzberger instituted a program of Management By Objective, another organizational tool stamped MADE IN HARVARD. The MBO program required annual self-examinations by senior executives. Similarly, when the Wall Street security analysts began setting "industry standards" of 20 percent annual return on revenues for newspapers, Sulzberger bent the *Times* toward more B-school expertise. Newspaper publishing became too important to be left to newspaper publishers. The *Times* convened a half dozen new committees—on readership, "the future of newspapers," color pages and photography, and new sections for the paper. Still later, Punch Sulzberger, with his son's enthusiastic endorsement, commissioned extensive polling surveys of so-called "light" readers and nonreaders. In-depth questionnaires and focus groups were employed to tease out what people wanted in their newspapers, and why they weren't reading the *Times* every day.

In more recent years, the younger Sulzberger became excited over Demingism—the ideas of the "quality pioneer" W. Edwards Deming. Demingism might be called Management-By-Obligation. Deming's fourteen-point plan for managerial behavior supposedly helped such companies as GM, Ford, and Xerox lift their myopic focus from the bottom line to a broader vision that included the customer. On June 6, 1991, some one thousand *Times* employes gathered (in two shifts) at the New Yorker Club to hear how Demingism was being applied "to every department and every employee" of the *Times*.

Many of these same employees took in their Arthur-flavored Demingism, and its dashes of personal discovery, team play, candor, and quality work-circles, with the same pose of weary skepticism that reporters usually adopt when invited to news conferences by promoters of "miraculous" self-help nostrums. But Arthur Sulzberger wasn't kidding about Management-By-Obligation. After the 1991 announcement that Demingism was here to stay, the *Times* held no fewer than five retreats for staff members in the period October 1992 to January 1993, at such "facilitating" locations as the Hyatt Regency of Greenwich, Connecticut. Amazingly, for a company with such a long institutional memory, few of the 1992–3 seminar participants recognized the Deming days as Argyris Part Two—the colorized re-run of the old black-and-white comic opera of twenty years before, with some of the same arias being sung by new divas. For example, in place of Abe Rosenthal complaining, back then, "Why do we have to get into this behavioral science crap . . . ", this time Max Frankel is the one who protests, "Let's not play these stupid games!" Through it all, the 1970s' Argyris and the 1990s' Deming, each Sulzerger in turn listened, nodded, squirmed, added his own recitatives—and picked up the check for the experts' services.

If, as Punch Sulzberger reminded his managers, "Dad"—Arthur Hays Sulzberger—didn't believe in poking around under the hood of a car that was running, the grandson no longer felt any such inhibition. At the modern *Times*, various mechanics swarmed all over the vehicle.

During all the changes at the *Times*, Punch Sulzberger was himself an adjudicator, the final authority when disputes couldn't be settled by his associates. No matter that he often took years to render his decisions. After Argyris packed his tape recorder and left, the *Times*—like many other news organizations in the 1970s—debated the usage of "Ms." as an alternative to the then-current style of designating women by Mrs. or Miss. Other publications, magazines as well as newspapers, adopted "Ms." with a minimum of fuss. At the *Times*, the Ms. question was studied like the Talmud. Max Frankel, then the editor in charge of the Sunday paper, was a proponent of change, and the right of women to be defined by something other than their marital status. Rosenthal, speaking for his news department, favored continued use of Miss and Mrs. The memos flew back and forth. The *Times* had to be consistent throughout, daily and Sunday: Frankel couldn't use "Ms." as long as Rosenthal forbade it in the news pages. Months, then years, went by, with no change in *Times* style. Each year, Sulzberger would side with tradition. In December 1974, in a one-sentence memo to Frankel and Rosenthal, Sulzberger wrote: "At the end of the year, like Solomon, I cast my vote 'No' for Ms."

The 1970s gave way to the 1980s, and Sulzberger remained unmoved. Not until 1986 did "Ms." become accepted *Times* style. The day of the change the writer and feminist Gloria Steinem showed up in the *Times* newsroom carrying the gift of a bouquet of flowers to mark the great event.

Another megastruggle of the 1970s centered on the so-called 6-on-9 decision. Like many established American dailies, the *Times* had for decades printed its pages in an eight-column format, the standard for broadsheet papers. Beginning in the early 1970s, a number of newspapers switched to a six-column format and a slightly narrower paper width. The difference in width per single page was microscopic, but the cumulative savings when tons of newsprint were consumed quickly added up. Walter Mattson, with his eye on costs, became the leading six-column advocate; he argued that the *Times*, printing a million copies a day, would save $2 million a year in newsprint expenses. Rosenthal opposed the six-column format, for all the expected reasons: It violated tradition, it meant fewer words per page, it "didn't look right." Mattson's figures at last convinced Sulzberger; he approved the project (long after both the *Washington Post* and the *Boston Globe*, among other broadsheet papers, had changed to six columns). As the day for the change neared, Sulzberger addressed a memo to Mattson and Rosenthal, urging them to get together and "close any open holes" on the six-column project. "I will be happy to play Solomon if you need me," he added. The Solomonic image pleased him: "I threaten my editors," he later said, smiling broadly. "If I can't get them to decide on their own, I tell them I'll cut the baby in half, and that moves them."

Sulzberger's air of judiciousness was admirable. But sometimes Solomon nodded when reading the *Times*, even as ordinary *Times* subscribers did. Nancy Newhouse, a serious and accomplished journalist, was the first editor of the Home and Living sections. In the early days, she was the recipient of the Punch Sulzberger memos about home furnishings and design—although she never realized it. Rosenthal, it turned out, redid the publisher's lists of story ideas for Home and Living. For example, in the Sulzberger memo listing eighteen suggestions, Rosenthal moved suggestion number one, urging coverage of the new rooms at the department stores, to suggestion number fourteen, thus burying—to some extent—the request for attention to major *Times* advertisers. Then the editor removed the publisher's name from the memo, and Rosenthal's secretary retyped the memo to make it a list of suggestions from Rosenthal to Newhouse. With a new addresser and addressee, the publisher's original list was sent on, "AMR" to "Nancy Newhouse."

Newhouse had no way to know who the actual source was. "Thank you for your recent memo giving me your thoughts about the Home section," she wrote Rosenthal.

Perhaps it was just as well that Newhouse and her staff were not apprised of the publisher's involvement. If Rosenthal had, in the pressure-cooker atmosphere of the new sections' start-ups, appropriated someone else's ideas for his own, the theft was no more than petty larceny. "Many of the story suggestions on the first list of eighteen stories actually have run," Newhouse wrote Rosenthal, "fourteen of them in Home and two in Living." She pointed out, for example, that the news about "awnings making a comeback was a page-one story in June." Furthermore, medical specialist Jane Brody had done "a definitive piece on medicine cabinets in Living." As for the big advertisers' promotions, "model rooms we cover regularly when they open."

The publisher and his editor were not reading Living and Home very closely, for why else did they miss all the stories that had run? Perhaps the two sections' presentation was so muddled that Sulzberger and Rosenthal, the two readers with the greatest possible incentives to follow the *Times*' coverage, quickly forgot what they read. Either way, the *Times*' efforts to be friendly required further work.

A DAY IN THE LIFE
1 1 : 1 0 A.M.—1 2 : 1 5 P.M.

1 1 : 1 0 A.M.

The sun burned away the clouds in Honolulu. Bob Reinhold began the first of his interviews on a feature he had been thinking about for weeks, should he ever get to Hawaii. The story revolved around the question of who owns the land under the buildings in Honolulu, a dispute with roots in Hawaii's feudal past. Reinhold interviewed people on both sides of the dispute, the landlords who owned land, and the leaseholders of the condominiums and apartments built on top of the land. Tuesday afternoon, his interviews finished, Reinhold flew back to Los Angeles, blocking out the story in his mind, organizing his notes so he could begin inputting the story on the office computer. But the article lacked a "today" angle—no court decision had been rendered. The national desk decided to hold Reinhold's copy a week. It ran as a "Honolulu Journal" on the national affairs page, A-14, Friday, March 10. Apartment Owners Live/On Time-Bomb Leases, the two-line, two-column headline read. The lead paragraph began: "A century and half after King Kamehameha III, under pressure from newcomers, declared the great division of crown lands, land ownership remains the ugliest issue in this most feudal of American states."

On the fourth floor of the *Times*, Stewart Kampel laid out the

Long Island weekly section. LI Weekly was one of the *Times'* four zoned sections for Sunday; the other three were for New Jersey, Westchester, and Connecticut. Like Sunday Main Part 2, the zoned sections represented a part of the *Times'* response to post-1960s changes in the New York area, specifically, the middle-class migration away from the city. Television not only claimed readers' time; these same readers had put down roots now in the suburbs, and developed new local interests and loyalties.

Kampel and the other zone editors worked against a midweek deadline. By Thursday, the sections were preprinted and delivered, along with other Sunday advance sections, to suburban distribution points to be "married" on Saturday night with the news sections of the paper. The fourth floor was once the *Times'* composing room, where twenty years before, in the era of linotype machines and hot type, 1,200 printers labored through around-the-clock shifts. When the press run was over at 4:00 A.M., apprentices stripped the forms used to print the paper, breaking up the metal type, throwing the lead-alloy pieces into receptacles called hell boxes; the type was molten, the room noisy, the air reeked of fumes from hot metal and ink—hence, the name. Later, hell-box type was melted down and used again.

Now the composing room was empty, save for Kampel, the two editors who assisted him on LI Weekly, and a half-dozen makeup people working on the other zoned sections. They were in shirts and ties, grouped around long, waist-high tables, similar to an architect's drafting board. They conferred softly as they pasted up the cold type—copy that has been set electronically. The stories came out of computer-run phototypesetting machines on white, sticky-backed paper, with one-column width settings. The editors used X-acto knives to cut and paste together the pages, making boards for the page-plater machines. The metal type long gone, the heavy fifty-pound plates that used to whirr on the presses had been replaced by thin aluminum sheets. But the computers of *Times* editors still have a "hellbox" command, to make a story disappear, and Kampel still refers to the photographs in his section as "cuts"—from the days when engraved plates were sliced with a bandsaw and placed by hand between rows of type.

The news department's regular 11:00 A.M. meeting began, as usual, a few moments late. Section editors described what they would offer for their dress fronts—the opening page of each section. The meeting lacked fire. The man nominally running it, managing editor Arthur Gelb, was in his final months in the news department; he was sixty-five, the normal retirement age for

Times executives. The department editors from Metro, Sports, Business Day, and the Living section spoke, hurrying through their presentations. Max Frankel, the executive editor, did not attend the 11:00 A.M. meeting. He came instead to the 5:00 P.M. news meeting, when page one was laid out and the strong pitches made to get stories fronted.

11:15 A.M.

In Boston, Anthony Lewis received a phone call from Menachem Rosensaft, head of the organization Children of Holocaust Survivors, and one of the participants in the recent meeting of Jewish leaders with Yasir Arafat in Stockholm. Rosensaft invited Lewis to a meeting to be held in Israel to follow up the Arafat opening. Rosensaft spoke feelingly about the ferocity of the attacks on him for advocating Israeli talks with the PLO leader. After Rosensaft rang off, Lewis phoned Andrew Rosenthal, a reporter in the *Times* Washington bureau (and a son of A. M. Rosenthal). The younger Rosenthal had been covering the Tower nomination story, and Lewis wanted the exact wording of a comment by Senator Bob Dole on the right of accused persons to cross-examine their accusers. Rosenthal relayed the quote to Lewis. That established, Lewis turned to a related matter. He had received a letter from a Cleveland woman who believed she was being persecuted because of her past "radical" views. Lewis talked about the letter with David Cole, a lawyer at the Center for Constitutional Rights in New York; Cole said he would look into the Cleveland woman's case.

The interviews that Sam Roberts wanted to arrange with Cuomo and Koch both came through. Roberts put aside the research for his backup column.

12:00 NOON

The Noon List, those stories considered probable candidates for page one, was assembled by desk editors and input on the Harris computer system. Senior editors scrolled through the list. Each story had a shorthand name, or slug—Tower, North, SCOTUS (for the U.S. Supreme Court), Caracas. Slug was another vestige of the old days when a small rectangle of metal was inserted in the linotype machines to create a title at the top of galley sheets.

12:05 P.M.

At the entrance to the Times Building, a group of twelve teenage boys, yarmulkes on their heads, gathered to take a tour of the plant. They were from the J.E.C. yeshiva in Englewood, New Jersey. Jim Morgan, tall and graying, a paper cup containing coffee in his hand, introduced himself as their guide from the *Times'* Office of Public Tours. To the east, two hundred feet down 43rd Street, a middle-aged woman huddled in the doorway of an empty office, formerly used by the Traveller Service company. Her possessions were stuffed in a shopping bag; she held out a cup similar to the one Morgan was carrying. She demanded of passersby, "a dollar, in change." Two hundred feet to the west, near the entrance of the scabrous Times Square Motel at the other end of the block, a second woman stood on the sidewalk, arms folded, not begging for anything. She was thin and pale, no more than thirty years old. She wore a cotton dress and a stocking cap; her legs were bare in the thirty-eight-degree chill.

Three rented limousines carrying Marco Vinicio Cerezo Arevalo, the president of Guatemala, together with his entourage of guards and aides, drove past the panhandlers and the yeshiva boys and pulled up to the entrance of the *Times*. The delegation was met by Joseph Lelyveld, then the *Times* foreign editor. President Cerezo, forty-six, was a lawyer by training; he had been elected almost four years before to head Guatemala's first civilian government "after 30 years of bloody and discredited military cliques," to quote a *Times Magazine* article, by reporter Stephen Kinzer, going to press that week (it appeared on Sunday, March 26).

Lelyveld escorted Cerezo to the tenth-floor conference room for a meeting with the editorial board. Rebecca Sinkler, the editor of the *Book Review*, had also been invited, as well as editors from the foreign desk. Sinkler was interested in Guatemalan literature. Lelyveld wanted Cerezo to understand the importance the *Times* placed on access for its foreign correspondents. Cerezo's security men, and two women with the Cerezo party, also crowded into the room. One of the women was introduced as a cabinet minister.

Kinzer's article described Cerezo as "the handsome young leader who was swept into office in December 1985, with two-thirds of the votes cast." The president lived up to his billing in his talk to the board. Cerezo animatedly explained his idea for a Central American peace plan built around a regional parliamentary body, something like the European Parliament. He complained that the United States had done nothing to help his project, that there was no firm Bush administration policy in the region as yet. He hoped the *Times* could begin to shape a sympathetic U.S. posture. He needed the *Times'* help. Cerezo explained that he believed he was being undercut by Oscar Arias Sanchez, the president of Costa Rica and author of his own peace plan for the region. Two *Times* editors exchanged glances; the Kinzer article, then on its way to the composing room, carried no mention of this infighting.

12:15 P.M.

In the third-floor newsroom, Mark Landler, twenty-three, had reached an improbable point in his career as a news assistant in the *Times'* business-news department. After eighteen months of answering telephones, running to the morgue for clips, and doing the other scut work of a copy person, Landler had worked up a big story on his own. Two weeks before, Landler handled one of the scores of daily calls that come to the *Times'* business-news reporters. Typically, public relations people are on the line, to request coverage or remind the *Times* of a press release or photo opportunity. This time, the caller was a private citizen. She introduced herself as Mrs. Terry Rakolta, of Bloomfield Hills, a suburb of Detroit. She said she wanted to talk to Randall Rothenberg, the *Times* advertising columnist. Her name meant nothing to Rothenberg, who was preparing to go on vacation; he handed off Rakolta to Landler. The story she passed on to the news assistant was now being pitched by the business-news desk for fronting on page one.

As Rakolta told Landler, early in the evening of Sunday, January 15, she was sitting in her living room with her three young children. They had been grazing across the television dial when she clicked to the local station carrying the Fox network's comedy hit, "Married . . . with Children." Rakolta remembered that she was "appalled" by a sequence featuring a woman, dressed only in bra, panties, and garter belt, being ogled by two men. Rakolta told Landler that she decided to monitor "Married . . . with Children," to see what else was going during television's "family" viewing hours. She observed, and duly recorded, "references to condoms and to homosexuality," scenes built around Barbie and Ken dolls in (toy) bed together, and locker-room jokes about sex and body functions ("Q: What do older women have in common with 'dog doo'? A: The older they are, the easier it is to pick them up"). "They are saying women are 'crap,' " Rakolta remembered thinking, angrily.

Rakolta tried complaining to the local station; the switchboard referred her to the Fox network offices in Los Angeles, where a sympathetic secretary gave Rakolta the name of a senior producer at the production company responsible for "Married . . . with Children." The producer told Rakolta the program was intended to be "a body show." If she didn't like it, she shouldn't watch. Rakolta then wrote to the CEOs of the companies who were among the fifty leading advertisers on national television, complaining about the sexual innuendo of the programs that carried their ads. A score wrote back; several said that they shared her concern. The president of Coca-Cola pledged that his company would review its commitments in the light of Rakolta's letter, and remove advertising on "inappropriate" programming. Rakolta told all this to Landler. Even a fresh-faced clerk could recognize a story with a strong narrative line: Lone, angry housewife takes on network television—and wins. The story appealed to *Times'* editors on many levels, including its unflattering portrait of television. Still, they worried; the story was the work of a news assistant. Landler was asked to make doubly sure that Rakolta wasn't "the point man for some larger movement." Satisfied that she wasn't, the senior editors ran the "Housewife" story on page one of the editions of March 2.

For all of Landler's checking, the *Times* missed the real story. Terry Rakolta, the "lone angry housewife," was married to one of the wealthiest contractors in Michigan. Her investment broker had supplied the corporate names and addresses (after assembling a computer list of the relatively small number of companies responsible for 70 percent of national TV advertising). Her letters went out with a professional polish supplied by her husband's staff and his office word processors. The CEOs had indeed responded soothingly to her letter; but the corporate promises of "review" proved meaningless. Only one advertiser changed its time-buying schedule—while a half dozen other new advertisers joined the line to buy commercial time on "Married . . . with Children." As for Coca-Cola, it ran twenty-three separate ads on "Married" over the next twelve months.

The *Times* was also unable to tell the story of the power of its own front page in the narrow, self-referential world of media. Rakolta had shared her story with the advertising-news department of the *Wall Street Journal* at the same time she talked to the *Times.* The *Journal* ran a one-paragraph item two weeks before the *Times* article. When Landler called to interview her, Rakolta concluded he was doing a short item as well. After she learned that he had called several people in the Detroit area to ask about her—including her congressman—she remembered thinking, "He's certainly going to a lot of effort for a three-line story." Then, on the morning of Thursday, March 2, the Rakolta phone began ringing at 6:00 A.M.; one after another, neighbors, relatives, friends from the country club, called to tell her that she was "on page one of the *New York Times.*" A Bloomfield Hills police squad car came to her door, and the patrolman delivered a message from Ted Koppel in Washington: He was trying to get in touch with her to invite her on "Nightline" (The Rakoltas' home phone was unlisted, and ABC News had asked the police to help out). In addition to "Nightline," her story was also featured on "The CBS Evening News with Dan Rather," the "Donahue" show, and the "Sally Jessy Raphael Show." The BBC did a special report. One of Rakolta's friends from Bloomfield Hills, in the Swiss Alps on ski holiday, saw Rakolta's face on television during a German-language news broadcast. Unable to understand what was being said, the friend concluded that Rakolta had been taken hostage by terrorists, "for why else would anyone put Terry on TV?"

4

—

THE CHANGES:
2. SAFE TIMES

"I DON'T LIKE IT in the *Times!*"

That was the unmistakable, proprietary Sulzberger style, expressed by the father, Punch, and mirrored in more recent years in the son, Arthur. Punch Sulzberger's comments about skimpy lingerie and the habits of lesbian couples set a tone for the *Times*; the father and the son's monitory notes influenced the words and pictures that made up the surface of the paper, at least for those subjects that interested each man. Important as these news pages were—hundreds of thousands of people each day relied on the *Times* for a reasonably reliable, and balanced, accounting of local, national, and world developments—there was another, enduring *Times*. Behind the daily face of the news existed the heart and soul of the paper, the ideas that were its animating spirit.

Formally, the principles of the *Times* were expressed on the editorial page of the paper, in endorsements for political office and stands on matters of public policy. As is the case at scores of other newspapers, the *Times*' publisher had the ultimate authority to make the paper's endorsements, set the paper's overall aims and decide its specific editorial campaigns. In practice, the publisher's real authority lay in the power to pick the editors to execute these tasks—the men (and one or two women) who carry forward the vision of the paper. The way this authority was exercised at the paper in the late 1980s and early 1990s made reading the *Times* a challenging task, and especially enjoyable if the reader knew what to look for. Punch Sulzberger continued to run the paper together with his top appointees, while his son was putting together his own team of editors and managers, Arthur loyalists, who comprised a government in waiting. The good Harvard doctor Chris Argyris, with his interest in living systems, would have profited immensely had he been conducting his interventions during this period. As it was, Argyris never probed quite deep enough to understand how the Sulzbergers' custodial role shaped the institutional *Times*, its "objective" news reports and its editorial policies.

Father and son both valued the power of the memorandum. The younger Sulzberger's interests were at once broader than his father's and more specifically focused. He involved himself across the board, and socialized with his employees in a way his father never did. The older Sulzberger was close to one or two associates at any given time. Young Arthur's shadow cabinet included: Lance Primus, the president of the paper and, like Arthur, only in his early forties; the columnist Anna Quindlen, whose work appeared on the Op-Ed page; the architectural critic Paul Goldberger (promoted to cultural editor in late 1990, and effectively allowed to consolidate the *Times'* arts and entertainment coverage under his control); and the managing editor—and next in line to be the top editor when Max Frankel retired—Joseph Lelyveld. The elder Sulzberger had been selective in his editorial interests. Not every subject captured Punch Sulzberger's attention— "very fortunately for those of us he didn't bother with," according to a member of the cultural staff. Punch Sulzberger seemed to concern himself with those areas, this reporter said, where "significant advertising was involved, for example, the theater and movies, two subjects related to the business health of the *Times*."

In his turn, Arthur Sulzberger worried less about advertising—he had others do that for him—and more about the *Times'* circulation and its hiring policies. These concerns were, as Arthur Sulzberger saw it, complementary halves of the same overriding social interest. The pursuit of a wider audience and of a racially and sexually diverse newsroom was part of his plan to broaden the *Times'* appeal as it moved into the new century. The paper was by tradition edited for the middle and upper-middle classes; Arthur Sulzberger wanted a more egalitarian *Times*.

The Sulzberger-family principles were never spelled out imperiously, in the manner of, say, a William Randolph Hearst. Hearst's messages enunciating policy for the Hearst newspapers were relayed over open wires from his lieutenants and usually began: "The Chief says. . . ." Punch Sulzberger spoke privately, obliquely, and at times with an element of guile. In a way, Sulzberger was a "Hidden Hand" publisher, to borrow the phrase the Princeton political scientist Fred Greenstein used in his revisionist view of the presidency of Dwight D. Eisenhower. The public Eisenhower appeared as a fatherly figure, friendly, and—with his fractured syntax and slightly out-of-it manner—a bit of a bumbler. According to Greenstein, however, "behind Eisenhower's seeming transcendence of politics was a vast amount of indirect, carefully concealed effort to exercise influence." The private Eisenhower was manipulative, letting others give the lecture, do the dirty work, or take the fall: "The Hidden-Hand Presidency." Punch Sulzberger developed a similar behind-the-scenes style, particularly when dealing with matters that touched on the *Times'* economic well-being. By contrast, his son's hand was seldom as hidden, perhaps as much because of the changed circumstances at the paper as the differing personalities of the two men. Punch Sulzberger, a social conservative in a tumultuous period, consciously lowered the *Times'* voice. Arthur Sulzberger, energetic and an activist at a time when American society seemed exhausted and wary of change, tried to push the *Times* into more high-profile stands.

The year 1963, when Punch Sulzberger took over as publisher of the *Times*, marked the beginning of what turned out to be a decade of unprecedented upheaval: assassinations, civil rights demonstrations, the unpopular (and ultimately unwinnable) Vietnam war, and the birth of the environmental movement with its demands for greater "corporate responsibility." In the early 1970s, the start of Sulzberger's second decade as publisher coincided with the Watergate scandals and the impeachment proceedings that forced the resignation of Richard Nixon. Then came the OPEC oil shock and the fiscal crisis in New York City. While these were exhilarating times journalistically, they were not cost-free for a newspaper of the *Times'* standing. The press during these years became an object of some hostility; feelings went beyond the old pattern of blaming the messenger for the bad news. Along with other leading news organizations, the *Times* invited anger when it departed from the political consensus that had held during the cold war years, and began questioning U.S. policy in Vietnam. The *Times* startled the establishment still more when the paper half turned its back on the official news it regularly processed and vigorously began generating important stories out of Washington. The tradition of independent journalism goes back to the early twentieth-century muckrakers and even earlier to the abolitionists and urban reformers of nineteenth-century America. But the establishment wasn't accustomed to seeing such investigative energy on the part of an institution, like the *Times*, considered one of its own. By then, of course, the establishment itself had split on Vietnam.

The *Times* started out as supporter of the American intervention. Editorially, the paper took a firm anti-Communist stance, backing the Gulf of Tonkin resolution (which opened the way for the full-scale commitment of U.S. armed forces to the Saigon government) and backing the candidacy of Lyndon Johnson against the Republican Barry Goldwater. John B. Oakes had resolved when he took over the editorial page in 1961 that he would abolish the old habits of inoffensive, finely tuned writing—what he called "on the one hand, on the other hand" editorials. Relatively early in the war, Oakes's editorials criticized the political corruption of the Ngo Dinh Diem regime. *Times* editorials began to oppose further escalation of American troop strength, mirroring the split in the American establishment. Members of the Senate and House, the faculties of prestige universities, and parts of the Wall Street financial community opposed the war, in many cases, well before the *Times* added its critical voice.

The *Times* moved to a more exposed position during the summer of 1971, when it took the lead in publishing the Pentagon Papers. Harrison Salisbury, in his semiauthorized history of the *Times*, *Without Fear or Favor*, regarded the Pentagon Papers case not just as a "great confrontation" between the press and the Nixon administration but also as a "metaphor" of the emergence of the *Times* into a new social role: the *Times* as nothing less than the fourth coequal branch of government. As Salisbury told it, the *Times* profoundly changed both the country and journalism with its courageous stand. With the passage of time, however, the whole episode has begun to shrink to a footnote in the narrative of the Nixon years.

The gray, ambiguous nature of the Papers may explain why the case wasn't the Salisburian seminal political event of the 1970s. The Pentagon Papers were documents written by a team of Department of Defense analysts, who had been assigned to assemble an historical archive of how the United States became committed to the Saigon government. The team produced a series of reports adding up to forty-seven volumes. *Times* reporter Neil Sheehan obtained a photocopied set of the documents from a military analyst named Daniel Ellsberg, a formerly gung-ho defense intellectual who had soured on the war. A protracted internal debate took place in Sulzberger's offices at the *Times*, with the paper's news editors in favor of publication, and the *Times'* outside law firm opposed on the grounds that the documents might compromise diplomatic secrets and military security. Punch Sulzberger sided with those who favored publication, after some sanitizing of the documents.

The first installment of the materials was published in the *Times* on Sunday, June 13, 1971, which meant that the edition was available to *Times* readers and competing news organizations on Saturday night. The *Times'* deliberately quiet "historical" presentation and the gray columns of text lulled many people. Gordon Manning, a network-news executive, remembered thinking, "This looks deep. I'll just put it aside and perhaps read it later, when I have more time." The two-line headline ran over four columns in the right upper half of page one. It read: "Vietnam Archive: Pentagon Study Traces Three Decades of Growing U.S. Involvement."

Most news organizations initially ignored the "archive" (the catchier title, "Pentagon Papers," wasn't used until later). The United Press International didn't put a story summarizing the materials on its wires until Sunday afternoon; the Associated Press waited until Monday afternoon. *Time* and *Newsweek* both had the opportunity to incorporate the *Times'* materials into their next issues due out Monday, but chose not to do so. CBS News skipped the story on its Sunday night newscast, although NBC News played it prominently. The most attentive readers were the *Washington Post* and the *Boston Globe*; they obtained their own photocopied selections of the documents (*Post* and *Globe* reporters and Ellsberg managing to find each other quickly).

The archives did become a "big story" . . . when Richard Nixon and his attorney general John Mitchell foolishly precipitated a constitutional case. Instead of standing aside and letting the dry archival materials continue to slip down the national memory hole, Nixon's Justice Department went to the courts and obtained an order of prior restraint. Sulzberger and the *Times* resisted the attempt to proscribe publication. A legitimate first amendment confrontation began, and the case quickly went to the Supreme Court. By a vote of 6 to 3, the lower court's restraining order was overturned: The *Times* and the *Post* could resume publishing without threat of civil or criminal penalties. Three members of the majority said there never could be a prior restraint, while three others said prior restraint would be appropriate in a proper case, but that these documents posed no real threat to national security.

On balance, the Pentagon Papers case strengthened the press's constitutional freedoms, as well as stiffening the spines of media executives. If the Nixon administration had been thinking coolly, it would not have charged ahead at its "enemies" in the press. Instead Nixon could have welcomed publication, making one thing perfectly clear: The Vietnam morass had begun not on his watch but on his predecessors', the Democrats Kennedy and Johnson. Even after the celebrated court case, few people ever bothered to read the papers. A book version of a set of the documents, made available by Senator Mike Gravel of Alaska, was brought out by Beacon Press and quickly forgotten. According to Erwin Griswold, who as U.S. solicitor general argued the government's brief before the Supreme Court, his boss John Mitchell had never seen the Papers and had no idea what was in them even after the case went to the court. Griswold himself didn't have time to read the Papers, relying instead on government briefers to point out what items the administration considered diplomatically or militarily sensitive. The team suggested about forty items; Griswold reduced the sensitive list to eleven. At most, only two or three of these actually appeared in newspapers once publication resumed.

Sulzberger doesn't dwell much either on Salisbury's grand themes. Twenty years later, he recalled the case as a threat to the *Times*' financial well-being. "It was a very scary thing because we were charting unknown waters," he remembered. "We had no idea of our liabilities. The courts could have found us guilty and fined us millions and millions of dollars, which we didn't have in those days." He adds, almost as an afterthought, "The company's reputation was on the line."

Nixon later explained rather lamely that he had moved against the *Times* because publication of the archive "was certain to hurt the whole Vietnam effort. Critics of the war could use [the Pentagon

Papers] to attack my goals and my policies." The explanation overlooks the realities of the "effort"; by 1971, U.S. public opinion had turned against the war. "Vietnamization"—the departure of American troops—and the defeat of the South were both assured: There was nothing of strategic value left to hurt. More than a decade after the last shots were fired in Saigon, however, unreconstructed hawks such as General William Westmoreland and William Colby, the former CIA director, would continue to insist that Vietnam was the first war in American history "lost on the front page of the *New York Times.*" That thought was somehow more comforting than the reality of a war lost on the battlefield.

History was an abstraction; economic survival was a more immediate worry in the publisher's suite of the *Times.* These were the same years during which the *Times* came to believe that its future was tied less to New York and more to a regional and national audience, a time when, as John Oakes says, "I kept hearing the phrase, 'We must go after the suburban housewife.' " In addition to the big push away from the city, Punch Sulzberger also was being urged to revive publication of a national edition of the *Times*—"to do it right this time," after the too-casual effort of the early 1960s. He was uncertain of its appeal: The rest of the country was not New York. One sales executive reported that among his industrial accounts beyond the Hudson, the *Times* was still considered "a Jewish paper." Sulzberger was hearing also from some of his advertising managers that the *Times* was "still perceived to be to the left" and "antibusiness." "The *Times* may be ready for the country," Sulzberger wrote in a memorandum to his associates during one of the discussions about a national edition of the paper. "But is the country ready for us?"

And not just Out There. Punch Sulzberger heard complaints about the *Times*' editorial stands from the nonfamily members of his board of directors. The *Times*, these in-house critics insinuated, was taking the "left-liberal" position on such issues as environmental protection and governmental regulatory powers. According to Oakes, "Punch's friends on Wall Street were angry at the paper. The editorial pages of the *Times* had antagonized 'The Club' "—Oakes's designation for the inner circle of the Wall Street investment bankers—"by advocating stricter federal controls of financial and corporate practices." Bernard "Bunny" Lasker, the financier and consummate Wall Street insider, "used to come to the publisher's lunches and raise hell about me," Oakes remembered. In the Reagan years, when government stood aside to let "the free market work," the insiders in the financial community got the regulatory relief they sought. Oakes took some satisfaction in the predictable results. "Their chickens came home to roost in the late 1980s with Ivan Boesky, Michael Milken, and friends."

Well before the Reagan years, Punch Sulzberger moved to counteract criticisms about the liberal tilt of the *Times*. On the most visible level he added William Safire as an Op-Ed page columnist. A New Yorker, Safire had begun his career at the age of twenty, as a legman— part assistant, part ghostwriter—for the public relations man and radio personality Tex McCrary. Safire's publicist's background earned him a backseat in Richard Nixon's entourage during the then vice president's visit to the Soviet Union in 1959. There, on the eve of the American presidential primaries, Safire contrived to set up the "kitchen debate" between Nixon and Soviet Premier Nikita Khrushchev. The Safire-inspired photo opportunity captured Nixon jowl to jowl with Khrushchev, wagging a finger in the Communist leader's face: the Republican hopeful lecturing the enemy, our tough guy standing up to their tough guy. Safire later joined the Nixon administration as a speech writer in the White House, where he composed the alliterative line about the press's "nattering nabobs of negativism" for Vice President Spiro Agnew. His speech-writing days ended after the president's men put a wiretap on him (they tried, unsuccessfully, to catch him leaking information to the press). Sulzberger recruited Safire, after the *Washington Post*, another of the elitist papers on the administration's enemies list, beat the *Times* out on its first choice for house conservative, the commentator George Will.

Safire started out rather slowly. The journalist Eric Alterman, in his study of Washington columnists, *Sound and Fury: The Washington Punditocracy and the Collapse of American Politics*, reported that Sulzberger was so unhappy with Safire's contributions that the publisher told the columnist, "This isn't working." Safire was supposedly so devastated that he returned to his office and buried his head in his arms. Then, looking up, his eyes locked on his desk phone: salvation—he would rescue his career by using his extensive contacts to do a reporter's column. "That's a good story but it never happened," Safire said when he was asked about Alterman's account. "It's some third party's version of what people imagined had happened." The closest he came to any "showdown," Safire said, was during a lunch with Abe Rosenthal, whose news department had no jurisdiction at all over *Times* columnists. "Abe told me, strictly as friend to friend, that he thought some of my columns were too shrill—that I was too tough on some people. After all, a *Times* columnist wields the enormous power of the *Times*. Abe was right. So I developed a good rule—kick 'em while they're up, not while they're down."

In 1978, five years after he was hired, Safire won a Pulitzer Prize for commentary; the Pulitzer judges were the same journalistic nabobs he had attacked a few years before.

The addition of a new columnist was a relatively quick way to achieve the appearance of "balance." Safire rather slyly suggested when he joined the *Times* that he and Anthony Lewis, whose *Times* column alternated with Safire's, were now paired: Like opposing U.S. senators, they canceled out each other's vote. But Sulzberger also had more fundamental changes in mind for the editorial pages. Beyond the adjustment of a sail here, and a rudder setting there, he steered the *Times'* editorials in new directions; some tacks were modest, others major, and all had the cumulative effect of moving the ship to starboard. Skipper Sulzberger didn't bellow out orders or make public pronouncements. Rather, he took a "Hidden Hand" approach.

In the late fall of 1974, just three months after the national trauma of Watergate ended with presidential impeachment proceedings and the resignation of Richard Nixon, Sulzberger shared what he called his "concerns" about the alleged tilt of the *Times* with his two top editors, Abe Rosenthal and Max Frankel. Rosenthal was in charge of the news department, Max Frankel was the Sunday editor. Sulzberger asked them to submit essay answers to a two-part question about how the paper was edited. First, Sulzberger wanted their written thoughts on whether the *Times* was fair in its coverage: Did the paper have adequate checking systems in place to insure accuracy and balance in the news? Second, he wanted his editors' reactions to corporate and business "perceptions" that the *Times* was "too left" or "anticapitalist."

Rosenthal and Frankel's replies were instructive; their memos offered a window into the two men's personalities as well as a display of their philosophies of the news. Rosenthal began defensively. He cited an article in the conservative magazine *National Review*, which declared, on the basis of an analysis of the *Times'* coverage of five major

news stories, that the paper set a standard for fairness worthy of emu-
lation by other media. These findings, Rosenthal wrote, came as a
surprise to the editors of the National Review, "who had assumed that
the Times, since it has a liberal editorial policy, was presenting its news
to suit a liberal bias." Rosenthal added his own gloss: "And yet we all
know that the Times is often attacked as biased. What is not generally
known is that the attacks come at least as frequently from the left as
from the right."

He then offered nine reasons—most of them self-serving—for these
attacks. In some cases, Rosenthal explained, the Times' critics were at
fault; there were readers who couldn't differentiate between fact and
bias. Other critics—from "the business community" that had supported Nixon—hated the press for hounding their man. Still other
businessmen-critics read the Times "even though they would prefer to
read other papers that more suited their opinions and tastes." Here he
mentioned the old New York Herald Tribune—"one of the most openly
biased newspapers . . . but a lot of people miss it precisely because its
bias fitted in with their own." Mainly, Rosenthal maintained, the
Times was the object of criticism for the simple reason that it was so
important, and so good: because the Times "almost always avoids
editorialization" in its news columns, every slip in the Times stands out
and provokes comment. "This attention is the price the Times must
proudly pay for its own commitment to its own ethic."

Rosenthal also wrote a second memo, three and a half pages in
length, explaining to Sulzberger how the news department employed
an "intricate plan of checks and examinations before and after a story
is printed" to insure that stories were "objective." Rosenthal detailed
how every reporter's work was reviewed before publication by layers of
editors. First the story was read by a news editor assigned to each desk
(national, international, business, metro, etc.). Then a "backfield"
editor looked for factual holes in the material, unanswered questions,
and matters of fairness. Next came the copy editor, who did the same
checking and also looked for grammatical errors. Finally, a senior
editor read every story designated for the front page as well as those
"takeouts"—major stories—written in advance or running over twelve
hundred words. As extensive as these editing layers were, Rosenthal
acknowledged, "It all starts with the reporter. . . . The rewards the
paper has to offer—promotion, assignments, merit increases—are
based not only on the reporter's ability as a writer and gatherer of

facts—but on his understanding of the paper's objectives and ethics and his devotion to them. Many a reporter, obviously talented, has been stopped in his advancement because his editors felt that there were times when consciously or unconsciously he wrote stories that were subtly biased." Rosenthal concluded on a self-satisfied note: "Virtually all reporters here are aware of the character of the paper and devoted to it—one reason why a slip stands out so vividly."

Rosenthal, the commander in the trenches, had offered a ground-level analysis. Frankel, the intellectual and learned expert of world affairs, took an opposite tack in his memo. "There is, first and foremost, no need to feel or be defensive," he began. Then came Frankel's wide-lens view of a world in crisis. His tour d'horizon makes painful reading today, considering what actually happened during the following decade in the two Germanys, the Eastern Europe of Havel and Walesa, Gorbachev's—and Yeltsin's—Soviet Union, and Ronald Reagan's United States. "Ownership is about to be redistributed in a major way," Frankel predicted, his crystal ball hopelessly clouded. "Capitalist institutions around the world have been shown to be inadequate. Populations want to reinvest some of their excess capital in public services and facilities."

Frankel then turned his attention to the *Times*. Given this atmosphere of change, he urged Sulzberger to remember that there would be demands for fresh ways to supply news and information. "If anything, as our more vigorous critics on the left have often contended, we have been more naturally and too easily 'pro business' and 'pro government' in our many routine and unquestioning reports on how politicians and corporate leaders define themselves and their works." In the future, Frankel wrote, *Times* readers will be demanding more accountability, including corporate accountability: "If fairness is taken to mean that we report business the way it sees itself, we are going to disappoint the complainants." Moreover, there are various definitions of fairness—first, "the definition of our grandfathers, handed down in the conventions and traditions of our business and of democratic debate in general." And then there is the definition of fairness supplied by the community: "Where there is a consensus in the community about right and wrong, we tend to reflect that consensus in our approach; when there is controversy, the requirements for journalistic neutrality tend to grow." Frankel concluded that homosexuals, blacks, the Pentagon, and the business community all were being treated differently today in the "community"—and therefore, in the *Times*—than they were a generation ago. Underneath the rhetoric, Frankel was offering the pseudo-profound wisdom of the folk singer Bob Dylan: The times, they are a-changing.

The two memos had little direct impact on the day-to-day operations of the paper. Punch Sulzberger did not circulate them, and *Times*-people were at most only dimly aware of the Rosenthal and Frankel essays. But Punch Sulzberger was not trying to influence the *Times* staff directly, through orders posted on newsroom bulletin boards. Instead, Ike-like, Sulzberger chose to cultivate a sense of his "concerns" in the minds of his two editors; their introspections were as much for their benefit as for his. Sulzberger didn't have to "plant" any conservative or centrist ideas with his editors. The *Times'* system of hiring people when they were young and then selecting only from within for advancement to the top helped assure that no unknown quantities were promoted to senior editorships. The soil was familiar and well tested; exotic flora could not grow too high, or survive very long. "I don't believe in telling editors or reporters what to do," Sulzberger summed up. "But I do believe in long, philosophic conversations with my editors about where the paper, the city, and the country are going. We had these discussions all the time."

The constant discussions also had the secondary effect of sharpening the competition between Frankel and Rosenthal. At the time of the essay exercise, the two editors were roughly equal in stature. Both had worked all their adult lives at the *Times*—Rosenthal, older by eight years, had been at the paper longer. Although Rosenthal held the title of managing editor, he ran only the news pages of the daily paper—the editorial page editor reported directly to the publisher, as did the Sunday editor. The title of executive editor had not been used since James Reston returned to Washington in 1970 and was not given to Rosenthal until later, after he "won" the essay contest.

When Sulzberger decided to make Rosenthal the executive editor, he also gave him power over the Sunday paper. That left Frankel without a job. But Sulzberger did not want to lose a *Times*man of Frankel's abilities. Frankel's argument that the *Times* ought to reflect the "consensus of its community" suited Sulzberger's temperament, as did Frankel's cautious, centrist positions. Sulzberger decided to put Frankel in charge of the editorial page. To open up the editor's job Sulzberger had to remove its occupant, his cousin John B. Oakes.

*   *   *

Perhaps in no other episode did the Hidden Hand reveal so much of itself than in the maneuvers to get Oakes off the editorial page. When Sulzberger asked his editors to respond to the question of *Times* "bias" he hadn't bothered to solicit Oakes's opinion. Yet Oakes, as the editorial page editor for the previous thirteen years, determined each day what the *Times* was saying about politics, business, and the state of the world. On the surface the decision not to involve Oakes in the discussions was bizarre. Considered from Sulzberger's point of view, the omission becomes understandable, indeed, inevitable.

Johnny Oakes was thirteen years older than Punch Sulzberger. Seemingly everything Oakes put his mind to, he did well. At Princeton he was an editor of the *Daily Princetonian*, was elected to Phi Beta Kappa, graduated magna cum laude, and was voted "most brilliant" by his classmates. He worked as a reporter on the *Washington Star*, served with distinction overseas as an army intelligence officer in World War II, and joined the *Times* after the war. By the mid-1950s, during the years when Punch Sulzberger was wandering the halls of the *Times* without any defined duties, Oakes was serving on the paper's editorial board; he already had a secure reputation as a leading conservationist and the *Times'* specialist on environmental policies. In April 1961, Arthur Hays Sulzberger, Punch's father, named Oakes editor of the editorial page. A *Times*man who has known both Punch Sulzberger and John Oakes for his entire adult life says that Iphigene Sulzberger, for one, was acutely aware of Oakes's achievements; "Punch heard from his mother more than once the refrain, 'Why can't you be more like Johnny?' " this *Times*man claims. In the 1960s, when Sulzberger took over as publisher of the *Times*, and became Oakes's boss, the two men had an outwardly correct relationship. But it was no secret that they represented different branches of the same family—the Ochs-Oakes side and the Sulzberger side.

Oakes's father, George Washington Ochs, was the younger brother of Adolph Ochs. Ochs had, as the *Times* put it in its article announcing John Oakes's appointment as editorial page editor, "Americanized the family name in 1917." Six decades later, the writer Stephen Birmingham suggested in a magazine article that George Ochs had changed the family name because the *Times* "does whatever it can to avoid creating the impression that it is Jewish owned." John Oakes replied that Birmingham could have easily ascertained, if he had been "interested in the truth," the real story: George Ochs had acted out of horror of German atrocities during World War I, and "did not wish his sons to bear a German name." John Oakes was justified in feeling aggrieved at the slur; as he pointed out, "It would not have been difficult for Birmingham to have discovered that I was brought up by my father as a Jew, was confirmed as a Jew as were my four children and have for years been an officer and trustee of my synagogue in New York." George Ochs, for his part, did not conceal his Jewishness in a career as an editor and public servant—he was mayor of Chattanooga. Nor were there any apologies because the Ochs-Oakes branches were the poor relations of the family, relatively speaking.

While control of the *Times* belonged to the Sulzberger side, John Oakes nevertheless was a highly visible presence. With his impeccable grooming and liberal humanistic views, Oakes came to personify the *Times* for many outsiders. Oakes could be seen shaping the *Times'* editorial pages. Punch Sulzberger, meanwhile, was otherwise engaged; he was preoccupied with the gritty business details of publishing—the shutdown of the western edition, the *Times'* new status as a public company, the price of newsprint, the fractious New York craft unions, and his own contentious editors. While the publisher maneuvered the retirement of the managers he had inherited and put in his own team, cousin Johnny Oakes was left free to run the editorial page during the late 1960s and early 1970s.

Most editorial pages in these years were dominated by white males, and the *Times* was no exception to this closed fraternity. When the seismic changes of the 1960s finally reached newspaper offices, Oakes shook up his page. The *Times* hired as editorial board members Ada Louise Huxtable, the architecture critic and a writer of grace and intelligence, and Roger Wilkins, a nephew of the civil rights leader Roy Wilkins and a former official in the U.S. Justice department when Robert Kennedy was attorney general. At many newspapers, too, the editorial pages were regarded as a dumping ground for journalists adjudged burned out by the news side. At Oakes's *Times*, however, the board attracted the best of the staff—for example, A. H. Raskin, the tall, angular specialist in labor relations, and Herbert Mitgang, who wrote on civil rights and constitutional law topics.

Raskin was born in New York City in 1913, the same year as Oakes; he grew up six miles north of Oakes's Fifth Avenue neighborhood and light-years away socially. His parents were poor Russian Jewish immigrants. Like many other young men of the era, he worked his way through the City College of New York, wangling the job of CCNY's campus stringer for the *Times*. He joined the paper after graduation in 1931, as a reporter. Raskin was a loyal member of the American Newspaper Guild, the newsroom union, and liked to boast that he held an honorary Guild card even after he joined the *Times'* editorial board in the late 1950s, and became "management." His affection for the ideals of the Guild did not prevent him from pulling together a stunning account of the New York City newspaper strike of 1962–63. The strike deprived readers of their papers for 114 days and ended in a "settlement" that settled little (it left unresolved, for example, the issues of work schedules and manning levels that had divided the unions and the owners in the first place). Raskin's report, a model of explanatory journalism, filled two pages of the *Times*; it meticulously documented how both the unions and the managements at the city's papers, including executives of the *Times*, had contributed to the disaster through incompetence and intransigence. "Both sides deserve each other," Raskin quoted New York mayor Robert Wagner as saying.

Herb Mitgang was also extending a distinguished journalistic career on the editorial board. During World War II, he was managing editor of *Stars & Stripes*, the Army newspaper. He joined the *Times* in 1945 and managed to produce a series of well-regarded books on his own time—novels, biographies, reportage, criticism, and a play, *Mr. Lincoln* (produced on Broadway). Mitgang left the *Times* in 1964, lured away by CBS to be its executive news editor. But Mitgang soon concluded that, as he later put it, "TV isn't a writer's medium." He returned to the *Times* three years later when Oakes asked him to help get the planned Op-Ed page started. When *New York* magazine profiled the Oakes board, it illustrated the article with the board members posed as "The Last Puritans," after the painting of the Flemish master Van Dyck. Mitgang, Raskin, and the other board members were zealous in their application of the notions of the good, the true, and the pure; but John Oakes was the foremost Puritan. The board members, Mitgang remembered, "always referred reverently to their editor as 'Mr. Oakes,' just as it was always 'Mr. Shawn' at *The New Yorker* magazine."

Like any editor of strong tastes and originality, Oakes had his blind spots. He could be stiff-necked; he became convinced that the news department had sided with farmers and hunters in a story about the killing of coyotes in Florida, and he refused to accept Abe Rosenthal's explanation that the overall Florida ecology was benefiting from control of the coyote population. Oakes also had a healthy ego, one that required stroking as much as other *Times*people's. Many executives, for example, later took credit for the Op-Ed page. Oakes did indeed first suggest the Op-Ed idea, but he was bothered by the prospect of "mixed voices" in proximity to his editorial page, and he worried that readers would think it was the *Times* speaking on the facing page, rather than an outside contributor. Punch Sulzberger went back and forth on the Op-Ed decision—one reason it took a decade to produce—but then so did Oakes.

Certainly, each man had plenty on his plate to occupy him in those first years of their collaboration: Sulzberger concentrating on business-side decisions, Oakes dealing with *Times* policies on Vietnam, civil rights, and the economy. They didn't crowd each other. "The compatible cousins," the trade magazine *Editor & Publisher* called them in 1970. "When we disagree, I'm in the fortunate position that I can win if I want to," Sulzberger explained to the magazine. "But I don't want to."

A few years later Sulzberger wanted a "win"—and badly enough to expose himself and his cousin to just the kind of public attention the family had so earnestly tried to avoid. The presumptive occasion for their highly publicized disagreement was the Democratic Party senatorial primary in New York during the summer of 1976. Sulzberger's choice was the centrist candidate Daniel Patrick Moynihan; John Oakes and the majority of his editorial board wanted to endorse the liberal Bella Abzug. Sulzberger got his way, but in a manner suggesting that Moynihan and Abzug were both somewhat incidental to the larger purposes of the publisher.

At the beginning of 1976, Oakes was still more than two years away from his sixty-fifth birthday. Sometime around that date, April 23, 1978, he would step down from his editor's job, if the *Times*' retirement policies were strictly applied to him. But the number sixty-five had no magic during Punch Sulzberger's reign. Specific departure times for senior men were—typically—left flexible: It could be any time in the calendar year, or in the case of one of Punch Sulzberger's latter-day favorites, the editor James Greenfield, more than a year after his sixty-fifth birthday date. (Punch Sulzberger himself stayed past his sixty-fifth birthday in 1991, as his own son tried to look patient.) In 1976 Oakes was a vigorous, healthy sixty-three-year-old, dedicated to the outdoors; on pleasant workdays, he liked to walk briskly some two miles through Central Park, East Side to West Side, before taking a bus to the *Times*. He didn't feel ready to retire when, one day in the spring of that year, his cousin called him in for a talk. Sulzberger, Oakes remembered, told him that he would have to step aside at the end of the year, a full sixteen months before his sixty-fifth birthday. "Punch forced me to quit," Oakes says. "I asked him, 'Is there anything in my editorials that you disapprove of?' He answered, 'Absolutely not.' Rather, Abe had gotten the job that Max competed for, and wanted. And now Punch told me, 'I'm afraid I'll lose Max.'"

The date of January 1, 1977, was picked for Frankel to assume control of the editorial page. The prospective move was doubly painful for Oakes. He had given his cousin a list of those editors that Oakes thought would make worthy successors. It was culled from the ranks of the Last Puritans. Fourteen years later, Oakes would not reveal his choices, though it's not hard to guess that Raskin and Mitgang were high on the list. Oakes did say, however, that the list did not include Max Frankel: "He was not my choice, and I said so to Punch. But I also said that if you reject my choices, I want you to know that Max is the next best qualified person, though he could use a year or more of training for the job." Sulzberger not only rejected the idea of more seasoning for Frankel, the publisher moved Frankel into Oakes's job well in advance of the ostensible changeover date. The editorial-page endorsements for the Democratic party primary became a handy vehicle for the publisher's putsch against Oakes.

The senatorial campaign that summer of 1976 had turned into pure New York theater. After the national shame of the Republican Nixon during Watergate, the 1976 general election was considered a walkover for the Democrats. New York Republicans were never numerous to begin with, and in the post-Nixon era, their party was in disarray. The incumbent Republican, Senator James Buckley, the decent, pedestrian brother of the writer William Buckley, Jr., had meager support. Punch Sulzberger and John Oakes agreed, along with everyone else, that victory in the Democratic primary would be "tantamount" to election. But the Democrats couldn't agree among themselves on their candidate; neither could the two cousins. Four men and a woman emerged as possible candidates: Daniel Patrick Moynihan, the former

Harvard professor and midlevel official in the Nixon administration; Abzug, the congresswoman from a left-liberal Greenwich Village district, and a leading figure in the woman's movement; Ramsey Clark, a former U.S. attorney general in the Lyndon Johnson years; Paul O'Dwyer, brother of William O'Dwyer, the former mayor of New York City; and the parking lot magnate Abe Hirschfeld. Abzug, Clark, and O'Dwyer clustered on the ideological left of the party, while Moynihan positioned himself as the candidate of the democratic majority (fifth candidate Hirschfeld was, and remained, a loose toy-cannon). The race, then, came down to whether the liberal-leaning Democratic electorate could unite on one candidate to oppose Moynihan. Practically speaking, that meant uniting behind Abzug, who was running well ahead of both Clark and O'Dwyer.

Moynihan had angered many New York liberals, and Oakes's editorial page, for a number of reasons. As the author of the "benign neglect" memorandum during his service in the Nixon administration, Moynihan was considered insensitive to the plight of blacks in America. Oakes saw in the memo a cynical retreat of government from its social obligations: a policy with the emphasis on "neglect" rather than "benign." Oakes also faulted Moynihan for his performance as Nixon's ambassador to the United Nations ("He spent his time bullying and baiting Third World countries," Oakes explained); for his military hawkishness; and for his general "florid adulation" of the disgraced president. Abzug, Oakes believed, "was a serious legislator of proven ability, a spokesman for urban liberalism and social humanitarianism."

Oakes, the lame duck editor, understood that the *Times*' endorsement of Abzug could swing wavering centrists and uncertain liberals to her line on the ballot. His predecessors, he recalled, had hung back from involvement in intraparty politics, considering the *Times* an "independent paper." "I was the guy who went against 'tradition' and first instituted the idea that the *Times* should take sides in every election," Oakes says. Even then, *Times* editorials were finely tuned—"judicious" assessments rather than clarion calls to party or faction. In the close Democratic primary race of 1976, however, even a mild *Times* endorsement—of either of the two leading candidates—could determine the outcome. But Sulzberger was not a fan of the assertive, "feminist" Abzug; he was leaning toward the brassy but "moderate" Moynihan. Knowing that his cousin had the final authority, Oakes tried a change in strategy. "Because this was a primary election and not the general election," he argued, "the *Times* could pass on its endorsement without violating its own rules." In Oakes's recollection, "Punch definitely agreed with me that there was no need for the *Times* to take sides. We had a clear understanding." Reassured that there would be no endorsement, Oakes remembered that he left in early August with his family for a month's vacation at their summer home in Chilmark, on Martha's Vineyard. The primary was on September 14, the second Tuesday after Labor Day.

In Sulzberger's memory, the cousins' conversation takes on a sharply different shading. "I don't know what Johnny thought when he went off to the Vineyard," Sulzberger said. "But the rules we had then are the same rules as now. Generally we don't endorse in a primary unless—" he paused and laughed "—we want to."

Oakes's vacation was not restful. On the August 30, 1976, cover of *Business Week*, he saw a picture of his cousin Punch, looking grim. The headline read: "Behind the Profit Squeeze at the New York Times." The reading inside was grimmer still. The article described how the Times Company's stock was down from $53 a share in 1968, the year public shares began to be traded on the American Stock Exchange, to $14.50 a share in the summer of 1976. The second paragraph of the story repeated a refrain that Sulzberger had grown tired of hearing: "Editorially and politically, the newspaper has also slid precipitously to the left and has become stridently antibusiness in tone, ignoring the fact that the *Times* itself is a business. . . ." The article angered Sulzberger. Three years later, *Times* economics writer Leonard Silk found Sulzberger still in an angry mood; *Business Week*, the publisher complained to Silk, "did a hell of a job on us. It hurt. It was not fair." Yet the magazine didn't say anything about the *Times'* politics that Sulzberger hadn't heard from some of his business friends.

A few days after the *Business Week* article appeared, Oakes opened a copy of the September 5 edition of the *Times*, delivered by ferryboat to the Vineyard. On the Op-Ed page, he read a sporty column by James Reston in praise of Moynihan. Reston likened Moynihan to a baseball pitcher of the moment: "Moynihan is to the Democrats what Catfish Hunter is to the Yankees—a flamboyant hardball, sometimes beanball, pitcher whose fastball is better than his control." Reston also called Moynihan "a hawk who sings like a lark."

Unknown to Oakes, at the same time that Reston was promoting

Moynihan for the U.S. Senate, Sulzberger was playing some hardball of his own. Sulzberger called in Max Frankel and gave him some notes that the publisher had jotted down in praise of Moynihan. The two men also discussed the shape of an editorial endorsement of Moynihan. Frankel had the job of putting the notes and the conversation into final editorial-page form (according to *Times*man Silk, Frankel at the time was "leaning toward Bella Abzug"). Neither did Oakes know that the Sulzberger-Frankel editorial was scheduled to run in the *Times* of Friday, September 10. On the morning of September 9—"the beginning of the worst day of my life," Oakes says—the Oakes family was packing to catch the ferry from Vineyard Haven back to the mainland at Woods Hole. The departure was hectic; Oakes's wife was having back problems, Oakes himself sensed that he ought to be back in New York as soon as possible. The phone rang. Sydney Gruson, Sulzberger's number-two man, told Oakes of the Moynihan editorial, by then ready to go to the composing room. Then, Oakes's deputy, Fred Hechinger, was on the line. "Fred read the endorsement to me," Oakes remembered. "And I damn near died. Aside from the choice of Moynihan, it was badly written."

The key passage in the editorial read to Oakes began: "We choose Daniel P. Moynihan, that rambunctious child of the sidewalks of New York, profound student and teacher of social affairs, aggressive debater, outrageous flatterer, shrewd adviser—indeed, manipulator—of Presidents, accomplished diplomat and heartfelt friend of the poor—poor people, poor cities, poor regions such as ours." Hechinger had been given the copy that morning, with a note from the publisher saying he wanted it to run in the next day's editions. "I like it the way it is," Sulzberger had written. Hechinger immediately interpreted that to mean, no changes at all, from anyone. Oakes nevertheless wanted to stop the editorial; and, if he failed at that, he would try to blunt its effects. "I protested, obviously. Yes, the publisher has the final say, but I thought to myself: I can't countenance this." He considered, and dismissed, the idea of a dramatic public resignation over the "forced" Moynihan endorsement: "Since I was already committed to leave, it would have been a silly gesture to quit." On the forty-five-minute ferry ride to Woods Hole he tried to compose his anti-Moynihan thoughts on a memo pad. Then, from a pay phone at the dock, his car parked alongside, his fourteen-year-old in the back of the car waiting for him, Oakes talked to Punch Sulzberger. "I told him, 'It's my responsibility to be heard.' " Oakes then asked Sulzberger, " 'What about me writing a rebuttal to appear on the page along with the endorsement?' " Punch thought about it for a moment, and then agreed. "Later I dictated a long rebuttal to Hechinger, giving Moynihan what for." (Candidate Moynihan, the rebuttal acknowledged, "is charming, highly articulate, and certainly intelligent; but then so are many other opportunistic showmen.") Hechinger sent Oakes's copy to the composing room; it was set for eight paragraphs, and ran just over 450 words. On orders of the publisher, it never appeared in the *Times*. Instead, the next day's edition, dated September 11, carried a one-paragraph, forty-word version of the original. It was signed by Oakes and appeared in the letters-to-the-editor column—Oakes writing to Oakes. The note simply expressed "disagreement" with the Moynihan endorsement. On Tuesday, Moynihan won the primary with 36 percent of the vote, to Abzug's 35 percent, a difference of around nine thousand votes.

The story did not end there. Roger Wilkins, the sole black member of the editorial board, wrote an article for the space sometimes reserved for editorial board members to speak under their own bylines. Wilkins attacked Moynihan's views of black America, and called his supporters "misinformed and generally quite wrong." He made no mention of the *Times* endorsement. Wilkins's Op-Ed piece was turned in to Oakes on Monday and scheduled for the editions of Tuesday, primary day. Monday night, Sulzberger stepped in again, and ordered Oakes not to run the Wilkins column until the following day, after the votes were counted. Wednesday's editions of the *Times* carried Wilkins's piece on the Op-Ed page and news of Moynihan's victory on page one.

The episode left a legacy of bitterness. Roger Wilkins decided that, as he put it, "I didn't want to write editorials any longer." He arranged with Sulzberger to do an urban affairs column under the jurisdiction of the news department and Abe Rosenthal (who had helped recruit him at the *Times*). Two years later, he decided to leave the *Times*. The paper's search for consensus from Wilkins's perspective as a black American looked less centrist than conservative. He was barely speaking to Rosenthal. Sulzberger and Wilkins continued to have a proper professional relationship; according to Wilkins, "If there was something serious to talk about, I could always go up to his office at the end of the day and he'd fix me a martini and we'd sit and talk." The Hidden Hand proferred a healing cocktail.

Moynihan, for his part, paid back the *Times* for its support in a particularly nasty passage in his memoir of his United Nations years, *A Dangerous Place*. As Moynihan told it, Oakes had run an "ethnic" editorial page that bore "the mark of German Reform Judaism." After the memoir came out, Oakes and Moynihan shared the dais at a fund-raising dinner held in one of the New York hotels. Moynihan expansively tried to shake Oakes's hand, as if nothing untoward had happened between them. Oakes refused to greet the senator. A decade later, Oakes still resented the reference. "I'll never forget that slur," Oakes said, with no trace of editorial-page politesse. "Moynihan was a drunk and a phony who had insinuated himself with Punch to get elected."

The Sulzbergers overlooked the Moynihan slur. He became a respected, effective senator, and his speeches were applauded in editorials for their intellectual vigor. But relations were never the same again between the compatible cousins. Punch Sulzberger's position, then and fifteen years later, remained consistent: "I wanted Moynihan to win." Sulzberger said he believed that his cousin "overreacted": "Johnny and I both knew the rules about the publisher's prerogatives." Narrowly, Sulzberger was right: The publisher makes the final call. But more than a senatorial endorsement was at stake. Sulzberger wanted to move the *Times* away from left-of-center stands. Oakes as well as Abzug no longer fit.

Sulzberger soon dropped the other shoe. Shortly after Frankel took over as editorial page editor, he purged Oakes's board, arranging for the transfer of some editors to the news department and speeding up the retirement plans of others. Wilkins and Huxtable were among the handful of Last Puritans who were left untouched, a form of conspicuous tokenism widely commented on by the staff. Punch Sulzberger, to be sure, wasn't sentencing Oakes and his colleagues to some Devil's Island of *Times* journalism. One board member remembered Oakes's new role as "a dream job: a column on the Op-Ed page, unlimited travel, generous expenses. The whole world as his beat." Oakes's assistant Fred Hechinger, the man at the other end of the Woods Hole telephone, returned to the news department and his old specialty, education reporting. Later, he was appointed president of the Times Foundation, administering the company's grants for social research and community service (the post paid a comfortable $150,000 annually). Herb Mitgang became the book-publishing correspondent, the first reporter any American daily had ever assigned to cover the publishing industry full-time. He traveled around the country to meetings of the American Booksellers Association and to Germany for the Frankfurt Book Fair, defining what became the "book beat" (and watching his work widely imitated when other quality newspapers created their own reporter-specialists). In 1981 Mitgang became a *Times* cultural correspondent, and in 1989 as he approached his sixty-ninth birthday, he was named a daily book reviewer. Mitgang wrote from home, seldom coming into the office; his reviews appeared regularly in the daily paper. He managed to keep his *Times* work in perspective; the purge of the Last Puritans served to remind him that *Times*people, whatever their stature in the eyes of outsiders, were still hired hands. "My books are my monument," he said.

Abe Raskin—whose byline, A. H. Raskin, served as a reminder of the old days at the *Times*—proved to be a kind of secret sharer of John Oakes's. In the spring of 1976, Raskin, like Oakes, was approaching the mandatory retirement age for *Times* executives. Sulzberger arranged a soft landing for Raskin, then marking his forty-fifth year with the *Times*. Raskin was asked to write a weekly labor relations column, to appear in the new Business Day section. The arrangement required Raskin's formal retirement, to be followed by the signing of a new contract with the *Times*; he would be an outside writer selling his consulting services to the paper. Raskin was happily anticipating his prospective status as a contract writer when the Moynihan-Abzug dispute occurred and then the purge of the editorial board. They were, he later said, "the most malign events in all my years at the *Times*." Raskin did little to conceal his feelings of outrage around the office: "Management knew how I felt."

As the date approached for Raskin's formal retirement party, the atmosphere soured still more. Parties for retiring executives and senior editors were typically held in the reception room outside the publisher's suite of offices on the fourteenth floor. The affairs brought one hundred or more *Times*people together at the end of the workday; there was a tradition of farewell remarks from the retiree, who was expected to be simultaneously witty and sentimental. Given the fact that there were usually large open bars at the publisher's parties, host Punch Sulzberger could be pardoned for preparing with some prudence. Just before the Raskin party, Sydney Gruson, Punch Sulzberger's chief aide, came up to Raskin, spoke of the festive nature of the occasion, and said, with a knowing look, "We hope you'll do nothing to spoil this affair."

Raskin had a vodka mixed with orange juice. His face reddened under the neatly barbered white of his hair. Raskin began his remarks with a tribute to his host, Punch Sulzberger. Raskin recalled his 1963 article on the New York newspaper strike. That the *Times* should commission it in the first place and then run it "at such great length with its conclusions for all to see," Raskin said, "well, that's what the *Times* is all about, that's what the First Amendment means." And so, Raskin continued, "I salute Punch for his role in all that." Then Raskin paused a moment, and continued in the same strong voice. "In the last few weeks," he said, "we have seen another face of the *Times*: the manner in which the editorial board has been handled, the sense that there is punishment for their views. That is not in the spirit of the *Times*. . . ." As Raskin paused again, preparing to make his final good-byes, he thought to himself: I'm raining on my own parade! Later, Sulzberger confronted Raskin. In his polite way, the publisher told Raskin how terrible his remarks made him feel, how "my heart sank, low, lower than the subbasement, the machine room of this building." Raskin remembers the publisher saying: "You let me down when I needed you." Unnerved, Raskin still managed to reply: "No, you let us down."

No more was said that day between the two men. They continued to smile and greet each other in the corridors in the months that followed. But Raskin sensed a change, a growing distance. The freeze is on, he told himself. Eight months passed; it was getting near the time to renew the labor-column contract. Raskin was eager to continue; he decided that because he had received so much praise for the column, he would ask for a raise. In the early negotiations, however, he was told "complications" had developed: The fact that Raskin had been allowed to stay on past the normal retirement date, even as a consultant, was causing "morale problems" among the staff. Raskin was told that others were angling for similar deals, both in the news department and on the business side, that there was a lot of "confusion and consternation." Raskin's journalistic ear detected a false note. He decided to check with Rosenthal, who told Raskin that he knew of no problems within the news department. Raskin made similar inquiries on the business side, speaking to Walter Mattson, the blunt and direct company president. While Mattson confirmed that some people wanted the same deal, he could offer no specifics. Mattson's uncharacteristic vagueness stirred Raskin to take his inquiries higher, to Sulzberger. Politely but firmly, the labor relations specialist put his question to the publisher: How come only the Raskin consultancy is causing "problems"? What about Scotty Reston, Raskin wondered. The columnist was well beyond sixty-five and continued to do his writing. Sulzberger, Raskin remembered, "looked at me with those lambent eyes of his, and said, 'You know, I was asking my people that same question. Why is it that only Abe Raskin is causing comments?' "

Why indeed? Since the farewell party, Raskin concluded, "Punch had been biding his time."

That was the end of the labor column, although Raskin managed to stretch out his contract another eight months, until the end of 1977. Good journalist that he was, Raskin continued to write free-lance articles and do reviews for the *Book Review* well into the late 1980s. In the fall of 1990, when the *New York Daily News* locked out its union workers and precipitated a long strike, a still vigorous Raskin returned to the labor beat; he reported and wrote a knowledgeable profile of Dennis Rivera, a rising young union leader in New York—not for his old paper but for *The New Yorker* magazine.

The *Times* never covered labor in quite the same way after Raskin's retirement. Starting in 1979 his old beat was filled for a few years by William Serrin. Hired from the *Detroit Free Press*, where he had already achieved an excellent reputation for his reporting and writing, Serrin was pointedly told he would be covering "work in America" rather than "labor." In 1986 Serrin resigned from the *Times*, convinced the paper didn't want to cover either work or labor with the same vigor it was devoting, for example, to the new life-style sections. "It wasn't so much that the *Times* was antilabor or conservative as that it was oriented toward the 'beautiful people,' " Serrin remembered.

John Oakes's post–editorial-page career offered a curious parallel to Raskin's experience. From 1978 to 1989, Oakes continued to supply occasional pieces for the Op-Ed page, under an agreement he had worked out with Sulzberger. In these pieces Oakes took up his familiar themes of conservation and social justice. He wrote feelingly, for example, of New York City's neglect of Jacob Riis Park in Queens. Many readers, including one editorial page editor who had joined the board long after Oakes left, found themselves wondering, as this editor put it, "where the *Times* news desks were on this one, and why it took Johnny Oakes to blow the whistle" on the city's dismal record of caring for its parks in the less fashionable neighborhoods outside Manhattan.

In May 1989, shortly after the parks article appeared, the cousins' arrangement ended. "Punch was making the transition to his son," Oakes said. "I would have gone on beyond, but Punch felt I should go. He didn't want any loose ends." Oakes lost his once-a-week secretarial help and his office space, where he kept his files of four decades. He put a positive face on his last years at the *Times*. "What the hell," he said. "I was there forty-four years. I have no regrets."

The *Times*man's spark remained. One winter morning, Oakes woke to see the Central Park trees outside his apartment window coated with ice, the aftermath of a storm. Without missing a beat, he called the *Times* photo desk to tell the editors of the lovely picture opportunity. In mid-January 1991, on the eve of the Persian Gulf war, as the deadline set by the United Nations for Iraq to leave Kuwait approached, the seventy-eight-year-old Oakes marshaled his editorialist's thoughts; as if by habit, he composed an Op-Ed page article. The Congress was about to vote on the resolution authorizing the president to go to war, a course Oakes thought unwise. Oakes called the *Times* Op-Ed page editor, Mike Levitas, to offer his view that the Congress, "If it couldn't say no, should say 'not yet.'" Unfortunately, the pages were fully committed. "You and about ten thousand others are trying to get in the paper," Levitas told Oakes. Oakes said he understood, hung up the phone, dialed the editorial-page editor of New York *Newsday*, explained what he wanted to say, and was asked to fax his piece over. It ran the next morning, January 11, two days before Congress's vote. Though both Houses said yes to war, Oakes was satisfied that he had the opportunity to make his argument. "The *Times*' loss was *Newsday*'s gain," he said jauntily.

Almost two decades after Oakes's removal and the great massacre of the Last Puritans, *Times*people still debated Punch Sulzberger's motives. Their explanations ranged from the silly to the grand, the practical to the political. Abe Raskin wasn't yet prepared to say there was a rightward shift. "There was a savaging of the board for its views," he says, "but those views were not all that liberal progressive. Is it anticapitalist to call attention to abuses in the system?" Another witness to events favored a psychohistorical analysis. Punch, he claims, "never said anything, but internalized the feeling that his family wanted him to be 'more like Johnny.' It obviously rankled and he waited his time."

Among the most thoughtful witnesses was Tom Wicker, the *Times* columnist. His office was on the same floor as Oakes's, but Wicker was reasonably detached from events (*Times* columnists of his era came close to having lifetime tenure on the Op-Ed page). Wicker put Oakes's ouster in the context of Sulzberger's efforts to unify the paper under Rosenthal, rather than as a strict left-right split. "But there was a rightward shift, and not only at the *Times*," he says. "After the 1972 [McGovern-Nixon] presidential election, it was easy for all of us to read the direction of country. In the 1980s, Reagan's election and reelection confirmed it all. My mail told me where the country was going, and I'm sure Punch's did too."

Punch Sulzberger blandly turned aside the suggestion that he, like the Supreme Court, was following the election returns. Every so often between elections, however, the Hidden Hand publisher picked up his own pen, or in more recent years, switched on his computer screen, to compose something for publication: Sulzberger speaking in his own voice in the pages of the *Times*. The occasions were rare. A Nexis data-base search of the decade of the 1980s produced three articles on the editorial pages carrying the byline Arthur Ochs Sulzberger. All three were in the format called "Editorial Notebook." All three related to jury duty; Sulzberger had been called to duty and the experience made an unfavorable—and patently lasting—impression on him.

The first "Editorial Notebook" with his byline appeared on May 7, 1983, under the headline "Why Try the Jurors?" Sulzberger's immediate point of departure was the New York State assembly's failure to pass a bill that would have reformed the jury selection process by speeding it up. He writes, from personal experience, of the "bitterness that the present system creates among the unfortunate jurors who must sit for countless, needless hours, waiting to fulfill their responsibilities as citizens." The waiting around continues to the point of numbness, "taking two days to seat a jury for a two-bit trial. If the legislature and legal profession want twelve good and true clothing-store dummies to grace the jury box," Sulzberger concluded, "Macy's would surely be glad to cooperate."

Less than a week later, on May 12, Sulzberger returned to the topic of juror selection and to his own experience: "It took more than eight hours to impanel a jury to determine the guilt or innocence of an alleged purse snatcher"—the two-bit crime. A juror is "treated like a schoolchild, [one's] time wasted and intelligence insulted." Sulzberger proposed three reforms: fewer juror challenges during the impaneling process, smaller juries, and once the trial begins, tighter rules about plea bargaining and out-of-court settlements (the first "Notebook" offered no suggestions at all). Five years later Sulzberger returned to the subject of jury duty again, this time in cases involving civil trials. He was still bothered by the two-bit stuff. "One would think, if the mind hadn't already glazed over, that the trial of a century was about to begin, rather than a dispute about whether Mr. Jones deserves some money after slipping on the pavement," he observed in the "Editorial Notebook" of February 7, 1988.

Punch Sulzberger sometimes used one other way of getting his words into the paper. He wrote letters to the editor of the *Times*, signing them with a pseudonym. The *Times'* news standards explicitly prohibit any resort to fakery or fiction-writing techniques. But the pseudonymous letter was something of a family tradition. Iphigene Ochs Sulzberger used the names of deceased relatives to write letters to the editor of the *Times* in her day on some of her favorite topics, such as the need to care for the treasures of Central Park. Arthur Hays Sulzberger, her husband, used the phonetic "A Haitchess." Their son's chosen nom de plume was "A. Sock." "That's for Punch," he explained, making a fighter's right hook motion.

A. Sock appeared in the *Times'* letters column on October 3, 1989. The headline over his letter read, "A Modest Proposal for Presidential Visits." Because it was obviously written from personal experience—and offers a window into the writer's mind and his sense of humor—it is worth quoting in full. A. Sock was responding to a *Times* editorial on a visit by President George Bush to the United Nations in New York. The editorial had noted that speeding motorcades, closed-off streets, diverted traffic, and the other security arrangements intended to insure the president's safety tied up the city and inconvenienced New Yorkers. A. Sock suggested:

"The President should fly to La Guardia Airport and immediately enter a yellow cab. As there are usually hundreds of such cabs there doing nothing more useful than waiting in line, he will be completely secure. No one will know which one he is in. As the driver is likely to be Russian, Israeli, or Ethiopian, he will likely have no idea of how to find the United Nations, and the President will be able to do no end of useful work on his way to town."

If A. Sock had engaged these amusing greenhorn drivers in conversation, he might have learned a little more about the time that they spent "doing nothing more useful than waiting" for high-powered executives to appear. The cabbies' long idle time at La Guardia and other area airports was one of the curses of cab driving in New York. As any number of drivers will willingly explain to anyone who asks, the time spent waiting in line—fareless and tipless, frequently for two hours or more—makes a tough way to earn a living a bit tougher.

A. Sock was never much of an investigative reporter, from that long-ago weekend in Le Mans to the present. He wasn't very curious about the taxi business, either. The proprietor of the *Times* had isolated himself from a lot of the grittier life of the city, as many wealthy New Yorkers do. These other super-rich don't publish the *New York Times*, of course. But then Sock/Sulzberger was able to hire people who knew somewhat more than he did about New York—and about the newspaper business.

A DAY IN THE LIFE
12:35 P.M.—2:30 P.M.

12:35 P.M.

Barbara Gamarekian finished a phone call from a public relations woman representing Clairol, the makers of hair shampoo. The company was holding its Seabreeze Award ceremony in the U.S. Senate caucus room on March 10, to honor teenagers doing volunteer work. Gamarekian told the Clairol woman that the Washington bureau of the *Times* "didn't cover that sort of thing." But this stood "heads and shoulders above other awards," the PR woman said, with no sign that she was aware of her pun. Besides, Gregg Petersmyer, the White House official in charge of promoting President Bush's "1,000 points of light" volunteers' program, would be on hand. Gamarekian made a perfunctory note to herself, and hurried outside to hail a cab to go to her appointment with Ambassador Margaret McDonald of the Bahamas. Gamarekian had turned in a feature article about Bushra Kanafani, the ambassador from Syria; but the Washington desk editors felt the piece should be broadened to include a second woman holding down an important job in the male-dominated world of diplomacy. Gamarekian arrived for the McDonald interview, and it went well.

In Boston, a Federal Express package was delivered to Anthony Lewis from David Runkel, an assistant to U.S. Attorney General Richard Thornburgh. Lewis had asked for Justice Department comment on the case of a Romanian exile named Emil Suciu, who had come to the United States as a student, graduated from MIT, married an American—and then was ordered expelled from the country. The Immigration and Naturalization Service claimed Suciu was "a risk to national security," but the INS would not elaborate on the charge. Runkel offered citations from court decisions as the statutory authority to withhold information of the government's basis for expulsion. Runkel did not, in Lewis's view, deal with the question the columnist had raised, specifically, "Why did Justice use an unfair process just because it had the discretionary power to do so?" As Lewis was turning over in his mind Justice's reasoning, he received a call from MIT; Sadik al-Azm, a Syrian scholar, would be giving a 4:30 lecture on Islamic revivalism. Lewis was pressed for time, but al-Azm was a critic of the mullahs, and had been a good source when Lewis was last in Damascus. The subject was timely as well: A few days before, the Ayatollah Khomeini had called for the holy murder of the novelist Salman Rushdie, author of the newly published *The Satanic Verses*. Lewis decided to eat lunch at his desk, to save time.

1:00 P.M.

The 43rd Street newsroom emptied, as if a whistle had blown: lunchtime. Carolyn Lee, the *Times* picture editor, had worked on papers in Houston and Louisville before coming to the *Times*. The eating habits of her *Times* colleagues reminded her of factory workers: "Everyone goes to lunch at one and comes back at 2:30."

1:05 P.M.

Along culture gulch in the third-floor newsroom, where the *Times'* critics and arts and entertainment writers sit, no more than ten of the seventy desks and cubicles were occupied. Walter Goodman, one of the *Times'* two television critics, planned a week of TV-viewing around the Tower hearings. The place was a jumble of cabinets, bookshelves, piles of magazines and newspapers, computer terminals, chairs and desks jammed too close together.

Wastebaskets overflowed with empty coffee containers and wads of discarded press releases. The desk of Larry Van Gelder, a *Times* veteran, looked as if it hadn't been cleared in the twenty-two years he had worked at the *Times*. The computer screens of Grace Glueck and Richard Shepard were separated by no more than thirty-six inches, and Glueck and Shepard talked into their phones in lowered voices, trying not to be distracted by each other's interviews. The door to the women's rest room was three paces from Shepard's desk. Directly overhead was the scratchy loudspeaker used by the editors to summon reporters to the metro desk—and by the *Times'* part-time fire marshal for periodic safety messages. Glueck, in pearls, covered the art world; Shepard, in sweater, was the ace cultural features writer. Between them, they represented over seventy years of *Times* service. Jim Morgan's tour came by, clogging the narrow aisles. Shepard smiled as Morgan embellished a few newsroom legends. The writer saw the bright side of the noisy, crowded word factory: It had been worse in the old days. In the late 1980s, the New York City ban on smoking in indoor spaces helped freshen the stale air a bit, and forced Shepard to break his cigarette habit. "Before," he said, "this was Pittsburgh in the 1940s here."

Two aisles over, Albin Krebs bent over his computer keyboard. For the last twelve years, Krebs had been a *Times* obituary writer—not the most joyful assignment. But because his obits set down a man's or woman's final record of achievement, Krebs felt moments of celebration as well. All morning he had been bringing up to date the stand-by obituaries of the television personality Alistair Cooke and the critic Malcolm Cowley. Early Tuesday afternoon, the paragraphs on his glowing green screen recounted the career of Walter Thayer, the long-time executive of the Whitney Communications Company, and a guiding light of the old *New York Herald Tribune*. The seventy-eight-year-old Thayer had been admitted to New York Hospital three weeks earlier. No announcement was made. All in all, these were the right circumstances for Krebs to update Thayer's obituary. At any given time, the obit bank at the paper held hundreds of appreciations of people who, in the editors' opinion, mattered to *Times* readers. These stories lacked only a few paragraphs on the cause of death, the immediate survivors, and the funeral arrangements.

Although just three miles separated the *Times* and New York Hospital, word of Thayer's illness had come to Krebs by way of the *Times* news bureau in Paris. In 1989 the *Times* owned a one-third interest in the *International Herald Tribune*, published in Paris and bearer of the name and logo of the *Times'* great morning rival in the first half of the century. Whitney Communications owned a second third of the paper; the third owner was the *Washington Post*. The three partners came together after the old *Herald Trib* vanished from New York City newsstands in 1966. It had been a strained union at first: the victor and the vanquished from the New York newspaper wars now business partners in Paris. But it worked, and Krebs's appreciation of Thayer deftly referred to the old days. In the nineteenth paragraph of his twenty-six-paragraph draft, Krebs quoted Arthur Ochs Sulzberger, the *Times* publisher and chairman: "Since the moment Walter Thayer and I shook hands on the merger, there have been no problems that the partners haven't been able to resolve through open and friendly discussion. . . . [Walter Thayer] was blessed by a good nose for news and high standards of journalistic excellence." Krebs also quoted Katharine Graham, chairman of the Washington Post Company: "We enjoyed a long, beneficial and harmonious partnership."

Before sending on the copy to his senior editors for their approval, Krebs allowed himself a small exercise in self-interest. Deep in the draft, he recounted the history of the labor-management disputes that hastened the death of the *Herald Tribune*. After the Newspaper Guild strike of April 1966, Krebs wrote, "Many of the *Herald Tribune*'s best journalists found other jobs." Krebs was one of them; he left the *Herald Tribune* to join the *Times* in mid-1966. The line survived the final editing. It appeared in print more quickly than Krebs expected. Thayer died on Saturday, March 4; the obit ran in the *Times'* Sunday editions (two years later, Whitney Communications dropped out of the IHT consortium).

The next day, Krebs announced to his editors that he had decided to take early retirement. Krebs had worked as a journalist since his student days at the University of Mississippi; he had never married and he was about to turn sixty. He decided to keep his Manhattan apartment but return to the South, to live at least half the year in the congenial resort town of Key West. He was fully vested in the *Times* pension plan, assuring him a comfortable monthly retirement check at 80 percent of his $65,000 annual salary. Krebs made his final decision while updating the Thayer obit. His work at the *Times* lived on, in a manner of speaking, as one after another of the men and women who were the subjects of the copy he had prepared succumbed to age or illness. A week after Krebs left the *Times* and the city, his obit of Malcolm Cowley appeared, up-to-date and literate.

2:30 P.M.

Three *Times* senior editors, returning from lunch at Orso, one of the executives' favored "company canteens" along restaurant row on West 46th Street, made a detour around the quiet, listless crowd in front of St. Luke's Church. The church soup kitchen began serving at 3:00 P.M. By 2:30, more than eighty men and women were waiting to be fed. The editors observed firsthand the editorial-page abstraction, "the homeless."

In the sports department, the dayside desk was quiet, the pace noticeably slower after the full schedule of weekend games. The football season was over; the baseball teams were in spring training, with opening day still more than a month away. Among local professional basketball teams, the Knicks and Nets were idle; so were the Rangers of the National Hockey league. Only the Islanders and Devils were on the NHL schedule Tuesday night. For the past two days, the big sports story hadn't involved a line-score at all. The three New York tabloids—the *News*, the *Post* and *Newsday*—featured stories about excessive drinking aboard the charter planes carrying the New York Yankees to games during the past season. The Westchester-Rockland Newspapers, the small suburban chain, had been on the story before the *Times* as well. The *Post* quoted Rickey Henderson, the Yankees' star centerfielder, who suggested that the carousing was one reason the Yankees didn't win their division pennant. For the approaching season, Yankees management had banned hard liquor on the team's charter flights. Michael Martinez, the *Times* reporter assigned to the Yankees, was in Fort Lauderdale with the team for spring training. Trying to get the *Times* back in the game, Martinez spent Tuesday morning looking for Lou Piniella, the former Yankees' manager, to get his comments or corroboration. Martinez had not yet found him. The dayside desk urged Martinez on.

5

THE CHANGES:
3. MONEY TIMES

"VICTORY HAS A HUNDRED PARENTS," John F. Kennedy is credited with saying, "defeat is an orphan." So too with the success of the modern *Times*, and the great "rescue" of the paper in the 1970s and 1980s, when the whole enterprise appeared to be sinking, along with the municipal fortunes of New York City. Between 1970 and 1975, for example, the *Times* suffered severe circulation and advertising losses. In one six-month period alone in 1971, daily circulation dropped by some 31,000 to 814,000. The *Times* had increased its newsstand price from 10 to 15 cents per copy, and the message seemed clear: Some people didn't think the *Times* was worth a nickel more. "I used to have a nightmare when I was editor," Abe Rosenthal recalled two decades later. "It's a Wednesday morning and there's no *New York Times*." In Rosenthal's recollection, "If no one did anything, and if we kept losing money, then the *Times* could have gone out of business. I'm not saying that it would have happened, but that it *could* have."

By the mid-1980s, however, all the trend lines had been reversed. Not only did the *Times* regain the daily circulation it lost in the early 1970s; it added another 100,000 readers between 1976 and 1982, then another 50,000 by 1984, and then another 50,000 more, to go over the one million mark in 1986. The city had come back, and so had its leading newspaper. The *Times'* shift to special interest coverage—its sectional revolution—became a model of the industry, and the faltering paper of the 1970s metamorphosed into the money machine of the late 1980s, throwing off operating profits of $200 million a year. The architects of its success were, in the commonly accepted accounting of events: Abraham Michael Rosenthal from the news department, and his opposite on the business side, Walter E. Mattson. Overseeing their work, leading the two leaders, was the third member of this pantheon of achievement, Arthur Ochs Sulzberger. They were, to be sure, a disparate team: Abe Rosenthal, son of immigrants, abrasive, driven, emotional; Walt Mattson, plain-spoken, curt, direct, a production specialist from western Pennsylvania, never wholly comfortable in New York; Arthur Ochs Sulzberger, the scion of privilege who had been treated rather dismissively by his family and associates in his earlier years. But, together, the odd trio remade the *Times*. They turned it into a contemporary guide to good living while maintaining comprehensive news coverage; they insured its continued preeminence in the new media landscape.

"Mattson and I worked together, but Punch had to make the critical decisions," Rosenthal remembered, rehearsing the company history. "That is, whether to change the *Times* by cost cutting or by adding more resources." Then Rosenthal, the word man, offered what has become known among *Times* executives as the "soup speech." Sulzberger, Rosenthal said, could have cut back on the *Times'* national and international coverage, diluting the daily news report—putting more water in the soup. Or he could maintain the *Times'* hard-news commitments while adding the new special sections—putting more tomatoes in the soup. Thus, as the *Times* presented itself, there was no conflict between the daily news report and the new feature sections. The *Times* did both hard and soft news, and did them superbly. "We never cut back on our news coverage," Rosenthal recalled. "The publisher never said to me, 'Since we're adding news about food, cut elsewhere.' Other places did cut back. It would have been easy at the *Times* to do so, too. We've got fifty foreign correspondents? Okay, we'll use twenty. We have seven music critics? Hey, keep two and we'll still have one more than the others. The same with the four daily book critics, and the seventeen national news bureaus for just five columns a day. That's 150 columns a month. Who'll notice if we do 130 columns?" The *Times*, Rosenthal emphasized, had to grow or atrophy. And so his metaphor of news-as-food. "Do we change by cost cutting, which was the solution of others? Or do we put more tomatoes in the soup, which was our solution? I wanted more tomatoes. So did Mattson. Punch had to say, 'Yes, I agree. Do it.' He did, and he became the best publisher the *Times* ever had."

So the official story goes. History, as usual, has been written by the winners.

The actual sequence of events was at once less dramatic and more ambiguous: The soup was a mixed brew. First of all, the changes were not revolutionary; nor were radical fixes even contemplated. The "new" *New York Times* was, above all, reactive—derivative of other journalistic models. Second, the *Times* never came close to shutting its doors, Rosenthal's nightmare to the contrary. Year after year in the previous decades, the newspaper demonstrated that it was possible to maintain journalistic standards despite minimal profit margins. That was, of course, before the *Times* became a public company, and well before its managers began worrying about whether the security analysts were recommending the stock. Third, the old *Times*—the hard-news Paper of Record—did suffer in the transition to the new, both absolutely and in comparison to others. Newspapers such as the *Washington Post* and the *Wall Street Journal* improved their own soups in the decades of the 1970s and 1980s. The *Post* produced a stronger national-news report, the *Journal* a better business-financial report. Not surprisingly, during all the soup stirring, the *Times* lost some of its most talented men and women, who were attracted to other news organizations with the promise of higher salaries and greater visibility (other talents turned down the chance to work for the *Times* in the first instance). "Once, the best people wanted to come to the *Times* to be a foreign correspondent or to write about American society," says Albert Scardino, who joined the *Times* in 1985 and left five years later. "They found they could do that elsewhere, and perhaps more effectively."

But neither did the *Times* devolve into a bland, suburbanized feature package, as some of its hard-line critics claimed. These revisionists presented the Rosenthal *Times* as an unfeeling Nero of New York, fiddling for the rich while the city burned. "To believe that the *Times* accurately reflects the world and then go out into the streets of New York is to be struck by a sense of the absurd," contributing editor Earl Shorris wrote in *Harper's* magazine in October 1977. And, in a reference to a notorious $4,000 dinner described by the *Times'* food writer, Craig Claiborne, Shorris asked plaintively, "Will the *New York Times* never stop eating?" (Rosenthal and his critics alike couldn't get away from thoughts of food.)

The revisionist critics had to suppress a large part of the past to make their case. The Sulzberger-Rosenthal-Mattson team did not suddenly turn its back on the blight of the Bronx and Brooklyn in favor of a cosmeticized view of New York as a wondrous place to live and work (and read a paper). The unbeautiful city of the poor and the dispossessed had not been within the *Times'* traditional ambit to begin with. In their times, Adolph Ochs and Arthur Hays Sulzberger passed quickly over the city—after giving close daily attention to its affairs of business and merchandising—to attend to the wider world of national and international news. The *Times* typically maintained more reporters in London or Paris than in the outer boroughs.

Both the official historians and the critics glossed over the essential point about the new, celebratory *Times*. It had not only come late to the consumers' party in the first place; once there, it looked around nervously to mimic what the others were doing. The *Times* was among the last major American newspapers to adjust their graphics and writing styles to a television-saturated society. In the late 1970s, an assertive young reporter named Anna Quindlen came to the *Times* from the *New York Post*. Fifteen years later Quindlen still remembered every detail of what happened when she turned in her first story to the metro desk. "Hot town. Summer in the city," she had written. The copy editor returned the story to her. "These are sentence fragments," he remonstrated, and proposed to insert before each "fragment" the phrase "It was a." The editor also wanted semicolons and other punctuation marks. "Look," Quindlen said, "you can't do that. These are the first words of a song." "What kind of a song?" the editor asked. "A rock 'n' roll song," Quindlen replied, challengingly. The editor, she remembered, was equally defiant. "His expression said, '*You* look. You're never going to get rock 'n' roll and sentence fragments into this paper.'"

The *Times* adapted itself—somewhat—to fresh styles, and memories like Quindlen's are intended to produce tolerant smiles now. The Sulzberger-Mattson-Rosenthal era changes actually were modest. Success came in part as a result of the failures of others: for example, the even more hesitant responses of the rival *Herald Tribune* to changes in the New York marketplace in the 1960s, and the self-destructive labor policies of another potential competitor, the *News*, in the 1970s and 1980s. Opportunism too played a part in the successes of the Sulzberger years, though few people normally associated that word with the *Times*. In the early 1970s, a group of former *Herald Tribune* journalists led by the editor Clay Felker developed so-called service journalism in *New York* magazine, with such features as "The Underground Gourmet," "Best Bets," and "The Passionate Shopper." Rosenthal lifted these ideas for the *Times*; to execute them, he also hired away from *New York* a cadre of editors and writers, including Nancy Newhouse, Mimi Sheraton, Suzanne Slesin, and Joan Kron, among others who had worked with Felker. (*New York* magazine, Rosenthal told the writer Stephanie Harrington, "used to drive me out of my mind": It was covering subjects around the city that the *Times* ignored.) The *Times'* roving eyes also fixed on the visual presentations and themed sections developed in regional newspapers such as the *Miami Herald*. When these features were adapted for the *Times*, they appeared fresh to readers and advertisers within the northeast corridor.

It was not an indictable offense for the *Times* to follow the lead of the more enterprising newspapers and magazines among the competition, especially when the *Times* subsequently produced many of these borrowed features in style, with sufficient financial and journalistic resources. "The *New York Times* hired real science writers, real music critics, and real architectural specialists, and they produced the best newspaper feature sections in the country," in the recollection of a friendly outside critic, Tom Rosenstiel of the *Los Angeles Times*. His own paper, he added, experimented with rotating themed sections in the late 1970s, and eventually decided that it couldn't find enough talent to execute all the sections properly.

In typical *New York Times* fashion, nothing was done "hastily." Fifty years before the introduction of the new sections, a member of the *Times* business department, Julius Ochs Adler, anticipated most of the "groundbreaking" ideas of the 1970s and '80s. Julie Adler was the nephew of Adolph Ochs and, as it happened, a rival of Arthur Hays Sulzberger (Ochs placed the two young men in separate departments at the *Times* and let them compete for his approval). In a five-page proposal headed "memo for Mr. Ochs" and dated December 31, 1924, the young executive recommended "supplemental additions to the daily *Times*." As Adler described them to his uncle:

"Monday—Financial, Economic and Commercial Review. Tuesday—Technical and Scientific Review. Wednesday—Mid-Week Pictorial Section. Thursday—N.Y.T. Shop Window (Women's Section). Friday—Review of the Professions (Law, Medicine, etc.) or Review of Sports (articles by golf and tennis stars etc. etc.). Saturday—Book Review."

A half century later, the architects of the modern *Times* used different rubrics on different schedules—though not all that different. The Business Day section of the 1980s appeared every weekday, the Science Times section on Tuesdays, Living and Home on Wednesdays and Thursdays, etc. Rosenthal referred to these sections as "daily magazines." Adler wanted true stand-alone magazines: sixteen-page, tabloid-size sections inserted into the daily paper.

The parallels between Adler's proposals and the ideas of his successors were the result of independent invention: There is a finite number of ways to slice the steak of a daily news report and market its sizzle. Consequently, Adler's arguments for the new section sounded very much like the arguments offered in support of the 1970s changes. They resembled as well the continuing efforts to remake the *Times* in the 1990s. Among his justifications, for example, Adler cited the changing "economic and intellectual" character of the 1920s audience. "People are more interested in a greater variety of matters and in turn these matters play a larger part in their lives," he wrote, making the "demographic argument" for change several decades before the first MBA specialists arrived at the *Times*. Adler also stressed that his proposed new features were "not of the cheap variety but are in keeping with the high intellectual plane which the *Times* has always striven to attain and maintain." Finally, Adler promised an added bonus: Some of the features of the daily would be shifted from the *Sunday Times*, "to relieve somewhat the size of [that] huge paper"—and help make the *Sunday Times* a faster read (another highly desired goal of his successors at the *Times*).

None of Adler's daily magazines materialized in his lifetime. Other *Times*people in subsequent years came forward with plans for changing the *Times*. One editor, E. Clifton Daniel, was more fortunate than Adler; he lived to see the realization of his ideas, though long after his departure from the paper. Clifton Daniel was the *Times'* managing editor from 1963 to 1969, a period that in retrospect served to mark off the "traditional" *Times* from the "modern" *Times*. The son of a drugstore owner in Zebulon, North Carolina, Daniel grew up during the Great Depression. He went to the University of North Carolina, and worked as a reporter at the *Raleigh News and Observer* and the Associated Press before joining the *Times*. He served as a foreign correspondent in wartime London and later married Margaret Truman, the only child of Harry S Truman, the thirty-third president of the United States. Daniel proved to be an ideal middleman during the period of transition at the *Times* in the 1960s. He was a man of modest background but well connected; Southern born and bred yet schooled in the ways of the wider world; reserved in manner though the possessor of a lively, inquisitive intellect. Daniel excelled as well at *Times* office politics; when he lost his managing editor's job, to Rosenthal, Daniel maintained his air of elegance (Rosenthal found a gift bottle of Scotch whisky waiting for him when he moved into Daniel's old office). Whatever pain Daniel felt during those years, he managed to put behind him, and he became an expert witness of the transition from the old regime of Arthur Hays Sulzberger and Turner Catledge to the energetic new team of Punch Sulzberger, Rosenthal, and Mattson.

"Some of us had ideas for 'modernizing' the *Times* long before it became an economic imperative to regain lost readers or attract younger readers," Daniel remembered, taking care to make the point that he wanted change for reasons of journalism rather than for reasons of marketing. Daniel's superiors resisted "modernizing." All through the Ochs and AHS decades, the *Times* was printed in two sections only. This effectively limited the prime display space to page one and to the second front page (known at the *Times* in the 1960s as the split page, and more recently, in the multisection *Times*, as one of the dress pages). When Daniel proposed dividing the paper into several sections to achieve broadened news coverage and better play of stories and photographs, he was told it couldn't be done. According to the production department, the physical limitations of the *Times*' presses prevented any such reconfiguration: the paper had to be in two sections of equal size. Daniel later concluded that "this attitude of it-can't-be-done" was a result of two factors typical of the *Times*' traditionalist thinking. "First, we had two sections and had gotten along all right. That is, the readers seemed to like them. Second, it would cost a lot of money to refigure the presses, and the *Times* thought it was a little short of money at the time."

Daniel nevertheless was able to make some major changes in the physical appearance of the *Times*. The second front page of the two-section paper was, by tradition, a miscellany: stories left over from page one, local and regional news, and inconsequential features, "usually about children or dogs." In order to open the second front for big photographs and major enterprise stories, Daniel decreed "no more kids or dogs." This caused objections from the editors who made up the page. The opposition was so fierce that the task had to be taken away from the Bull pen, as the imperious chief layout editors were known at the time, and given to Abe Rosenthal's lieutenants on the metropolitan desk. The new page, Daniel was happy to see, was an immediate success: "We got only one letter of complaint; it came from a cousin of one of the former editors of the page."

Daniel was eased out of the newsroom in 1969; Punch Sulzberger wanted his own man, Rosenthal, in charge of the daily news report, and not a holdover from his father's regime. Two years before Daniel's removal, the *Times* became a public company, its stock traded on the American exchange. Daniel knew that there were new pressures to change the traditional can't-do attitudes. A good case might have been made that the *Times*, of all newspapers, could ride out the shifts in the New York market. Would its well-educated readers really be lured away to suburban papers or to the intruder television? For years, the old management felt confident it knew the answer: There would always be a need for the authoritative voice of the *Times*. No other paper, over the years, attempted as much journalistically as the *Times* did, and no other paper succeeded the way the *Times* did (more often than not). But if the *Times'* typical readers were not likely to be lost to more trivial pursuits, they were inevitably going to be claimed by the actuarial tables. Older readers had to be replaced with new readers, specifically, those younger, affluent consumers desired by the advertisers. A company whose shares were publicly traded could not afford to be too smug, or appear to be too passive.

And so the new dynamic took over. Decision making focused on improving stock price-earnings ratios. The production departments solved the challenges of a four-section paper. The editors filled the newly opened space with fresh features designed to attract the right audience. Between 1976 and 1978, the *Times* introduced its daily, consumer-oriented C sections (Sports Monday, Science Times on Tuesday, Living, Wednesday; Home, Thursday; Weekend, Friday) and the Monday-through-Saturday Business Day, a stand-alone section offering expanded coverage of business and finance. The new features became testimony to the endurance of the *Times*—and to the team of Rosenthal, Mattson, and Punch Sulzberger. In a 1983 interview, Mattson described these years of change as "the highlight of the careers of a lot of people. Abe and Artie [Rosenthal's deputy, Arthur Gelb] were so involved that they'd just bubble over."

At the time, many of the participants didn't appreciate just how much they were supposed to be bubbling along, enjoying themselves. This victory had one hundred parents, many of them constantly fighting with each other. Mattson and Rosenthal were the chief antagonists, although with the passage of the years, the more jagged edges of their bureaucratic and personal disagreements became smoothed over: Collective Memory, like corporate history, dwells on success.

A protracted great struggle between Science and Fashion, for example, occupied the energies of the news and advertising departments for the better part of two years, beginning in the fall of 1977. At that point, the C-section format was four-fifths complete: Only a theme for the Tuesday paper needed to be selected. Sulzberger and his lieutenants, Rosenthal and Mattson, couldn't agree on what that theme should be. Narrowly considered, the fight pitted the editors against the sales staff in an argument about news content. The editors wanted the fifth and final C section to cover science and technology; the business side wanted a section of fashion news.

Rosenthal was then executive editor; Mattson, executive vice president: two strong-willed men leading the two factions. Science and technology ranked in the editors' minds as an "intellectual" subject, befitting their image of the *Times*, and of themselves. On the other side, the sales staff argued that a section devoted to fashion was just as newsworthy—and also effectively lent itself to the selling of ads. With his habit of florid self-dramatization, Rosenthal kept telling Sulzberger and Mattson that the "character of the paper" would be defined by their fifth choice. He left unspoken the other issue: which side would prevail over the other, a matter of some importance to men of great ego.

Mattson, however, now says, blandly, that "there was no real debate." According to Mattson, "Abe said he was going ahead with science, and we should sell advertising for the section." In memory, the business side's magnanimity transcended egos, as well as its responsibilities to the bottom line. "We tried to sell ads and couldn't at first," Mattson said mildly, the practiced executive used to defusing aggressive questions from stockholders and investment analysts. "But we went ahead anyway. We felt we owed Abe one." Rosenthal's "merry henchmen"—Mattson's quietly mocking term—joyously threw themselves into the job, Mattson remembered.

Rosenthal's recollections were more pointed: Boy, did they ever owe me one! In his memory, he and his "henchmen" had reluctantly but uncomplainingly soldiered on through the new Weekend section and Sports Monday, both with the stress on leisure-time news. Then they produced the Home and Living sections focused on upscale "lifestyles." Taken together, the "character" of the first four sections was unabashedly light and consumer-oriented. "That was not my world," Rosenthal remembered.

But he and his editors were nothing if not realists. Sulzberger expected the new sections to pay their own way, not only by bringing in readers but by concentrating on subjects that would appeal to the advertisers as well. "Our first major effort," Sulzberger told Rosenthal, "must be to answer the following: What is it that we can add to the news content of *The New York Times* that will make the newspaper, in addition to being the best in the world, more marketable and a better advertising medium. That, after all, is the pressure under which we are working." A few months later, in a memorandum about the proposed Living section to Rosenthal and Mattson, Sulzberger became more specific: "If we continue to grow, we are just going to have to adapt the added material in *The New York Times* to the desires of our advertisers. If we want to get the business, we just can't give them circulation which they do not find useful, and we, in turn, cannot afford the luxury of carrying that material free."

The "material"—news, reviews, features, columns, guides, and similar service articles—shouldn't be too grim or downbeat. Content had to be aimed at gaining "useful circulation"—read, the affluent and the suburban readers. When the *Times'* research department conducted a poll to find out what readers wanted in a Weekend section, interviewers were instructed to go to "upscale areas" for their sample. The poll results indicated these upper-end readers wanted listings of movies and entertainment; they were so eager for this service that they said they would turn to such a section on Thursdays for "early planning purposes." The C sections were supposed to be about fun, and advertising. The morning after the debut of Weekend on April 30, 1976, Rosenthal told his staff how much he liked the pace, writing, and design of the pages—the tone was "sophisticated but not nasty." Weekend was an "up." It was "light."

Rosenthal was less certain about Home, with its food and entertaining tips threading through large display ads for D'Agostino's, Sloan's, and other supermarkets. He believed that "recipes lowered the quality of the paper"—though, he says, he recognized Sulzberger's argument that the *Times* needed the advertising. Rosenthal remembered that he became reconciled to the publishing side's economic arguments by convincing himself, like a good *Times*man, that if the *Times* was going to do soft journalism, it should do *superior* soft journalism: "We would cover food the way we did foreign affairs, with the best writers and reporters." True, the subject was "only" food—and later, "only" design—and not topics with the resonance of Mideast politics or Soviet military affairs. And so he had a second nightmare: "I was terrified at the idea that people would pick up Home or Living, decide they were soft, and throw away the whole section." Consequently, he insisted that the *Times'* reviews of theater, music, dance, and motion pictures and its arts coverage be carried in the interior pages of each C section. "With our culture material in the back C pages," he reasoned, "no one could throw the section away."

While Rosenthal worried about too many recipes in the *Times*, some members of his staff were skeptical of the overall project. Rosenthal and his deputy, Arthur Gelb, informed midlevel editors that the new Living section would be, to quote from their planning documents, "a cheerful presentation of life-style" and "a glamorous, upbeat overview of living." The goal would be to tell readers "how to get greater enjoyment out of life." Joan Whitman dissented. Whitman, then in her fifties, was married to Alden Whitman, a *Times*man who was ending his career at the paper by turning the dreary routine of the obituary into a minor journalistic art form. In the 1970s, Whitman was one of the very few high-ranking women editors at the *Times*; in fact, she was editor of Family/Style, as the female-oriented pages were called before those pages—and Whitman—became casualties of the sectional revolution. But Whitman, a thin, self-contained woman of high intelligence and experience, did not allow herself to be carried out silently in the tumbrels of the revolutionaries. "I think we should be presenting the news in our fields," she told Rosenthal. "If it's glamorous, fine. If it's cheerful, terrific. But when the news isn't quite so chic, we should report it. And when goods are shoddy or we're being ripped off we should alert readers." Whitman then offered as an example of the unglamorous and uncheerful, a news story she was planning for the next week. The story asked whether women should have mammograms, given new evidence that there was a risk of breast cancer from the radiation. "That's on the news," Whitman said. "It's the best service possible, and it's solid. But it sure isn't trendy."

Rosenthal did not have to win over the Whitmans on his staff; Punch Sulzberger was the one whose approval counted. And Sulzberger had his own recurring worries about the sections. In particular, he dreaded the possibility of too much "sociology"—a label he used for all those topics that made him feel uncomfortable. Rosenthal had to hold Sulzberger's hand and reassure him about Home. "I am absolutely not contemplating a heavy section full of sociological pieces," the editor told the publisher. "Quite the contrary, we are contemplating a section that is intimate, helpful, and service-oriented." Whitman ran a feature story about the efforts of women who lived together to raise children on their own, either through adoption or artificial insemination. The story became a kind of shorthand for what Rosenthal wasn't planning to do. Not every subject in Home will be "frothy," Rosenthal assured Sulzberger. "But it will definitely not be a section devoted to lesbian mothers."

Sulzberger wanted not just light materials but marketable ones. Thus, the big Fashion-Science battle of the mid-1970s. The business side's interest in expanded fashion coverage, with its potential for readily available advertising, dated back almost a decade. The idea had been pressed on Punch Sulzberger by a number of outsiders, including Charles H. Revson, chairman and CEO of Revlon Inc., the cosmetics company. Sulzberger had invited Revson for one of the periodic "publisher's lunches" with *Times* executives in the private fourteenth-floor dining room. Rosenthal was traveling and missed the meeting. Waiting for him when he returned was a note from one of his associates, Seymour Topping, who apprised Rosenthal of the thrust of the cosmetics king's remarks. According to Topping, "Mr. Revson strongly urged that the *Times* give more space to fashion and beauty news" (including presumably news of Revlon's products). Sulzberger himself followed up with his own memo about the lunch discussion to Rosenthal, noting that "there was some truth in Mr. Revson's statement that we are not handling enough fashion news."

Sulzberger took up Revson's idea in character: the publisher ordered an in-house study of the subject. A grandly named task force, "involving all the necessary departments," was told to review past studies and take "a new look at what we might do for the future." The task force produced no discernible decisions over the next eight years. By 1978 the time for more studies had past; the four-section paper forced the issue. Weekend, Sports Monday, Home, and Living were in place, and Rosenthal was being pushed to create the final daily magazine for Tuesdays. "Fashion interested me," he remembered. "But I felt that three consumer sections in a row—Home, Living, and now Fashion— would tip the paper." As it was, he said, "Women were saying to me that the *Times* was looking down on them. My friends were kidding me about the paper." Equally to the point, Rosenthal's enemies also were making jokes at the expense of Living and Home; the critics passed around stories about the paper's investigative report on the best rigatoni in town and about the competition between two hotshot reporters for the job of *Times* restaurant critic, with the loser exiled in disgrace . . . to be the *Times* chief of bureau in Moscow. Always impassioned when it came to public perceptions of the paper, Rosenthal grimly informed Sulzberger and Mattson in a confidential memo dated January, 11, 1978: "What we select as the topics for Tuesday will affect not only Tuesday, but the totality of the image of the paper."

In his memo, Rosenthal proposed that the *Times* "break new journalistic ground" with a Science and Health section—"an exciting opportunity that seems to coincide with the interests of the kind of readers we are after . . . young people, more women, more students on the campuses, more professionals in every field." The new Tuesday section, Rosenthal assured Sulzberger and Mattson, would be "the final piece of the mosaic that will result truly in the new *New York Times*." As an inducement to get the business side's approval, Rosenthal promised expanded fashion-news coverage in the back of the new section. He would produce a news report with something for everyone.

While the idea for a special Science and Health section in the *Times* dated from Julie Adler's memo of 1924, even ignoring that archival record, the proposed coverage didn't represent new journalistic ground. Beginning in the late 1950s, Walter Sullivan, the *Times'* star science writer, sent to Turner Catledge a series of proposals to enlarge Sullivan's column in the Sunday Week in Review into a separate section. Sullivan suggested that the expanded science coverage be packaged with "advertising from the science/technology field." According to

Sullivan, "Nothing came of the scheme." The sales staff couldn't get any ads. Worse, Sullivan remembered, his Sunday science column itself was later eliminated in the aftermath of some since-forgotten study. In the mid-1970s, the old doubts about science remained.

Rosenthal's attempt to co-opt the business side by adding a fashion-news caboose to his science-health train left the publisher unimpressed. Punch Sulzberger repeated his "serious reservations as to the viability of such a section." Sulzberger added: "I don't think I can go beyond this right now until I get some feedback from Walter on his business perceptions." Rosenthal tried once more. He assured Sulzberger that the news department shared the business side's concerns for "economic viability." He repeated his arguments about the need to think of the "totality" of the *Times* rather than of its individual parts. Then the editor appeared to signal his withdrawal from the combat; he let the publisher know that the news department was turning its attentions to "expanding and refining" Business Day, the new business/financial section. He said nothing about a fashion-news plan. "Rosenthal was, as usual, a sore loser," Donald Nizen, one of Mattson's associates, later remembered.

Rosenthal was also resourceful. He recognized that "the *Times* didn't start these sections to lose money." When the news department and the business side couldn't come to an agreement, "We left our disagreement at that for a while, at an impasse." Adolph Ochs's *Times* devoted major resources to cover science; it provided financial support for Commander Richard E. Byrd's expedition to Antarctica and later serialized the commander's account (he returned the favor by naming Antarctic geographic features after the Ochs family). "I loved science. It was timely, and it belonged in the *Times*," Rosenthal said. He made a calculation based on his years of working for Punch Sulzberger: "I had my own strengths. The publisher wasn't going to push something down my throat. We were not a paper where someone descends from above and says, 'We must do this.' " Then in the summer of 1978, the pressmen's union struck the *Times* as well as the other New York papers. It was the last big labor-management dispute at the *Times* over the manning levels of the 43rd Street presses. The *Times* was shut for eighty-eight days. "I had time on my hands, and I wanted something to welcome readers back," Rosenthal said. "So on my own time, and on my budget . . . only at the *New York Times* can you talk that way, 'my budget' . . . I worked on a science section."

Rosenthal thought he knew the secret to win over Sulzberger and Mattson: "I would not add any more staff." I reminded Rosenthal of Russell Baker's description of the newsroom in the old days: idling firemen waiting for a Titanic-sized alarm to sound. Mattson, uncomically, had hammered in the same point. The newsroom, he insisted, should do the new sections with existing people. "Perhaps we were overstaffed," Rosenthal said. "I hired a designer, but that was all. Basically I mined this place for staff." Then he shuffled his allotment of pages, again staying within the newsprint budget set by the business side. "I took the first six columns of the existing Tuesday space. I added the three or four columns we were doing anyway on science. These were quote my unquote pages. I got another three columns elsewhere. Then I found four more. I put culture in the back and that did it. I went to the publisher with The Science Times."

Mattson, by Rosenthal's testimony, was not happy with the section. But Mattson was preoccupied with the byzantine negotiations to end the great strike. Dealing with the fractious New York press unions was draining enough for Mattson; in addition, Rupert Murdoch, the Australian newcomer to the city, broke ranks with the publishers' association and resumed publication of his *New York Post*. Rosenthal sensed that the business side, already doubly distracted by its dealings with the unions and the renegade Murdoch, could not fight on a third front. Specifically, Mattson would not be able to reverse Rosenthal's coup if the editors had the new Science Times package ready to greet readers when the *Times* resumed publication. "That was me," Rosenthal said. "The last of the Red Hot Mamas."

The first post-strike *Times* was published on Monday, November 6, 1978. Science Times appeared on Tuesday, November 14, 1978. Mattson may have since come to regard it as the section he "owed" Rosenthal; but there was little civility on either side at the time. Rosenthal turned out to be a sore winner as well. Science Times was only two weeks old when Rosenthal complained that Mattson's people weren't promoting the section sufficiently. Two weeks later, Chuck Greenburg of the promotion department responded with his own complaints. Science Times was too highbrow, Greenburg declared; it didn't carry topics that "the average reader could identify with." Greenburg also announced that his department was going to conduct a telephone survey after the first of the year to collect information from both readers and nonreaders on their "attitudes" toward Science Times. Rosenthal reacted angrily, dictating a memo to Mattson about the business department's "very grudging attitude" toward Science Times. "The very idea of promotion people deciding to 'survey' the news report . . . without consulting in advance shows that some of your people simply do not understand their role or the news department's role on this paper," Rosenthal said. When the memo was typed for his signature, Rosenthal decided not to send it to Mattson. Relations were bad enough without dispatching the B-52s.

Rosenthal didn't always behave with such restraint toward Mattson during this period of change at the *Times*. Mattson's business side, Rosenthal came to believe, was encroaching on the editors' authority to determine what cultural-news stories were covered. Rosenthal seemed to exempt Mattson from the complaint, excoriating instead some of his "executives who simply [don't] understand the nature of journalism . . . or the essence of this paper." The unnamed "executives" were in the *Times* advertising department. They had done what ad people usually try to do: sell ads—in this case, by proposing that editorial matter for a special issue of the *Times Magazine* be "tied in" to the release of a forthcoming motion picture from one of the major studios. Ads for the picture and related promotions would be inserted throughout the *Magazine*, which would carry stories about the film's stars and production. The idea was bad enough, Rosenthal told Mattson, but it was made worse by the "effort to keep pushing it once the editors had said they were not interested."

The special *Magazine* tied to the film did not appear. But the sales department never gave up on the idea of tie-ins, and a few years later, a more adaptable Rosenthal came around to the ad people's approach. In the early months of 1982, the Science Times section was almost four years old and it still lacked an advertising base. However, John Pomfret, a former *Times* reporter who went over to the business side to become the chief assistant to Mattson, noticed that a few retail ads offering a newly available product called the personal computer were beginning to "dribble" into the section. The whole field of small-business technology and home electronics, Pomfret told Rosenthal, "seems to be substantial and growing." Pomfret included in his list "the business computer, electronic game, data base, cable TV, hi-fi, [and] visual tape business." Pomfret wasn't much of an audiophile: in the early 1980s, consumers were buying stereos, not "hi-fi" equipment; and by "visual tape," he had meant videotape. But Pomfret understood the advertising market well enough. "There seems to be some affinity between the Science Times audience and this equipment," he told Rosenthal.

A week later, Rosenthal met with Pomfret to discuss the business side's idea of adding a weekly column on personal computers to Science Times. The column ought "to cover the whole explosion of home and small business information," Rosenthal subsequently told Arthur Gelb. "The advertising people think they can get a lot of advertising for this. As far as I am concerned, it is a good, solid venture because it is an interesting, expanding, and useful field which we do not now cover." Rosenthal also relaxed his vigilance against the advertising department's ideas for promotional tie-ins. When a major Richard Avedon exhibit was due to open at the Metropolitan Museum of Art, the *Times Magazine* ran a lavish selection of Avedon's work. Avedon was one of the great fashion photographers, and the *Times* sales force solicited advertising from the department stores that sold high fashion. The feature turned into a trifecta: Punch Sulzberger at the time was on the board of the Met. Later, as economic conditions worsened in the early 1990s, tie-ins appeared regularly in the *Times*. In the Arts and Leisure section of February 2, 1992, there was, for example, an appreciation of the new upper Madison Avenue retail space opened by the clothier—and major advertiser—Ralph Lauren. (Lauren was reported to be unhappy because his store didn't get an even grander spread in the *Times Magazine*; instead he had to be satisfied with carefully calibrated treatment that began on page one of the section and ran to over nineteen hundred words.)

There was indeed a "new" *New York Times*. Sulzberger had named Mattson president of the Times Company in 1979; Mattson was also appointed to the board of directors. Science Times began paying for itself, thanks to home-computer advertising. The editors learned to stop worrying and begin to love the fashion business. The *Times'* balance sheets were now reasons for joy. Mattson encountered less trouble in his drive to develop more new "editorial products" around which advertising could be sold—inserts and magazine supplements such as the Sophisticated Traveler, Good Health, and Business World. All of them became money-makers though none did quite as well financially as the special magazine section called "Fashions of the Times," or FOTs.

FOTs were ingenious tie-ins. Adolph Ochs's *Times* long ago understood the importance of the clothing manufacturers and the big stores to the economic health of the paper. Ochs courted Seventh Avenue. Retail ads for the "rag trade" ran throughout the daily paper and the *Times Magazine* on Sunday. But the FOTs offered a pure "dedicated" format: The news department supplied the fashion-editorial matter and the advertising department sold the fashion ads around the copy. The Fashions of the Times supplement which appeared on March 3, 1985, for example, totaled 158 pages; 68 percent of those pages represented paid advertising, including a gatefold ad for the cover. The total advertising revenue for that single section on that one Sunday totaled $2,322,100. This revenue was in addition to revenues from the ad lineage scattered through the regular edition of the *Times Magazine* and the rest of the Sunday paper. The direct expenses to produce that Sunday's Fashions of the *Times* totaled $1,618,500, mainly for printing and paper (the editorial staff costs, to prepare the copy, were listed as $150,000). The "gross contribution margin" was $703,000, a 33 percent return on revenue. The Fashions of the Times supplement of the year before had done even better; the FOT section of March 4, 1984, totaled 224 pages; its contribution to profits was $1,533,000, a 44 percent return. Later FOTs were developed for men's fashion and for children's clothes, in addition to the women's FOTs. Supplements also appeared seasonally for the spring and fall fashions.

By 1990, the *Times* was publishing eight special magazine supplements on fashion and related feature subjects each year. All of these were edited by Carrie Donovan, who first joined the paper in 1955, left in the mid-1960s, and came back in the 1970s. In addition, Donovan edited the weekly features of the *Times Magazine* covering fashion, style, beauty, design, and food—in effect, more pages offering desirable "advertising adjacencies" to the fashion industry. In the fall of 1990, in a long profile of Donovan, *Vogue* magazine described her as "the most powerful and influential newspaper fashion editor in America, perhaps in the world."

The *Times* had discovered in the FOTs a new way to print money. Through the flush years of the 1980s, however, some of the old tensions festered; prosperity, perversely, didn't produce total peace between the advertising and news departments. The *Times* advertising-sales staff complained that Donovan featured fashions that were "elitist," "fantasy," "impractical for ordinary people." Worse, from the sales staff's perspective, the FOTs concentrated on the same select upper-end designers, principally Yves St. Laurent, Karl Lagerfeld, Calvin Klein, Chanel, and Norma Kamali. In the advertising department's view, the editors were "ignoring major societal changes such as the professional working woman." As an example, the sales staff cited an article urging women to rush out in June to the department stores because the racks would be empty when they returned in September; it was "unrealistic," a business-staff memo declared, for the *Times* to assume that the typical woman reader "took a three months' vacation in the Hamptons."

The most vocal protests came from Herbert Shapiro and Brenda Racoosin, two salespeople responsible for selling to the mass-market manufacturers—rag trade companies as opposed to couturier houses. The *Times* needed "broader, more practical fashion coverage," Shapiro told Rosenthal. Shapiro refrained from attacking Donovan directly. But he alluded to her high-fashion tastes, reminding Rosenthal that "only 8 percent of our weekday readers and 7 percent Sunday have household incomes of over $100,000." Further, there were many working women in the *Times* audience for whom the couturier prices were out of reach: "Probably more than 95 percent of our readers can appreciate our fashion news only vicariously." Racoosin, for her part, did a tally of the women's Fashions of the Times for the spring of 1983, and reported: "YSL was mentioned 67 times, Calvin Klein 22x, Lagerfeld for Chloe and Chanel 44x . . ." Similarly, Racoosin analyzed the children's FOT for the summer of 1984. "Why are we directing our editorial credits to less than 10% of our readership?" she asked. Racoosin calculated the average cost of the children's clothes in FOT's twenty-three photo spreads. The outfits featured, she complained, cost on average $125.25; there was only one "mass market" outfit—"a lonely jumpsuit from Health Tex for $16."

No one could mistake Shapiro and Racoosin for objective analysts; they both made their livelihood selling the "mass market" accounts. Shapiro was particularly sensitive to what he judged Donovan's "editorial swipes" at his accounts. The men's and the women's FOTs in the spring of 1985, he declared, were "the two worst editorial sections I can remember." Shapiro listed the offending features: " 'City Styles' is so damaging I can only hope that because it is also so boring and uninformative it goes unread. In one sentence we're told the Palm Beach suit was banished 'into mothballed oblivion' and a Dacron shirt 'is looked upon with the same disdain. . . .' Both Palm Beach and Dupont, among our very biggest advertisers, will love it." Another advertising department report summed up the "perceptions of the trade" about the *Times'* fashion staff: "Does not return phone calls, does not acknowledge letters and invitations, does not explore merits of product lines, sign up for shows and never show up and don't even call to say sorry; doesn't have enough people to get out and really dig into and explore the trade."

Still, the fashion trade gritted its teeth and continued to advertise in the *Times.* Eli Dyan complained that the *Times* was "just not tuned in"—and bought a twelve-page schedule. Another major advertiser, Paul Marciano of Guess Jeans, increased his company's schedule, after expressing his "disbelief" at the *Times'* "devotion to the same select few." The advertisers had few other places to go: The *Times* so dominated the upper end of the newspaper audience in the Northeast that space buyers could only turn to V*ogue*, G*Q*, and the glossy magazines for alternative print options. As the decade of the 1990s approached, the fashion-sales troublemakers, Shapiro and Racoosin, were both shown the door by the *Times.* Offered early retirement, both accepted. Donovan carried on. The *Times'* "quintessential Fashion Person"—as V*ogue* called her—worked well into her seventh decade (she was born in 1928). The FOTs rolled forward, as did Science Times. There was something for everybody in the new *New York Times.*

The same V*ogue* article that praised Donovan as fashion's most powerful newspaper editor also sketched the contrasts in the life of a *Times* department editor. In her public persona, Donovan represented the *Times.* As V*ogue* described the official Donovan: "In a white-sequined Bill Blass jacket and Karl Lagerfeld dress, she took a limo to a benefit at Carnegie Hall and sat in a box with Oscar de la Renta, Nancy Kissinger, and some foreign aristocrat." The private Donovan, however, appeared in V*ogue* as a lone, unmarried woman who had recently been through a sad "relationship": "In for the night, [Donovan] curled up in the bed of her small one-bedroom rental on Sixty-fifth Street with Chinese takeout, a glass of wine, and MTV." Wrapped in the rich mantle of the *Times,* V*ogue* suggested, ordinary, otherwise unremarkable people come to wield extraordinary authority among the moneyed and the celebrated. Power came with the *Times* job, of whatever kind: theater critic, architecture writer, executive editor, publisher.

＊　　＊　　＊

In the mid-1970s, when the *Times* was being treated as a faltering enterprise, *Business Week* magazine had criticized the paper's "leftist" bent and Punch Sulzberger's apparent disdain for profits. In the magazine's issue of April 26, 1986, *Business Week* couldn't find enough compliments to pay Sulzberger and the *Times*. Acccrding to *Business Week*, the *Times* was "flush with record profits." The company had spent some $400 million on acquisitions in 1985, and was still a "hugely profitable engine for growth." With the "flagship paper throwing off cash," *Business Week* concluded, Sulzberger now presided over a company with "an embarrassment of riches."

Punch Sulzberger's elliptical managerial style seemed vindicated. The tensions at the *Times* were papered over (a winner's habit, too). Indeed, while the odd trio of Sulzberger, Mattson, and Rosenthal remade the institutional *Times*, they also reinvented themselves. Abe Rosenthal engineered perhaps the greatest make-over.

A DAY IN THE LIFE
2:45 P.M.—3:00 P.M.

2:45 P.M.

Allan M. Siegal, one of the *Times'* assistant managing editors, normally juggled the column allotments among the news desks. Siegal had the authority to swing space toward or away from national, or foreign, or business, or metro, depending on how the news developed on any given day. February 28 was shaping up as a moderately quiet news day, and so no extra demands were placed on the news hole—the daily budget of sixty-six pages that the editors controlled. The news department worked within an annual allotment; each time the editors determined that breaking events required an increase in the size of the news hole, that decision took them over budget, and they had to draw from the "bank," subject to the publisher's approval. In any given week, Siegal knew just how much the news department owed the bank, and how much it could still borrow. (Eighteen months later, during the extraordinary run of news beginning with the Persian Gulf crisis, the news department received permission to increase its news hole to sixty-eight pages per day. In all, it went seventy-two pages over budget for 1990, an expense that added several million dollars to the year's costs.)

Siegal was a *Times* lifer; he joined the paper as a copy boy in 1960 after his graduation from NYU, and never left. Smooth-faced, intelligent, intense, he lost a battle against weight early in his *Times* career. He sometimes ballooned to 240 pounds, then contracted to a relatively svelte two hundred. By newsroom legend, Siegal's poundage was a measure of executive-office turmoil: the greater the bureaucratic tumult among the top editors, the larger Siegal's girth.

He was the *Times'* arbiter of taste as well as of its space allotments. If there was one editor who made the *New York Times* the *Times*, it was Al Siegal. Readers might not recognize his name, but the journalistic brotherhood knew him; most of the day of February 28, Siegal was at Columbia University, helping judge the Pulitzer Prize competition.

3:00 P.M.

The day-side editors in the newsroom were joined by the night shift of backfield editors. Each of the sections in the news department—national, business, foreign, sports, culture, life-styles, media, and so forth—was run by three desks. The first, or day, desk consisted of the section head, the section deputy, and their assistants. These editors determined what stories should be covered and made the reporting assignments. In the Frankel years, they had been instructed to look for a mix of stories, trends as well as spot news. A second desk, known as the backfield, came in after lunch and stayed through the lockup of the first edition later in the evening. Backfield editors monitored copy flow, determined story lengths, and edited leads and opening paragraphs—actually, *re*edited them, since the day desk already had made its input on stories. Backfield work followed a predictable pattern. In the words of editor Carolyn Lee, "the reporters call in and mutter, 'What do you mean you want more information?' Or, 'What do you mean I've got to cut ten inches from my story?' " A third desk, made up of the copy editors, was the *Times'* "experts in style, grammar, and arcana," to quote the *Times'* handbook for new employees. The copy editors were charged with searching out errors and inconsistencies in the reporters' copy—another layer of editing.

6

—

LAST OF
THE RED HOT MAMAS

ABRAHAM MICHAEL ROSENTHAL was describing his City College days as a commuter student during the early 1940s. He was so poor, he said, that he had to eat "ketchup sandwiches" in the school cafeteria. As Rosenthal explained it, the sandwich consisted of two slices of white bread, available for a few pennies, smeared with ketchup, free, from the condiment table. The audience let out an audible sigh, a collective mixture of admiration and remembrance. But then Abe Rosenthal's listeners were with him even before he began speaking. It was a soft New York evening in June 1988, and history of a sort was being made. Rosenthal's appearance at the Sutton Place Synagogue at 225 E. 51st Street was his first speaking engagement since leaving the post of executive editor of *The New York Times* and becoming a *Times* columnist.

Well before 8:30 P.M., some four thousand men and women had quietly filed past blue wooden police barricades, and filled the synagogue sanctuary as well as the adjacent social hall, where closed-circuit televisions had been set up. In one of the front rows of the sanctuary a few seats were reserved for Rosenthal's guests, including his wife of eleven months. She was the second Mrs. Rosenthal, listed on the masthead of *Vogue* magazine as Shirley Lord, beauty/health editor. Shirley Hussy Lord Anderson Rosenthal was born in London (her second husband, the textile magnate Cyril Lord, was known as England's "Carpet King"; her third husband, David Anderson, was the architect who built the Lords' Caribbean beach house). She was the author of two steamy novels; blonde, buxom, and at five feet, eight inches, the same height as her new husband. W, the fashion paper, referred to her as "that great marzipan creation." In 1985, shortly after Rosenthal had ended his marriage of four decades, two mutual friends of Rosenthal and Lord's, the television personality Barbara Walters and the former operatic singer Beverly Sills, introduced the *Times*man to the *Vogue* woman. The couple soon became part of the New York celebrity scene, or at any rate that part of it known as New Society (to distinguish it from the more traditional society based on "old money" and "breeding"). Abe and Shirley Rosenthal were seen at all the New Society places; they attended such roaring '80s affairs as the fiftieth birthday party of the financier-corporate raider Saul Steinberg, which featured tableaux vivants—elaborate replications of great works of art, with hired actors posing in the "pictures."

Not many in the audience that Rabbi David B. Kahane welcomed were likely readers of Lord's novels; some of them probably were familiar with the tabloid gossip columns that chronicled the high life of the newly rich and infamous. Mostly, though, they were sober-minded New Yorkers, the kind of people who have read the *Times* all their adult lives. They were spending their evening as a *Times* reader might, participating in "the Jewish Town Hall," in Rabbi Kahane's words. Their guest speaker for the evening, the rabbi said, "was a towering giant of journalism, who would take the audience along on an intellectual journey." "Our speaker," the rabbi said, "although born in Canada, is a true New York success story . . . a poor immigrant boy who attended CCNY, where the tuition was free, but as he has said, it was still a little more than his family could afford. . . ." Rabbi Kahane referred to Rosenthal's assignments abroad as a *Times* correspondent in Poland, India, and Japan, and to his steady advancement at the *Times*, from metropolitian editor to managing editor to executive editor and then, after his retirement from the newsroom, to his new life as an Op-Ed columnist. "Tell us about your journey from Sault Sainte Marie, Ontario, to the *Times*," the rabbi said, yielding the lectern to Rosenthal. The audience settled back, ready to hear the narrative of a plucky boy's rise from poverty to power, a good Jewish success story.

Rosenthal began by declaring that he was making his first public speech in twenty years. "When I was the *Times'* editor, I didn't think I should make speeches, because the *Times'* news department has no politics. But now I'll speak my mind, because I'm a columnist, and I'm paid to pop off." If some congregants were skeptical of the notion of the apolitical *Times*, they didn't show it. The audience saw one of its own: a Jew and a New Yorker. The man standing before them was, like many of the men in the audience, in late middle age, conservatively dressed in a bankers' blue suit, white shirt, blue silk tie, and black-tasseled loafer shoes. He appeared neither tall nor short, neither fat nor thin. Rosenthal's most distinctive feature was his full head of hair, still black in his sixty-seventh year and styled over his forehead. The yarmulke he wore kept slipping to the side of the mass of hair, and Rosenthal had to keep righting the cap as he talked.

Rosenthal moved quickly through the early Ontario years. He skipped mention of the original family name, Shipiatsky, and of its roots in Byelorussia. He passed over his own painful medical history; osteomyelitis, an infection of the bone marrow, crippled him in his early teens. The audience would have admired the story of the boy who had to walk with a cane during high school, who did not get proper treatment and the needed corrective surgery until he was accepted as a charity case at the Mayo Clinic in Minnesota. Understandably, the audience might have had different reactions to the other details that unsympathetic biographers—for example, Rosenthal's former colleague and longtime ill-wisher, Harrison Salisbury—were careful to include: that Rosenthal's father, Harry, who had settled the family on a farming commune in Canada, was an atheist; that Rosenthal, the youngest of six children and the sole male child, was babied and fussed over by his five older sisters; that his sister Ruth had become a member of the Young Communist League and married another young Communist, the dashing George Watt, who fought with the Lincoln Brigade in Spain ("God how I admired that man," Salisbury quoted Rosenthal as saying); that Rosenthal was raised in a socialist household, learned no Hebrew, and was never bar mitzvahed; that he eventually married an Irish Catholic and brought up his three children without religious training. Still, his listeners would have understood that Abe Rosenthal always considered himself a Jew, as Salisbury told it, because he was perceived as Jewish.

None of Rosenthal's red-diaper background was surprising, given the secularist ideals of the time among many immigrant Jews. What made it relevant to the poverty-to-power narrative were the adult Rosenthal's politics. He despised the Gomulka government when he served as the *Times'* Warsaw bureau chief in the late 1950s. His tour of duty came during the height of the cold war, at a time when the suffocating air of the police state hung over the Communist-bloc countries of Eastern Europe. Part of Rosenthal's reaction grew out of his competitive journalist's feeling that Poland was a "second-rate story in the suburbs," too far removed from big events. In 1960, however, Rosenthal won a Pulitzer Prize for his Polish coverage, and realized he hadn't wasted his time. But the honor didn't make him mellow or less ambitious. Contrary to his opening disclaimer, he was no more apolitical than he was bald.

The Shipiatskys moved to New York in the mid-1920s, to live in a Bronx cooperative apartment complex sponsored by the Amalgamated Clothing Worker's Union. The family name had been changed to Rosenthal, and the father had found work as a house painter. Around the boy's thirteenth birthday, Rosenthal told the Sutton Place audience, his father died from injuries suffered when he fell from a scaffold. There were audible groans. (Four of Rosenthal's sisters died at relatively young ages—two from cancer, one from pneumonia, and one shortly after childbirth—though this too was omitted from the family narrative.) When Rosenthal talked of his college days, recounting how he had only five cents to spend in the CCNY cafeteria, he began to choke with emotion, as if telling the story for the first time. One of Rosenthal's classmates from the CCNY days, Robert Schiffer, has stayed in touch through the years, and Schiffer takes the ketchup story with a pinch of salt. "I've heard it many times," says Schiffer, who served as a demographer at the United Nations in New York. "Since everybody was in the same Depression-era boat, no one felt he had anything less. We were not all that poor."

Rosenthal asked for questions from the audience. A questioner expressed concern about the "unfair" coverage of Israel. Rosenthal acknowledged that some of the images of Israel on American television were harsh, "but you have to pay a price if you're an open democracy, and a free press is part of that price." He disposed of a question about Kurt Waldheim quickly. "He's a liar," Rosenthal said, to loud applause. He had more difficulty when asked about the Reverend Jesse Jackson and black attitudes toward Jews. Jackson, Rosenthal said, had visited the *Times* in the weeks before the New York Democratic primary the past April. "I advised Jesse to make a healing gesture," perhaps by meeting with Jewish leaders to counteract the effects of his "Hymietown" reference to New York. "But he couldn't rise to it, and that was a pity. The proper question is, 'What can we do to heal the rift between these historic allies, Jews and blacks?' " Several members of the audience were visibly displeased; Rosenthal sought to reassure them. "The Hymietown remark was disgusting," Rosenthal said. "But has no one in this room ever made an antiblack remark?" A woman quickly shouted, "No!" Rosenthal just as quickly turned to her, and said with the fast mouth of a New Yorker, "Then you should run for president."

He was asked about his choices on the eve of the presidential campaign (both parties' political conventions would be held in the next two months). "I sat out 1972," he began by way of context. "I wouldn't vote for Nixon. McGovern made me ill and Norman Thomas wasn't around." At the moment, he was still "very lukewarm" about the 1988 front-runners, George Bush and Michael Dukakis; Rosenthal wished that Mario Cuomo or Bill Bradley were running. There was time for only a few more questions, and Rabbi Kahane said he would ask them. Tell us, he said, turning to Rosenthal, the major influences in your life, the most memorable story you covered, and the most memorable person you ever encountered. They were a fan's questions, but Rosenthal's answers were not the usual stuff of a *People* magazine interview, any more than he was a standard *People* celebrity. He mentioned "the many influences on a person, such as family and religion." Then added: "In my case, what influenced my life and, I believe, is the reason I'm alive, is the United States of America." The answer produced more applause, though some puzzlement as well. The Shipiatsky-Rosenthals were not a refugee family (as some in the audience were); his parents emigrated well before Hitler's terror against European Jews; they settled initially not in the United States but in Canada.

Rosenthal surprised his auditors once again with his choice for most important story. "News is usually so depressing; it's about wars, disasters, and so forth. But the story of men going to the moon lifted the heart." He had an "inspired idea" during the *Times'* editorial planning for the first Apollo lunar-orbit flight in December 1968, he remembered. "I asked Archibald MacLeish to write a poem to appear on page one for the *Times* in celebration of the occasion. We had him on an open line during the countdown, to dictate a new lead for his poem if anything went wrong."

The audience didn't pick up on the journalist's humor about the poet laureate of the United States standing by, at his farm in western Massachusetts, ready to phone the desk with a "top" for a page-one story in the *Times*. Rosenthal's remembrance of the "most memorable person" was equally puzzling, except perhaps to those who had worked for Rosenthal or had encountered him during his years at the *Times*. The Indian leader Jawaharlal Nehru was his choice, he told the men and women of Sutton Place Synagogue. "Nehru was mean. He went around yelling at people. He was not a lollipop. He was not warm and cuddly. But he was beautiful, a great man, a father to his country. He could have been a dictator, but he kept India a democracy and he was accessible to his people. He was a leader."

With that, the man who ran the news pages of the *New York Times* for two decades finished and sat down, to sustained if perplexed applause. Two members of the audience who knew Rosenthal exchanged glances. Their looks conveyed the same thought: Describing the beautiful, mean, shouting, great Nehru, Rosenthal was describing as well how he saw himself.

The efforts to "explain" Abe Rosenthal became a cottage industry during the years he edited the *Times*. Alexander Cockburn, Geoffrey Stokes, and other columnists of the *Village Voice*, the weekly newspaper in New York, conducted a Rosenthal watch in the 1970s and 1980s, documenting his alleged depredations, regularly updating the infamous Rosenthal "shit list" of *Times* staff people said to be in disfavor. Rosenthal and his news department were fair game. The *Times* was the most important journalistic force in town, and a subject as worthy of regular scrutiny as City Hall or the New York theater. It made good journalistic sense for the *Voice* to act as jeer leaders; the *Times* was a competitor, and the columnists could assume their readers also read the *Times*, and were familiar with what they were writing about. A major complaint was that Rosenthal had moved the *Times* news columns to the right. From the *Voice*'s left-liberal position, the charge was accurate. Rosenthal later acknowledged "a grain of reality" in the criticism. The *Times*, he said, had been pulled temporarily "off course and to the left" in the late 1960s and early 1970s by some reporters and midlevel editors. "In the absence of any countervailing intellectual thrust," he remembered, "the paper was not always where it should have been—in the center." By the 1980s, Rosenthal said, he was satisfied that he had taken full control of the news pages and was supplying the needed balance. The *Times* was once again on course, "not right wing but as close to center as possible."

The thunder from the left bothered Rosenthal. Another editor, with a different temperament perhaps, might have ignored the *Voice* writers, putting their criticisms down as one of the costs of being in charge of the journalistic standard by which other news organizations were judged. Rosenthal, however, thundered back. The *Village Voice*, Rosenthal told Jonathan Beaty, a reporter for *Time* magazine, "was an urban ill like dog shit in the street—to be stepped over."

Rosenthal also attracted the attention of Joseph Goulden, a Washington-based investigative biographer. In the mid-1980s, Goulden conducted over three hundred interviews with present and former *Times*people in the course of his research for a book on the *Times* during the Rosenthal years (*Fit to Print; A. M. Rosenthal and the Times*). Rosenthal parried Goulden's requests for an interview for over a year. Finally, in 1986, after Goulden reminded Rosenthal that two hundred people had already been interviewed, Rosenthal's "curiosity apparently got the best of him." Rosenthal sat with Goulden for four sessions totaling over twenty hours. The sum of Goulden's efforts was less than the individual parts. Goulden hectored Rosenthal through 460 pages, describing the *Times*man's alleged near-constant drinking and womanizing. Goulden's Rosenthal was a tyrant, and a petty one at that. Goulden also said that Rosenthal did indeed keep a shit list of errant reporters. Once on the list, their careers were stalled: They could leave the *Times*, or keep a low profile and hope that Rosenthal would forget their offense.

Somehow the angry, profane, list-making Rosenthal described by Goulden also found the time to wield power "equaled by few in American journalism" and to affect "the course of his country's history and the world's." But Goulden offered little evidence of how Rosenthal reached out and touched history. As one example of the *Times'* supposed national agenda-setting power, Goulden cited the Bitburg episode—Ronald Reagan's decision in 1985 to visit a German military cemetery where Nazi SS troopers were buried. Had it not been for "Rosenthal's rage" over the president's insult to the memory of the

Jews, and the *Times'* subsequent coverage, Goulden reported, the Bitburg story would have died in a day or two. To make that argument, Goulden had to ignore all the stories that appeared in the rest of the media. He also had to ignore all the public opinion polls. In the days after Rosenthal "raged" about Bitburg, one third of the public said it was in favor of the visit; another third said that it was indifferent whether Reagan went or stayed away. Only one third opposed the trip. If Rosenthal was so powerful, and if the *Times* did set the agenda, why then did Reagan go ahead with his Bitburg visit anyway? The journalist Lou Cannon, the definitive biographer of Reagan, provided the answers. Helmut Kohl, the West German chancellor, had pleaded with Reagan, telling him that cancellation would be a personal embarrassment and possibly cause his government to fall. Cannon also ran through the list of the important voices that opposed the trip; he included Senator Bob Dole, representatives of the American Jewish community, the Nobelist Elie Wiesel, and some of Reagan's own advisers, such as Edward Rollins. Cannon did not mention Abe Rosenthal or the *New York Times*.

The Reagan White House did attend to the *Times'* views—when they supported its own agenda. Rosenthal visited Manila in 1985 before the Marcos dictatorship was overthrown, and interviewed Corazón Aquino. According to Raymond Bonner, a former *Times* foreign correspondent, Rosenthal was unimpressed; she was not sufficiently anti-Communist, and Rosenthal said so publicly. Reagan was soon quoting Rosenthal in White House conversations.

All the talk of national agendas was largely pro forma. Goulden wasn't so much interested in public policy as he was in the private Rosenthal. When Rosenthal made the transition in 1987 from editor to Op-Ed page commentator, his initial column appeared under the headline, "Please Read This Column." The head was written by Rosenthal. The unsuspecting Op-Ed page reader might regard this as a harmless, even larky, way to begin; not Goulden. "The pathos of Abe Rosenthal may be summarized in these sad words," Goulden concluded. "The little boy on the center of the stage shouting for attention."

Goulden had conducted an exercise in overkill. His relentlessly mean tone undermined his credibility. When alternative explanations for Rosenthal's news decisions presented themselves, Goulden invariably chose the worst possible interpretation, and then presented it as if self-evident. For example, on the same day that City Hall announced a multimillion-dollar city project for the renovation of Yankee stadium, it also announced cutbacks in funding for day-care centers serving working mothers. "The Yankee story ran [in the *Times*]; the day care story did not," Goulden reported, and immediately added: "Rosenthal is a chum of George Steinbrenner, the Yankees' owner." No evidence of this chumminess was presented. No mention was made of the background that made the stadium project newsworthy. Steinbrenner, a major league blowhard with a reputation for greedy self-interest, had pumped up public concern by hinting that he might move the Yankees out of New York unless the stadium was refurbished with help from the city—just as other team owners in other cities had threatened to move their franchises, without those inducements to stay that they regarded as their due. As for the *Times'* omission of the day-care cuts, no consideration was given to the possibility that such a decision might have been made not by Rosenthal but at a much lower level, by the *Times'* City Hall bureau or by metro-desk editors—or that no decision was made, that the story was simply missed by a large, imperfect news-gathering machine. Rather, a directive to suppress had come from the very top, the tyrant *Times* obliging the bureaucracy, while the poor suffered.

"It didn't do me any good to talk to Goulden," Rosenthal complained when I interviewed him. "He had made up his mind about me. So I appear as a villain and a terrible person, whether that's true or not." Rosenthal added, almost softly: "I think of myself as a very successful editor, but I come across as a Hitler." Two years earlier, at the time of publication of *Fit to Print*, *Time* magazine called Rosenthal for his comments on the book. "It's like walking into a mess on the street," Rosenthal said. "You step in it; you try to wipe it from your foot." The quote echoed the "dog shit" line of six years before; this time, *Time* ran it.

Yet Goulden's nasty account could not be casually stepped over as if it were a pile of dog litter. A. H. Raskin worked alongside Rosenthal for more than thirty years. Raskin's career at the *Times* began in 1932, when he was the paper's campus correspondent at City College (the same stringer's job that Rosenthal had a decade later). Raskin watched admiringly when Rosenthal arrived at the *Times* during the war years and began his steady ascent up the newsroom hierarchy. Raskin thought he knew "almost everything there was to know about who did what to whom on West 43rd Street and why." But he said that he learned a lot of "solid new information" from Goulden. For all of Raskin's admiration of Rosenthal, and for all his distaste for Goulden's decision to "sex up" the narrative with stories of Rosenthal's extramarital affairs, Raskin concluded that Goulden's interviews and research were too strong to shrug off. Given a chance to trash the Goulden narrative, Raskin chose instead to applaud its "provocative findings."

Harrison Salisbury in his memoirs of his career at the *Times* left out the sexual tales about Rosenthal but not much else. Salisbury's Rosenthal is, at heart, an angry, argumentative, supremely ambitious egomaniac. Salisbury's view of Rosenthal the journalist was not much better than his opinion of the man. Salisbury concluded that Rosenthal was not really a reporter of, say, the stature of Harrison Salisbury; rather he was a writer, and an "overemotional" one at that. Salisbury praised with not-so-faint damns Rosenthal's best-known journalistic work—his account, during Rosenthal's tour of duty in Poland, of his visit to the Nazi death camp at Auschwitz. Salisbury called it Rosenthal's finest story, and then reported that the original theme was "suggested" to Rosenthal by a colleague; moreover, while Rosenthal's superiors back in New York found the article moving, they judged it unsuitable for the news pages. The editors published it instead in the *Times Magazine*—as a feature.

Salisbury also added his version of the *Times'* rightward turn, even giving it a date: the students' occupation of the president's office at Columbia University on the night of April 29, 1968. Rosenthal, the onetime poor City College commuter student, assigned himself to the story of the rampage (as the *Times* told it) by the Ivy League children of the middle class. Rosenthal had been enjoying the beautiful New York earlier that night, sitting in the *Times'* house seats at the Broadway opening of *Hair* (like the Columbia student occupation, a celebration of the new Age of Aquarius, but put to music, and safely confined to the stage). On the campus, the editor turned reporter for a night surveyed the damage done to the office of Columbia president Grayson Kirk. Rosenthal's account focused on Kirk's books, "spines ripped and pages defiled." Kirk was quoted: "My God, how could human beings do a thing like this?" Editor Rosenthal's associates placed reporter Rosenthal's story on the front page of the *Times* the next morning. According to Salisbury, however, Rosenthal's Columbia reportage was more imagined than factual. He all but accused

Rosenthal of "piping"—making up—the story. Kirk, Salisbury reported, later said he had no recollection of the scene as described in the *Times*, or of seeing Rosenthal that night. Furthermore, a Columbia University investigative committee subsequently dismissed the office damage as "trivial."

Salisbury called Rosenthal his "friend," someone he knew "better than any man." Yet no good Rosenthal deed went unpunished. His successes at the *Times* were explained—more accurately, explained away—as a by-product of obsessive ambition (to escape from poverty and his roots) combined with a nimble ability to borrow from others. Salisbury moved from the newsroom to supervise the start-up of the Op-Ed page in 1970. Rosenthal, Salisbury remembered, initially had nothing but ridicule for the graphics Salisbury introduced in the page, "but within a year, graphics, drawings, artwork blossomed throughout the paper. [Rosenthal] designed and redesigned section after section until the paper had an open and inviting aspect."

One of Rosenthal's often-stated credos involved the ideal of "objectivity," and the need for the *Times* to present "both sides of issues." "We live in a time of commitment and advocacy," Rosenthal wrote in a memo to his staff, later adapted and published as a full-page statement in the *Times*. " 'Tell it like it is' really means 'tell it like I say it is' or 'tell it as I want it to be.' For precisely that reason, it is more important than ever that the *Times* keep objectivity in its news columns as its number one, bedrock principle." Later, Rosenthal admonished his staff that the *Times* shouldn't "use a typewriter to stick our fingers in people's eyes just because we have the power to do so." But the Rosenthal-watchers accused him precisely of misusing the power of the *Times* to reward cultural favorites and strike out at putative enemies. Rosenthal's friendship with Beverly Sills was well known. A poster of the singer hung in Rosenthal's outer office, moving Salisbury to wonder how this "affected the [*Times*'] music critics." Salisbury didn't follow up by asking the critics directly; nor did he consult their published reviews for any clues to whether their critical opinions were influenced by the editor's choice of office decoration. In fact, the *Times*' files show that John Rockwell, the *Times*' lead music critic, did not hang back from negative reviews of Sills's performances.

The critics also trashed Rosenthal for his role in the Kosinski affair, a bizarre episode that roiled the New York literary-social-media world in the early 1980s. Salisbury suggested that Rosenthal's friendship with Jerzy Kosinski inspired a "ponderous essay" about Kosinski which appeared in the *Times* in November 1982. The "essay" was actually an investigative report describing how the Polish-born writer, novelist, and celebrity-around-town had been victimized by a long-term disinformation campaign that apparently originated with the security services of Warsaw's Communist regime. The campaign, the author of the *Times* article, John Corry, implied, eventually found an American outlet in the *Village Voice*. The *Voice* article stated, among other things, that Kosinski had invented many of the more dramatic details of his life in wartime Poland, that he had major "assistance"—uncredited—in writing his books, including his best-known novel, *The Painted Bird*, and that the Central Intelligence Agency may have been his "sponsor" in the United States. The *Voice* called its article "Jerzy Kosinski's Tainted Words." By implying that the *Voice* article was somehow "linked" to the Polish government, the *Times* all but announced that the real tainted words were those of the *Voice* writers, Geoffrey Stokes and Eliot Fremont-Smith.

In outline, the Corry story did look like a "*Times* editor's special"— the Arthur-ized Version, as the newsroom wordsmiths liked to joke. Rosenthal and his chief deputy, Arthur Gelb, were much too smart to try to influence a critic to write a puff review; they knew what a scandal it would create. But they did not hesitate to push for favorable mentions of friends in the news pages. "Please make sure that we give some decent quotes from Betty Friedan in our ERA series," Rosenthal told James Greenfield, a senior editor. "For one thing she inspired us to do it, and secondly, she really is, still, a paramount figure in the woman's movement and one who, I believe, is a bridge among many women and men." Sometimes the back-scratching produced hilarious results. Gelb and his wife Barbara wrote a biography of Eugene O'Neill in 1962, nine years after the playwright's death in 1953; ever since the Gelbs' biography, the *Times* never seemed to run out of stories to tell about O'Neill. At the time of the centennial of O'Neill's birth, the *Times* published a story about plans to demolish the New London, Connecticut, house where O'Neill lived one winter; five weeks later, the *Times* ran a picture of a plaque being dedicated in Provincetown, Massachusetts, site of the first performance of O'Neill's play *Bound for East Cardiff*.

The Kosinski affair was far more tangled. Rosenthal and Gelb were both friends of Kosinski. Abe and Ann Rosenthal dined with Jerzy and Kiki Kosinski on the Rosenthals' Central Park West terrace; the Kosinskis in turn entertained the Rosenthals at dinner. Barbara Gelb wrote a glowing literary appreciation of Kosinski in the *Times Magazine* four months before the *Village Voice* attack appeared. Her article included a quotation, from an unnamed "friend," describing how Kosinski had visited the friend as he lay sick and despondent in the hospital. The anonymous admirer quoted by Barbara Gelb was Abe Rosenthal. There were other complicating circumstances. The writer of the *Times* article, John Corry, was not the original reporter assigned to look into the *Voice's* "Tainted Words" story. Gelb initially gave the assignment to Michiko Kakutani, a young Yale graduate who joined the *Times* as a cultural reporter in 1979. Kakutani worked on the story for six weeks, growing increasingly anxious about her abilities to do the investigative journalism her editors expected (at one point she thought Kosinski was following her). Corry, sitting a few desks away, watched in silence as Kakutani struggled. She finally asked to be taken off the story. "She didn't understand the assignment," Gelb later said. (Kakutani's career at the *Times* didn't suffer from the episode; she became one of the *Times*' regular book reviewers.) Corry said that he then volunteered for the assignment. He had been at the *Times* twenty-six years; like Rosenthal and Gelb before him, he was energetic, ambitious, a working-class boy of the outer boroughs. Corry sensed a "big story" and hurled himself into the reporting.

A few *Times*people believe that Rosenthal had second thoughts about his conduct in the Kosinski story, given all the charges that he used the *Times* to play favorites. (In a *Newsweek* article about the Kosinski affair, an anonymous "senior *Times* critic" was quoted as saying: "It's real Louis XIV time. It's 'I am the newspaper and the newspaper is me.' ") When I asked Rosenthal if he regretted his part in the Kosinski episode, he quickly acknowledged that he did. "Kosinski was raped by the *Voice*," he said. "The only thing I'm ashamed of is that we didn't do the story sooner." Only later, said Rosenthal, after other newspapers took up the *Voice* story, did the *Times* weigh in. "I walked away from Kosinski at first. I was afraid to be seen coming to the aid of a friend. But then I decided that I wouldn't be a 'thirty-ninth witness.' " This last was a reference to one of the major stories of Rosenthal's tenure as metropolitan editor of the *Times*. In 1964 a young Queens woman named Kitty Genovese was stabbed to death in her Kew Gardens neighborhood; according to a *Times* reporter's reconstruction of the murder, thirty-eight people heard her screams or glimpsed the attack but failed to come to the young woman's aid.

Rosenthal often used explosive words in conversation, and in his writings: Critics treated him like "a Hitler," Kosinski was "raped." Emotional language aside, Rosenthal's facts were accurate. The *Los Angeles Times* and the *Chicago Sun-Times*, among others, critically examined the *Voice*'s "Tainted Words" article before the *Times* did. Without question, the story had news value: celebrity scandal, literary politics, international intrigue, and a strong narrative line. It was a New York story; it belonged in the *Times*. The extraordinary length of the Corry piece—some 6,500 words, running through sixteen columns of the Arts and Leisure section—may have warranted some of the critics' hand-wringing. But the defense of a friend, however belated, didn't make Rosenthal an editor unique in the annals of journalism; it did undercut his public declarations about the *Times*' purity. As with Kakutani, so too with Rosenthal and Gelb: They somehow failed to "understand the assignment." Perhaps Punch Sulzberger should have advised them to remove themselves from all aspects of the *Times*' coverage, as Kakutani did. He might have started with the suggestion that Barbara Gelb's profile not be published in the *Times Magazine*; she easily could have gone elsewhere to get it into print. But the lit-crit world didn't interest him (as did, say, Macy's designer windows). Sulzberger was the publisher who asked his book editor John Leonard to recommend cruise-ship reading he could toss overboard when done. He left Rosenthal's authority unchallenged in such matters.

Salisbury thought he knew why Rosenthal became blind to the ways he used that authority at the *Times*. "Once ambition began pounding in [Rosenthal's] veins, it was ambition unlimited," Salisbury concluded. "Lord Acton, I think, was right." Goulden employed "Geraldo!"-style talk-show analysis to "explain" Rosenthal (the editor as attention-craving little boy). Salisbury spoke in the more measured cadences of MacNeil-Lehrer. Both critics ended up with the same ugly picture. Not surprisingly, Rosenthal thought Salisbury's account to be as untrustworthy as Goulden's. "Harrison was a part of some of these events, yet his reminiscences are wrong time after time," Rosenthal said. Rosenthal had his own behavioristic explanation for Salisbury. "Harrison is an intelligent man who grinds axes at all times. We all do that to some extent. But not as he does, as a way of life."

*   *   *

Outsider Goulden and insider Salisbury, for all their fascination with Rosenthal's personality, never conclusively demonstrated how the man shaped the paper. They credited Rosenthal for livening the news report, bringing in writerly reporters (and requiring critics and writers to do reporting), and creating a more magazine-like *Times*. In short, they applauded him for trying to keep the *Times* up to date with the times. Did Rosenthal's changes make the *Times* in the decades of the 1970s and 1980s measurably different from what it might have been in the hands of another editor, operating under the same competitive media pressures and in the same volatile New York marketplace? Was its conservative turn "because of" the editor? Or did it have more to do with the wishes of the Sulzberger family, and with the general political climate as well?

Editors can put their unmistakable imprint on publications—depending on the editors' abilities and the size or frequency of publication. Magazines appear weekly, or monthly; the chief editor is responsible for "only" sixty thousand words in any one issue. Book editors normally supervise perhaps ten to twelve titles a year for their publishing houses. And so it has been possible to speak of "Harold Ross's *New Yorker*" and, for a time, of an "Alice Mayhew book" at Simon & Schuster. At the *New York Times*, however, almost one thousand journalists deal with millions of words a week, collecting, sorting, editing, and printing 240,000 words a day, and three times that many on Sundays. Can any one editor direct this Niagara of words, channeling them toward desired goals? If so, how? Was there, in fact, the Rosenthal *Times*?

The evidence that Rosenthal sought iron control of the news pages exists, in abundance. He has never been a guarded person, or modest about his accomplishments. The interviews he gave to Goulden and Salisbury, despite his misgivings about their intentions, testify to a combative openness—the Last of the Red Hot Mamas, as he described himself. In 1988 Rosenthal deposited his office memos, personal letters, and working papers in the Times Archives on lower Fifth Avenue. He placed no restrictions on their use. By contrast, all the files of Punch Sulzberger and Walter Mattson, including those dating back to the 1960s, were still classified as "active" in 1991, and not made made available at the Archives. The Rosenthal materials fill thirty linear feet of boxes. They reveal Rosenthal's unceasing efforts to involve himself in every aspect of the *Times'* news operations. They also show the gap between intention and accomplishment in an institution the size of the *Times.*

No detail of the *Times'* news report was too small to attract Rosenthal's eye. After the new Weekend section appeared, Rosenthal worried that the picture rules—the hair-thin, black lines around photographs—were unnecessarily heavy: "If it is a light, up section, it seems to me that too much blackness is contradictory," he told the *Times'* graphics designer Lou Silverstein. Nor was any subject too trivial for a Rosenthalian postmortem. "I have enjoyed reading your pieces in the past few months, and I have said so," he told fashion writer John Duka. "I didn't enjoy the second paragraph of your last story. It used a stylistic device that is quite outmoded . . . staccato, repeated, short sentences. 'Blass, that is. Bill Blass. William Ralph Blass, to be exact.' Et cetera. John, that is not writing, that's stuttering."

Variations on the theme of control occur through the years. Before 1976, when the news and Sunday departments were separate, with Rosenthal in charge of the former, and Max Frankel the latter, Rosenthal became convinced that "his" reporters were not working as hard as they should for "his" daily news report. "We sent Frank Lynn around the country with [Mayor John] Lindsay. Why hasn't he done the sum up for us that he did for the Review of the Week? . . . We must not be in a position where the reporters begin saving the meaning of their stories for the Review and giving us the scattered detail." Later, when the work of feature writer Jean Hewitt appeared in the *Times Magazine,* Rosenthal ordered an assistant to find a bookkeeping method to charge Hewitt's salary to the Sunday department. Five months later, Rosenthal asked one of his deputies if "our" Washington bureau reporters, in particular, John Herbers and R. W. Apple, Jr., were "being forced to do too much work for the Review or are kind of saving up their best thoughts and writing for the Review." Two weeks later, an article by Robert Reinhold in the Review, on a new approach to the teaching of physics, angered Rosenthal. The article was "precisely the kind of piece that I have been asking Reinhold to do for years," Rosenthal complained. The story "should have appeared in the daily before it appears in the Review. . . . As far as I'm concerned, Bob Reinhold appears to have disappeared from the *Times.*" Reinhold was not the only *Times*man who, in Rosenthal's opinion, was not contributing enough. After a Supreme Court analysis by Warren Weaver of the Washington bureau ran in the Review, Rosenthal wondered what had "happened" to Weaver as far as the daily news report was concerned. Was Weaver "coasting"? Rosenthal asked.

None of these complaints matched Rosenthal's explosive reaction when, in the spring of 1975, he learned that Harrison Salisbury was trying to get a visa to go to North Vietnam and to Cambodia. Salisbury was by then working as a Sunday special correspondent, no longer under Rosenthal's control. Salisbury was "stupid" to apply before checking with the news department, Rosenthal informed Max Frankel. "Salisbury knows damn well that this is not permissible." Hanoi was on the verge of victory in Vietnam and, as Rosenthal explained, he was trying through Washington, Paris, and other diplomatic channels to get visas for one of his own reporters (either Seymour Hersh, Flora Lewis, or Fox Butterfield). Rosenthal found out about Salisbury's encroachment onto news department turf only by accident; an alert foreign-desk clerk brought Rosenthal the cables that Salisbury wanted sent to his various Cambodian and North Vietnamese contacts. Worst of all in Rosenthal's view, Salisbury sent effusive personal greetings to the neutralist Prince Sihanouk "in the name of the *Times*."

Rosenthal's elbow-in-the-eye managerial style affected lower-echelon editors. When his assistant Allan Siegal was detached to study the plans for the *Times*' new computer system in early-1975, Siegal reported that the Sunday Arts and Leisure staff wanted an electronic device in the system "for hiding their stories from Rosenthal's departments." Sunday editor Frankel disowned the request, calling it "silly and destructive," the result of "a childish playing out of normal competitiveness."

The merger of the two departments with Rosenthal in control in 1976 settled who was working for whom. Rosenthal quickly turned to the planning of the new C sections, trying to shape each daily magazine to appeal to leisure-minded younger readers. The first Weekend appeared in April 1976; Rosenthal liked it. The tone was just right, "sophisticated but not nasty," he told the supervising editor, Arthur Gelb. Still, Rosenthal fussed with the details, asking that one of the shorter reviews on the Books of the Times page regularly be about arts or leisure activities, "since this is an entertainment and leisure section." When the Living section appeared in November 1976, Rosenthal advised editor Joan Whitman: "As we are aiming for wider audiences in the suburbs, could we not . . . in the future (1) Indicate where possible the branches that sell the items. Bloomingdale's, Altman's, Macy's all have such branches. (2) Spread the joy a little by trying to select some suburban stores where some of these items may be purchased."

Home came next, in March 1977. At a Manhattan party in late 1976, Rosenthal met the author Lois Gould; she talked about what people usually talk about when they have the attention of the editor of the *New York Times*. The *Times*, Gould said, needed a "special forum" where intelligent, involved women could be heard. From that conversation, Rosenthal developed the "Hers" column. Gould helped in the planning and was the first "Hers" columnist. Following Gould, "Hers" writers were rotated periodically from among a pool of women not on the *Times* staff.

Ideas as well as people caught Rosenthal's eye; he distributed to his editors copies of *The Good-Natured Gardener* and *The House Book*, the latter by Terence Conran of Conran's (a major home furnishings advertiser). After the first Home section appeared, Rosenthal conducted a postmortem. He instructed his editors to make sure that a Letters column always appeared in each Home (as well as in Living and Weekend). He wanted a minimum of three items in every Joan Kron column, "About The House." He changed the page position of the "Design Notebook," and ordered a New Haven dateline on a column by contributor William Zinsser, a former book editor of the *New York Herald Tribune* and a visiting professor at Yale. Three weeks later, the column still did not have a dateline and Rosenthal repeated his order. He fussed at Home editor Nancy Newhouse for allowing Kron and food writer Mimi Sheraton to have double bylines—two stories carrying their names in one edition of the paper. He pounced on a minor feature about the disruptions created by the building of the East 63rd Street subway tunnel. The story, he informed his editors, was not right for Home, the headline was wrong, and the writing bad. The writer, Tony Kornheiser, used "repeated gimmicks," Rosenthal complained (Kornheiser left the *Times* in 1979 and became a much-praised columnist for the *Washington Post*). In June, Rosenthal ordered Zinsser dropped; the three-month-old column wasn't "leading us anywhere." In September, he admonished Newhouse for hiring a free-lance writer to cover a topic that "an ordinary [staff] reporter" could handle. Later that month, he protested the use of a double byline again. In Home, right before the Thanksgiving holiday, he was dismayed to see a "Design Notebook" column on a cemetery; at the same time he complained that Linda Bird Francke, in residence as the "Hers" columnist, had become funereal herself, writing constantly about the trials of divorce and separation. Couldn't she give all the female depression a rest? Rosenthal asked Newhouse for stories more "appropriate" for Home, specifically, a feature on winterizing plants and shrubs for the suburban gardener and for apartment-house dwellers who have their own terraces (one percent of the city's population—at most). Three weeks later, Rosenthal complained to Newhouse that Home was too "Manhattan-oriented." He asked her to include more references to suburban shops and services in stories, repeating the request he had made of the Living editor, Joan Whitman.

Rosenthal knew what materials pleased the publisher; but he was guided as well by his own instincts. He trusted his judgment. In Poland as a correspondent, he had found a way to write about Auschwitz with a fresh eye (Salisbury's sniping to the contrary). Back in New York as metro editor, he looked at the city as a foreign correspondent might, and saw startling changes. One result was a long feature, commissioned by Rosenthal, on homosexuals in New York. It brought together in one story a fuller picture of homosexuality than had ever before appeared in any general daily paper. In 1971 Rosenthal argued for the publication of the Pentagon Papers. On the Op-Ed page of June 11, 1991, in a column marking the twentieth anniversary of the episode, he explained how he had come to his position: "If you know in your stomach" that government information stamped secret is essential to public understanding, then go ahead and print it. In January 1986, when the space shuttle *Challenger* exploded moments after launching, Rosenthal relied again on instinct. He cleared all advertising from the first ten pages of the *Times*, to give the story the "open" columns he felt it needed. Later, he detached a team of reporters to reconstruct the events leading up to the disaster. A half dozen reporters worked full time on the *Challenger* story for twelve weeks, traveling around the country, interviewing NASA scientists, visiting the builders of the rocket booster engines. "There was a lot of head shaking in the newsroom; all this cost, all this waste of manpower," recalled David Sanger, one of the reporters Rosenthal assigned to the story. But the reporting produced the *Times'* "O-rings" story, which pointed to the probable cause of the rocket-booster explosion. "That won us a Pulitzer Prize," Sanger said. "Rosenthal knew next to nothing about the space program or rocket technology, but he resolved to get 'the story.' He understood in his gut there was something there."

Rosenthal's stomach also enabled him to make decisions on the spot, often with excellent results. Anna Quindlen, who joined the *Times* as a general assignment reporter, flourished under Rosenthal— once past her first sentence-fragments story. In 1981, just four years after she was hired, she began writing the "About New York" column and building a loyal audience. In 1985, at the age of 35, she took a maternity leave. When the time came to return the next year, Quindlen wasn't sure what she wanted to do. Rosenthal heard that Quindlen had another offer. He called her to his office and asked her not to leave. As Quindlen tells it, "Abe said, 'Why not do a new column? We need a column. . . . Let's see . . . Thursdays we have something. How about Wednesdays? In the Living section? We need a name . . . Let's see, how old are you? . . . 36? 37? . . . Good, we'll call it Life in the 30s.' " Quindlen adds: "People later said to me that all kinds of market research must have gone into it. I tell them, 'Abe did it in three minutes.' "

The supportive Abe could give way at any time to the furious Abe. Les Ledbetter, one of the handful of black reporters in the *Times* news department in the early 1970s, sent a memo to Rosenthal about the *Times*' longstanding policy of denying the honorific "Mr." to anyone convicted of a felony. "I find this paper's style of taking the title 'Mr.' away from convicted felons to be offensive, archaic, and snobbish," Ledbetter began his memo to Rosenthal. "If nothing else, I would hope that the lesson learned from Attica and similar uprisings is that you only make men more bitter when you deny them their common claim to humanity." Rosenthal replied to Ledbetter: "I find your note to be offensive, arrogant, and snobbish. I find that your tone appears to put you on the side of those who do not know the difference between discussion and aggression and who, having decided on the validity of their own point of view, regard others as not worthy of being treated with dignity and thought. Do you like that? I don't suppose you do. Not any more than I like being addressed in a haranguing tone of typewriter." Rosenthal went on to say that *Times* editors had for years discussed "this whole Mister business" and that he was still not happy with *Times* policies. Rosenthal added that he welcomed hearing from his staff but "only on condition that you discuss things with me as you would wish me to discuss them with you." Les Ledbetter was not the only black reporter to feel the heat of Rosenthal's blast-furnace prose. C. Gerald Fraser, a *Times* reporter on the metro desk, obtained a wide-ranging interview with Roy Innis, the leader of the Congress on Racial Equality (CORE). Fraser's article covered, among other things, Innis's views on President Idi Amin of Uganda, on American Jews and their relations with Israel, and on racism in America. The article incensed Rosenthal; he told Mitchel Levitas, then his assistant, of his objections and asked Levitas to draft, in Rosenthal's name, a memo to David Jones, Fraser's editor. Levitas's draft began: "The Fraser piece today was both incompetent and vicious and I'd like to know how it got into the paper. Let me itemize my objections. . . ." Levitas listed six criticisms and concluded: "The only germ of a story here, and the only justification for devoting three-quarters of a column to this claptrap is in the last paragraph." Rosenthal edited out the first sentence, in order to begin, "let me itemize my objections." He also pared Levitas's conclusion to "The only germ of a story here is in the last paragraph."

Mostly, Rosenthal spoke in his own voice, without prompts. The Washington bureau became a regular target of his complaints after he was named managing editor in 1968. He was convinced that certain reporters tended to "editorialize" in their news stories. For example, they quoted congressional liberals more than conservatives, or more favorably. During the anti–Vietnam war rallies in October 1969, he complained of the "painfully loaded" words used by E. W. Kenworthy (Kenworthy described a speech as "portentous" in a story about the Nixon White House). A few weeks later, Rosenthal found what he called an "awry picture of America" in the *Times*. He singled out the editions of November 7: "On page 7 we have a story about the G.I. trial at Ft. Dix. On page 8 we have the MIT sit-in and on page 9 we have the moratorium. On page 13 we have the Army memorandum about the anti-war protest. On page 22, the Chicago trial. In between, two stories about poverty and housing demonstrations. On page 27 a story about job discrimination. There are others. This was not a particularly outstanding day for that kind of thing. But I get the impression, reading the *Times*, that the image we give of America is largely of demonstrations, discrimination, anti-war movements, rallies, protests, etc. Obviously all these things are an important part of the American scene. But I think that because of our own liberal interests and our reporters' inclination we overdo this. I am not suggesting eliminating any one of these stories. I am suggesting that reporters and editors look a bit more around them to see what is going on in other fields and to try to make an effort to represent other shades of opinion than those held by the new Left, the old Left, the middle aged Left and the anti-war people."

From the reporters' point of view, however, the editors were imposing their conservative views on the news. J. Anthony Lukas was the *Times* man assigned to the Chicago Seven conspiracy trial in the fall of 1969. Then thirty-seven, Lukas was already a Pulitzer Prize winner for his reporting of the Greenwich Village "hippie murder" case (the only Pulitzer for local reporting that the *Times* won during the Rosenthal years). A painstaking reporter and a perfectionist, Lukas was unhappy with the constraints he believed Rosenthal's editors put on his reporting. He complained that he couldn't cover the trial with the same freedom Nicholas von Hoffman of the *Washington Post* had. From the start, von Hoffman treated the story as a political show rather than a criminal trial. The *Post* man called the trial "a shoddy parody of jurisprudence," and he reviewed it as if it were street theater— produced by the country's richest backer, the U.S. government, directed by Abbie Hoffman ("public relations genius"), and starring Judge Julius Hoffman ("an aged hobbitt . . . with the voice of a man reading horror stories to small children") and Jerry Rubin ("free-lance wild man"). Von Hoffman, said Lukas, caught the trial's "tone and flavor in a way that has been almost impossible for those of us operating under tighter editing restrictions." While Lukas said that he understood Rosenthal's demands, nevertheless the *Times'* doctrine of "objectivity" made it difficult to give a true picture of the judge's erratic behavior in the courtroom. Lukas objected to the *Times'* display of his reporting—while page 22 was too prominent for Rosenthal, for Lukas it represented indecent burial. Moreover, the desk edited his copy with a leaden hand. One memorable day, Lukas reported, one of the defendants shouted "Chicken shit!" at Judge Hoffman. The desk deleted the "un-*Times*-like" language and substituted the phrase a "barnyard epithet."

When Lukas returned to New York, he shared some of his discontent with other *Times*people. One result was a bit of street theater at the paper itself, a series of informal after-hours meetings in the early months of 1970, attended by some of the *Times'* better-known reporters, critics, and middle-echelon editors. Part gripe session about the way stories were being handled and part social hour, the meetings involved at one time or another Tony Lukas, theater critic Clive Barnes, women's news editor Charlotte Curtis, and reporters Joseph Lelyveld, Martin Tolchin, William E. Farrell, and Paul Montgomery. Barnes was unhappy with his editors, in particular, the cultural desk's handling of his review of *Inquest*, a play about the Rosenberg "atom spy" case. Curtis thought the *Times* had failed to present a rounded picture of the Black Panthers (the group's separatist rhetoric usually was reported and not its self-help programs). The *Times*people at the meeting called themselves, self mockingly, "the cabal."

Rosenthal heard out some of the cabalists later at a dinner meeting one of his assistants arranged; he liked a good argument, though he was unlikely to change any of his beliefs. Political opinions didn't belong in cultural reviews, he argued, "Otherwise we would have ten extra political commentators on the paper." He talked about how decision making at the *Times* had broadened over the years; but newsrooms weren't democratic assemblies. Authority couldn't be diluted: "The news columns will not be made into a political broadsheet—period."

The cabalists didn't actually disband; they were never banded in the first place. "At our big meeting, at Bill Farrell's apartment on a Sunday, we went around the room airing our gripes, one after another, and found no two people had the same concerns," Joe Lelyveld remembered twenty years later. "I was worried about how my beautiful, flawless prose"—he smiled here—"was being treated. Others couldn't care less about me; they wanted to talk about their own troubles." Curtis moved out of the news department to the Op-Ed page. Barnes left the *Times* to become chief drama and dance critic of the *New York Post*. Montgomery went to the *Wall Street Journal*. Lelyveld stayed. His *Times* career was not hurt by his cabalistic role; in 1989 he became managing editor, the number-two position in the news department. Tony Lukas left the *Times* to free-lance. He had a last word of sorts, incorporating the chickenshit episode into a book, *The Barnyard Epithet and Other Obscenities: Notes on the Chicago Conspiracy Trial*. He also became a founding editor of MORE, a journalism review that regularly monitored press performance, including the *Times*', in the early years of the 1970s. When MORE ceased publication, Lukas became a full-time author, winning a second Pulitzer Prize for his book *Common Ground*, a thoroughgoing, humane study of the effects of school desegregation on three Boston families.

Post-cabal, Rosenthal remained vigilant, undeterred in his campaign to "keep the *Times* straight." He complained that a Washington story by Warren Weaver was "politically loaded." He thought metro reporter Frank Lynn injected an "editorial needle" into a City Hall story. He was preoccupied with the *Times'* coverage of student activism. Four years after his own Columbia bust story, he registered his dismay about a campus roundup story by Robert D. McFadden. The report was "editorialized in the extreme and terribly naïve," Rosenthal complained to Gelb. "The whole thrust of the first few paragraphs is to equate lack of political action and demonstrations on the campuses with sleepy-headedness, social indifference, and boredom. Who says so? Did it not occur to McFadden that a great many people believe that the purpose of a campus is not political action at all, but study? I really couldn't believe my eyes when I read those first three paragraphs."

By the mid-1970s, the war in Southeast Asia had been pronounced "Vietnamized" by the Nixon administration. The Congress ended the military draft, and college students returned to their books (and beer blasts). Rosenthal still had to contend with "editorialization" by some of his reporters. For the Sunday paper of August 12, 1979, Robert Reinhold did a feature timed to the tenth anniversary of Woodstock. Rosenthal didn't see Reinhold's story until early Saturday night, when he received the first edition of the paper. He immediately called the news desk to order removal of some of Reinhold's "vacuous politicalization." Reinhold had called Woodstock a symbol of a "national, cultural, and political awakening," and the event itself the "culmination of a decade-long youth crusade for a freer style of life, for peace and for tolerance." In the decade of the 1970s, Reinhold continued, radical politics "reverted to more conventional politics and even apathy." On Monday morning, Rosenthal did an exegesis of the story for his editors. Reinhold was implying that "there was a downward scale from radicalism to conventional politics," Rosenthal said. The editor's comment: "Good God!"

Rosenthal, clearly, tried to control the outputs of the *Times* word factory. A phone call from him could excise a displeasing phrase in a story; a note could insure the inclusion of a friendly name. He had the power to reward his favorites, someone like Quindlen, with prized assignments, while the force of his anger could drive a Lukas to consider another line of work. The pattern was unpredictable. The editor had powerful weapons to achieve consent; many of his staff were convinced that he had a shit list, and kept all the names fresh in his mind. Even if the paranoia was justified, Rosenthal was constrained by the tenure system of the *Times*, mandated by its contracts with the News-paper Guild. Once beyond a relatively short probation period, news department people could not be fired absent clear criminal behavior, such as a conviction for drug possession. Les Ledbetter and Ned Ken-worthy, both tenured, resigned on their own; Gerald Fraser and Robert Reinhold remained in the newsroom long after Rosenthal had left. Both the reach and the limits of Rosenthal's office were never better demonstrated than in the editor's long, painful dispute with Richard Severo, a member of the news department and a first-class reporter and writer.

If Rosenthal was a list keeper, then so was Severo. The descriptions applied to Rosenthal could just as well be applied to Severo: intelli-gent, determined, energetic, quick to anger, sensitive to slights (Severo said he discerned anti-Italianism in the attitudes of *Times* editors toward him). Severo and Rosenthal were, in many ways, more alike than either man would acknowledge. Each characterized the other with words eerily the same. Severo on Rosenthal: vindictive, stubborn, a bearer of grudges. Rosenthal on Severo: difficult to work with, ar-gumentive, enjoys feeling persecuted. Their dispute eventually be-came a formal arbitration procedure, and engaged lawyers, the Newspaper Guild, and the *Times'* senior management and outside counsel. It stretched on for seven years, longer than World War II. The arbitrator took ten thousand pages of testimony. Severo's attorney died shortly after the decision was announced. So did the arbitrator, who was suffering from cancer during the hearings.

Severo joined the *Times* in 1968, after working at the *Washington Post*, the Associated Press, the *New York Herald Tribune*, and CBS News. A science specialist, he had little to do with Rosenthal for twelve years, other than working in his newsroom. That all changed in De-cember 1981, when Severo did a two-part article on Lisa H., a young woman suffering from the disfiguring effects of neurofibromatosis, pop-ularly known as the Elephant Man's Disease. Severo decided to write a book on Lisa H., and share part of his earnings with her family ("I want to help Lisa, she is the bravest woman I have ever met," Severo said he told Rosenthal; the young woman had taken terrible abuse because of her looks, and yet remained "a bright, cheerful, well-adjusted person.") Severo's agent conducted an auction for the book rights. One of the auction participants—a losing bidder, it turned out—was Times Books, then part of the New York Times Company. From this point on, the narrative grows murky, clouded by lawyers' obfuscations. Rosenthal, both sides acknowledged, ordered the auction stopped on the grounds that the Lisa H. story was the *Times'* "intellectual property"—less pretentiously, Severo had collected the facts on company time. The point was narrowly correct but without real meaning: Scores of books written by *Times*men and -women developed out of *Times* assignments (including Rosenthal's own two books, compilations of *Times* reporters' published work). Severo's agent went ahead with the auction. Harper & Row's bid was accepted. According to Severo, Rosenthal then struck back: "He kicked me off science and sent me to the gulag of the metro desk, where I was given only cub reporter assignments." Severo's union, the Newspaper Guild, brought a formal grievance action against the *Times*, charging the editors were using the assignment process to punish the reporter for taking his book elsewhere. For three and a half years Severo was on an unpaid leave of absence while the case lurched forward. To him, the fight was about principle. He spent much of his free time reporting and writing a new book, on the use of Agent Orange in Vietnam.

During the arbitration hearings, Rosenthal acted by turns provocative and bemused. On several occasions, he responded to the questions of Severo's lawyer, Philip D. Tobin, by calling Tobin "boy" ("Get on with your questions, boy"). Other times Rosenthal played the part of the busy executive inconvenienced by the proceedings. "The book story was a pure concoction. Severo's transfer had nothing to do with the book," Rosenthal testified. "They were two separate episodes." The *Times'* science editors felt they could not work with Severo, Rosenthal explained. Severo was endlessly adversarial. He argued about being edited. He took too long with stories. Further, how Rosenthal's editors dealt with Severo was their business; as executive editor of the *Times*, he didn't have time for such newsroom minutiae. The *Times* also said principle was involved; its counsel argued that any limit the arbitrator put on management's right to assign its employees where it wished would be a violation of the freedom of the press provisions of the First Amendment.

In September 1988, the arbitrator ruled for the *Times*, accepting the argument that Severo's transfer was within management rights by the terms of its Newspaper Guild contract. The next month, Severo exercised his rights of tenure, and returned to the *Times*. "I fought the good fight," he said later. "It would have been cowardly not to return." Rosenthal, too, remembered himself on the barricades of personal honor. "Severo was disruptive, and his editors begged me to get him out of science," Rosenthal said. "If the editor of the *Times* doesn't have the right to move a reporter from one desk to another, then that's the end of the paper." By then, Rosenthal had left the newsroom, and was enjoying his new life as a columnist.

Severo's story did not end as happily. Four years after the arbitrator's decision, Severo said he was still being punished. In the new regime of the "benevolent" Max Frankel, Severo said, he finally got transferred from the metro desk . . . to the job of preparing death notices for the obituary desk, a gulag colder and more demeaning than metro. He also had another bitter fight with the *Times*, again over a book, his study of Agent Orange. The book, praised by reviewers around the country, was dismissed in the *Book Review*, as we will see. Severo believed he was being pursued by his doppelganger from beyond the grave. His victim's fantasy was understandable. Rosenthal reacted to the Lisa H. deal all out of proportion to the "offense"— though consistently with his behavior through the years. The issue, as usual, was doing things his way.

The legend of Rosenthal's infamous shit list still left unresolved the more compelling narrative. Was the product of the word factory different in significant respects in the Rosenthal years than it might have been under the control of another editor? Broadly put, the question defied answers. Limited to a specific example of coverage, it became more manageable. The *Times'* treatment of the subject of homosexuality, and later, of AIDS, has been amply documented. It was said, on the record and off the record, by the staff and by outside critics, that Abe Rosenthal was a homophobe. Supposedly, the newsroom explicitly understood this, and as a result, the *Times* initially "ignored" the AIDS epidemic. Supposedly, too, the *Times'* AIDS coverage didn't measurably improve until Rosenthal was succeeded by Frankel (an executive praised by the same staff and critics for his enlightened attitudes). If an editor can be said to make a difference, then the evidence should emerge in the contrasting ways the *Times* dealt with AIDS in the Rosenthal and Frankel years.

*　　*　　*

"Rare Cancer Seen in 41 Homosexuals," read the headline over the first *Times* report in its coverage of the AIDS pandemic. The story appeared on July 3, 1981, on page A-20; it ran for the length of a column and carried the byline of Lawrence Altman, the *Times'* chief medical reporter. Altman had an M.D. degree; before coming to the *Times*, Altman had been on the staff of the Centers for Disease Control, part of the U.S. Public Health Service. His specialty was epidemiology, and the July 3 story was written from materials in *Morbidity and Mortality Weekly Report*, a CDC journal for which young Dr. Altman once wrote. Noting the appearance of Kaposi's sarcoma—the "rare cancer," hardly ever seen in otherwise healthy young men— Altman approached his first story from the point of view of the medical epidemiologist-detective: the sudden onslaught of Kaposi's "could have as much scientific as public health importance because of what it may teach us about determining the causes of more common types of cancer."

Altman's theoretic frame for the story served to downplay its human interest aspect. Yet one of the principal efforts of the Rosenthal years was aimed at getting more such stories in the *Times* news report. Typically, the old, pre-Rosenthal *Times* stressed "policy" over "people." Rosenthal received his first major attention as an editor when he ordered up the front-page feature of December 17, 1963, on New York's homosexual community. That story talked of the "problem" of homosexuality, and explicitly spoke of homosexuals and other "degenerates" (in the spirit of the early 1960s). While the story quoted police officials who had to deal with such "outlaw" behavior, homosexual spokesmen received a sympathetic hearing. Seven years later, Rosenthal's metro staff reported on the growing militancy of homosexuals, again with a degree of empathy, and again on page one.

Rosenthal experienced that militancy directly, beginning in the early 1970s. Representatives of gay and lesbian groups complained to him that the *Times* did not give adequate coverage to Gay Pride parades, that it neglected to carry news of violence directed at homosexuals, and that it routinely turned down story suggestions from gay and lesbian groups. An exchange between Rosenthal and Ronald Gold, communications director of the National Gay Task Force, was typical of the back-and-forth correspondence of the 1970s. Gold faulted the *Times* for a reference to a "homosexual torture ring" in a news story from Houston in the editions of July 1, 1974. (A "heterosexual torture ring,"

Gold told Rosenthal, "is a big circle of editors all telling fag jokes.")
Gold also criticized the *Times'* coverage of the Gay Pride Parade two
weeks before. According to Gold, the *Times* reporter assigned to the
story counted the number of marchers at the beginning of the parade
rather than at the end, thus underrepresenting the size of the parade by
a factor of four. Gold thought the *Times* should have done an article
summing up the events of Gay Pride week; further, the *Times* missed
a good story about a Solemn High Mass held by gay Roman Catholics
at an Episcopal church. Then, adopting a conversational tone, Gold
told Rosenthal of "my three-year-old dream. Perhaps it was too much
to think you'd print a schedule [of the gay community's plans for the
week] like the free ad you ran for the Newport Jazz Festival. Just a nice
compressed local feature. . . ."

Rosenthal replied brusquely, waking the dreamer from his reveries.
Gold just didn't understand how the *Times* was edited; "You are balancing your desires in coverage as against what we do and deciding that
since your desires are not fulfilled there must be something wrong with
us. . . . We will not substitute your judgment for ours any more than
we would substitute the judgment of any industry, community, or
special interest group." Rosenthal did concede Gold a point on the
Houston story. "I agree that the expression 'ring' is an unfortunate one.
This is a large paper with a great many people writing under a great
many pressures of time, and occasionally expressions get through that
we would prefer not to see."

The Gold-Rosenthal exchange was typical. Through his years as
editor Rosenthal kept sounding the theme of "news judgment." While
he talked in public about the need for objective standards in the *Times*,
he made clear to his editors that such judgments were, in the end,
personal. Homosexuals, and later AIDS, were treated as news stories,
he said, "no more, no less." But because "it did come down to what
goes in and what stays out," only the editor can make those decisions.
Rosenthal exercised that power whenever he could. In the fall of 1977,
for example, Sydney Schanberg, his distinguished overseas service
behind him, was back in New York, on a senior editing track, and
being talked about as the "next Abe Rosenthal." Like Rosenthal a
decade before, Schanberg was running the *Times* metro desk and
seeing New York with the fresh eye of a foreign correspondent. In a
memo to Rosenthal, Schanberg proposed major new treatment of the
homosexual community of New York, which he described as "large

and increasingly middle class." According to Schanberg, "many people still think of homosexual life in terms of interior decorators, Fire Island, and leather bars, but increasingly it's also very much a world of lawyers, physicians, teachers, politicians, clergymen and other upper-middle-class professional men and women who, aside from their sexual preference, live like their 'straight' counterparts."

Rosenthal replied that while he would always give attention to Schanberg's ideas, he didn't "want a whole bunch of stories or a series. A great amount of coverage at this time would simply seem naïve and déjà vu." It was "a question of perspective" for the *Times*: "Yes, there are many homosexuals, just as there are many of almost everything in New York. I have a gut feeling that if we embark upon a series for now or a bunch of pieces, it would be overkill." And here he set down his principle of inclusion-exclusion, old hand instructing the new man: "There is also the question of exactly what it is we want to do with our space. Space is gold. The proper use of space is the essence of our existence, because it reflects our taste and judgment. . . . It is the areas of taste and judgment that, in the long run, are our most important areas of responsibility." Schanberg's ambitious series never appeared.

There is still a leap from "gut feeling" to "phobia." Journalist James Kinsella investigated the Rosenthal years at the *Times* in his study *Covering the Plague: AIDS and the American Media*. Rosenthal's fractious personality and his imperious newsroom behavior engaged Kinsella principally as they affected his larger interest, how the *Times*—in his words, "the agenda setter for major national news"—and other news organizations covered the rise and spread of acquired immune deficiency syndrome in the 1980s. Kinsella argued the general thesis that AIDS went uncovered in the early years first and foremost because mainstream journalists didn't know any of its victims. In Kinsella's view, journalism actively pursued the story only when personal connections were made—specifically, when "people like us" succumbed to AIDS. Thus the death of Rock Hudson in October 1985, at the age of fifty-nine, put AIDS on the front pages. A popular, well-known actor, someone "like us," Hudson was actually a closet homosexual. Now that was news! Implicit, too, in Kinsella's argument was the notion that mainstream journalism initially regarded the deaths of homosexual men and IV-drug abusers as not worth reporting in detail.

The argument was flawed. Mainstream journalism's indifference to the first AIDS deaths reflected not the victims' marginality but their ordinariness. In America, and in the *Times*, all men do not die equal. Contemporary journalism celebrates celebrity; the AIDS cases, pre–Rock Hudson, failed the media test of social status. The early narrative also lacked the hot-button elements that make events involving the uncelebrated newsworthy. When the modes of virus transmission were more clearly understood, editors had the sensational charge the AIDS story needed (though they were often too tongue-tied to speak up, as the record will show). Logically, too, Kinsella was on uncertain ground. If New York City in the 1980s had, by Kinsella's own (wildly improbable) estimate, a population of 600,000 to 1 million homosexuals, then it's hard to accept that no one at the *Times* knew anyone with AIDS or was likely to be at risk himself. Even if New York's homosexual population was half or a third Kinsella's estimate, it was still unlikely that no one at the *Times* would know what was going on in the city.

Nevertheless, Kinsella raised valid questions. If the *Times'* staff wasn't ignorant of what certainly was going on outside its doors—and just as certainly, inside—why the failure to give the AIDS story the attention it deserved? Several factors inhibited every news organization's coverage, starting with the federal government's initially slow response to AIDS, and the significant areas of medical ignorance about the origins of AIDS. But the *Times* had one hundred reporters and editors working for the Metro pages (looking for "trends" in the city, Rosenthal said). Besides Larry Altman, the M.D., there were ten other specialists on the medicine-science-technology desk, the largest such reporting staff in American journalism. The staff put out Science Times every Tuesday. Kinsella offered a number of explanations for the reporters' performance. Some had their own priorities. According to Kinsella, Altman was intrigued with artificial-heart research and became convinced that it would be the medical story of the decade. But Kinsella looked beyond the reporters, the desk editors, and the staff to the top editor. Kinsella heard the same voices every *Times* monitor encountered; his principal explanation for the *Times'* inattentive coverage was that Abe Rosenthal fostered a "homophobic atmosphere" in the newsroom. As a result, homosexual men at the *Times* kept their distance from the editor, and heterosexual reporters shied from proposing stories about AIDS.

Kinsella made a serious allegation, one with much greater resonance than whether Rosenthal's friends—a Jerzy Kosinski, a Beverly Sills, or a Betty Friedan—were treated as cultural icons, or whether the designer windows of a *Times* advertiser like Macy's were accorded special news coverage. By mid-1991, 20,000 New York City residents had died from complications resulting from AIDS. As of the same date, more than 30,000 New Yorkers had been diagnosed as having AIDS and an estimated 150,000 other New Yorkers were HIV-positive—their blood, when tested, indicated the presence of the AIDS virus. No vaccine or curative treatment was then in sight. Indifferent or tardy reporting of AIDS by the presumptive journalistic agenda setter would affect the federal health establishment's own responses. But Kinsella marshaled no direct proof of Rosenthal's homophobia. He cited "reports" of the use of the words *faggot* and *queer* at editorial meetings, without attributing these slurs to Rosenthal. Kinsella interviewed Max Frankel, who also passed on second-hand information: Some staff people had told Frankel of their belief that "if reporters [during the Rosenthal regime] got to be known as excessively interested in homosexuals or were themselves thought to be homosexuals, something would happen to them."

Kinsella offered indirect evidence of homophobia, such as the *Times'* treatment of the news about a virus affecting the dancing Lippizaner horses of Austria. The story of the illness of the horses, a Viennese tourist attraction, appeared on page one of the *Times* of March 28, 1981. The prominence of the account, juxtaposed with the modest attention given the Kaposi's story by Altman and his editors two years earlier, made for obvious irony. It did not advance a theory of the *Times'* willful neglect of AIDS. The Lippizaner treatment proved only that on one day, one offbeat "medical mystery" caught the interest of a single page-one meeting.

Larry Kramer, the playwright and a founder of the Gay Men's Health Crisis organization, went over some of the same ground, collecting examples of what he considered to be the *Times'* selective attention to AIDS in the Rosenthal years. Thus, Kramer compared the *Times'* initial AIDS coverage with its coverage of the Tylenol tampering case in 1982. Containers of the nonprescription drug Tylenol had been opened, laced with cynanide, and returned to supermarket shelves in the Chicago area. Seven Tylenol poisoning cases were reported over a three-month span. By Kramer's calculations, the *Times* wrote about the Tylenol contamination story on fifty-four separate occasions; on four days, the story made page one. By contrast, said Kramer, in the first nineteen months of the AIDS epidemic, with the number of cases totaling one thousand, only seven AIDS stories appeared in the *Times*, none on page one. Again, the "pattern" demonstrated little other than the fact that *Times* editors judged the Tylenol story to be big news. Tens of millions of consumers take over-the-counter pills for headaches and minor pains each day; hundreds of products lie on supermarket shelves, vulnerable to criminal tampering (the makers of such products have since developed "tamper-proof" containers). Kramer assembled other such examples. He compared the *Times*' AIDS coverage with the coverage in other big-city newspapers, including the *Washington Post* and the *Philadelphia Inquirer*. In one period in 1983, New York City was reporting more new AIDS cases each week than the *yearly* totals for Washington and Philadelphia combined. Yet, according to Kramer, the *Times* lagged behind the *Post* and the *Inquirer* in both the number of AIDS stories published and in the quality of the reporting. To him, the case for Rosenthal's and the *Times*' homophobia was obvious. Rosenthal was a "monster" and the *Times* "the enemy of gay men and women," Kramer declared. Seven years later, Kramer explained his anger at the *Times* in an interview in the magazine *Tikkun*. "If the public had been told that a transmissible disease was going around and that they had to start cooling it, an awful lot of people who are dead would be alive today," he said. "I harp on the *Times* because . . . it has the most influence."

In my own interviewing of *Times*people I heard many of the same charges; one editor remembered being present in a group when Rosenthal complained about "the place being full of Ivy League fags." The man, an Ivy League graduate *and* a homosexual, nevertheless had been hired by Rosenthal and his career had flourished during the Rosenthal years. Still, it's easy to accept the argument that a "perception" of homophobia existed among the *Times* staff. Anyone who has worked in a newsroom—Kinsella served as editorial-page editor of the *Los Angeles Herald Examiner*—understands that what Rosenthal thought mattered perhaps less than what the *Times* staff *believed* Rosenthal thought. Consequently, no knowledgeable outsider has difficulty accepting the *Times* reporters' belief that their proposals for stories about AIDS, and about the homosexual victims of AIDS, stood a poor chance of being published. At the same time, no executive, however energetic, is able to take every supervisory editor aside for instruction, let alone every staff member. In large news organizations, the institutional values filter down from the top to the bottom: They are "in the air." The word "osmosis," not so incidentally, often came up in talks about news work with *Times* reporters and desk editors.

Subtly or unsubtly, the newsroom atmospherics began shifting at the *Times* in 1983. The staff's gut perceptions, and the day-to-day news coverage, changed as well. Punch Sulzberger and his editor Rosenthal were under renewed pressures from gay and lesbian organizations to pay more attention to AIDS. The homosexual "community" in New York was, as Schanberg suggested, mainly young, white, middle class, and well educated (in many ways, its members resembled the model reader of the "new" *New York Times*). By the spring of 1983 it also had gotten organized. Sulzberger's assistant, Sydney Gruson, held a meeting at the *Times* with representatives of homosexual organizations. Rosenthal later met separately with the representatives. One of the participants at both meetings, Virginia Apuzzo, then executive director of the National Gay Task Force, later described the session with Rosenthal as "Gays and AIDS 101."

Rosenthal was a good student. He came out of the meetings with several story ideas, including a suggestion for a story on Apuzzo, who worked in the administration of New York Governor Mario Cuomo. Always the news hound, constantly pushing the *Times* to be on top of trends, Rosenthal "began to demand more on AIDS," according to Kinsella. Within three months of the Gays and AIDS 101 meeting, the *Times* produced a two-part examination of the impact of AIDS on "ordinary people." Each article ran almost 3,500 words on consecutive days in June 1983.

Gradually, staff fears of retribution because of too-close "identification" with gay and lesbian topics dissipated—at least sufficently for story suggestions to flow up the newsroom hierarchy to Rosenthal. *Times* reporter Susan Heller Anderson was told by a friend—a man she described as a homosexual and a physician—to expect a surge in AIDS cases. Anderson passed on her friend's views to Edward Klein, then editor of the *Times Magazine,* and offered to do an article for the *Magazine*. Klein, in turn, told Rosenthal of the doctor's expectation of "tremendous" death tolls "among homosexuals in the creative areas of life, such as dance, fashion, advertising, music, etc." Klein said he was prepared to give the assignment to Anderson but thought that

Rosenthal might want the story instead for the news pages. Rosenthal sent on Klein's memo to Richard Flaste of the science desk, calling the information "interesting." Rosenthal added: "It seems to me to be a daily story and one that should be handled by your department."

Rosenthal's *Times* continued to irritate some of its angrier critics. Spokesmen from homosexual groups complained about the paper's refusal to use the word gay as a noun in its news columns. Rosenthal replied that the usage was "too politicized." *Times* editors also elided—for reasons of "good taste"—some of the specific facts of virus transmission. The omissions contributed to the "mystery" of AIDS; what did the phrase "intimate sexual contact" actually mean? Clifton Daniel, long retired but still a careful reader, chided Rosenthal when the *Times* missed the story of Esmé O'Brien Hammond, "a socially prominent New Yorker," as Daniel described her, who had died of AIDS as a result of a blood transfusion. Both New York tabloids, the *Post* and the *News*, included that information in their stories; the *Times* made no mention of AIDS. "I take the trouble to mention this to you," Daniel wrote, "because I had difficulties with a certain squeamishness on the *Times* when I was there, and I keep hoping someone will overcome it, while maintaining the paper's standards of good taste." Rosenthal replied in his elbow-in-the-face style. He turned the letter over to his associate Allan Siegal, who did a Nexis search; it produced forty-eight references to "anal intercourse" in *Times*' stories about AIDS in the period 1981 to 1986. The printout was sent on to Daniel with a covering note signed by Rosenthal. "Dear Clifton: 48!" the letter read in entirety. Daniel replied that while he was "gratified to learn that the subject of sodomy is being so well covered these days, and that, journalistically speaking, the *New York Times* has come out of the closet," the number of references to anal intercourse "is not exactly responsive to the question I raised" about Mrs. Hammond.

The *Times* was not alone in its initial squeamishness. Other newspapers also discreetly drew the Victorian curtain across too-graphic references to sexual practices that caused tears in the rectal tissue, or to the swallowing of semen during oral intercourse (both possible ways of HIV transmission). But the *Times*' elisions invariably attracted more attention than the parallel shortcomings of other news organizations—such was the burden of being the standard of journalistic performance. Some AIDS organizations had adopted the slogan "Silence Equals Death." The obverse was, in their minds, "Publicity Equals Funding."

Late in 1986, when Punch Sulzberger announced his decision to appoint Max Frankel executive editor, Rosenthal began the shift to his new role of columnist. AIDS activists shifted their focus a bit. Larry Kramer, for example, moved from the Gay Men's Health Crisis center to Act Up (AIDS Coalition to Unleash Power). Kramer no longer denounced "the *Times*" or "the editor." Rather, he criticized individual *Times* reporters, for their supposed failures in AIDS coverage. The criticism took highly public form. Kramer acknowledged "creative responsibility" for the Act Up campaign aimed at *Times* medical writer Gina Kolata. In the late winter of 1990, Act Up members affixed stickers on *Times* vending boxes around New York City. "Gina Kolata is the worst AIDS reporter in America," the stickers read.

A year later, the guerrilla attacks let up. The *Times* was no longer regarded as the enemy. Allan Siegal amended the newsroom stylebook to allow the word "gay" to be used interchangeably with "homosexual." Reporters came out of the closet, sometimes right into the columns of the "About Men" feature in the *Times Magazine*, to talk of their sexual orientation and HIV-positive status. The new publisher, Arthur Sulzberger, sent a message of support to a national association of gay and lesbian journalists, the new *Times* publicly aligning itself with its cause.

Perhaps the most dramatic "outing" at the *Times* involved Jeffrey Schmalz, a 1975 graduate of Columbia University who began working for the paper while still a student. Schmalz is a homosexual, "a reporter with AIDS who covers AIDS," he informed *Times* readers in a remarkable article that appeared in the Week in Review section on December 20, 1992. He is also a self-described "by-the-book *Times*-man." He rose quickly through the ranks to become one of the youngest city editors at the paper; by 1980, he was a regional editor. Then, he says, his career trajectory stalled: "The executive editor at the time, Abe Rosenthal, was not comfortable with homosexuals, and so I was reassigned in 1984." Pressed to be more specific, Schmalz conceded that Rosenthal "never made his homophobia explicit to me. My understanding is, he called in my editor and said, 'I want that guy off the desk.' " Schmalz returned to reporting, and got a somewhat lateral assignment, career-wise, to cover politics out of the state capital in Albany. After Rosenthal left the newsroom, Schmalz returned to New York and to editing, this time on the national news desk.

One day in late 1990 Schmalz rose from his computer terminal and suddenly fell to the newsroom floor. He was having an epileptic sei-zure—an early sign of the advance of the AIDS virus. Max Frankel was among those who rushed to Schmalz's side. Over the next several months Schmalz rallied, returned to the paper, and fell sick again. "In February 1992, I almost died," he says matter-of-factly. He had brain surgery, took the drug AZT, and by the fall was well enough to cover the presidential campaign. In March 1993, his T-cell count stood at 0 to 2 (the normal count is 1,000); but he was working full-time again—in fact, he was writing and talking about his own experiences as a gay, HIV-positive man in the *Times* newsroom, breaking the informal barriers *Times*people ordinarily throw up around their work. "I am going to die of AIDS—so my life's now a gift," he explained. "That's why I speak now. When a homophobic editor took me off the desk, I didn't fight it. I was cowardly. When I got AIDS, I decided not to be cowardly anymore. I would speak out."

There was also a practical side to his decision. "AIDS is a good news story. I was and am a child of the *Times*. I know how to work the paper, how to get play for stories, what language to use." For Schmalz, too, the *Times* was more than a way to get good display for his stories. He didn't march or contribute to AIDS groups: He was a *Times* reporter first, an AIDS sufferer second. He was single, he lived alone; "The newsroom is my support group." The paper, he said, was changing under the younger Sulzberger, Frankel, and Lelyveld—"They've hired more women, blacks, gays." A listener, skeptical, wondered about the *Times'* new enlightenment; perhaps demographic factors—the size and relative affluence of the homosexual community in the city—made "gay news" more compelling to management, and to advertisers. Schmalz appeared to consider the idea for a long moment. Well, "Frankel was sincere—there were real tears in his eyes" as he bent over the fallen Schmalz. But yes, perhaps "the *Times* is an institution driven by trends and politics."

As for Rosenthal, after Schmalz went public with his illness, the former editor took the reporter to lunch. "He said there had been a ter-rible misunderstanding on the part of the middle-level editors," Schmalz reports. *Imagine them thinking that he was homophobic!* Schmalz did not challenge Rosenthal's account. "I thought to myself, The fact that he took me to lunch 'to clear things up,' that was enough for me."

There were no more complaints about the "homophobic" Abe

Rosenthal. Columnist A. M. Rosenthal began referring to the AIDS epidemic as "the story of the decade" in his Op-Ed page space. He, as much as anyone, could read the new spirit of the day. By 1992 the transformation was complete. Together with his wife, Shirley Lord, he became a regular at the charity balls and fashion-industry cocktail parties intended to raise funds for AIDS research and care.

To their credit, the activist critics avoided overly glib analyses of Rosenthal's psyche. But the proposition that Rosenthal somehow kept the AIDS story from being reported nevertheless misrepresented the news department's overall record, and failed to take into account how the *Times* worked. A more thorough analysis would have included the Sulzberger family and its attitudes about "Gays and AIDS 101." The role of the publisher was ignored by Kramer and mentioned only in passing by Kinsella, who reported that Punch Sulzberger—and his mother Iphigene Sulzberger—were furious after the *Times'* Sunday Travel section of April 6, 1975, ran a free-lance writer's rollicking article about a week-long all-gay cruise from Florida to the Yucatan. The marketing strategies of the *Times* and their effects on Rosenthal's news judgments also remained unexplored. The *Times'* energies in the early 1980s were still being channeled into its new sections and the related drive to build suburban circulation. An upbeat news report in the *Times* would please a number of crowds—among others, affluent readers and upper-end retail advertisers. If Rosenthal's *Times* was slow to move on the AIDS story, it was not solely "because of" Rosenthal's homophobia; there were other reasons: reporter Altman's interests, the editors' efforts to keep the paper "light and up"—as Sulzberger desired—and, probably, lower-ranking editors' beliefs about Rosenthal's homophobia. But Rosenthal was too much the competitive newsman to leave out the ingredient of serious news from his soup. He began giving the AIDS pandemic the attention it deserved.

In the end, too, the efforts of the cottage industry to "explain" Rosenthal fell short because the quest was poorly framed. It was never "his" *Times*; he was an employee. He worked for the Sulzbergers' *Times*. Even as a hired hand, Rosenthal served as junior member of the team. He and his merry henchmen of the news department were pushed, prodded, and pulled along by Walter Mattson on the business side. The critics concentrated on Rosenthal, snarling and aggressive, king of the third-floor newsroom. They didn't see Rosenthal, the serv-

ing man, attentive to his ringmasters. Rosenthal was not a paper tiger.
He wasn't a monster, either. A midregister interpretation would sketch
a competitive, angry, exuberant journalist, always looking over his
shoulder, worrying about his prerogatives, fearful of those he believed
out to challenge his authority. He constantly dramatized. He would
have made a good tabloid journalist if he hadn't gone to work for the
Times: the Bronx boy's tale of the ketchup sandwiches, beautiful Nehru
and tacky Poland, poor Kitty Genovese, the rape of Kosinski. He con-
fided to his friend Gay Talese that 1968 was the worst year of his life.
He was "sitting shivah" (the Jewish practice of mourning the dead).
What events of 1968 had driven him into a mournful state? The Robert
F. Kennedy assassination? The mounting American casualties in Viet-
nam? The turmoil on university campuses? The street riots at the Dem-
ocratic National Convention in Chicago? Richard M. Nixon's election?
No. His friend, James Greenfield, wasn't the new *Times* bureau chief
in Washington. Punch Sulzberger had rejected Rosenthal-candidate
Greenfield at the behest of James Reston, who conspired to put in his
own man, Tom Wicker. Reston had won the *Times'* great New York–
Washington power struggle. A decade later, in the fall of 1978,
Rosenthal wrote his friend Jerzy Kosinski about another "worst time" of
his life. The *Times* was shut by a strike; he had torn his knee cartilage
and was (again) on crutches; a group of women at the *Times* was bringing
a class-action suit against the paper, charging sex discrimination; his
wife, Ann, was going in for a doctor's appointment, and "if she turned
out to be pregnant, I was going to kill myself." And then the boy-from-
the-Bronx punch line: "She wasn't and I didn't."

Perhaps the best character analysis of the stormy, emotional
Rosenthal came from Tom Wicker, who observed Rosenthal for over
three decades. According to Wicker, "Rosenthal succeeded not because of his brilliance but because of his tenacity. Over the years, he
shot down all possible rivals. He was the great infighter, who wanted
power." Wicker said he noticed a new Rosenthal since the passing of
his power. Others, too, commented upon Rosenthal's new wife, his
newly styled hair, his Paul Stuart suits, the calm demeanor and the
ready smile. "The Most Happy Fella," the writer Jeanie Kasindorf
called him in a *New York* magazine feature article illustrated with
photographs of Abe and Shirley Rosenthal in black tie at a Costume
Institute gala at the Metropolitan Museum of Art.

Rosenthal signed a book contract in 1987. Six years later, he had not produced a manuscript. The project remained vague. "It's not really a memoir," he told me. Then abruptly rising, and looking down at the tips of his tasseled shoes, he added: "I don't know what it is right now. I don't know the publication date. . . . Well, it's a book." Whatever the project's final form, it will allow him to talk back to the axe grinders and the writers of dog shit—when he can find the time. Abe and Shirley Rosenthal are out four or five times a week during the New York social season.

A DAY IN THE LIFE
3:05 P.M.—3:45 P.M.

3:05 P.M.

Carlin Romano, a forty-year-old critic and journalist, arrived for his appointment with the managing editor, Arthur Gelb. After four decades with the *Times,* the sixty-five-year-old Gelb saw himself as the exuberant, excitable newshound, still on the prowl for new talent. Romano and Gelb had met at a party; Gelb said that he knew, and admired, Romano's writings, particularly some of his free-lance critical essays. Gelb asked Romano to come in for an interview, "if you're looking." At the time, Romano was a fellow at the Gannett Center for Media Studies at Columbia University, on leave from the *Philadelphia Inquirer.* The year-long Columbia fellowship gave him the breathing space, as he told friends, "to consider my options." Romano had been a philosophy major at Yale; after college he worked as a reporter for the *Washington Post.* In 1980 he joined the *New York Daily News* as a feature writer and later became the book editor of the *Inquirer.* He and Gelb talked for forty minutes, mostly about books and how cultural news should be covered. Romano spent another thirty minutes with John Lee, an assistant managing editor responsible for supervising the *Times'* arts and cultural coverage.

Romano was unsure whether he wanted to write criticism or do cultural reporting for the *Times.* On one side, he told himself, "There's the prestige of the place: no other book review outlet commanded as much attention." Against that, he counted the drawbacks: "First, the careful, constrained, 'balanced' way that *Times* people have to write, even as critics. Second, the authority-bound system"—all those editing layers. "And now there were the new rules on outside work." Much like the Washington bureauman Steve Roberts, who wanted to build up his regular panelist's role on public television, Romano hoped to continue writing for magazines and other journals. The *Times'* "free-lance noose" made him hesitate. Still, he was curious to see the inside of the institution, and he enjoyed his interviews with Gelb and Lee. They agreed to talk again, and arrange for Romano to meet other *Times* editors.

3:10 P.M.

On the street below, the one-ton newsprint rolls that *Times* driver Mike Casanova trucked down from the Bronx were carted to the laydown area, preparatory to being loaded on the presses. Casanova backed his rig away from the bay carefully; he had exactly six inches of clearance on each side of his truck. His workday was over. In the laydown area, the rolls were lowered to the reel room in the subbasement.

The reel room work crew placed the newsprint rolls on Y-shaped reels. Each reel carried three rolls of paper. Pressman Richard Manning began making up the paster pattern. These strips of tape joined one roll of paper to another roll, so that the paper continuously feeds into the presses, located one floor above. Working in the pressroom, Ed Gruneberg webbed up the presses, leading the newsprint sheets into the equipment that printed the pages. The *Times* had nine presses in all. Both Manning and Gruneberg wore the flat paper hats that pressmen have used for generations to keep ink out of the hair (and declare their pride of craft).

3:30 P.M.

Anthony Lewis finished half of a draft of his Tower column before leaving for MIT across the Charles River.

The *Times* editorial board heard from its second visitor of the day: the U.S. Ambassador to El Salvador John Walker.

Ambassador Walker arrived on crutches. He had gone sky-diving, broken his leg, and wound up in Walter Reed Army hospital in Washington—in the same wing where General José Napoleon Duarte, the president of El Salvador, was being treated for cancer of the liver. Walker gave the *Times* editors his reading of the political situation in El Salvador. The leftist guerrillas had proposed elections in September rather than March, the ambassador said, adding that he didn't believe the guerrillas wanted elections at all. Duarte's precarious health further complicated the outlook. Walker was told of the visit of Guatemala President Cerezo to the editorial board earlier in the day, and the ambassador added a small footnote about the president's entourage: The woman cabinet minister was Cerezo's mistress; so was the other woman in the group (another gap, the editors realized, in the *Times Magazine* article).

Barbara Gamarekian read through the afternoon pile of press releases and invitations from, among others, the Smithsonian, the Library of Congress, the Folger Shakespeare Library, and the National Capital Children's Museum. She began her rewrite of the women-diplomats feature, interweaving the materials from her interview. Three phone calls interrupted her work. Her calls from the morning, seeking comment on the private lives of the Congress, were being returned. Gamarekian had begun as a journalist in Washington in the 1960s, and her contacts were excellent. She talked to Gary Hymel, a lobbyist who once worked on the staff of Representative Thomas "Tip" O'Neill, the former Speaker of the House; to Horace Busby, a former assistant to Lyndon B. Johnson, and now a Washington consultant; and to Marty Davis, the high-profile wife of Congressman Robert Davis of California.

In New York, David Jones, the editor of the National edition, answered his phone. He wasn't able to talk: "The afternoons are killers here," he told his caller. The National edition of the *Times* was transmitted via satellite to eight plants around the United States, where the signals were reconverted into printed pages. Jones and his overworked staff were publishing a full-sized paper, every day. They took the copy and photographs from the "basic" *Times*—the four-section paper, available in the New York area and the Northeast corridor—and reedited the materials to produce the two-section paper for satellite transmission. It was no cut-and-paste job. Some days, several stories had to be recast, to make the materials "more national." There were as well changes of position and display: What was judged of page-one importance for the "basic" paper might not be so judged for the national edition. Jones did the editing with the help of a full-time staff of four. The national paper reached almost one in every five *Times* readers, and was gaining circulation at a faster rate than the basic paper on sale in New York and the corridor.

3:45 P.M.

Albert Scardino, a reporter specializing in stories about the media, finally accepted that Tuesday would be a lost day for him. He had just returned from Amelia Island, a pleasant resort on the Florida-Georgia border, where he had participated in the *Times'* Big Brother program. That was the newsroom's somewhat mocking name for the *Times'* latest corporate management venture. In

1987 the Times Company had designated Seymour Topping, a former *Times* foreign correspondent and later an assistant managing editor, to be director of editorial development for the company's thirty-five regional newspapers. Topping was supposed to help sharpen the journalistic skills of the news staffs at the regional papers. He had the idea of inviting *Times* reporters and editors to speak on their specialties to regular gatherings of the little brothers (and sisters). The *Times'* newspaper properties were located mostly in smaller towns with a heavy concentration in the South. Scardino once owned and edited a small weekly in Augusta, Georgia—and won a Pulitzer Prize for his editorial writings. He was invited by Topping to Amelia to speak on the topic of "enterprise reporting."

Ordinarily, Amelia Island in February would be a welcome assignment for a transplanted Southerner, but a snowstorm hit Florida, bringing northern temperatures to the resort. Scardino faced rough weather on another front as well; the previous Big Brother speaker, an assistant editor on the metro desk, chose to talk about the *Times'* coverage of the Tawana Brawley case. The editor described how the metro desk assigned no fewer than eight people for a good part of 1988 to investigate the story of the black teenager (Brawley had claimed she was abducted and raped by a band of white men, some of them law enforcement officers; the *Times* team presented evidence to demonstrate that her story was a hoax). As the metro editor reprised the *Times'* handling of the case, a hand shot up. The questioner said he had to put out a paper every day, including Sundays, with a news staff of eight people. What possible relevance could the Brawley example have to his experience? Scardino was sympathetic. There is no way you *can* relate to the behemoth of the North, he told the little-brother editors when it was his turn to speak. "The *Times* is like the U.S. Post Office."

Back in the newsroom on Tuesday, Scardino sprayed his desktop with Fantastik cleaner and swiped at it with a rag. Judith Miller was rejoining the paper as the new deputy editor for media, and she decided to set up shop in the cubicle until then assigned to Scardino. A former *Times* foreign correspondent and more recently a deputy news editor of the Washington bureau, Miller had been on leave to finish a book on the Holocaust (published in 1990 as *One by One by One*). Miller was now Scardino's supervisor, and so he spent the day moving his files in order to turn over his desk to her. He was not a happy *Times*man. The paper ran a feature under his byline called "Press Notes," though not as regularly as he would have liked. "It appears as frequently as the *Scholastic Quarterly,*" he joked. Scardino complained that his last column sat in his editors' computer directory for almost a month. "They ask, 'Is this exclusive?' If you reply, 'It's ours alone,' then they hold it a few weeks."

7

—

CHOOSING MAX
(AND JOE)

IN THE FALL OF 1985, Max Frankel decided he had to advance his bid
to become executive editor—the top news post at the *Times*, and one
widely described as the most important journalistic position in the
world. He asked Punch Sulzberger to have lunch with him. Using a
technique he had initially perfected in his years as the *Times* Washington bureau chief, Frankel during the lunch made it clear that,
while he was making his case for the job, he wasn't pressing for an
immediate answer. When dealing with the ambitious, sensitive men
and women who worked for the *Times*, Frankel found, words might be
spoken in haste and later regretted, especially if the reporter had come
to talk about career advancement. Frankel learned to include a cautionary preface: "Listen to me, but don't reply; then go away and reflect
on what I've said." The implication was that the smart *Times*man or
-woman ought not to say anything hasty, like "No" or "I quit," that
would close off options. A colleague grew to admire the editor's approach to staff matters. "Max is always thinking, thinking. He has lots
of *sachel*," the colleague said, using the Yiddish word meant to convey
shrewd common sense.

Sachel was prized at the *Times*. In his Op-Ed page column, William
Safire once admonished Secretary of State James Baker about his Middle East diplomacy; Baker, Safire wrote, has the "smarts" of a Texas
lawyer and Washington insider but not the *sachel* that gives "a feel for

the way human beings react." At lunch with Sulzberger, Frankel used his *sachel*, applying the same deft touch he had brought to dealings with his subordinates. Before making his case, Frankel lightly told the publisher that he had the right to remain silent. Sulzberger readily accepted the ground rules. Frankel put forth his arguments; Sulzberger listened in silence. Before they rose to leave, Sulzberger said he was glad to hear that Frankel was available. Furthermore, the publisher said, "You know I think the world of you." That was it. Not another word was exchanged between the two men on the topic of the top editor's job for the next eighteen months.

From Frankel's point of view, his case was airtight. He had been at the paper all his adult life, almost thirty-three years; the executive editorship was, logically, the culmination of his life's work. The *Times*, indeed, was his life: Not for Frankel the television talk-show circuit or the journalistic memoir for a book publisher. He had given the *Times* his full-time, seven-days-a-week devotion. But Frankel faced an obstacle to his quest, actually several obstacles. To begin with, the editor's job that Frankel wanted was already occupied, and by the formidable Abraham Michael Rosenthal. After fifteen years of running the news department of the *Times*, Rosenthal seemed a part of the environment as fixed as the fluorescent ceiling lights that burned day and night in the third-floor newsroom. The newsroom denizens, at any rate, believed Rosenthal was ready to defend his authority to the end; they claimed to see no evidence that he wanted to relax his grip. For his part, Rosenthal gave every sign that he regarded the executive editorship as the most important journalistic job in the world, and one that he perhaps alone among men was qualified to do. In his early sixties, he still relished running the *Times* fortissimo.

In late 1985, Rosenthal seemed more energetic than ever. The *Times* was producing creamy profits for the Sulzberger family, its circulation was still growing, its reporters were regularly represented when the Pulitzer Prizes were awarded each spring. The story of what happened when the force of Frankel's ambition collided with the entrenched authority of Rosenthal reveals a great deal about the workings of the *Times*. Moreover, the way the *Times* selected its new editor also suggests why the paper has come to look and read the way it does, and how misguided are some of our notions of "the news"—and of the eager, egocentric men and women who do newswork.

*　　*　　*

Frankel, as a good *Times*man, knew enough to keep word of the lunch with Sulzberger and, indeed, of his own plans, as quiet as possible. He understood that Sulzberger wanted it that way. Sulzberger's family by temperament as well as tradition valued their privacy. It was somewhat awkward for Sulzberger to suppress all talk about the *Times*. He was, after all, in the news-gathering business, and his employees worked zealously to find out about other people's affairs. But Sulzberger was not pleased with the kind of news the *Times* had made: the Washington bureau revolt against New York in the late 1960s; the ouster of John B. Oakes and his editorial board in the mid-1970s; the reporters' cabal and the Kosinski and Severo episodes—the list went on. Sulzberger kept asking his executives to "calm down the place," but to little avail. Abe Rosenthal had been at the center of many of these fights. The Red Hot Mama positively radiated danger to those who crowded his authority.

In late 1985 the *Times* was about to create more unwanted headlines. Although Rosenthal was approaching the *Times'* mandatory retirement age of sixty-five, there was speculation he would not willingly let go. Perhaps, some of the staff suggested, he wanted to be editor for life.

In the early 1980s, Rosenthal instituted an elaborate procedure to select, as he put it, "the next generation of *Times* leadership." A baker's dozen of top *Times*men—no women were included—became part of this next generation. At one time or another, the list involved: the imposing Hedrick Smith, a Pulitzer Prize–winner for his reporting from Eastern Europe and a frequent guest sage on public television's "Washington Week in Review"; Sydney Schanberg, the impassioned correspondent whose Pulitzer Prize work in Cambodia was the basis for the motion picture *The Killing Fields*; Bill Kovach, the *Times'* Washington bureau chief, with an unusual background—he was an Albanian-American from East Tennessee and, more improbably for the *Times*, an editor who was well liked by his staff; the metropolitan editor, John Vinocur, an aggressive former foreign correspondent brought back from Europe for bigger assignments; and Craig Whitney, a kind of composite of the *Times* senior editors on their way up in the mid-1980s: Ivy League scholarship boy (Princeton), major overseas experience (Moscow, though not yet a Pulitzer), and quite tall. All of the candidates in Rosenthal's "next generation" seemed to be six feet or over.

A half dozen other *Times*men were part of the next generation as well, though not as it happened, Max Frankel. Some people thought Frankel was the logical choice to be the next editor by background, abilities, and length of service. But Rosenthal had organized the process for the editors in the news department. Frankel was in charge of the editorial pages, where the *Times'* opinions are fashioned. According to one of the most frequently enunciated canons of the *Times*, the paper's editorial-page staff had to be kept isolated from the news department. There was one notable exception: As we've seen, the Sulzberger family moved back and forth between the two departments, involving itself in *Times* fact and *Times* opinion to a greater extent than most *Times*people suspected. The news-editorial separation rule existed for everybody else at the *Times*, and it could be a convenient barrier if anyone wished to block off Frankel from the editor's post. The editorial page editor was automatically excluded from a competition organized for the news department.

Other factors were working against Frankel, specifically, the baggage he carried from his days in Washington. Frankel had been the bureau chief in 1972 when the Watergate revelations began appearing in print and the public learned of the full extent of corruption in Richard Nixon's White House. The stories appeared first in the *Washington Post*, the *Times'* keenest competitor. Some *Times*people defended Frankel and the bureau, arguing, rather loftily, that Watergate began as a "police story" and that the *Post*, as the "local" paper, had a natural edge over the *Times*. The surface logic eased some of the sting, but the fact remained that on the biggest story during Frankel's watch, his bureau was soundly beaten. The defeat might have been enough to sink the career of a news executive. Only Sulzberger could say how much permanent damage Frankel's reputation had sustained in the publisher's mind.

While Frankel's editorial-page post conveniently excluded him from Rosenthal's competition, other traditions of the *Times* narrowed the field still more. Potential candidates from outside the paper were excluded. This ruled out an admired former *Times*man named Eugene Roberts. Gene Roberts left the *Times* in the early 1970s, after chafing under Rosenthal's rule for almost a decade, to become editor of the *Philadelphia Inquirer*. Roberts flourished at the *Inquirer*; the paper's record of investigative triumphs, Pulitzer Prizes, and soaring newsroom morale led many *Times*people to conclude that they had lost the better man. Among Roberts's fans, for example, was Tom Wicker, the columnist. Wicker would have urged Sulzberger to pick Roberts, "if I had been asked." But that wouldn't have been the *Times*' way, for it might have been perceived as a tacit admission of weakness within the paper. "The *Times* just doesn't bring in people from outside, even if they worked here once, and are great editors, like Roberts," Wicker said.

Though Roberts was beyond recall, Frankel remained very much alive as a possibility. The same wall of quarantine between the news and editorial page departments that excluded him from Rosenthal's "process" also afforded Frankel some protection. The system designed by Rosenthal presented so many danger zones and dead ends that some candidates making their way through it ended up out of the running and gone from the *Times*. There was some question about whether Rosenthal—and more important, Sulzberger—would feel bound by the results. The choice of a new editor was not a minor occasion at the *Times*. There had been only five in the eighty years that the Ochs-Sulzberger family had owned the paper. Many signs flashed "go slow" to Frankel.

Not that Frankel needed much cautioning. He was by nature a careful man. He grew up in Washington Heights in upper Manhattan, a German-Jewish refugee boy attending public schools. After bigger neighborhood toughs beat him up, he transferred to another school. Later, in his years as a Washington bureau chief and a senior editor at the *Times*, Frankel had learned how to survive in the *Times*' tribal society. He understood the advantages of privacy as well as of accommodation. He knew how to stroke—to use a word heard frequently from *Times*people. He understood that journalists as a class possessed fragile egos. Artisans if not artists, they were nevertheless quick to perceive personal slights and shifts in status. Their insecurities were well known. They required stroking.

Individual hurts, thwarted ambitions, blasted careers—all classified under the heading "personnel matters"—often occupy the days of *Times*' executives as much as the ostensible main business of collecting and printing the news. Turner Catledge spent forty-one years at the *Times*, through the Great Depression and three wars, serving as managing editor and then executive editor, from 1951 to 1968. Yet in his memoirs Catledge noted that his hardest decisions were those within the *Times* "family"—another term frequently heard at 43rd Street. "I was not dealing with abstractions, but with people, talented, sensitive, ambitious men and women," Catledge recalled. "I had to work with and through them." In a word, he had to know when to stroke the egos of his reporters and editors. In none of Catledge's stroking did he exercise more care than in his relations with his superior, Arthur Hays Sulzberger, Punch's father and the publisher of the *Times* from 1935 to 1961. Catledge recounted in his memoirs how his future executive role at the *Times* was assured after he and the publisher traveled together, and drank Scotch together, across the Pacific during World War II. For good *Times*men, the personal bond was paramount.

As with Catledge in a more paternalistic time, so, too, with Frankel in our therapeutic age. A shortish man with a round, open face, in his earlier years he used to puff on a pipe at *Times* meetings: the good listener, picking up on the emotional clues. Indeed, he looked a bit like a respected psychiatrist with a successful Manhattan practice. Frankel knew how to deal with Sulzberger, and with the staff. By late 1985, Frankel had been part of *Times* management for almost two decades. His practice of asking staff members to listen to him in silence while he tried to address their concerns was only one of his techniques. Frankel had concluded from his own handling of personnel matters that people tend to listen more conscientiously when they know they don't have to respond immediately. The general principle was clear: Hasty actions should always be avoided by *Times*people.

Frankel had learned that firsthand, and painfully, earlier in his *Times* career. In 1964 Frankel actually resigned from the *Times*. He was then thirty-four and a star correspondent covering the State Department. His letter of resignation, addressed to Turner Catledge, then the paper's editor, came shortly after Tom Wicker was named Washington bureau chief in one of the *Times*' periodic reorganizations of the bureau. At the time, Frankel had an offer to write magazine articles and essays as national correspondent for *The Reporter*, a small-circulation, liberal-left fortnightly published in Washington. At the magazine, he would be doing *reportage*, rather than daily journalism. Frankel's letter to Catledge linked the decision to a desire to get away from the demands of deadlines and the constricting forms of newspaper reporting rather than to any disappointment at being beaten out by Wicker. But Frankel soon had second thoughts. Unhappy as he was at the *Times*, he faced the prospect of trading its daily audience of over 800,000 readers for the relative handful of people who subscribed to *The Reporter*. In a matter of days, Frankel readily agreed to reconsider when approached by his immediate superior, James Reston, who was turning over the bureau chief's duties to Wicker in order to concentrate on his own twice-weekly column. Reston also persuaded Catledge and the other executives in New York to withdraw acceptance of Frankel's letter. As it turned out, haste would have been waste for Frankel. *The Reporter* ceased publication in 1969.

Frankel was wiser in the ways of the *Times* when he opened his campaign for the editorship during his lunch with Punch Sulzberger. He was fifty-five, and had spent two-thirds of his life as a *Times*man. He started as a campus stringer while still at Columbia University, joining the staff upon his graduation, reporting from Washington as well as overseas, winning a Pulitzer Prize for his coverage of Nixon's 1972 trip to China. His career at the paper had not suffered fatally from the bungled resignation episode, however immature—or worse, "disloyal" to the family—it may have seemed at the time. The bureau's performance during Watergate was another matter. Sulzberger made Frankel editor of the Sunday edition of the *Times* while the Watergate scandals were still unfolding; that was read as a mixed judgment of Frankel's status. The editorship was one of the top three news posts at the paper but it also meant he was running the softer, feature sections, such as the *Times Magazine*, the travel pages, and the *Book Review*. Four years later, Frankel suffered a terrible blow to his prestige and power. Sulzberger abolished the position of Sunday editor. Authority over both the daily and Sunday paper was consolidated in the hands of the new executive editor, Abe Rosenthal, eight years' Frankel's senior and always one step above him on the pyramid of *Times* power. Frankel moved laterally, in the best interpretation, out of the news department entirely, to become editor of the editorial page, succeeding John Oakes. This new post removed Frankel from the gritty world of day-to-day hard news coverage.

In late 1985 Frankel carried the burden of his decade removed from hard news. What's more, Frankel's own life was unsettled as the new year approached. His wife, Tobi, was ill with cancer (she died several months later). He was nearing his tenth year in the editorial page job, and had ten years more to go before the normal retirement age for executives at the *Times*. The executive editor, Rosenthal, was still two years away from the same retirement age. Once before, Frankel had thought the top job might be his. A decade earlier, when Frankel was still Sunday editor and Rosenthal had the title of managing editor, the post of executive editor had not yet been filled. A few *Times* handi-cappers also thought Frankel had an outside chance to beat out Rosenthal. When Frankel lost out, there were no wounding moments of resignation and sudden regret, as there had been in Washington twenty years before. This time, Frankel had a strategy. He wanted Sulzberger to hear face to face how much he wished to be the top editor, and how "vigorous" he felt despite his private anguish. He also wanted the publisher to know that if he wasn't made executive editor, he would consider "something else." This could be a column on the *Times'* Op-Ed page. Or it could be—the thought was left unspoken—moving on from the paper. The thrust of the lunch meeting was clear. Frankel explained how much he loved the *Times* and his editorial page job, but his time had come for greater things.

This was not unfamiliar ground for Sulzberger. However uncom-fortable Sulzberger felt when making grand policy in his earlier years, especially decisions on the direction of the paper and its leadership, he had by 1985 been in similar situations before—in fact, several times before. Sulzberger had moved up, down, around, and aside a series of executives—men older, more imposing and experienced than he, jour-nalistic titans such as Turner Catledge, E. Clifton Daniel, Lester Markel, and James Reston, among others. Sulzberger also had, again with a great deal of agonizing and demarches, closed off the rise of other *Times* eminences, such as Harrison Salisbury.

Through it all, one editor seemed immune from the laws of exec-utive motion. Abe Rosenthal's rise had been steady and undeflected. Other bodies colliding with him were destroyed as he bounded ahead. Through the years of the 1960s, 1970s, and 1980s, Rosenthal tight-ened his hold upon the *Times'* lines of authority with a tenacity con-sidered fierce even for that level of management. A series of stars had fallen in their turn: Catledge, the poor Mississippi country boy who learned to move easily within the journalistic establishment; Daniel, another small-town Southerner metamorphosed into elegant foreign correspondent, and son-in-law of a president of the United States; Salisbury, the quintessential hard-charging reporter, whose unim-peachable sources extended inside the Kremlin and the Chinese Po-litburo, or so he claimed; Markel, the imperious editor who ran the Sunday paper like a private fiefdom for thirty years. Each of them had been pushed from Rosenthal's newsroom. Even Scotty Reston, merely the nation's opinion-page conscience and confidant of whatever administration was temporarily in residence at the White House, had gone reeling back to Washington as Rosenthal consolidated his power. In the summer of 1983, at a *Times Magazine* editors' conference considering topics for the magazine's new Sunday column, "About Men," one participant suggested that the emotional trauma faced by some men when forced to retire at sixty-five might make a good subject. Rosenthal agreed that he wanted more such personal materials in "About Men." Then he added: "By the way, I'm never going to retire."

Seven years later, when Rosenthal was asked about the events of the succession, he insisted that the whole "editor for life" story was a joke. "The most I was expecting was to stay on as editor for an extra year, until I was sixty-six." At the time, however, not everyone waiting below Rosenthal was willing to laugh it all off. Frankel wasn't at the "About Men" meeting, but Rosenthal's punch line was repeated throughout the building. Rosenthal had been in charge for fifteen years, the gossipers around the office water coolers told each other, why not fifteen more?

Why not, indeed? These had been grand years for the *Times*. A major editorial make-over brought in fresh advertising revenues and readers. Rosenthal deserved credit for the new daily sections; but he also had to take responsibility for the petty, tyrannical atmosphere in the newsroom, the Severo episode, the reports of homophobia, the departure of so many journalists during his drill-instructors tenure. One of the best of the departees did a two-year hitch in the U.S. Army before working at the *Times*. Compared to Rosenthal's *Times*, this man remembered, military service was like toddlers' day care (in fairness, his was peacetime service). A second *Times*man, still at the paper, offered another metaphor: Rosenthal, he said, was "the iron fist in the iron glove."

Did Punch Sulzberger want the authoritarian, though successful, regime to continue? It all seemed at odds with his public persona: the polite proprietor with a lively sense of humor. Sulzberger had grown up in a Jewish family whose ancestral roots were in Germany. They lived as privately as a wealthy family could in New York. The Sulzbergers were old money. One conducted one's affairs quietly, avoiding public attention and, in particular, shunning the kind of ostentation endemic among some of New York's new monied class. Sulzberger was conservative in his social attitudes, and moderately progressive in his politics. As might be expected, the *Times'* editorial positions on policy issues and its endorsements for public office over the span of the 1970s and 1980s reflected that outlook. Yet Sulzberger was still something of a puzzle to his own newshounds, with their sensitive noses for story angles and hidden agendas. Few people in the newsroom could honestly claim to know him. If Sulzberger the man was as open-minded as claimed, then why was the place run in such an authoritarian fashion all those years? If the old ethos valued decorous quiet, why was there so much vulgar noise? A plausible answer gradually occurred to a number of *Times*people: Sulzberger was not deaf, dumb, and blind to the *Times'* newsroom atmosphere. That was how he wanted it. The *Times'* support of civil rights, economic equity, and liberal Democratic candidates across the land was one thing. Inside the building, he was management, and the staff the hired hands.

This didn't prevent the worker class in the newsroom from exercising its rights of speculation. Years in advance of the date for Rosenthal's prospective retirement, succession scenarios were widely discussed and written about. The *Washington Post* ran a three-part series on "the twilight of the Rosenthal years." Rosenthal had barely turned sixty-two when the *Washington Journalism Review* examined "The Royal Succession" in its issue of January 1985. Two years before that, the freelance writer Craig Unger, in *New York* magazine, offered a very early morning line on Rosenthal's likely replacement. Frankel was described as a "bitter rival" of Rosenthal's. His appointment would "drive Abe crazy." Because Frankel was the oldest of the prime candidates, closer in age to Rosenthal than to most of the others, he was treated as an afterthought. *New York* magazine returned to the story frequently during the mid-1980s, its Intelligencer section carrying a string of items about one or another of the *Times* "princes" who were, as one 1986 headline put it, "Running Hard for the *Times* Crown."

The royal trope was overwrought. Still, the particular editor who wore the *Times* "crown" had the power to control directly an impressive dominion. While a weekly magazine, or a smaller newspaper or a television news program, often bears the individual mark of its editor or producer, the *Times* tries to present itself as a collective. The institution, the *Times*, is supposed to be too big and too serious to be the extension of any single mind or ego. Yet readers, when they think about it, recognize that one editor's *Times* may be different from another's, however many bows are made in the direction of the institution and its "objectivity." The personality of the editor shapes the paper through allocations of resources, hiring choices, decisions about coverage, and, equally important, the decisions not made.

Turner Catledge, the good old boy and establishment insider, ran a congenial *Times*, one that dawdled on many stories—though it did make major contributions to the coverage of the paramount domestic news event of the postwar years, the civil rights struggles of black America. Catledge's successor, James Reston, envisioned a lofty "intellectual" *Times*, where good writing and clear thinking on the big issues of the day would be enshrined. Reston's successor, Abe Rosenthal, created a third kind of *Times*. The Monday-through-Friday life-style sections begun in the 1970s moved the paper away from the mean streets of the city—away, interestingly, from Rosenthal's own roots. Rosenthal also took the paper in search of the political and cultural consensus of the country during those same post-Vietnam years, effectively moving the *Times* to the right. The individual editor mattered to readers as well as to staff.

With the power of the editor came the prestige attached to the *Times*. Not so incidentally, the salary was good as well; the position paid around $350,000 a year, plus generous benefits, stock options, and bonus incentives. Rosenthal was a rich man by 1985.

The candidates for the *Times* editorship would have wanted the job at a half or a third of the pay. They were all hugely ambitious as well as upwardly mobile. The editor's job would be the only fitting cap to their careers. They were similar in other ways as well: middle-aged, of middle-class origins, and each typically with Washington or foreign reporting experience. They were all, finally, white males. Eileen Shanahan, a *Times* reporter with extensive Washington experience, was in the opinion of many *Times*people, men and women, extremely well qualified to lead the paper. But the *Times* wasn't moving women ahead then, and she had left in the early 1980s to become editor of the *Pittsburgh Post-Gazette*. Her departure still rankled her supporters.

Underneath the apparent professional conformity of the leading candidates, however, were some striking differences of ideology and temperament. Sydney Schanberg, born in 1934, appeared possessed by the zeal and idealism of the Roosevelt New Deal. "By nature, I identify with an underdog," he once offered, by way of explaining his work. Lean, intense, bearded, Schanberg in 1985 was writing a twice-weekly column for the *Times'* Op-Ed page, concentrating on New York City affairs. He had been in Cambodia for the *Times* covering the bloody Khmer Rouge years (the experiences that won him a Pulitzer). Schanberg came from Massachusetts, from a family of modest circumstances. His voice grew sharp and his eyes blazed when he worked up his columns on the latest development schemes of New York landlords, as if he was witnessing again the destruction of Cambodia. The Schanberg *Times* would never lack for targets, many of them among the establishments that ran the city.

Bill Kovach, less than a year older than Schanberg, ran the *Times'* Washington bureau with distinction. He was an apostle of tough reporting and investigative journalism, and in the bargain, an excellent manager of people. With his close-cropped salt-and-pepper hair and pleasant down-home drawl, Kovach conveyed a sense of integrity. Daily journalism was his life. He looked the way the editor of a distinguished newspaper should look: tall, graceful, with a direct gaze.

Another possibility, John Vinocur, had been brought back from his foreign correspondent's post by Rosenthal and soon was supervising the *Times'* metropolitan coverage. The way Vinocur pushed reporters for more "exciting" stories and more "vivid" writing reminded *Times*people of the younger Abe, who came back from abroad and stirred up a somnolent metro staff in 1963. Vinocur had the wide shoulders of a football player; his large hands looked as if they could easily throttle any reporter slacking from Vinocur's standards for metro coverage. He was, without doubt, the hard charger among the candidates.

A fourth possibility, Hedrick Smith, would have easily won the job if appearance and energy alone were the determining factors. Rick Smith was the same age as Kovach and was Kovach's predecessor in the Washington bureau. Smith possessed the knack for the grand Restonian phrase. He could sit in his office in Washington and write about "the mood of the country." He also could claim a Pulitzer for his reporting from the Soviet bloc and a best-selling book, *The Russians*, to back up his amour-propre. In addition to his accomplishments in Moscow, Smith already had earned a small place in journalistic history, literally a footnote. During the American presidential campaigns of the 1970s, bureau chief Smith frequently appeared on the candidates' planes or in the press bus, dropping in for a few days to do interviews and write a "mood of the primaries" analysis for the *Times*. A big man, well over six feet tall, Smith would drape his size-13D shoes over an armrest or aisle seat, in the self-assured pose of a man who owned the plane and the story. The regular reporters assigned to the campaign were known to resent such intruders. They hit upon a name for Smith that became generic, applicable to other high-powered chiefs who rode for a time on the political trail with the pack. Since Smith, they have been designated "Big Foot."

Schanberg, Smith, Kovach, and Vinocur all could boast strong reporting experience, as well as considerable personal presence. Together these "hard news" men contrasted strongly with Max Frankel, who had been away from the daily grind since 1973. They promised excitement and change. Frankel suggested stability, the timelessness of *Times* tradition. Not only had he been at the paper longer than any of the others, Frankel's whole demeanor—the Talmudic mind, the compact body, the pipe he puffed on—helped contribute to the image of the journalist-scholar. Possibly he had been too slow to pick up on the Watergate story, perhaps he was too thoughtful to run the news operation; but he seemed perfectly cast for the editorial page.

While Frankel calculated his chances of succeeding Rosenthal, one after another of the hard-news candidates stumbled. Schanberg's views were not trimmed to the shifting political direction of the *Times*, which had grown increasingly conservative in the later Vietnam years, and he fell hardest. His first post-Cambodia assignment, the job of metropolitan editor, did not work out. He clashed with Rosenthal; the two strong-willed men could not learn to get along. Schanberg left the news department entirely, for the Op-Ed page, where his opinions appeared for four increasingly contentious years. One Monday in August 1985, the day after he returned from a two-week vacation, Schanberg was notified by Sydney Gruson, the chief assistant to Sulzberger, that the publisher had "not been happy with the column for some time" and had decided to "discontinue" it. A two-paragraph story in the *Times* the next day informed readers of the end of the column, in the noncommittal manner of a communiqué from the Chinese Politburo.

The immediate cause of the column's demise was hardly mysterious. Before Schanberg went on vacation, he had written scathingly in the *Times* of July 27 about the Westway Project, a $4 billion plan to redevelop real estate and the highway on the West Side of Manhattan along the Hudson River. Schanberg called Westway a "scandal" and "a megaboondoggle." Westway had been pushed by the city's developers, and supported on Frankel's editorial pages. Sulzberger was a Westway enthusiast. Schanberg also criticized the news columns of New York's newspapers, including by implication the *Times*, for being "strangely asleep" in their coverage of the "shame of Westway." Sulzberger's decision ended Schanberg's twenty-six-year career at the paper. He rejected an offer to be a roving correspondent for the *Times Magazine*, and early in 1986 left the *Times* and became a featured columnist for *New York Newsday*. (*New York Newsday*, now separate from the Long Island edition, was trying to be the fresh, liberal voice in the city.)

Rick Smith also left the *Times*, pursued by rumors of a scandal of his own—the story of a married bureau chief having a torrid love affair on the bureau premises, during office hours, with his secretary. Smith went on to appear on public-television documentaries and to write a book, *The Power Game: How Washington Works*, published in 1988 and dedicated "to Susan, and the spark of renewal." *The Power Game* ran on for 793 pages and managed, astonishingly, to avoid any mention of the *New York Times* as a player in Washington, while devoting two long sections to the power of the television networks' news shows and to the "MacNeil/Lehrer NewsHour" on public TV. Ingenuously, Smith gave more space in *The Power Game* to Bill Regardie, publisher of *Regardie's*, a Washington monthly with a circulation of forty thousand, than he gave to the *Times*. ("Powerful" *Regardie's* ceased publication in 1992.)

Schanberg and Smith may have been too smart to see themselves as realistic choices for the editorship. Bill Kovach, however, was not the kind of a candidate who would take himself out of the competition. Like Frankel, Kovach wanted the job and wanted Sulzberger to know that he wanted it. Like Frankel, too, Kovach met privately with the publisher. Kovach talked mainly about his views of the paper in the years ahead. Kovach wanted to point the *Times* toward a future consistent with his career as an advocate of news-driven journalism. The *Times*, he argued, should not be soft and featurized. It should aggressively pursue investigative stories. Sulzberger heard him out and made no comment. Kovach now says that while other people may have considered him a strong choice, he soon came to realize that Sulzberger was not going to give him the job. "The direction I wanted to take the *Times* was not the direction it was going in," he recalled, diplomatically.

Kovach let some of his wide circle of friends know that he was interested in moving on; one friend, Tom Winship, a former editor of the *Boston Globe*, did some matchmaking. At the end of 1986, Kovach left the *Times* to become editor of the *Atlanta Journal-Constitution*, the morning and afternoon papers owned by the Cox family. The papers were boosters of the "New South," the business-minded, racially harmonious South that was "too busy to hate," in the glib slogan of the day. Under Kovach's prodding, the *Journal-Constitution* produced a thorough, meticulously documented exposé of Atlanta's banks and their Old South practice of redlining—turning down mortgage applications for black prospective homeowners. Kovach was in Atlanta less than two years. He had a series of clashes with Jay Smith, the paper's publisher. Kovach thought Smith was overly sensitive to the feelings of the clubby, downtown establishment—all-white, naturally—that "ran" Atlanta. After one argument, Kovach quit—and Smith accepted the resignation. The *Times* gave special attention to the stories, far beyond the interests of non-Atlantans. It carried two long stories, each with two-column pictures, and quoted Smith as saying that neither Kovach nor anyone else "is bigger than the newspapers themselves." In the summer of 1989, Kovach became curator of the Nieman journalism program at Harvard.

That left the "new Abe," John Vinocur. He arrived in 1985 in the third-floor newsroom, a man shot out of a cannon. Like Abe Rosenthal, Vinocur had been a star reporter. The *Times* twice nominated the work he did in its Bonn bureau for the Pulitzer Prize competitions. His *Times* stories were credited with helping change American perceptions of West Germany, from a country bound to U.S. policy to a resurgent power entering a new and more fractious relationship with its old mentor. In New York, Rosenthal made Vinocur his assistant—Rosenthal called the assignment "a good place to get a fast look at the paper." Soon, Vinocur was deputy metro editor, helping run the staff of eighty. Rosenthal talked of new career moves. Other editors translated that to mean Vinocur was going to be the next executive editor. A *Times* editor offered a characterization typical of the paper's self-image: "There was a laying on of the hands of Vinocur," he remembered. The newsroom congregation watched as Rosenthal and his associates, managing editor Arthur Gelb and assistant managing editor for personnel James Greenfield, introduced Vinocur to the social activities that are the due of *Times'* executives:

invitations to the fourteenth-floor editorial lunches, dinner parties, and nights at the opera. Vinocur also received some unsolicited marital counseling (to marry the woman he was living with) as well as advice on a new wardrobe.

Vinocur deciphered these signals as well as he could in after-hours talk with other *Times*people. He shared his feelings with his friends, Craig Whitney and Warren Hoge, two other *Times* editors still in their forties. Vinocur thought, and his friends agreed, that he was faring quite well within the *Times* culture. With the metro desk assignment, he had an excellent opportunity to enliven the *Times*' rather pallid local reporting, and "showcase" his managerial talents.

The showcase turned out to be something of an open coffin for Vinocur's career at the *Times*. In the summer of 1985, while the humiliation of Sydney Schanberg was going forward on the Op-Ed page, deputy metropolitan editor Vinocur supervised a story written by reporter Jane Perlez. The subject of the Perlez story was the developer and publisher Mortimer B. Zuckerman. The article was revised extensively before publication. When it finally appeared, no one could accuse Perlez of the customary metro-page blandness. Zuckerman was described as "flamboyant . . . a shortish figure, with receding dark hair. . . ." He acquired the prime Coliseum site at Columbus Circle on the West Side after five years of "plotting." According to Perlez, he entered "the publishing ranks" by buying the monthly *Atlantic* magazine and the weekly *U.S. News & World Report* and then "befriended writers, editors, and television personalities in an effort to win a place in their world." This portrait of Zuckerman as arriviste was accompanied by an analysis of several Zuckerman business deals that ended in litigation. The article ran in the editions of August 5.

Within forty-eight hours, an "Editors' Note" appeared on page three of the *Times*, in the space occupied by the regular "Corrections" box. The "Editors' Note" heading in the *Times* was pure Rosenthal: He had initiated it as part of a dogged, decade-long effort to establish a magisterial "canon" for journalistic performance at the *Times*. Notes did not appear often, but when they did there was no way for readers, or *Times*people, to miss them. The "Editors' Note" on the Perlez article found it to be "opinionated, pejorative, and unbalanced." The note concluded with a judgment about the story's use of anonymous sources that was as blunt as a blow to the head: "They should not have appeared."

Vinocur had not been back in New York long enough to realize that Zuckerman's litigious ways could extend to the *Times*. The editor's grooming for bigger things had left out an important lesson: Among Zuckerman's acquaintances in the news-lit world, he counted Abe Rosenthal. Zuckerman sent a three-page, single-space letter to Rosenthal by hand the afternoon of August 5. Two days later, the "Editors' Note" excoriating Perlez was in type.

Perlez's career at the *Times* was not fatally damaged. She rode out the episode and eventually received a prized assignment to be the *Times*' East African correspondent, based in Nairobi. Vinocur never rose any higher at the *Times* than his deputy editor's job; he could no longer move up, only out. But his fallback position was one that journalists fantasize about: He became the editor of the *International Herald Tribune*, a post of near-legendary status (one's own paper, and in Paris!). The appointment suggested how highly regarded John Vinocur was. He did not let down his remaining *Times* supporters in his new job, and remained reasonably free of rancor about his "New York adventure." In retrospect, Vinocur says that while he saw himself as a candidate for the *Times*' top editor's job, "I didn't see myself as a successful candidate." He declined any other public comment, on the grounds that he was "a member of the *Times* family" (the *International Herald Tribune* is partly owned by the New York Times Company).

Kovach made a similar point about his own chances. Kovach believes that he "didn't quite fit the image of what the *Times*' leader should be." But then who did fit? For that matter, what were the attributes that added up to make the proper leader? One or another of the several candidates appeared to be running with a handicap: too aggressive, or not aggressive enough; not sufficiently polished, or a bit too pompous; light on administrative experience, or not enough service in the field.

One man, however, not only matched the profile of ideal editor, he was the editor in reality. Once the notion had taken hold around the newsroom that Abe Rosenthal did not intend to step aside at sixty-five and that the whole selection process was illusory, the editor-for-life story became difficult to spike. It wouldn't go away. Rosenthal impatiently dismissed the allegations of his unwillingness to give up the editor's post. What kind of executive would have to be prevailed upon to groom his successor? he asked an interviewer in 1983. It was meant as a rhetorical question, with the clear message that Rosenthal *was* preparing to find the next editor. The process had been thorough. He put in motion an elaborate administrative structure. He gave his senior editors "a chance to see the workings of the paper," as he put it in a memo to managing editor Gelb and assistant managing editor Seymour Topping. When one or another of this editorial troika was away on vacation or traveling on the periodic trips to visit bureaus in the field, editors from the executive level immediately below handled the absentee executive's duties. Because Gelb and Topping were in Rosenthal's age group, and therefore not considered realistic candidates to succeed him, Rosenthal reasoned that the three friends could act as a panel of judges, assaying the men working with them. In this way, "the next generation of leadership," in Rosenthal's favored phrase, would emerge.

There was some snickering in the newsroom about "Abe's game of musical chairs," but if anything Rosenthal intensified the process. On February 1, 1983, Rosenthal announced in a memo, marked Confidential and addressed to Punch Sulzberger, that the effort to find the successor generation would be at the top of "my MBO list."

Sulzberger understood the shorthand. The 1970s' Argyris experience behind him, Punch Sulzberger had swallowed hard once again and approved a new administrative exercise for senior executives of the *Times*: the practice of annual written declarations of work goals, or Management By Objective. The idea had emerged from the Harvard Business School. (Not until the arrival of Demingism in the 1990s was the *Times* apparently able to find expertise from beyond Cambridge.) The *Times*' MBO memoranda required executives to set down at the beginning of each new year their personal and organizational goals for the months ahead. In his February 1, 1983, memo to the publisher, Rosenthal announced that he was tearing up his earlier MBO for 1983—a proposal to hire the management firm of McKinsey and company to do a study of *Times* staffing (more B-School expertise). In its place, Rosenthal offered a new MBO: "to prepare and put into operation, with the agreement of the publisher, a specific plan that would enable him subsequently to select the next top leadership of the paper." Rosenthal's accompanying explanation for the change sounded a strange, elegiac note, as if he had sat down to compose a formal business memo and wrote instead a "September Song." "As the years ahead for personal MBOs on my part dwindle," Rosenthal declared, "they become rather more important to me than less. It becomes a matter of personal satisfaction and obligation to make sure that the MBOs I undertake have meaning for me in my job and contribution."

Seven months later, Rosenthal announced a series of six "promotions and assignment changes" in the newsroom, including the elevation of Craig Whitney and Warren Hoge to new positions. The selection of a new Pope could not involve more *in camera* intrigue. Rosenthal summoned each of the six editors affected to private meetings. He also met with a half dozen others who were, as Rosenthal put it, "editors of importance to the paper not involved" in the promotions and therefore likely to feel "wounded in spirit" because they had been passed over. After these one-on-one sessions, Rosenthal summed up for Sulzberger what he had said to each editor: "I told every person [that] there is no list of 'ins' or 'outs.' There is no race to be the executive editor after I retire. What is taking place is the continuation of a process that started years ago and will continue for the next three or four years—a natural process of management growth." The editors, Rosenthal informed Sulzberger, were also told: "All jobs from now on are to be considered stepping stones." Finally, Rosenthal reported to Sulzberger, "I told them to discourage gossip among their colleagues because that gossip could only hurt them and each other." Rosenthal concluded on a note of delusive self-satisfaction: "I feel now that there are no secrets, that everybody understood that there are no lists, that the procedure is open and understood."

Rosenthal was not a very good reporter covering his own story. Others involved contradicted his account of the supposedly open, noncompetitive, straightforward procedure. A number of editors grew convinced that just the opposite was true. Bill Kovach, who can now look back on the succession maneuvering with a degree of dispassion, says, mildly: "I'm not sure to this day how the 'contest' worked." Another editor thought there was a "search only in the formal sense—that Sulzberger knew what he intended to do all along." Others take an exquisitely conspiratorial view of Rosenthal's visiting editor program, arguing that it was actually an invitation to self-immolation. Each guest editor in turn would, by reason of inexperience or temperament or flawed performance, fall short of the ideal, or be perceived to have failed. They would be returned to their departmental editorships, or to foreign assignments. New aspirants would then be brought up. The "nonexistent list" could stretch through the newsroom's next "next generation," younger editors in their forties such as Allan Siegal, Joseph Lelyveld, and Howell Raines. A perpetual motion machine, in short. Yet the competition, endless as it was, would never be an open one. Max Frankel, an editor of acknowledged stature, as well as the strongest Rosenthal rival, was conveniently excluded.

A number of people thought the biggest secret of all might be that Rosenthal was cleverly prolonging his stay, adding to the Rosenthal legend. If the *Times* saw itself as the indispensable paper of the elites, then perhaps its leader was the irreplaceable editor of the elites. Rosenthal may never have consciously accepted this. He may have believed in his personal MBO. It wouldn't be unusual if there were two Rosenthals who showed up every day in the editor's office, one convinced he was preparing the succession, the other at some deeper level unwilling to surrender his post. Public life is full of examples of such executive schizophrenia.

Five years after the succession process, Rosenthal dismissed all such talk. "Why the hell would I expect to stay on," he said. "We had the age sixty-five retirement rule. Did I want to go at the stroke of sixty-five? No. But I knew the most I could expect was to stay until I was sixty-six." He felt happy, and amply rewarded, doing his twice-weekly column for the *Times*. Still, Rosenthal added, who could turn down a lifetime tenure in the greatest job at the greatest place in all of journalism. "If anyone asked me, do I want to be editor for life, and sit back forever in the job, like Bradlee, or Shawn, I'd say 'sure.' But it was never in my mind that it could happen." The evocation of the names of Benjamin Bradlee of the *Washington Post* and William Shawn of *The New Yorker* suggested that, at the least, the idea of staying had occurred to Rosenthal, if only to match the record of two other leading editors of the day. Shawn remained the reclusive editor of *The New Yorker* until he was eighty; he yielded his editorship only reluctantly in 1987. Bradlee became top editor of the *Washington Post* in the same era that Rosenthal was consolidating his power at the *Times*—and Bradlee continued to run the *Post* until his seventieth birthday in August 1991.

In retrospect, too, Rosenthal acknowledged second and third thoughts about his succession process. "It became screwed up, a hodgepodge," he said. "The reason was the overcomplicated attempt on my part to give everyone a chance, but there were too many people involved." He continued to defend his handling of Frankel. "If I was intelligent enough to be the executive editor, I was intelligent enough to know that the leading candidate was Max. He did not have to prove anything. He was not my choice or my non-choice." Rosenthal now says that he did have a favored candidate, a "logical choice." This editor was not Abe Rosenthal or Max Frankel but Arthur Gelb, Rosenthal's longtime associate. It was not to be: "Arthur was too old, though in my mind, I suppose I was hoping for Artie to get a crack at it." In Rosenthal's recollection, "My biggest mistake was not to have a candidate. I should have picked one younger man."

As the "process" actually played out, the power of selection did not belong to Rosenthal. While there may or may not have been two Rosenthals at the paper, there were certainly two Sulzbergers. One, of course, was the publisher, Punch, who had run the paper since 1963; the other, his son, Arthur Jr., born in 1951—the family heir already chosen to succeed his father. The formal transition from Sulzberger to Sulzberger didn't take place until 1992, after the father marked his sixty-fifth birthday. But by the 1980s the younger Sulzberger was beginning to cast critical votes, if not to exercise explicit veto power. He was not reluctant to use his authority, tactfully, to be sure. From the heir apparent's point of view, the best resolution of the succession would insure that the older generation of editors did not stay on too long, and that the younger generation did not move up too quickly. An interim arrangement would be ideal.

In early November 1986, the succession issue was resolved publicly. Rosenthal stepped aside, and Frankel, the *Times*man who never was a part of Rosenthal's elaborate visiting editors' program, became executive editor. Many *Times*people expressed their surprise, though not Tom Wicker, who believed that Frankel was always the front-runner. With the clarity of hindsight, it was easy to understand why Frankel was the perfect candidate. He had not been overly aggressive during the early Watergate days, or a bomb thrower later over Westway. His personal interests and tastes insured a continued comfortable course for the softer sections started in the Punch Sulzberger years. Frankel himself would later say that the publisher didn't give him the job "to make radical changes." Rather, his assignment was "to make a good paper still better." When changes did occur in content or format during the first years of his editorship—for example, the shortening of news stories and reviews, the use of more graphic signposts to entice readers into articles, revisions in the captions under pictures—they were so slight that only the most attentive students of the *Times* noticed them. Frankel took that as proof of his success: "I've done things that I hope you haven't noticed," he told a visitor in late 1989.

The atmosphere in the newsroom remained much the same in the Frankel years. Supposedly, the Sulzbergers wanted their new editor to ease tensions and encourage calm after the turbulent Rosenthal years. Frankel did bring a different style to his dealings with people. His first memo to the staff upon being appointed acknowledged the turmoils of the past and suggested a new page was being turned; "We are hurtling into a time of new definitions of news," he said. Expansively, he urged everyone to enjoy the "fun" of newspapering at the *Times*. The wordsmiths at the paper puzzled over that one; the newsroom had been called many things, but never a fun place. In fact, some of the old ways continued, with fresh variations. The *Times* reporter who had characterized the Rosenthal years as "the iron fist in the iron glove," offered a mordant description of the new Frankel regime: "With Max, the fist is still iron, but the glove is velvet."

Frankel was fifty-six at the time of his elevation. In the *Times'* long view, he fit neatly into the family continuum. Frankel's period in office until his retirement at sixty-five would be split roughly in half: four-plus years under the elder Sulzberger's gaze, then four-plus years reporting to the younger Sulzberger. The son thus preserved some valuable options of his own in the course of moving up Frankel. In particular, young Sulzberger retained the authority to chose a successor to Frankel relatively early in his tenure—something that would not have been possible if an editor younger than Frankel had been chosen. Perhaps equally important, the younger Sulzberger could do so with a minimum of consultation: The interim Frankel would be hearing the ticking of his retirement clock, and the elder Sulzberger would no longer be the preeminent force on the premises. The next editor would be young Arthur's man—or woman. All of Arthur Sulzberger's talk about the value of "diversity" stirred the newsroom to speculate on the managerial future of, say, an Anna Quindlen. After Frankel's term, it was said, Arthur Sulzberger would make sure that two white males would never again simultaneously occupy the positions of executive editor and managing editor.

When the *Times* in 1990 announced that Joe Lelyveld, forty-nine, was succeeding Arthur Gelb as managing editor, the younger Sulzberger had the best of all worlds. He could work with Lelyveld in the remaining years of the Frankel regime, and take his time about the succession: Lelyveld, Raines, Quindlen, whoever. There would be no musical-chair charades in the newsroom. The *Times*people and the outsiders who watched the succession "struggle" at the paper in the Rosenthal years were caught looking in the wrong direction. The visiting editors' program and the excitement created by Rosenthal distracted everyone in the way a magician's assistant engages in side business while the master conjures the trick.

The entire Rosenthal selection process was a sideshow. To the extent that any of the participants believed that it mattered, they were fooling themselves. If Rosenthal, deep down, hoped to emerge from the process as the choice to stay, he was deluding himself as well. The Sulzbergers had their candidate, Frankel, in hand all along. There was no contest, because only the Sulzbergers made the rules. From beginning to end, Rosenthal was excluded from the real decision making, along with everyone else. Outsiders need not apply; Rosenthal's men, older and younger, were never in the running; neither was Rosenthal. A publisher at a rival newspaper watched the succession with a mixture of interest and bemusement; he extracted a moral from the story. People in the newsroom think they "run" the *Times*, but they are mistaken. It is the Sulzbergers' newspaper; the family does what it wants without staging popularity contests or collecting employee ballots.

A DAY IN THE LIFE
3:55 P.M. — 4:45 P.M.

3:55 P.M.

From Moscow, Bill Keller was offering the paper a feature, datelined Kiev, about the Ukrainian leader, a Brezhnev-era holdover named Vladimir Schherbitsky. Unlike the majority of candidates for the new Congress of Deputies to be elected March 23, Schherbitsky was running unopposed. Also from Moscow, correspondent John Burns filed an eleven-paragraph story quoting Gennadi I. Gerasimov, the foreign ministry spokesman. Gerasimov said Moscow could play a part in resolving some of the tensions between Iran and the West brought on by Salman Rushdie's *The Satanic Verses*. The bureau knew that the editors in New York had an appetite for stories involving free-speech issues; they were also interested in stories about publishing, especially book publishing, a major industry in New York. Keller and Burns punched their copy into the IBM desktop computers in the Moscow office; the impulses sped over leased wires to *Times* computers in New York, where the copy appeared again on computer screens, ready for editing by the backfield.

In recent years an informal system had developed among the New York desks as evening deadlines approached. Backfield editors were instructed to address first the "difficult" stories; these might involve complex and/or sensitive materials—or, occasionally, writers and reporters with a reputation within the *Times* of being "difficult." The difficult *Times*people were a mixed group: late filers, complainers, the overly stubborn, and so forth. Most were caring journalists zealous about their original copy. Correspondents who filed difficult stories, or were considered difficult themselves, were instructed to remain next to their computers for backfield editors' questions. When the backfield was satisfied, the correspondent normally got a "good night": a sign-off on the story, and permission to go home. Some reporters had their own variation of the nightly routine: They waited . . . to make sure the multiple levels of editors didn't introduce errors or "corrections" that changed the thrust of the story. These reporters worried about "all the futzing around"—as they saw it—by the desk. They stayed to give a "good night" to the editing process.

Because of the time differences, the "good night" sometimes came for Keller and Burns after midnight Moscow time. Some reporters in New York or Washington often didn't fare much better. Because the easiest stories were dealt with last by the desks, a "nondifficult" writer who had filed a straightforward piece of reporting was apt to get the latest "good night."

4:00 P.M.

Editors on the copy desk and in the backfield began glancing at their wristwatches, conscious of approaching deadlines. The computer age was supposed to ease the pressures of editing and printing; but at the *Times* a combination of factors instead forced *earlier* deadlines on the news staff.

Punch Sulzberger and his associates on the business side of the *Times*, desk editors came to realize, had tied the future of the paper to regional and national distribution. Since the 1970s, circulation had been growing beyond New York City, until only one third of the paper's total daily circulation of 1.1 million came from within the city. Another third was accounted for by the suburbs within a fifty-mile radius of the Times Building. The final third came from sales in the corridor—the Northeastern coastal strip, from Maine to Virginia—and from the National edition, printed at satellite plants in Chicago, Los Angeles, San Francisco and five other distribution points. The *Times* plants on 43rd Street and in New Jersey printed the corridor papers, and trucks delivered the bundles to New England and to Pennsylvania, Maryland, and Washington, D.C. Computer technology may have shortened the printing process and made later closing possible, but the Sulzbergers' national ambitions—and the low-tech provisions of the drivers' union contract with the *Times*—canceled out the gains.

As non–New York circulation grew, news deadlines were moved up. In the old linotype days, before the *Times* began its drive for national circulation, the filing deadline in the Washington bureau for the first edition was 7:30 P.M. Now the rule was off the desk and to New York by 5:00 P.M. That in turn meant reporters had to finish any interviews by early afternoon, begin writing, and, if necessary, hand in their copy in takes—one or two pages at a time. New York waived the 5:00 P.M. rule occasionally for major news developments. More often, though, there were no dispensations. At the Oliver North trial, late-afternoon developments had kept Michael Wines, the *Times* reporter, in court following the testimony. He missed his deadline. The desk in New York ran an Associated Press account of the trial in the first edition. The embarrassment was palpable: Wines was taken off the story.

The Wines decision was made by the new bureau chief, Howell Raines, still in his first months on the job. Raines arrived from the *Times* London bureau in 1988, at the beginning of the presidential campaign. His predecessor in Washington, Craig Whitney, was sent to London—to unsuspecting outsiders, a straight exchange of dream assignments. *Times*people knew better: Whitney had been exiled. London was a step backward after Washington. Whitney had signed the bureau's notorious "fishing expedition" letter to the presidential candidates on the eve of the 1988 primaries—the letter asking each candidate to supply the *Times* with his income tax forms, medical records, lists of contributors, and other personal data.

Once, the Washington bureau of the *Times* was among the leading cheerers of the candidates. Arthur Krock, Turner Catledge, James Reston, and Tom Wicker were all courtly men with small-town newspaper backgrounds; they came to Washington and flourished in the *Times* bureau chief's job. They enjoyed being drinking companions and, sometimes, confidants, of the political figures they covered. That was now a times past.

4:45 P.M.

The page-one meeting, the key meeting of the day, began in the executive conference room along the north wall of the news-room. Though it usually started at 4:45, it was still referred to as the 5:00 P.M. meeting. Managing editor Artie Gelb conducted it, as he had the 11:00 A.M. meeting. In his day, Gelb was a brilliant, fast-thinking M.E.; good as he was, his successor Joe Lelyveld, proved to be faster and brighter still. But true authority lay with the man at the opposite end of the table, the executive editor. Max Frankel was the arbiter of what the *Times'* front page would look like the next morning. Page one of the *Times*, he once told a questioner, "is what I say it is." He claimed that he valued collegiality; but the final decisions were his. The 5:00 P.M. meeting also gave Frankel the chance to raise queries about the stories he had read and alert the backfield to pursue his questions in the next hour before deadline.

The page-one elements for March 1 offered no surprises: Chi-cago mayoral primary results, developments in the Tower nom-ination, the Shoreham nuclear reactor agreement. Summaries of these stories were in the computer directory, and available to senior editors. Because everyone at the meeting had read the factual summary, department editors used their time to argue why their stories deserved page-one attention. Usually, seven or eight department desks sent representatives, depending on what they had to offer for fronting. The sports desk attended only occasionally; the national and foreign desks showed up for ev-ery meeting.

In the days before Frankel and Lelyveld, department heads made their pitch and left. A core group composed of the exec-utive editor, Abe Rosenthal, the managing editor, and three or four of their assistants, then made the decisions. Under Frankel and Lelyveld, the meetings opened up a bit. Department editors remained to debate story decisions. In Washington, the bureau chief regularly participated via speakerphone. Overseas corre-spondents on home leave came by, sitting in a rear row of chairs and listening to the give-and-take.

The meetings grew more fractious. Frankel let it be known that his editors "ought to be able to say anything, even dumb things," in the interests of a better page one. Still, Frankel was a majority of one and meetings seldom went past 6:00 P.M., while the Rosenthal meetings often ran eighty minutes or longer. In both regimes, page-one meetings sometimes became stuck on a point of journalistic arcana; like a broken record player, they lurched on for thirty or forty minutes without resolution. Rump sessions frequently followed as department editors drew senior editors aside and privately lobbied to reverse the decisions made a few moments earlier.

A jumble of hunches, conventions from the past, untestable assumptions, hard facts and unstated principles shaped page one. Senior *Times* editors agreed that, as Al Siegal said, "the lead stories virtually chose themselves." The bigger the story in the editors' judgment, the bigger the headline. This day, the 5:00 P.M. meeting deemed nothing worth more than a one-column head: "Cuomo and LILCO/Sign a New Accord/To Shut Shoreham." It was not earthshaking—rather, a minimally passable choice, "a story that won't embarrass us," one senior editor remembered thinking. As the lead story, Cuomo-LILCO was placed on the top right-hand side of the paper. The *Times* always tried to lead its front page with spot news. The off-lead, or second most important story, went on the left: "Bush Fails to Win Any New Votes/As Senate Fight Over Tower Boils." It was a story of nonmovement, rescued in part by the accompanying photo of Bush and Tower, smiling. The Venezuelan riots story was placed in the middle of the page. *Times* market research suggested that page-center was a Bermuda Triangle for readers: Few people could recall what appeared there when asked by the researchers.

The rest of the page was unremarkable, if not outright boring: no reader-friendly features, no exclusives, no trend stories, no news analyses, no fallback to the Frankel rule, "If there's no spot story, then go with the next most interesting story, period." There was nothing, in short, to cause concern on the part of old-time editors wary of the intrusion of "un-*Times*-like" stories in the Frankel-era paper. This page one on this particular day did not violate the traditionalists' rule: "The *New York Times* should report the news, it shouldn't make news."

One visiting correspondent came away from the page-one meeting thinking he had observed "the best and worst of the *Times*." He was impressed by "the great collegiality of the meeting and the good paper that results from it." At the same time, he was bothered by a process that "put such a premium on glibness." Well-spoken, well-prepared editors, able to argue for their stories clearly, won the contest for space. Other editors— "the ones who don't give good meeting"—found that their offerings were rejected. The styles of individual editors, as much as the content of the presentation, subtly influenced story selection, or so the correspondent thought. A deputy editor from the correspondents' desk tended to mumble his presentation, and on those days that the deputy represented the desk, its stories received less attention.

8

THE NEWSROOM:
THE TIMES THAT
TRIES MEN'S SOULS

JOHN ROTHMAN, who spent forty-two years with the *Times*, the last ten as director of its archives, was explaining to a visitor in his office not long ago why some well-regarded journalists had left the paper. Most of the reasons offered were general to the point of opaqueness: Sydney Schanberg resigned shortly after "a publisher's decision" to discontinue the New York City–affairs column that Schanberg was contributing to the *Times'* Op-Ed page; Richard Eder, the theater critic, was removed from his reviewer's post after "bad evaluations of his work." The explanation for the departure of John Leonard, once the editor of the *Book Review* (as well as a daily book critic), unexpectedly cut through the bland recitation. "Some people just aren't good *Times*men." Then, aware perhaps that he had revealed more about how the institutional *Times* sees itself than he wanted, Rothman corrected himself. "Some people aren't good *organizational* men," he said.

Schanberg went on to write a column for *New York Newsday*, continuing the same adversarial approach to the city's real estate developers that upset publisher Punch Sulzberger. Eder spent a short time in exile in the Paris bureau of the *Times* before leaving the paper entirely to become a critic at large for the *Los Angeles Times*. There, in after-hours conversations, he shared with fellow workers his musings about the differences between the two *Times*es. On his way to meetings with top editors at the *New York Times,* Eder remembered, "There was always a sinking feeling in my stomach. I felt my bones afterward to see which ones might have been broken." Later, after he joined the *Los Angeles Times,* Eder recounted, "I went to the editor and asked him what he wanted me to write, and I was told, 'Anything you want. . . .' Two years later I won the Pulitzer Prize." The brilliant, erratic John Leonard struggled for a time with depression and alcoholism, but organized a productive career post-*Times.* Through the 1980s and into the 1990s, Leonard balanced regular assignments from *New York* magazine (where he wrote television reviews), his column for *New York Newsday* (personal essays about literature and politics), and weekly appearances on the CBS program "Sunday Morning with Charles Kuralt" (more commentary).

No one had to pass the hat for these three former *Times*men, or for ninety-nine out of one hundred other journalists, well known or unsung, male or female, who over the past two decades decided, or had it decided for them, that they were not "good *Times*men" and so moved on to other news organizations, to free-lance work, or out of journalism entirely.

Yet such experiences provoke curiosity about what the qualities of "good *Times*men" were. More generally, they raise questions about what it was like to work in the *Times* newsroom and why some men and women flourished and others left, in failure or frustration.

There is also a connection between the conditions of news work at the *Times* and the news output of the *Times*—that is, the content of the stories themselves. *Times'* editors proclaim their efforts to insure fairness and balance. No one questions their intentions; but they work at a subjective task. From the multiplicity of events in any given day, the collective newsroom extracts the stories it wants to tell, believes should be told, or thinks its readers are eager to hear. Journalists call this "news." It is not "reality" but an artifact, someone's story of what happened. In the *Times* newsroom, the selection is done by a company of almost one thousand men and women working under agreed-upon procedures. Who they are and what they are trained to value matters in the collection and publication of the news. This is not a stop-press bulletin. The cultural historian Robert Darnton points out how "the context of work" shapes the content of the news: The stories the newspaper tells depend on certain "inherited techniques of storytelling"— conventions passed on from older to younger journalists. Long before

Darnton, too, Walter Lippmann explained how the "processes" of journalism are intended to produce news as distinct from truth.

One of the most visible processes of the *Times* is the bureaucracy: The newsroom is vast and hierarchical. Many, many people oversee the output of many, many other people. Another obvious characteristic is the *Times'* journalistic self-image; these are people who describe their work as stressful, competitive, and—above all—"important." The editors' attitude is that, as I've indicated, there's no fundamental connection between the conditions of news work and the outputs of work, at least not one that they can't anticipate and correct. The news is the news, and anyway, the *Times* is not that different from other places where intellectual work is done; it's only bigger and better. Thus, when the behavioral scientist Chris Argyris conducted his interviews at the *Times*, he discovered that most *Times*people regarded any introspective analyses of their "condition" as a waste of time—the same complaint Max Frankel would voice a generation later. Yet reporters described themselves and their colleagues to Argyris as "highly competitive," "partially paranoid," "out to show the emperor to be without clothes." Some reporters, intent upon succeeding within the *Times* system, said that they would be willing to commit "shady acts" to get a story. They acknowledged that, under pressure and vying for the attention of their superiors (and for good display in the paper), they might sometimes "magnify" certain elements of the story.

When Argyris then inquired how such predispositions affected the way the *Times* reported reality—how it covered "the news"—the line went dead: His subjects professed not to know what he was talking about. They argued that all reporting was incomplete and subjective because it was done under daily pressure. In Argyris's words, "They polarized the issue"; they exaggerated the depth, pervasiveness, and inevitability of distortion—and then dismissed the subject. "There was no sense discussing 'subjectivity' because nothing could be done about it." The reader must take the *Times* "as is." This exasperated Argyris. To stretch the point a bit, assume the consumer was not a reader of the *New York Times* but rather a passenger flying TWA. The airline and its unionized pilots are involved in a contract dispute over seniority. The passenger remains unconcerned about the details as long as the disagreement doesn't affect overall TWA flight operations or the crew's performance in getting the aircraft from city A to city B. So, too, with the conditions of work at the *Times* (absent any life-threatening possibilities). When the product, the news, is reliable and complete, the operations of the bureaucracy and the morale of the newsroom are not of great concern to the reader. They are the grist of insiders' gossip, the stuff of Page Six of the *New York Post*, or *Spy* magazine. The personal becomes public only when it affects the outputs of paper.

Robert Darnton is on the Princeton faculty, where his specialty is French history; he also knows the *Times* newsroom. His father was a *Times* combat correspondent who was killed during World War II (a wall plaque near the foreign desk commemorates his death). His brother, John, a *Times* senior editor, supervised the paper's metropolitan coverage from 1988 to 1991. Beginning in 1959, Robert Darnton worked as a police reporter for the *Newark Star-Ledger* and the *Times* before leaving journalism in 1964 for a scholar's career. Ten years later, Professor Darnton reflected on what reporter Darnton had learned of the "sociology of the newsroom." The *Times*, he concluded, was "an editor's paper." New arrivals—young, eager, malleable—quickly pick up the not-so-hidden clues to what the news desks want. They learn, through the patterns of rewards and punishments, the values of "the good *Times*man"—just as employees of large companies like IBM or Citicorp learn what's expected of them. The editors mete out plum assignments and public pats on the back, or withhold these reinforcements. The carrot or the stick, observed by one's peers, an important audience, led as well to their approval, or scorn. Among the editors' most tangible rewards are merit pay increases and bonuses. All organizations use the power of the purse; the *Times* has enshrined the process. The Publisher's Awards, cash prizes for the best work each month, are posted on all bulletin boards. In the years after Robert Darnton left, and particularly during the Max Frankel era, the editors' favorites were assiduously cultivated. In 1990 Frankel created a new "senior writer and photographer" category, outside the provisions of the *Times* contract with the Newspaper Guild. This allowed him to single out nearly two dozen men and women and pay them $15,000 to $20,000 more than the Guild's top scale. (In 1993, the minimum salary for beginning reporters at the *Times* was $60,264.)

Similarly, punishment for "bad" *Times* behavior is sometimes done so openly that the names might just as well have been posted on bulletin boards. *Times*people, after their trial period, have lifetime tenure; according to the Newspaper Guild contract, they cannot be fired except if convicted of a felony, such as theft or possession of drugs, or for reasons of overwhelming economic need (in which case the Times Company would have to open its financial books to Guild lawyers to prove its case). But if it is hard to remove the "difficult" *Times*men, they can quite easily be moved around, or made so miserable that they resign. Prickly, stubborn Richard Severo challenged the hierarchy and was sentenced to the lowly obit desk. The Ray Bonner case shows how the "difficult" can be made to go on their own.

Raymond Bonner was one of the *Times'* best and hardest-working, though most unorthodox, foreign correspondents. A lawyer by training and a Vietnam veteran, he worked for a time for Ralph Nader in Washington before going to Latin America to try his hand as a freelance journalist. In December 1980 Bonner, then thirty-eight, was in El Salvador writing about the civil war between the rightist military government, backed by the United States, and the leftist opposition forces (supplied, the Reagan administration insisted, by Communist Cuba and the Nicaraguan Sandinistas). The *Times*, in a sharp departure from its institutional ways, hired Bonner in San Salvador—"in the field"—for a two-week tryout. It turned into a staff job, and a spectacular mismatch. Bonner, compact, intense, committed, had no rabbi/sponsors in New York; he had never "done lunch" with the editors. His stories from the battle zone earned him the enmity of the U.S. embassy people, the Reagan White House, and its supporters in the press—in particular the hard-conservative editorial page of the *Wall Street Journal* and a right-wing press watchdog group called Accuracy in Media. In the winter of 1981–1982, Bonner and Alma Guillermoprieto of the *Washington Post* were escorted by the guerrillas to the village of Mozote, where, the journalists reported, they found the human remains of a massacre carried out by government troops. Bonner placed the death toll at between seven hundred and nine hundred men, women, and children. The progovernment right in the U.S. immediately smelled a Marxist plot, intended to undermine support for aid to the Salvador government. Accuracy in Media devoted two issues of its *AIM Report* to Bonner's stories and his "suspect" background (Nader, and also for a time, Consumers Union!). In June 1982 Reed Irvine, editor of the *AIM Report*, arranged a meeting with Punch Sulzberger; Irvine told the publisher, according to the *AIM Report*, that "Bonner was worth a division to the Communists in Central America." Two months later, Bonner received a call from the

Times foreign desk, telling him he was being reassigned to the home office. (Later, responding to a reporter's question, Abe Rosenthal scoffed at the idea that the *Times* "knuckled under" to the Reagan White House or to right-wing pressure; rather Bonner was "self-taught," and so he needed desk work in New York to be a "totally trained reporter.") Bonner took a leave to finish a book—and never returned to the newsroom. He has since refused to discuss his short, unhappy *Times* career, in part because that is his nature, and in part because his companion, later his wife, was a *Times* reporter on a good track at the paper. Friends of Bonner were not so circumspect. "The *Times*'s treatment just broke his spirit," a friend remembered. "He seemed like 'damaged goods' after he left the *Times*—no newspaper would have him." Bonner wrote books, contributed to *The New Yorker*, and did free-lance pieces. In March 1993, more than a decade after the Mozote story, a special United Nations commission of inquiry confirmed that Bonner and Guillermoprieto were correct: the massacre had taken place, though the Salvador military and U.S. officials tried a clumsy cover-up. The *Times* gave the UN report modest treatment; worse, it said nothing of Bonner and the Reaganauts or the AIM campaign of character assassination. "The *Times* just disappointed him again," says the friend.

For every Bonner or Severo-like public spectacle, dozens of other men and women endured penance quietly. Robert Stock was one of them. Stock never was judged difficult or contentious by the senior editors—indeed, he was one of those editors for most of his first twenty-three years at the *Times*, in the Travel section, and at the *Times Magazine*. He was the editor of the *Times* supplement, Business World, in the summer of 1991 when his own world collapsed. Advertising pages fell as the northeast region's recession deepened; the Sulzbergers decided for reasons of economy to discontinue the supplement. Stock declined to apply for the one of the so-called buyouts management offered in a related effort to lower operating costs. *Times*-people over fifty-five and with a minimum of fifteen years' service at the paper would receive as severance the equivalent of seventy-eight weeks of salary. For someone at Stock's pay level, the buyout would average around $130,000. "We are offering a humane nest egg," Punch Sulzberger claimed at the time. Stock thought otherwise. A fit, lively man whose taste in clothes ran to tweed sports jackets and chino slacks, Stock decided that, at sixty-two, he was not ready to retire. A few days after the deadline for applying passed, Stock was told to report to the metro copy desk, to work the 4:00 to 11:00 P.M. shift. He had to learn story formatting and other computer operations that, in the past, he had left to his assistants. His shift permitted twenty minutes for dinner. The lesson of his transfer to the nightside was not lost on other *Times*men. But Stock, like Severo, took a certain pride in surviving his personal Siberia.

No one starts out to be "difficult." They strive, as Robert Darnton did in his day, to be good *Times*men. Darnton quickly learned how to write to please his immediate editors. He grasped the process of fitting a story to the editors' preconceptions, mastering what he calls "the standardization and stereotyping" of news. Working in the London bureau of the *Times* in 1963 and 1964, he produced copy that followed accepted journalistic clichés about England. As Winston Churchill lay ill, Darnton wrote about the crowds gathered outside the great man's window. One man catches a glimpse of Churchill: "Blimey, he's beautiful," Darnton has a mythic average Londoner say. Whether or not the reporter actually heard the quote was beside the point. It was harmless enough, and it matched expectations. "The combination of cockney-Churchill could not be resisted," Darnton remembered. The editors played the story on page one.

The reporter intent on being a good *Times*men understood both the breadth and limits of editor power. The desk men were sticklers for language and the enforcers of *The New York Times Manual of Style and Usage*, a 230-page handbook described as "the rules or guides to insure consistency" in such matters as spelling and abbreviations in the pages of the *Times*; but the manual went far beyond whether, in its own example, the word *martini* should or should not be capitalized. Several entries explained "matters of policy and objectives of the *Times* that members of its news staff are asked to keep especially in mind." Under the heading "obscenity, vulgarity, profanity," for example, the manual noted that "a *hell* or a *damn* is really not offensive to a great degree. But if the paper is peppered with such words, the news report is cheapened. . . ." When a story left the good *Times*man's typewriter—or today, the computer queue—it passed into the control of the copy editor. These desk editors, in Darnton's words, treated stories as "segments of an unremitting flow of 'copy' which cries out for standardization." The *Times*' reporters were unhappy to see "their" work in the hands of such "humorless zombies." Class, race, and gender as well as the conflicting roles of writer and editor also contributed to the tensions. In Darnton's day, the desk men were likely to be City College graduates, the sons of poor immigrants; the younger reporters, by contrast, just as likely came from Columbia, Harvard, or other private universities. By the 1990s, the older desk men were editing the copy of not only the sons of the affluent—as the editors saw it—but also the copy of younger women and blacks, who often had gone to the same Ivy League schools. These more recent hires perpetuated rather than weakened the paper's class divisions. The *Times*' efforts at affirmative action, a national-desk editor complained to a friend in the fall of 1991, "had made the place more boringly homogeneous: All the 'minorities' seem to be the children of doctors and teachers." (The editor asked that his name not be used; rather he suggested he be identified as a *"Times* veteran.")

The resolution of reporter-desk conflicts depended on the top editor. In Turner Catledge's newsroom, the values of order and hierarchy prevailed, and the copy editors' authority went unchallenged. One Catledge-era hire, David Halberstam, was a Harvard man and had worked at two other papers before joining the *Times*. Assigned to the Washington bureau, Halberstam supposedly was made to rewrite the first story he filed five times by bureau desk man Wallace Carroll. Halberstam has a different but equally telling memory. "The story is way off," he says. In his recollection, "I was hired to the Washington bureau because Scotty Reston wanted reporters who could also write"—the Max Frankel quest thirty years later—"and I was judged to fit in that category. To my memory there was no rewriting [in the bureau] at all. The great obstacle was the New York desk system. In those days the power of the desk was immense, in comparison to the New York *Herald Tribune* and the Nashville *Tennessean*, where I had worked. The New York copy editors felt free to do anything to your copy that they wanted. The reporter was powerless to fight back and did not even see what had been done to his story until they next day." As for Wallace Carroll, Halberstam said, the editor was "on the side of the reporters. I had no trouble with him, found him to be a considerable help and have no recollection of anyone else having a problem with him." Halberstam adds: "Gradually over the years, in no small part because of the pressure from television, the paper's definition of what constituted a story and what levels of freedom a reporter was given was expanded." By then, it was too late for Halberstam. Though he went on to report from the Congo and Vietnam as a *Times* correspondent, he eventually quit and became a best-selling author.

The good *Times*man, then and now, got along by going along. Catledge himself was the model of correct behavior. He said that he learned early in his career how to work harmoniously with others and "get them to like me and listen to me." When Darnton was at the *Times*, Abe Rosenthal was beginning to consolidate his power. Rosenthal wanted a staff in his own aggressive image: The good *Times*men of the Rosenthal era were the reporters who "hustled" and produced snappy, original stories. They got the best assignments and the promotions. In the *Times* of Max Frankel, the definition of a good *Times*man shifted again. The meditative Frankel rewarded the more writerly storytellers; he elevated the stylist—man or woman, black or white, Ivy or City College—over the stickler copy editor and the hustling street reporter. Through all the changes, the values of the top editor determined the ascendancy of one faction or another, as well as the tilt of the news. Because the shifts were gradual, the paper outwardly continued to appear in its familiar institutional shape, the eternal *Times*.

The acculturation of the good *Times*man observed by Robert Darnton actually begins before the new hire enters the building. A good *Times*man, first of all, ought to feel that he has arrived at the top of his field on the day he joins the paper. The *Times* is highly selective in its hiring, and no one is allowed into its ranks casually. When a young journalist named Martin Levine left a well-paying position at *Book Digest* magazine to join the *Book Review* section, the discussion of his starting salary went quickly. Levine had been on the *Crimson* during his undergraduate years at Harvard; later he was a book critic at *Newsday*. The *Times* assistant managing editor dealing with Levine asked him what he was being paid at *Book Digest*, and more than matched it. According to Levine, "He told me, 'No one takes a pay cut to come to work for the *Times*.' Even if it meant just a few hundred symbolic dollars, they were determined to underline the 'importance' of the *Times*." The *Times* insisted on paying more to someone coming over from the competition and it also volunteered added benefits. The paper, for example, paid for language lessons for reporters and photographers prepping for new assignments, and in some cases for their spouses as well. In one typical calendar year, the news department underwrote such training for sixteen correspondents and two wives. Later, when a reporter told his editor that he was unable to accept an assignment because the story required driving and the reporter had let his license lapse, a staff memo asked that everyone make sure their permits were current; the memo concluded, in the best paternal manner: "Let me remind any of you who don't know how to drive that we will pay for lessons."

Levine was hired in the Rosenthal era. In Frankel's time the attitude was no different. A "stylish" writer that Frankel wanted to recruit bridled at the newspaper's rules against writing for other outlets, even those not competitive with the *Times*, such as special-interest magazines. The writer calculated the rule would cost her $15,000 to $20,000 annually in "lost" earnings. Frankel was adamant about outside writing; but he agreed that the *Times* would make up the shortfall, by adding a "signing bonus" to her base salary. Similarly, in 1989, when the book critic John Gross was leaving the *Times*, the editors saw an opportunity for progress on the pledge Frankel made to hire more minority journalists. Margo Jefferson, a fortyish black woman who had been an editor at *Newsweek* and a contributor to *Vogue*, was being actively courted by the *Times*. Three senior editors took turns calling her, offering counsel, describing the part she could play at the *Times* and, by extension, in the cultural life of the country. At the time, she was teaching in the journalism department at New York University while continuing to write criticism and magazine articles. Jefferson was uncertain whether she wanted to continue as a free-lance journalist or become an "important" critic. Independence or prestige? Perhaps she could continue to do some outside writing? She learned that was not the thinking of a good *Times*man. "This is a special place," the senior man on the interviewing team told her. "Nothing in your career can be like being at the *Times*. All other assignments pale." Jefferson and the *Times* remained apart. "I was unsure that I wanted to surrender to the institution," Jefferson recalled. In the spring of 1991, she decided instead to accept a teaching post at Columbia University. But Frankel didn't forget Jefferson, or his vow to make more minority hires. The editors kept sweetening the pot, promising her more money, prime display, and choice assignments. In June 1993, at the end of the spring semester at Columbia, the *Times* announced Jefferson's appointment as its newest cultural critic.

Like Levine and Jefferson, the prospective new hire has typically accumulated several years of experience at other newspapers, or in related work, before the *Times* will consider an application. When James Reston was chief of the *Times'* Washington bureau, he instituted a system of news clerkships; Reston hired bright young men from the Ivy schools to serve as his assistant, sorting mail, clipping newspapers, keeping files—and observing Reston close up. After a year, Reston's news clerks graduated to reporting jobs. A number of *Times* stars came up in this manner, including Robert Darnton's brother, John Darnton. In the mid-1970s, a Yale graduate named James Brooke served as Reston's clerk and achieved a dubious first: The *Times* did not make him a reporter after his Reston clerkship. The competition for *Times* reporting slots was so keen, Brooke was told, it would be better if he went out and "got a reputation" if he wanted to work at the *Times*. And so Brooke, tall, slim, dark-haired, well-groomed, fluent in French and Spanish, left Washington for Rio de Janeiro, where he had talked himself on to an English-language paper, the *Brazil Herald*. In Rio, he also served as a stringer for the *Miami Herald* and the *Washington Post* and worked himself onto the *Herald* staff. Finally, in 1984, he was hired by the *Times*. In 1986, at the age of thirty-one, he became the *Times'* West African bureau chief, and three years later, the *Times'* man in Rio, covering all of the South American continent.

A good *Times*man also must be prepared for a lengthy—sometimes ludicrous—mating dance once the *Times* shows interest in hiring him. The courtship of Margo Jefferson sputtered on and off over a period of four years, and it was not all that exceptional. John Crudele joined the *Times* in 1985 as a financial-news writer. Crudele worked for Reuters, making his reputation as an astute reporter of Wall Street during the 1980s boom years. The *Times* sought him out: "They wanted me, I wanted them," he says, "and it still took six months." Crudele sat through four separate interviews, each one higher up the *Times* chain of command. Two editors told him they were unsure why they were interviewing him: "It's the editor of your section who really cares. He's the one trying to hire you. The rest of this is bullshit." The interviewing process culminated in a session with the executive editor, in Crudele's day, Rosenthal. As Crudele remembers the interview, "Rosenthal was sitting at a desk with these toys . . . I think, plastic guns . . . on his desk. He doesn't look me in the eye. He says, 'I'd like to hire you.' Then he calls in my section editor, and says to him, 'You've made a good choice.' And then to me, 'Glad to have you aboard.' There's more chitchit about my specialty, the financial markets. Then he says, 'We would like to have you do more interviews, but we've streamlined the process.' " Crudele later told his wife, "Streamlined, hell! It was crazy." Rosenthal explained why the process was so extensive. "It's because we're giving people tenure here. . . . This is for life." Crudele found himself thinking, Nothing's for life.

Later Rosenthal invited several recent hires, including Crudele, to the executive dining room to celebrate their induction into the *Times*. To reach the reception, the new *Times*men and -women walked down a winding corridor; on the walls on either side were framed pictures of the *Times*' winners of the Pulitzer Prize, a display connecting the *Times*' past to the present (history looks out on *Times* workers wherever they are; the walls of the Tokyo offices are decorated with photographs of Adolph Ochs and past chiefs of the bureau). At the reception, Crudele recalled, "we new boys and girls had cheese and wine and tried not to get drunk in front of the boss. In Rosenthal's speech, he said he would like to welcome us all to the *Times*, but since the *Times* was now our home, 'it seemed inappropriate to welcome someone to one's own house.' A group of us in back snickered. It sounded so presumptuous that we should consider the place as dear to us as it was to him and the older editors. We were there to feed our families, not to join a priesthood." (Crudele left the *Times* two years later).

Many younger journalists were prepared to suspend some of this generational skepticism in order to become good *Times*men. Anna Quindlen eventually rose through the ranks to achieve in 1990 one of the best prizes the *Times* can bestow—a twice-weekly column on the Op-Ed page. Quindlen joined the *Times* in 1977 after working as a general assignment reporter for the *New York Post*. Her column reflected a feminist sensibility on such contemporary "women's issues" as abortion, sexual harassment, and the limits of equality in the workplace. In her own ascent at the *Times*, however, Quindlen chose accommodation rather than trying to smash through the "glass ceiling" that thwarts women's ambitions. "Fifteen years ago at the *Times*, our tendency was to try to blend in, to be 'another one of the boys,' " she recalled for a group of university students (80 percent of them female) in the fall of 1991. Good *Times*men and -women were aware of the importance of behaving responsibly. When Quindlen worked at the *Post*, she said, "The feeling was, 'If we get it wrong today, there's always tomorrow.' At the *Times*, you feel that if you make any mistake, a bolt from above will strike you. You know what they say about journalism being a first rough draft of history? That's the *Times*." Some of Quindlen's audience were skeptical. Go to the public library, she said, and look around the reading room. "When I see some fifteen-year-old reading the *Times*—*my* words—on microfiche, I feel that weight of history."

The *Post* had the sporty, big-mouthed style associated with New York City tabloids; but it also had, in Quindlen's day, a newsroom where the majority of reporters were women (52 percent by Quindlen's count). At the *Times*, by contrast, women made up no more than 15 percent of the newsroom during the late 1970s and early 1980s. The *Times* actively sought more women, propelled along by a sex discrimination suit brought in 1974 on behalf of a group of *Times* women employees. The newly recruited women, like the new male hires, were encouraged to regard the *Times* as an institution above and apart from all others. "The editors acted like the *Times* was a 'calling' and a form of higher service," says Alex S. Jones, who regarded the editors' arrogance with a certain sly compliance. Jones joined the *Times* in 1983. He came from a publishing family in East Tennessee, where newspapering for him was a real calling. He had been the editor of the *Greenville Sun*, the paper his family had owned since the early 1900s. He became a Nieman Fellow at Harvard in 1981, and in his first week in Cambridge met Susan Tifft, a Duke graduate who was studying at the Kennedy School of Government. When the couple decided to marry at the end of the Harvard academic year, Jones knew he would not be going back to Tennessee, to the family business. Tifft wanted to write about national politics, and so they concentrated on job hunting in Washington and New York. Jones had attended the annual meetings of the newspaper owners' and editors' professional associations and met *Times* executives socially. The *Times* was looking for a reporter to cover the press; Jones, with his newspaper-business background and his Harvard training, seemed like an ideal candidate. Nevertheless, he, too, went through the elaborate interviewing process, culminating in a meeting with executive editor Rosenthal, who insisted on making the formal offer to all new hires. Jones met Rosenthal in the editor's sitting room, next to his office just off the newsroom. The sitting room was done in Japanese-style, homage to Rosenthal's Tokyo bureau days. There was a shoji screen and scrolls on the wall. They talked twenty to twenty-five minutes and then Rosenthal leaned forward. He put his hand lightly on Jones's knee, and asked, "Would you join us?" Jones answered yes; Rosenthal leaned forward again toward the new *Times-man*, and with a broad smile asked: "Who's the first person you're going to tell?"

Jones, Quindlen, and Crudele were among the prospective new hires who managed to avoid the series of test assignments that the *Times* uses to winnow out people who don't meet the editors' standards for good *Times*men. Not long ago, a white, male Ivy League gradu-ate—who does not want his name used—sent a letter of application for a reporter's job, along with clips of his articles, to the editor of one of the *Times'* major sections. Later the applicant spoke on the phone with a deputy editor, who sounded only moderately encouraging. The *Times*, he was told, had been looking for minorities ("Max Frankel says that we've got to have some blacks"). The applicant persisted; he was given a test assignment, to write a feature story. He did well on the test, according to the detailed commentary sent to him by one of the editors. He then was asked to write a critique of the section's pages. He gave the assignment considerable attention; in his words, "I didn't pull any punches." He wrote that he found many stories predictable, and the writing stilted. The editor liked his comments and moved the applicant on to the next assignment, a list of story ideas for the section. He submitted twelve proposals, which were judged good enough to take him past this third hurdle. He was told that while no reporting positions were available for him, an editing job might open in a few months. Four months had passed and he still had not managed to arrange a face-to-face interview. Finally, eight months after he first applied, the man was invited to New York to meet the editors; six weeks later they offered him an editing assignment on the section desk.

At this point, new hires may still be required to go through an extended trial, or probation period. Both the *Times* and the tryout look each other over, although the arrangement favors the institution. The outcome may be uncertain until the end, as probationer Michael Gross discovered. A 1974 graduate of Vassar College, Gross built a solid free-lance career in the years between his twenty-first and thirty-first birthdays. He wrote books on rock and folk musicians (including a life of Bob Dylan), and also tried his hand as a mystery novel writer, an advertising copywriter, a contributor to *Manhattan Inc.* and *Vanity Fair* magazines, and a reporter for the *East Side Express*, a short-lived Manhattan weekly. He began writing about the fashion business ("to meet models," he says now). One afternoon in early 1985, in his thirty-third year, he bolted upright in his Manhattan apartment. "I read in Liz Smith's gossip column that John Duka, the fashion/style columnist for the *Times*, had quit what I considered a dream job." Gross's older sister, Jane, was a valued *Times* reporter. She urged him to send his clippings to James Greenfield, at the time an assistant managing editor. Greenfield, Michael Gross remembers, "was very charming. I suppose it was because he had once worked for the State Department." Next Gross met Nancy Newhouse, the editor of the Home and Living sections. "She made it clear that this was going to be a long process." Four months passed. "My life goes on," Gross says. "Then I'm told I am a finalist, but that there is no reason to cheer yet. Two more months pass and I get a call to come in to see Abe Rosenthal. We spent at least an hour together. It's clear from his questioning that there was a 'Duka problem.' " The *Times* was unhappy with Duka: He was considered to have behaved in an un-*Times*-like manner, apparently abusing his *Times* privileges by, among other things, bringing his girlfriend to fashion shows and passing her off as a *Times* staff person (a "crime" probably every reporter has perpetrated in one context or another). Nevertheless, Rosenthal did not commit himself to Gross during their interview. Later Duka resigned from the paper. Two more months went by. In late 1985, Gross got an offer, but not of a job. Rather, the *Times* gave him the chance to work as a free-lance "contract writer" for six months at a salary twice what the *East Side Express* paid him. Gross was told the arrangement was a way around the Newspaper Guild rules, which required the *Times* to make its decision to hire and confer job security after a fourteen-week trial. The good pay also came with a trip to Paris to cover the showings (the assignment "would clarify questions about his ability to cover fashion," noted his editor, Newhouse). Two days shy of the six-month mark, the *Times* formally notified Gross he had made the staff. He was assigned to the Style pages, to write a column called "Notes on Fashion." The end of his tryout came with another bonus. While Rosenthal and Greenfield were careful about who they admitted to the ranks of the *Times*, Gross discovered, the editors had little interest in what a fashion writer actually wrote once at the *Times*, short of embarrassing them as Duka apparently had. "They thought fashion was squishy soft. The pages were about personalities and parties and fun, and not 'real news.' And so they didn't pay much attention to us."

Still, Gross says, "the self-importance of the place" nagged at him. He was not adapting: He wasn't becoming a genuinely good *Times*man. Gross developed a "thirty-month plan." At the end of two and a half years at the *Times*, he would consider his options again. As Gross's private deadline approached, he found himself sitting on the balcony of the Beverly Wilshire hotel in Los Angeles, on assignment from the *Times*. "I was doing my column. I could pick up the phone, and get anyone—they would respond to 'The *Times*.' I had my expense account. It was intoxicating. I rethought my plan. Maybe I'm wrong about the *Times*. This is a great life. I'm in love with the world." Three days later, Gross was told that the new editor, Max Frankel, had much firmer ideas about fashion coverage than his predecessor. The Style page, where Gross's "Notes on Fashion" appeared, was being changed. Frankel wanted a new column focusing on the business of fashion— sales figures, marketing strategies, tie-ins of the couturiers with department-store chains, hirings and firings. Frankel also wanted the column to be "more national"—to work in references to fashion-business news from Dallas and Beverly Hills—in keeping with the *Times'* new plan to make its pages attractive to an audience outside New York.

The column's name was changed, to "Patterns." Gross changed too. He attended a retirement party for a fellow fashion writer, a good *Times*woman. She was sixty-five; she had been at the *Times* forty-one years, and never wanted to work anywhere else. Elsewhere in the room were a half dozen others just like her, except at earlier stages in their *Times* career. Some people, though not Gross, regarded them, uncharitably, as "the coven," and members of a closed culture. Six months later, he left the *Times*. He has burnished his reputation, and makes a very good living as a magazine writer.

In a notorious passage in his novel *Scoop*, Evelyn Waugh described the offices of the London newspaper *The Beast*, where neurotic men in shirtsleeves and green eyeshades spent their days "insulting and betraying one another in surroundings of unredeemed squalor." Many *Times*people made the point that the real-life *Times*, albeit in ways more benign than the fictional *Beast*, was a place of high ambition and sharpened rivalries—for stories, for bylines, for play on page one, for new and more glorious assignments. Former *Times* reporter Michael Norman served with the Marines in Vietnam, one of the very few

*Times*men with a full tour on the battlefield. No stranger to turmoil, Norman brought a cool eye to the *Times* "experience." He likened the *Times* newsroom, where he worked from 1981 to 1986, to a kind of department store, say, Filene's basement, during a big clearance sale: Reporters were jostling for the top jobs, like a roomful of people grabbing for a few pairs of socks.

In the Catledge era, the newsroom was considered an orderly, even congenial place. Reporters sat according to rank. The best men— Meyer Berger, Peter Kihss, Murray Schumach, later, Homer Bigart (the stars were invariably male then)—occupied the front desks, closest to the city editor and his assistants. The middle-level reporters sat behind the stars; far to the rear of the room were the newest staff members. When Russell Baker first walked into the *Times* newsroom in November 1954, he was shocked by how different it was from the *Baltimore Sun*, where he had worked the previous seven years. At the *Sun*, anyone who had been around five years was considered an old hand; at the *Times*, Baker got the impression that everybody intended to stay "until life's sunset." The *Sun* was a rough-and-tumble place; the contented middle-aged *Times*men in business suits, Baker thought, gave the newsroom the aspect of an insurance office. Darnton the cultural historian filled out Baker's sketch, describing how clusters of *Times* reporters grouped together according to age, life-style and social background (in his day, Harvard versus City College). These sub-groups held off the copy editors and helped the reporters deal with their own insecurities. Darnton remembered how four or five of his friends, all private-university men, gathered informally to decipher a City Hall document on some newly issued welfare regulations. The man assigned the story by the editors had to do a rush job, but was mystified by the impenetrable bureaucratese in the report (some things never change). The group collectively agreed on what it thought the regulations meant, and the reporter wrote the story accordingly.

The place was tense enough, even in these supposed good old days. "There has always been 'low morale,' " said John Corry, who joined the *Times* in 1956 and stayed until 1988. "There's no such thing as 'high morale.' " A good *Times*man like Corry, intent on adapting, looked on the bright side. "I liked the old linoleum floors in the newsroom and the sense of one vast space. I liked the pecking order of the reporters, beginning with that front row of talent; the people sitting on each other's desks, schmoozing." While Rosenthal stirred up the newsroom, rewarding the younger, eager hustlers (including Corry), the old habits were hard to break. *Times*men continued to drift into work at 10:00 A.M. or later. The newsroom emptied around noon, and luncheons sometimes stretched lazily into the mid-afternoon. "We simply cannot run a newspaper if all the top executives are out to lunch until 3 P.M.," Rosenthal complained in a confidential memo to his top deputies after he became executive editor. "Time after time other desk editors look for their superiors and can't find them." Five years later, Rosenthal was still unhappy about the length of the lunch hour. "Day after day, top editors and their deputies, sometimes whole groups of editors, are gone until 3 P.M. or later."

These efforts to shape up the staff were paralleled by a succession of "improvements" of the third-floor newsroom. The floors were carpeted to cut down noise; the introduction of computer terminals was accompanied by rearrangements of the news desks. Specialized departments, such as science-technology news, were moved one floor up. The Sunday departments had traditionally been on another floor; but even within the same departments, jurisdictions were carefully demarcated. A former *Chicago Tribune* reporter, Terri Brooks, found work at the *Times* in the mid-1970s in the Sunday Week in Review section. In the next aisle was the Sunday *Book Review* section, Brooks remembered, "but no one ever talked to you; it was just like an invisible wall ran down the aisle." Brooks was gone from the *Times* in less than a year. The segregation extended outside the office, to the lunchtime eating places frequented by different groups and specialties. The top editors patronized the Century (a male-only club until the 1980s), Orso's in the theater district, and sometimes, for dinner, the Russian Tea Room. Younger editors chose inexpensive Greek, Chinese, and Thai restaurants along Eighth Avenue. A floating group of reporters on the arts and cultural desk, led by Richard Shepard and Gerald Gold, had a regular table in the restaurant of the gone-to-seed Edison Hotel a block north of the *Times*. As a good-natured needle to the upscale dining habits of the top editors, Shepard renamed the Edison luncheonette, with its delicatessen-style food, "The Polish Tea Room."

More managerial layers were added by Max Frankel, when he became editor. By 1992 the number of different news desks had reached twenty-seven . . . and still counting. The good *Times*man knew how to live in the shadows of this vast bureaucracy. The sports columnist Dave Anderson joined the paper in 1966; after almost three decades, he accepted, as a fact of *Times* life, his detachment from his fellow workers. "If Vincent Canby or Anna Quindlen got on the elevator with me today, I wouldn't recognize either of them," he said cheerfully. Design consultants, called in to rearrange the workspace to reflect the new editing desks, made separate what had been whole. "They put in clusters, dividers, islands, cubicles, walls," says John Corry. "We no longer had the old interchange." He understood how much the newsroom had changed one sour morning in late 1988. "I came in and found a memorandum from the publisher, about the current hard business climate and the need to keep costs down, stuffed in my mailbox. They would never do it that way in the old days." Frankel also created new supervisory titles, partly for reasons of "affirmative action"—to promote a number of women and minorities—and partly because Frankel, as a colleague put it, "has a Germanic penchant for organizational boxes." The colleague added: "the place was physically unattractive, crowded, and practically windowless to start with, and as more partitions went up, there was less room, and you were more removed from daylight."

By the late 1980s, the good *Times*man's attention had turned inward, to the computer screen of his partitioned work module. Modest cooperation gave way to undisguised careerism. Michael Norman says experience taught him never to leave anything useful out on his desk: Once, someone lifted his dictionary. At one point, Norman was assigned to the metropolitan news desk as a rewrite man, shaping reporters' work into acceptable *Times* stories. The work excited and energized him—he was on the desk at the time of the explosion of the *Challenger* space shuttle and the U.S. retaliatory stroke against Qaddafi.

The competition to make page one, "P-1," as they called it, and the "second front," the front page of the Metro section, was keen—and not only for the reporters. Editors competed for the space as well; metro wanted more "starts" on P-1 than national and foreign, and vice versa. The new Metro editor that year was John Vinocur, a hard-driving, often hard-headed former reporter who had covered Europe. Metro controlled the *Times* rewrite desk and Vinocur calculated that one way to wield more influence on the front page was to involve rewrite in as many of the big breaking stories as possible. Sometimes "his" rewrite men—and they were all men—would completely refashion a piece: literally rewrite it and give it the shape Vinocur demanded. This often infuriated the editors on the other desks; how dare Vinocur rework "their" stories. Frequently, on a big breaking story, Vinocur ordered rewrite simply to take the piece over—the rewrite men did most of the reporting by phone—and thus important stories, such as the Tylenol poisoning or the Liberty Bicentennial, came under Vinocur's control. None of this, of course, endeared the rewrite men to the rest of the staff, especially, said Norman, "the young ones from the Ivy League, pups with thin skins and literary ambition who hated having their copy touched." Vinocur's style of management soon created chaos in the newsroom. To survive, the staff actually drew close. Reporters began to hang together in Dartonian self-selecting groups—by age, by beat, by common gripe and ambition. To Norman, it was like men on the battlefield "looking for a steady hand, someone to keep them from going under."

The *Times* stirred military images as well for William Serrin, a contemporary of Norman's. Serrin had been hired in 1979 by the *Times* national desk. While a reporter for the *Detroit Free Press* he had shared in the paper's award of a Pulitzer Prize in 1968 for its coverage of the Detroit ghetto riots. A pleasant, open man, Serrin used to nod good morning to people he passed in the newsroom. He received no response and, after a while, stopped trying to make eye contact. Soon he set his own eyes straight ahead. The gaze of the *Times* staff, he remembered, recalled a passage in one of the World War II novels of James Jones. "Jones wrote about 'the one-thousand-yard stare' of combat infantrymen under fire too long," Serrin says. "That's the kind of look I was getting." Serrin adjusted to the *Times*' ways. During his early years, Serrin convinced himself that he had one of the two or three best jobs in all of journalism. "The editors told me I was being hired to be a star, that I would have the opportunity to write for the *Times Magazine*, where my articles would be read by the most important opinion makers in the country." Life at the *Times* dazzled Serrin at first. Detroit was a major media market, and the *Free Press* one of the better papers in the country. But nothing in journalism had prepared Serrin for the *Times*' expansiveness. "I'm given an out-of-town assignment. An editor asks me, 'How much do you need for expenses?' What do I know? I pull out a number: 'What about $3,000?' 'No problem.' I take the elevator to the eleventh floor, go to the accounting-office window, and put in a chit for $3,000. That's impressive for a baker's son from Saginaw, Michigan."

Serrin picked up on the changes in the newsroom atmosphere—this was the 1980s, high noon of the Rosenthal era, with its emphasis on reporters' hustle. He joined the Filene's clearance-sale frenzy. "Ninety-five percent of the stories I did were self-generated. An older *Times*man took me aside and told me, 'Don't start too fast.' That is, don't burn yourself out. But I thought, I have to. This is the big chance for stardom, to be one of the hot shots." The older man's advice proved sound. Serrin began to sense that his editors thought he was "pro-worker" and "too opinionated"—specifically, that his stories were somehow failing to meet the *Times'* unspoken centrist standards. A top executive admonished Serrin for "quoting too many pro-labor people" in his stories—for example, the writer Michael Harrington. Serrin was reminded by the executive that he was supposed to cover "the workplace in America, not unions." The editor was a company man, and like a good *Times*man, strove to impress his superiors. Serrin watched and learned. He was invited to present article ideas during a meeting with the editors of the *Times Magazine*. He told them of a story that had fascinated him. It was about "work in America," in this case focusing on a group of black women who plucked chickens in a Southern factory, and their perseverance despite unspeakable conditions. "As soon as I saw the stricken faces, in a flash I knew what they *didn't* want." As the cultural historian Darnton would put it, Serrin was learning "to internalize the norms" of the *Times*.

The baker's boy from Saginaw chose to go along in the part of a good *Times*man; "I took pains to dress like them and act like them. I had my own standards for what I wanted to accomplish." The editors wanted "trend stories" about the workplace and not stories about the AFL-CIO and working-class people. Such stories had to be done in the field and, says Serrin, "they were time consuming—that bothered editors." He obliged them to a point, and within the limits of his interests, producing coverage of such big-picture matters as the plight of the American steel industry and changes in the family farms of the Midwest. In early January 1984, he wrote about the Homestead Works in the Monongahela Valley of Pennsylvania, the center of American steel-making for over a century. The week before—just after the Christmas holidays—U.S. Steel announced the closing of two dozen plants around the country; 3,800 workers in the valley lost their jobs, and Serrin told one part of the story through the remembrances of one family, operators of a candy store in Homestead. Many of the steel workers had migrated from Europe to America early in the century and were members of the Eastern Orthodox Church; they brought with them their customs, including a taste for hand-dipped candy, fashioned into chocolate rabbits and baskets, at Eastertime. Serrin quoted George Couvaris, owner of the Sweet Shoppe on Eighth Avenue in Homestead; he described how the mill produced rifles for the Union soldiers during the Civil War as well as the rails that railroad workers used to build the West. Now Couvaris's old customers "can't afford to buy candy anymore." Two years later, in July 1986, Serrin returned to the valley to report on the final closing of the Works; he interviewed two of the twenty-three men who had shut off the maintenance equipment for the last time in a plant which, as late as the Second World War, employed twenty thousand people. The story appeared in the *Times* under the headline, "A Chapter of Industrial History Closes with the Homestead Steel Works."

Homestead stayed in Serrin's mind. He began considering alternative futures to the *Times*. Though he was married, with two children and a mortgage, he realized that he didn't want to move up in the newsroom "to become an editor and control people." He liked reporting, but he doubted his desire to sustain indefinitely the output of a *Times* hotshot. He produced the kinds of workplace stories he thought the *Times* should run—for example, a profile of the acclaimed artist Ralph Fasanella, a painter who worked in a United Electrical Workers local. The story sat for weeks in the editors' queue, and then, says Serrin, it was buried in the Sunday paper "back with the truss ads, as they used to say." In October 1986, three months after his Homestead story appeared, Serrin resigned from the *Times*, started a book on the collapse of the American steel industry for Random House, and began a new career as a university professor. Looking back, he explains: "What bothered me about the *Times* . . . and what bothers me today, is that I think I have been forced out of my own profession, and this saddens me to this day. The bureaucracy, the old-boys network—the Harvard guys, the guys who started as clerks—whose members can almost never do any wrong, the terrible in-fighting between desks, the concentration on reporting high-level government and the establishment: All this combines to force one out." Serrin adds: "The strange thing is, I still miss the place immensely and sometimes wish I were back."

Still, competition helped make many people good *Times*men, and they were grateful. Steven R. Weisman joined the *Times* in 1971, after

Columbia and the Associated Press. Quickly, his *Times* career stalled. "My writing was considered too soft, I was judged not productive enough," he says. "They put me on the rewrite desk, banished me there for three years, not only to rewrite, but on the night shift, until 3:00 A.M." Help arrived from an unexpected direction; John Leonard, the *Book Review* editor, asked Weisman to review the new Theodore White book detailing the author's disenchantment with Richard Nixon. "Leonard could have assigned the review to a heavyweight, but he liked to make some waves," Weisman says. "He wanted to get something unpredictable into the *Review.*" The review stirred things up for Weisman; he was noticed. The editors moved him off the night desk and sent him to the City Hall bureau. He became the number-four reporter in the four-man bureau, just as the public was becoming aware of the extent of the municipal fiscal crisis in New York. "I had paid my dues," Weisman says, with pride. He was back on the good *Times*man's fast track. The rewards followed. His explanatory coverage of the fiscal story received prominent play and wide praise. He became the *Times'* New Delhi correspondent, and then was posted to Tokyo as the chief of bureau for four years beginning in 1989. His tour of duty coincided with the period of heightened tensions in the U.S.-Japanese trade relationship. Weisman's dispatches made page one regularly. In his early forties, he achieved visibility inside and outside the *Times.* The parallels in his career with another former foreign correspondent were not lost on his peers; Abe Rosenthal had also been stationed in New Delhi and Tokyo before returning to New York to begin his ascent to executive editor.

High-pressure workplaces are not easy on people already under great stress, and the good *Times*men understood that personal demons couldn't be brought in to work. If they forgot it, the short unhappy life of reporter Fay Joyce served to underline that lesson. Joyce began her newspaper career after graduation from college in 1970, when she was hired by the *Savannah Morning News.* She later worked for the *Atlanta Constitution*, covering the Jimmy Carter campaign. She joined the *Times* in 1983, the year after her marriage broke up. The *Times* assigned her to cover national politics during the 1984 presidential races, and she reported on the campaigns of Walter Mondale and Jesse Jackson. Joyce had made the big time journalistically, but she was developing a reputation among her editors for being—yes—"difficult."

She initially asked that her byline be "Fay Joyce," using her former husband's name. Then she suggested "Fay Smulevitz," her name before she married. After a series of arguments with her editors, everyone agreed on the byline, "Fay S. Joyce." An affair begun with a married man during the political campaign ended badly. Joyce grew more depressed after her editors moved her from the national desk and assigned her to local stories. In the summer of 1985, she applied—using the stationery of the *New York Times*—for a job on her first paper, the *Savannah Morning News*. "The *Times* is not what you think it is," she wrote Wally Davis, her first editor fifteen years before. "Nobody around here ever smiles." She eventually accepted a reporter's position at her old Atlanta paper. On November 15, 1985, Fay S. Joyce resigned from the *Times*. Two weeks later, she shot herself to death. Her body was discovered in her apartment when her super let in a prospective renter. Some of her friends complained about the *Times'* treatment of Joyce, although they can point to nothing specific, other than the wording of the short obituary the paper ran. It described her as a "former" reporter of the *New York Times*. She had killed herself the day before she was scheduled to report to work at the *Atlanta Constitution*.

To some *Times*people, the bureaucracy was the *Times*, and the *Times* was the bureaucracy. The editors' authority has a physical locus—the news desk for the Washington bureau, the foreign desk for overseas correspondents and, above all, the "North Wall" where the senior editors sat, near the executive editor's office suite at the north, or 44th Street, end of the block-long newsroom. When the whole place was repainted not long ago, some newsroom people began calling those editors "The Boys Along the Blue Wall." In 1990 they became the boys and one woman, Carolyn Lee. Lee helped integrate the ranks of the senior editors when she was appointed an assistant managing editor. Today, the usage has been simplified, to The Wall.

New reporters learned to regard these ranks as a collective on matters of policy. Martin Levine, while an editor for the *Book Review*, received assurance of a desirable promotion from his section editor. A few weeks later, though, a Wall editor explained to Levine that the promise had no standing: "It was personal, because no one can speak for the *Times*." The idea of the *Times* collective extended beyond internal administrative decisions. E. R. Shipp, a black woman reporter for the *Times*, accepted an invitation from Fred Friendly of the Columbia Graduate School of Journalism to appear on a television program about the Tawana Brawley case—and then abruptly canceled. Shipp had gone to Columbia and covered the Brawley case for the *Times*; Friendly thought she was an ideal choice and he spoke to her supervisor, metro editor John Darnton. "The drift of Darnton's conversation," Friendly remembered, "was that 'we can't have a reporter speak for the *Times*.' " Friendly thought that Darnton was really saying, "a young black woman couldn't speak for the *Times*." But every good *Times*man is expected to reflect institutional opinion. Tokyo correspondent Steven Weisman, home on leave, happened to remark to a senior editor that the expanded national edition of the *Times* was "boring, a cut-and-paste job." Not so, the editor replied, "the correct view now is that the national edition is a good product for the *Times* company." The correspondent looked for a sign that the editor was being sarcastic about the *Times*' ways: "But no, he said 'the correct view' with a straight face, without irony."

The editors have the formal means to enforce their views of journalistic correctness. Most publicly, the boys along The Wall spoke through the "Editors' Note" and "Corrections" boxes that regularly ran on page three of the *Times*. Until 1992 a two-page newsletter called *Winners & Sinners* was distributed to the staff twice a month. *Winners & Sinners* described itself "as a bulletin of second-guessing issued occasionally from the newsroom of *The New York Times*"; but the good *Times*man knew it was the voice of The Wall. The supervisor was the formidable assistant managing editor, Allan Siegal; for a donation of $25 to the *Times*' Fresh Air Fund, non-*Times* people could subscribe. The newsletter consisted of a series of short, post-facto commentaries on news stories. Entries were instructive; *Winners & Sinners* bulletin no. 530, dated May 19, 1991, for example, informed readers that the *Times* style book requires "all right" to be two words, and not "alright," as it was published in the newspaper of March 20. More substantively, no. 530 critiqued a feature story of April 19, which gave *Times* readers some suggestions on where to take visitors. One of the tips recommended fried chicken at Sylvia's in Harlem, adding: "Ask the cab to wait." The *W&S* comment: "Do all our readers have to take a cab to get to 126th Street and Lenox?" Further, "the snide aside" about asking the cab to wait sounded like, "Get out of there as fast as you can." The *W&S* conclusion: "If we did want to offer the opinion that the area is unsafe or unsavory, we should have said just that." In 1992 Frankel drastically changed the format for *Winners & Sinners*, dropping the name and outside subscribers. Instead, The Wall began circulating a daily memo among the top editors, with strictly internal comments on the sinful and the winsome stories. Selected news stories from that morning's edition, each with The Wall comments stapled to them, are pulled together into a small packet. Grammar, style, and questions of fact and interpretation are all covered. Reporters and midlevel editors usually saw these packets in a weekly collection called "the Greenies" (for the color of the paper). Some of the grunts in the newsroom decreed a different name: the "Daily Slam Sheet."

Good *Times*men were never far from the reach of The Wall, no matter where they were stationed. Every foreign correspondent received a daily fronting cable, describing the page-one lineup of the current edition and telling where all foreign stories appeared in the paper. If the Nairobi correspondent was traveling to Dar Es Salaam, then the cable was sent to her hotel. In addition, every ten days or so, overseas correspondents got an air shipment of a week's worth of the regular paper. As the sociologists would explain it, the correspondent read the status system of the *Times*, along with the air mail edition, and assimilated the ethos of the institution.

The growing bureaucracy of the Frankel years affected the good *Times*man's daily routines. The daily miracle of each edition, with its heft and sense of comprehensiveness, is more wondrous considering all the meetings the staff attends; the meetings give the workday the appearance of one extended story conference. "The challenge is to survive the bureaucracy, not get frustrated, and find time to be productive," Josh Mills explained to an interviewer. An editor on the *Times'* business-news desk since 1986, Mills offered this outline of a typical day, from his own schedule in the spring of 1990, working for the Business Day section:

9:00 A.M. Pod conferences; meetings of the specialists who do the stories and pages on media, technology, real estate, advertising, marketing, and the other "pods," or subjects.

11:00 A.M. Forward planning meeting; the Business Day editor has the choice of either attending or staying away to prepare for the 11:15 news meeting involving all the desks.

11:15 A.M. News meeting.

11:50 A.M. The noon list; stories being offered for the next day's edition are cued and available on editing screens. In effect, another meeting, via computer.

12:00 noon to 2:00 P.M. (or later). Lunchtime.

2:15 P.M. "Time for about forty-five minutes of work."

3:00 P.M. Departmental news meeting; Business Day layout and story selection determined.

4:00 P.M. "Another chance to work."

4:45 P.M. The page-one meeting, held along The Wall. Only the Business Day editor attends, but the other editors "await word of any changes."

Within this formal framework are the multiple editing sessions among reporters, writers, and desk people. For example, an article about the press—an Alex Jones report in the summer of 1990 on, say, the decline of newspaper reading in America—was edited by the media-cluster editor, Martin Arnold, and/or his assistant, at the time, Judith Miller. Next the Business Day backfield looked at Jones's copy for gaps, inconsistencies, and other matters of substance. Then the Business Day copy desk read over the story for proper grammar and style. In addition, the Business Day editor, or his deputy, might ask to see the edited version and request changes. This can cause a turf war. The Business Day editor can say, "It's my department," and the media-cluster editor can reply, "But it's my page." Higher editors then have to intervene. Finally, if the story contains any mention of the *New York Times* or the Times Company, no matter how peripherally, a copy must, without exception, be sent out to The Wall for an assistant managing editor to read and formally initial.

This, then, was the institutional *Times* that tried the souls of even the most ardent loyalists. People with no desire to be anything other than good *Times*men nevertheless suffered the pains of the *Times'* tough love. "Three things have dominated my life," the columnist James Reston wrote in his memoirs, published in 1991. He listed them in order as the teachings of his parents, the love of his wife, and the "integrity of the *New York Times*." But Reston diplomatically skipped over his unhappy tenure in New York, excising the memory of his months as executive editor with the brief comment that he didn't realize how much he would miss Washington when he accepted the editorship. Reston's fellow columnist Russell Baker felt no need for such tact. Baker treated the *Times* with the same sardonic humor he used in his column. He mocked, gently to be sure, the bureaucratic habits of the *Times'* newsroom and treated "the news game" itself as a shallow enterprise. Reston wrote a love letter to the *Times* and to the role of the press in the American democracy. Baker grew tired of being a *Times*man; on the White House beat, considered the plum assignment in the *Times'* Washington bureau, Baker said the news was so tightly managed that a reporter's only intelligent defense was boredom or cynicism. And so Baker accepted an offer from his old newspaper the *Baltimore Sun*, to write a column. When Baker informed his bureau chief, Reston, of the decision to resign and return to the *Sun*, Reston's reaction was: "That's a kick in the balls to me." Reston took Baker's resignation personally, though Baker wasn't sure whether Reston really wanted him to stay or was more upset at the notion that anyone would actually leave the *Times* for another newspaper, and a provincial one at that. At Reston's instigation, the publisher immediately telephoned Baker to persuade him to remain. In quick succession Baker was asked if he wanted to be the chief of the *Times* bureau in Rome, in London, or in New Delhi. After the fourth offer, to have his own column in the *Times*, Baker withdrew his resignation. Even then, he maintained his distance from the bureaucracy, occasionally writing satirically about it in his columns. Eventually, he transferred himself out of the Washington bureau to work at home, and came into the office no more than once or twice a year.

The search for the perfect *Times*man ended in a roundabout way at Columbia University, in the office of Pamela Hollie. At the time she was director of the Knight-Bagehot Program, which offers fellowships for journalists to study economics and business subjects for an academic year. Hollie was an exemplar of what the modern *Times* said it wanted on its news staff. She is an African-American with a graduate degree, trained both as a business-news reporter—she worked at the *Wall Street Journal* for four years—and as a specialist in Southeast Asian history. In her career at the *Times*, Hollie moved up from metro and business desk assignments in 1977 to become a *Times* national business correspondent in the Los Angeles bureau for three years. She was the *Times'* Manila bureau chief beginning in 1981; after four years covering the Philippines and filing stories from Bali, New Guinea, Singapore, Australia, and New Zealand, she returned to the newsroom in New York to write a Sunday financial column for two years. In 1987 she resigned from the *Times* to take the Knight-Bagehot director's job. According to Robert Semple, the *Times*man who hired her in 1977 when he was foreign editor of the paper, "Pam Hollie was terrific, but she fell between the cracks."

Hollie was interviewed not too long after she left the *Times*. She had just turned forty, a confident, vibrant, intelligent woman, tall and sturdy, with long straight hair (she grew up in Kansas, and among her ancestors on her mother's side were Native Americans). Hollie was forthcoming about the *Times* and frank about how she did, indeed, fall between the cracks.

She began with praise for the *Times*. "I got to do a lot of high-visibility big stuff. The *Times* does a good job of bringing you along. The problem comes at the senior level, in getting those promotions. That's something it doesn't do too well. I was an administrator. I ran a bureau. I was a national correspondent. I worked in the home office. But the *Times* couldn't accommodate me. I couldn't move up. And not just me. Look at Reginald Stuart, who just left after thirteen years." Stuart is an African-American, too. Was Hollie suggesting racial discrimination at the *Times?* "Well, there was a minority suit," she replied, "and the *Times* settled it out of court. As a result, I get a check for $400 a year." But had not Frankel publicly announced his intentions to hire more minorities? "I know what he announced, but I felt he didn't make much of an effort to talk me out of departing. He told me, 'I'll miss your energy and great spirit.' That's fine, but I wanted to hear something else. I just wasn't getting great stateside assignments. Overseas I was on a fast track. I'm not sure who derailed whom. Did I leave? Was I pushed? I just couldn't be around another ten years without my managerial skills being used."

Hollie had, in the *Times* newsroom phrase, "rabbis"—senior editors, such as John Lee, the Business Day editor, who advised her and helped her. "Bob Semple recruited me, and then he was gone from the foreign desk. No one is excluded from the screwing. At the time, I had an Asian Studies fellowship at the University of Hawaii. Early in 1977, the program administrators prepared an advertisement showing the photographs of the prospective graduates, me included. Three white males used it as part of their job applications to the *Times*. Semple saw me in the others' materials and arranged an appointment. Ask yourself, 'How many Mandarin-speaking black women journalists, with business training, are on the market?' " The *Times* was just about to start its Business Day section, while the *Wall Street Journal* was starting its Hong Kong edition. "I would be a feather in someone's cap, so a bidding war got under way between the *Journal* and the *Times*. I went to the highest bidder.

"Sometimes the *Times* makes promises it won't keep, but they lived up to their promises to me. I wanted an Asia assignment and they eventually gave me one. I had a brief training program, I was only in New York for three months. I did the stations of the cross—you know, three weeks on the metro desk, three weeks somewhere else. Then, in May of 1978, I went to Los Angeles. It was an assignment where I could be a self-starter. I don't need direction, and I was left alone with thirteen states to cover. I was used to being alone, and I was used to leading; in college in Kansas I was the student council president and the president of my sorority. I got to the office at 5:00 A.M. Robert Lindsey was the bureau chief. We didn't get in each other's way. There were plenty of stories for both of us to break.

"I became bureau chief in Manila at a time when the Marcos regime was on the edge. Bob Semple sent me as promised but then Semple was replaced as foreign editor by Craig Whitney, who had different ideas about coverage. He was more Euro-centered. Each time a new foreign editor comes in, he has his own worldview, and the correspondents get shifted around. Of course the *Times* denies it, but the editors shape world coverage to conform to their vision. Whitney's background was as a reporter in Moscow and Bonn, and so there were more Soviet stories and less about the Pacific Rim. Then, without any discussion with me, they decided to close the Manila bureau—this was right before the Aquino assassination in July 1983! Whitney wanted me out of there. The bureau was closed without so much as a phone call to me."

(Because Hollie was dismissing out of hand one of the bedrock pretentions of "objective" *Times* journalism, it seemed appropriate to get other correspondents to respond to her charge about the importance of the "worldview" of the foreign editor to them. Three foreign correspondents agreed, separately, that the attention their beats received rose and fell depending on the home editors' own foreign experience. As a Pacific Rim correspondent explained, "We worry that the Far East is not 'understood' the way Russia is by the editors back home. Take Frankel, who has been stationed in Moscow. His knowledge of Japan, for example, is intellectual not emotional.")

Hollie remembered telling herself, "If they don't appreciate what I've done for them, then OK, fine. I'm transferred to New York, and guess what? Whitney's out and a new foreign editor, Warren Hoge, is in. Next, he's out. And each time they make these changes, a lot of other people get moved around. When Aquino was shot, I'm sitting twenty feet away from the foreign desk, but I'm not called or consulted. After all the expertise they invested in me, nothing. If the foreign desk is not thinking of me that day, then they're not thinking of me, period. I'm pissed off. I'm tired. I'm buying a co-op. I went to the business desk, to do a financial column. But I made plans to leave. I was lost sight of." Again, what about the *Times'* investment in her, and in minorities in general? "I don't blame 'racism' or the 'system,' " she said. "Still, Max never made an effort to discourage my leaving, despite the fact that I hadn't made any secret of it. I knew I was wasting my talents, and a lot of other people knew too."

Hollie had no regrets about leaving "the big time." "It was just a job," she said. "I always had great jobs. This past year, I won two Fulbrights to return to Asia and lecture. I had no pangs. I hated that neighborhood." The newsroom, she added, was not a friendly place either. "Not due to its bigness, not due to the dailiness, but I think perhaps because you are dealing with many people who worked their way up in life. The *Times* represents all the social status they have in their lives. Toughness is their badge. They had to be tough to leave their past behind."

In the Frankel years, too, Pam Hollie's experience was mirrored in the career of Paul Delaney, an African-American who seemed to be a committed *Times* lifer. Through the 1970s and 1980s Delaney worked his way up to deputy national editor. In 1989 Frankel—signaling his commitment to "diversity" and more black hires—appointed Delaney senior editor for minority recruitment. Delaney accepted the job with the expectation that, in three years or so, he would be able to leave administration and move up to line responsibilities along The Wall, where the big rewards were. The Wall proved only marginally more responsive to Delaney than to Hollie, and Delaney quit the *Times* in 1992 to accept a journalism professorship at the University of Alabama. Discouraged, he told the writer Robert Sam Anson: "We haven't accomplished anything. The fight is the same we had thirty years ago. . . ." (Frankel was later quoted as saying that such charges by black staff people were "like a dagger in my heart . . .")

Delaney and Hollie, in the end, did not qualify as good *Times*men. The same day Hollie was interviewed, that morning's *Times* carried a full-column obituary on Philip H. Dougherty, the paper's advertising columnist, who had died of an apparent heart attack at the age of sixty-four. Phil Dougherty, Hollie said, lived and died in "pure *Times* style—he went to work in 1942 at the *Times* as a nineteen-year-old copy boy, straight from high school, and he never worked anywhere else, or wanted to do anything else except be at the *Times*."

The obit, written by Dick Shepard, filled out the rest of the picture of a *Times* lifer. Dougherty was born in the Bronx in 1923 and raised in Manhattan. He left the *Times* for World War II service in 1943, and was discharged in 1946 with the rank of master sergeant in the U.S. Army Military Police. He returned to the *Times* as a clerk in the managing editor's office and took night classes at the Columbia University School of General Studies. In 1949 he was promoted to the society news department and, later, to the metro desk. His advertising column began in October 1966, and appeared five days a week. "It was the substance of his column that made Mr. Dougherty an influential figure in the advertising world," Shepard wrote. Shepard also quoted Mark Stroock, a senior vice president at Young & Rubicam: "He gave everyone an absolutely fair shake, and he once told me that he knew if he was writing for the *Hoboken News* and not the *New York Times*, his phone might never ring." Two weeks later, George Lois, at the time chairman of Lois Pitts Gershon Pon/GGK, offered his affectionate farewell. Dougherty, Lois said, "always arrived at our early morning appointments bearing a bagel and his own herbal tea. I finally put in a supply of chamomile and red zinger and made sure his beloved bagel awaited him. This was his only compromise with integrity." One Christmas, Lois's firm sent roses to Dougherty's wife. The columnist called and angrily ordered Lois never to do it again.

Pamela Hollie added her own appreciation of Phil Dougherty. "He died in his sleep, having written his column for the next day," she said.

He was the perfect *Times*man.

A DAY IN THE LIFE
5:15 P.M. — 6:00 P.M.

5:15 P.M.

In Cambridge, Massachusetts, in an MIT seminar room, columnist Anthony Lewis decided he had made the right decision to attend the Al-Azm lecture. Lewis heard a brilliant, sarcastic interpretation of Islamic fundamentalism, an antidote to much of what he had been reading in the papers, including in the *Times.* The Ayatollah Khomeini's brand of fundamentalism, Al-Azm argued, has not taken hold in the Arab world.

Mark Landler, the news assistant in New York, waited for his "good night." The Terry Rakolta piece would run, without his byline. *Times'* news assistants, during one month of their fourteen-month tryouts, did a reporter's work for a reporter's pay and byline. By the *Times'* same rules, anything published outside that one-month period appeared unsigned, even on page one.

Free of the deadline-news crush in the Washington bureau, Barbara Gamarekian took a phone call from Lori Heise, a senior researcher at the World Watch Institute. Heise described a new report that gave a global overview of violence against women, from bride burning to female circumcision. Gamarekian asked Heise to messenger over the report, promising to read it within a day and discuss it with her editors. Another call came from David Chikvaidze, counselor at the Russian embassy on Sixteenth Street. He invited Gamarekian to a "Spring tea" with Mrs. Dubinin, the wife of the ambassador, on March 10 at 5:00 P.M. No special reason was given, but Gamarekian had been trying to get the embassy to cooperate for the past three years on an article about how Soviet diplomats live and work in Washington. Gamarekian accepted the invitation, polished her redo of the women-diplomats story, and turned it in to her editor, David Binder.

Karl Meyer finished reading the Amnesty International report and began his "Topics of the Times" editorial for Sunday's paper. "Saddam Hussein's Baghdad dictatorship is one of the world's most barbaric tyrannies," Meyer wrote. The headline was also blunt: "Horror in Iraq."

6:00 P.M.

David Jones laid out page one of the national edition, and gave the lead right-hand column space to the Tower nomination, demoting the Shoreham story that was leading the "basic" paper. He phoned Frankel to inform him of the switch. Jones's office, along the same wall as Frankel's, was a little bigger than a broom closet. Overhead, half the acoustic ceiling tiles had been removed, exposing a large, white-plastic elbow pipe leading out of the old composing room one story above. A cold-water leak from a clogged drain had soaked through the ceiling; the new tiles, recently installed because of a previous leak, had been removed. Metal wastebaskets served as makeshift drip buckets to catch the water. Taped to Jones's door, an oversize strip of computer printout paper carried the hand-scrawled warning: "Do Not Use This Room—Engineering Dept."

At home, Anthony Lewis worked on his column until 7:30. The draft began with the Tower nomination and used the Suciu case as an example of how secret evidence, untested by cross-examination, led to injustices. Lewis was not satisfied with the draft, and broke off for dinner.

Barbara Gamarekian circled the room at the reception celebrating the Wilderness Society's twenty-fifth anniversary year, hoping perhaps to pick up an item for the *Times* "Washington Briefing" feature.

9

OPINION TIMES:
ANNA AND ABE AND BILL
AND MAUREEN AND GARRY

IN RECENT YEARS the news coverage of the modern *Times* has told a story of subtraction. A. M. Rosenthal and later Max Frankel, together with Joseph Lelyveld, cut back on the complete texts of governmental reports, presidential news conferences, and other official transcripts that, in the past, gave the *Times* its reputation as the Paper of Record. Years before, too, their predecessors discontinued the shipping-news column, the listings of garment-center buyers in town, and the other now-quaint ledgers of an earlier era, in the life of the city and the *Times*. The routines of congressional legislation no longer wended their way day after day through the *Times'* news columns as they had as recently as twenty-five years before. According to Lelyveld, the "official" *Times* of the 1960s had several excellent writers—he singled out Russell Baker for his coverage of the U.S. Senate and Claude Sitton's dispatches from the South during the civil rights marches. Still, said Lelyveld, "By the standards of today, that *Times* would be unreadable. Then we'd do eight page-one stories on a Senate crime bill, and chart its legislative snail's-progress from hearings to committee votes to passage in each house to White House. Today, by contrast, we would do two or three page-one stories at most: when the bill clears committee, and when it's passed and/or vetoed." The same held true for the international-news report. Early in his career, Lelyveld was the

Times bureau chief in New Delhi; good foreign correspondent that he was, he understood that the foreign desk wanted to hear from him regularly. As late as the 1970s, Lelyveld remembered, when there was a shake-up of the Indian cabinet, that used to be front-page news. Today, Lelyveld says, "a cabinet shake-up would scarcely rate a short. That was the 'official' *Times*. Now it's a different *Times*." He adds: "That's not a downgrading of news from India. It's a redefinition. We want more significant themes."

In place of the Record, as we've seen, the modern *Times* expanded its coverage of "softer" specialized news, life-style features, and trend stories. By far the most unremarked increase, however, was in the space the *Times* devoted to opinion. Through all the years until the late 1950s, there were never any more than four or five columnists in the *Times*—two or three Big Thinkers appeared alongside the editorials on the editorial page; another, usually less reverent, graybeard ruminated on "Sports of the Times" in the sports section, and, on the metro pages, the revered Meyer Berger wrote the "About New York" column. By the 1990s, however, almost four dozen columnists were being published throughout the pages of the modern *Times*, from the critics' contributions in the arts and culture section to the columns devoted to society and fashions. The editorial page itself was opened up, with the chin-tugging columnists given their own new page and the old space turned over for "Letters to the Editor," and for "Editorial Notebook," a series of short, informal signed opinion pieces by the previously anonymous members of the editorial board.

The subjects of these columns, editorials, and "Notebooks" changed as well, just as the hard-news coverage had changed, to reflect the new interests of the *Times*. To describe the new content as "trivial" was too harsh; but it was nevertheless true that many of the columns and commentaries concentrated on "light" subjects. They were certainly a soufflé in contrast to the old, "serious" *Times*. The 1990s sports section alone, for example, offered more commentary than had appeared in the entire 1950s-era paper; the *Times* of April 17, 1992, carried four sports columns, including one devoted solely to commentary about sports events on television. In the paper run by Arthur Sulzberger and edited by Frankel and Lelyveld there was, in fact, a column for just about every reader's taste; hints for "The Practical Traveler" in the Travel section, "Peripherals" (for owners of computers), "Economics of Health" (in the Business Day pages), "Personal Health," "Pop

View," "Keeping Fit," "Parent and Child," "Coping," "At the Bar" (about lawyers), "Runways" (on fashion). The final enshrinement of consumerist journalism—or for nostalgists of the old *Times*, its reductio ad absurdum—came in May 1992, when Arthur Sulzberger and Frankel et al. introduced a new Sunday section called "Styles of the Times." Styles consisted almost wholly of columns about people, fashions, nightclubs, eating, drinking, and other consummatory pleasures. Styles had attitude . . . spread out over almost two dozen pages. There were features on bondage trousers and children as a fashion accessory. "The Night" reported on the club scene of the moment, mainly Downtown. A typical column began: "Monday. Mambo Monday. Again the pink flamingos are out in front of SOB's in Tribeca . . ." The standing column-heads cried out for attention: "The Sexes" (about men and women), "Egos & Ids" (celebrity gossip), "Things" (how various new consumer products work, such as caller ID).

The advent of Styles marked the resolution of the editorial infighting that had been waged for almost two decades over the contents of Sunday Main Part 2, the second news section with its mix of society news, wedding announcements, late radio-TV listings, and arts reviews. In the new Styles some of these old Part 2 staples were repackaged with trendy graphics and self-consciously "spritely" writing. "On the Street" and "The Evening Hours" featured big photographs of the fashionable at play. The formulaic wedding pictures were also given a postmodernist make-over; in the late 1980s the *Times* began encouraging the groom as well as the bride to pose for their marriage announcement pictures (and make the point that wedding news was no longer about "lucky" young women who had caught their man). Styles took the new wedding pages another step away from the old sexism with "Vows." The story of one couple from the forty or so wedding notices carried on average in the *Sunday Times*, "Vows" recounted details of the couple's initial meeting, courtship, and marriage.

Other Main Part 2 news offerings, such as "Campus Life," were dropped entirely from the new section. A series of stringer reports from colleges around the country, "Campus Life" touched on unusual courses and curriculum changes, manifestations of political correctness (and, on the other side, yahooism), and social tensions among students (clashes between blacks and whites, for example, or feminists and fraternities). "Campus Life" carried actual news. Now, in the space where "Campus Life" formerly appeared, Styles featured a two-page account of "The Arm Fetish," writer Molly O'Neill's speculation of the effects of fitness routines on body image ("the sculptured body is now the foundation of fashion," she announced). Styles writers cultivated their individual voices; the presentation fairly cried out, "Pick me up, caress me (with your shapely arms), read me. I'm so fabulously adorable."

Styles was introduced shortly after Arthur Sulzberger succeeded his father in early 1992. When the new publisher was asked about these changes by a university teacher—who said that he missed "Campus Life," and the sense it gave him of what was going on at other colleges—Sulzberger replied, pleasantly, "Styles isn't intended for you. You're too old. It's for different readers, for those between thirty and forty years old." He paused and laughed, "Maybe I'm getting too old for it, too" (Arthur Sulzberger was forty-one at the time). More seriously, he half-apologized for some of the unbearable lightness of Styles, explaining that the new section was a departure from the usual news-gathering work of the *Times*. It would take a period of adjustment before the form was mastered by the "hard news" people. "We're not there yet. It hasn't been our franchise. We're not used to this kind of thing at the *Times*," he said. After the first few Styles appeared, Enid Nemy, a *Times* fashion reporter since the early 1970s seemed unusually quiet when asked about the new section. "Downtown isn't going to read Styles. Those children just don't read the *Times*," she said, echoing what the Polish Tea Room crowd had said when it discussed the culture pages' romance with rock, rap, and "the pop life."

Arthur Sulzberger and his lieutenants Frankel and Lelyveld did not abandon the traditional franchise. The same Sunday the first Styles appeared, a new Sunday Metro section was also introduced. It brought together in one place coverage of the city and its suburbs; the new section was the first step toward zoned editions, a publishing plan that would segregate still further metropolitan-area news: Connecticut news for Connecticut subscribers only, for example. But the main marketing energy of Arthur Sulzberger's *Times* was channeled into softer features with "voice" and into commentaries of all kinds.

The emphasis on opinion began well before Arthur. As far back as the early 1970s, the *Times*' Op-Ed page, with its daily chorus of public-policy voices, proved to be a crowd pleaser. Readership surveys indicated that the Op-Ed page was the best-read part of the paper, after page one, just as the same surveys reflected the popularity of "Critic's

Notebook," the variant of the column idea of the culture pages. On any given day, the Op-Ed page offered two contributions from the *Times'* own columnists, including Anthony Lewis, Russell Baker, William Safire, and, in more recent years, Anna Quindlen and A. M. Rosenthal. In addition, two or three outside contributors usually appeared each day, so that on average about sixteen to twenty nonstaff pieces were published each week. A four person Op-Ed–page staff commissioned about half of these contributions, after the approval of the page editor (the editor and an art director increased the size of the staff to six). The same person who suggested topics to selected writers then worked with the writer to get the article in shape. By far the most time-consuming part of the staff's work, however, involved digging out from under the avalanche of unsolicited manuscripts—known as the "slush pile," a phrase borrowed from book publishing. Hundreds of opinion articles arrived from people eager to be published in the *Times*, for reasons of ego, ideology, or an interest in contributing to "the public dialogue." It certainly wasn't the money that made outsiders want to be in the *Times*: Throughout the 1980s and into the 1990s the Op-Ed page paid an inflation-proof $150 for the standard 750-word article (double-length contributors earned $300).

The Op-Ed page was a popular hit with these would-be contributors. At first a trickle and then a rush of manuscripts came in by mail, by messenger, and more recently, by fax. When the page observed its twentieth anniversary in September 1990, as many as sixty unsolicited manuscripts were arriving each workday. In the early years of the 1990s, the slush pile passed one hundred daily. "It was as if the Gray Lady had hit the dance floor," Robert B. Semple, Jr., dryly noted on the occasion of the anniversary. Semple was the editor in charge of Op-Ed from 1982 until mid-1988, when he moved across the page to join the editorial board. The Op-Ed page attracted so much attention, Semple said, "I developed a fantasy about all the would-be contributors. There were all these Op-Ed assembly lines across the land at the think tanks and the universities. Rooms full of professors and experts writing Op-Ed pieces for submission. Harvard, Yale, Stanford, Columbia, the Carnegie Endowment, the Brookings Institute, the Heritage Foundation. They had a paragraph in their employment contract, stipulating, 'You will write X number of Op-Eds a year.' " Considering that no more than two unsolicited pieces are normally published in the *Times* on any given day, Semple added, "There must be a lot of unfulfilled agreements out there." Mitchel Levitas, who took over the page in late 1990, said he noted a fallback pattern among the rejects: "They showed up later in the *Washington Post* and the *Wall Street Journal*."

Many of the Op-Ed assembly line writers moonlighted by writing to "Letters to the Editor." In the 1980s, according to R. A. Barzilay, the editor in charge of selecting the letters that appeared on the *Times'* editorial page, some seventy thousand letters came in annually; by 1992, the figure had risen above 100,000. Typically, three hundred letters a day were arriving, without any sign of a dropoff, a remarkable volume considering that seven or eight letters on average were published daily on the editorial page. (The editors of other sections of the *Times*, such as the *Times Magazine*, the *Book Review*, the Sports section, and Arts & Leisure, received their own heavy volume of mail as well; they accommodated a few of these in their pages.) According to Barzilay, there were some souls—eager? lost? pathetic?—who corresponded with the *Times* daily and many more who wrote "excellent and informative letters at least weekly." But the *Times* was firm: As a rule no outsider could appear on the Op-Ed page or the letters columns more than two or three times a year. For a time, Henry Kissinger was an exception; eventually, the rules were applied to him as well.

The popularity of Letters and Op-Ed proved double-edged. As Barzilay explained, "All letters get a viewing"—a policy that reflected the *Times'* good manners but one that put an awesome burden on the three-person Letters staff. The same was true of Op-Ed submissions. Levitas liked to boast that his staff brought a bracing diversity to the task of selection and editing, consisting as it did of "men and women, blacks and whites, and Jews and Christians." The staff lost some of its diversity when Kathleen Quinn left in 1992 to write a novel; Quinn, an Irish Catholic, voted for the Reverend Jesse Jackson in the 1988 New York presidential primaries. Mostly, though, the staff was united by the unremitting pressure of 365 deadlines a year. Susan Lee, who served as deputy editor of the page after Bob Semple left, once offered would-be contributors six rules of the "Op-Ed page game." Only one of her rules dealt with substance: "Do not be too complicated, or too sophisticated," Lee admonished. "Newspaper readers do not want to pause while they are reading. . . . The simpler the idea, the better." Lee's other rules all had to do with what the newspaper's editors wanted. Contributors should keep in mind "one simple fact: the Op-Ed editor only wants to fill his or her page efficiently and quickly." Consequently, do not phone before submission (rule one), do not waste time getting to the point in the essay, and do not send messy, unstapled manuscripts ("loose pages make it difficult for the Op-Ed editor to stack your manuscript in the manuscript pile efficiently and quickly"). Her final rule reprised some of the earlier advice: Do not phone the editor after submission—you'll get an answering machine, Lee explained, and if you do reach a live human, the response is likely to be, "Oh dear! I haven't seen it yet. I hope it didn't get lost."

Lee intended her advice to be lighthearted. But her "amusing" sketch of beleaguered editors, checking for staples, behaving as if they were clerks in a substation of the U.S. postal service, rather than serious-minded professionals of the world's best newspaper, squared with other accounts. As in any bureaucracy, an internal system for handling Op-Ed submissions had to be developed. It was the staff that informally let would-be contributors know outsiders were restricted to two Op-Ed appearances a year. Those manuscripts that survived the first culling were coded and circulated to the Op-Ed staff. The circulating editor's ballpointed red dot in the upper right-hand corner of a manuscript signified "good." A six-pointed star meant "excellent." (The publisher was not in the circulation flow, but as I was told by a member of the Op-Ed page staff, "after a while you know his causes and his dislikes.") The volume of manuscripts and the unrelenting deadlines left no time for thorough fact-checking. After a six-pointed manuscript made the final cut, the editor handling it usually selected one representative idea or factual statement in the copy and picked away at it, calling the author, checking reference books. The final edited copy was faxed to the author—a last line of defense against error. The Op-Ed page operations fit Anna Quindlen's broader description of the paper. The *Times* was like the Frank Morgan character in the *The Wizard of Oz*, Quindlen said. "We want you to pick up the paper every day and think of the wonderful Oz; we don't want you to peek behind the screen and see the actual men and women involved."

The modern *Times'* decision to give new importance to market-pleasing, personality-driven columns made this amiable Ozian deception harder to sustain. With the shift to opinion and individual voice, it was only natural that some of the audience looked behind the curtain, at both the magicians and the smoke-and-mirrors operations of the editorial page, the Op-Ed page, and the columns.

*　　*　　*

Of all the departments of the *Times*, the editorial page editors tried hardest to hold up the institutional screen of their work. "It is a great forum, a place for balance, consensus, and enlightened dialogue," said Karl E. Meyer, a third-generation newspaperman and an editorial board member since 1979. Meyer acknowledged that the *Times'* twelve-person editorial board was no democracy. The board reported to the publisher—Arthur O. Sulzberger, senior and junior, during Meyer's time—and the publisher's authority resided in his power to appoint the editorial-page editor and the board members, and review their work. Decisions about what subjects to take up and the shaping of views were made "collegially," according to Jack Rosenthal, who became the editorial-page editor in late 1986, succeeding Max Frankel. Three times a week the Jack Rosenthal board met in its tenth-floor conference room to discuss topics for editorials and to divide up assignments. Rosenthal made the assignments, did his share of lead editorials, and also rewrote and edited the copy of his board. On the rare occasions when Punch or Arthur Sulzberger submitted editorials, Rosenthal edited their copy as well. One fall morning in 1991, just before he stepped aside as publisher to make way for his son, Punch Sulzberger arrived at the *Times'* offices in an agitated state. He was appalled at the sight of overflowing garbage cans and trash left out overnight by two fast-food restaurants up the street, at the corner of 43rd and Seventh. He logged on his desk computer and wrote the draft of an editorial, which began: "Times Square vomited last night. . . ." The editorial ran, but not before Jack Rosenthal called up the publisher's handiwork on the editing screen and changed the first sentence to read: "Times Square was a mess last night. . . ."

Much like Mitch Levitas on the Op-Ed page, Jack Rosenthal took pride in the "diversity" of his page. "The editorial board used to be a bunch of sixty-year-old white males," he said over lunch at his club (Harvard) in the winter of 1991. "Of the dozen of us now, 4½ to 5½ are women, depending on leaves and their half-time schedules. Two are blacks. Our ages range from thirty-two to seventy-two. Roughly half of us are journalists, the others former academics recruited specifically for their specialties." Still, it was a narrow kind of diversity. The editorial board's middle-aged white men typically came from the same place—the third-floor newsroom. In some ways, Jack Rosenthal himself was a transitional figure.

His father was a judge in pre-Hitler Germany.

Jack Rosenthal was born in 1935 in Tel Aviv, and grew up in Portland, Oregon. He was graduated from Harvard College and was a reporter for the *Oregonian* newspaper before going to the Department of Justice as an assistant to Attorney General Robert F. Kennedy in 1961. Rosenthal regarded government as a detour; he always wanted to return to newspapers. He joined the *Times* in 1969. His mother had gotten upset at his choice of a career. "It wasn't a status occupation then and when I told her of my newspaper plans, she complained to me, 'Why waste your Harvard education?' To be a journalist then was like being a cab driver." At the *Times*, Jack Rosenthal helped develop the coverage of urban affairs for the news department—this was the period following the ghetto riots—and began his career-long interest in "the problems of the cities." In the years of the Bush administration, Rosenthal did not hold a high opinion of the news department's treatment of his old beat. Some of his reservations were the usual ones that older hands often have about the work of their successors. In the Sunday, December 1, 1991, editions, for example, metro correspondent Sara Rimer wrote of suburbia's split from the central city; Rimer quoted suburbanites who said that they lived, worked, and relaxed near their homes, never feeling any need to go into New York for its shops, plays, museums, restaurants, or other urban amenities. "Give me a break," Rosenthal commented, "I did that story twenty years ago." Rosenthal did offer some praise for the new Metro section. "I see the heading 'Connecticut,' I know I don't have to read it." Rosenthal lived at the time in Westchester county.

He was impatient with Metro's coverage of the city as well, in particular of Harlem, and what he called the *Times'* "Talk of 139th Street" story form. A "139th Street Story," he explained, focused on the despair of the scene: corner drug dealers, crime, abandoned tenements, the homeless. "The message is, 'Things are worse, worse, worse.' The implication is that we're pouring money down a rat hole, that nothing helps," Rosenthal said. "So, while you may feel guilty, white America, you can't do anything about 'the problem.' However, the truth of 139th Street is, many blacks are making it in America, and our journalism has to communicate that life is not hopeless." Rosenthal recalled that the Harlem of the 1950s had a population of 1 million; by the 1990s, it was 600,000. If Rimer or other *Times* reporters bothered to check the cars parked outside the Abyssinian Baptist

Church on Sunday mornings, they would have observed a sea of New Jersey license plates. Old Harlemites had moved out and up; they were living the suburban life themselves: "The civil rights revolution worked." But, Rosenthal concluded, the news department too often took the attitude, "We did that story, the one on the black middle class in Atlanta. . . ." The story of the parking lot, perhaps, was news from too far Uptown, not the sort of happening thing for the hot new Styles columns.

Jack Rosenthal left the urban beat in the early 1970s and began the ambitious *Times*man's climb up the newsroom ladder to the top editing posts. In the classic pattern too, he was pushed out of the *Times Magazine* by Abe Rosenthal in one of the recurring coups of those years. The two men are not related, and while they often saw eye to eye on story ideas, Jack Rosenthal was not hired by Abe Rosenthal—and the executive editor wanted one of his own loyalists in the job. But Jack Rosenthal was deemed too valuable for the Sulzbergers to lose; by the Frankel-Lelyveld years he had been rehabilitated. A bright, intense man, Rosenthal shrewdly sized up the 1990s shifts. The *Times'* editorial-opinion strategy was in step with its marketing plan—"elitist" and "specialized," much like the audience it coveted.

"Once newspapers were a popular medium, directed to the general audience," he said. "Now in my own time at the *Times*, the newspapers' old role of provider of immediate hard news has been taken over by television." There has been a change in the audience as well. According to Rosenthal, when he left Portland for Harvard in the early 1950s, only 20 percent of high school graduates went to college. The figure has more than doubled since. "The new audience is informed and sophisticated; it wants a selection of materials, it wants to use its judgment. It looks to the *Times* for expertise, in foreign news, arts criticism, whatever." In 1966, Rosenthal said, "Clifton Daniel was mocked for hiring Craig Claiborne to write about 'mere' food. Now we have four food specialists, one writing on the culture of food, a second on nutrition, a third on restaurants, a fourth on food as food. The same with science. Twenty-five years ago, Walter Sullivan wrote about black holes. Today there are six science/technology writers; another writer covers psychology, exclusively; two more with M.D. degrees write about medicine. On the business staff one person specializes solely in medical economics." The *Times* was elitist, Jack Rosenthal concluded, "in the best sense of that word."

The changes on the editorial and opinion pages mirrored the overall changes at the *Times*. In the space of fourteen months beginning in the spring of 1989, two of the older, journalistically trained board members stepped down, and Rosenthal hired specialists in their place. Michael Weinstein, a younger (41), white male, had a Ph.D. from MIT and was chairman of the economics department at Haverford College; Rosenthal recruited him to comment on business, finance, and public policy. In June 1990, the *Times* announced that the veteran foreign correspondent and Op-Ed columnist Flora Lewis, then sixty-seven, would retire by the end of the year. Lewis was a generalist of the old school. She worked for the Associated Press and the *Washington Post* before joining the *Times* in 1972. For two decades, she covered foreign policy, mostly from her home base in Paris, but also moving around, filing from two dozen different countries. Her replacement on the Op-Ed page, Leslie Gelb (no relation to Arthur Gelb), was a Harvard Ph.D. and Washington insider (less politely, bureaucrat). Gelb had worked on Capitol Hill, at the Departments of State and Defense, and at public-policy think tanks; he joined the *Times* in 1973 as a diplomatic correspondent and eventually became Jack Rosenthal's editorial-page deputy. Gelb's move to the Op-Ed page opened up room on the board in the summer of 1990 for Brent Staples, a thirty-eight-year-old African-American with a Ph.D. (in psychology, from the University of Chicago). Staples was brought in to write about politics and culture.

Staples's hard-news experience was limited. He had been with the *Times* just five years, part of the time on the *Book Review*. His stay on the editorial board was also short. Staples got close enough to the top at the *Times* to figure out "the values system." The senior editors of the news department, like Frankel and Lelyveld, had come up through the reporter ranks. Staples could have stayed on the board, in its university-like setting, far removed from the third floor. He would hold a comfortable chair, perhaps until retirement; but he could never aspire to the best posts—in Washington, as a foreign correspondent, or as a senior editor. The truly ambitious among *Times* lifers still needed to get their career tickets punched in the newsroom. Within two years, Staples left the board, and became a Metro section reporter.

Fortunately, too, for "balance" there were still some well-trained journalists on the *Times* editorial board. The board's public-education specialist, Diane Camper, grew up in Flushing, Queens, and attended city public schools before going away to Syracuse University, where she majored in journalism and political science. Camper was hired by *Newsweek* in 1968 as a fact checker; only one other African-American woman was on the magazine's editorial staff at the time. Camper went to *Newsweek*'s Washington bureau in 1972 as a general assignment reporter, just in time to cover the Watergate scandals. She took a year's leave to earn a Master of Studies of Law degree from Yale Law School in 1977. Six years later, Jack Rosenthal hired her (they first met while both were serving on a journalism-awards committee). Another experienced board member, Joyce Purnick, had New York City roots as well. A 1967 graduate of Barnard College, she covered politics for the *New York Post*, wrote on urban affairs for *New York* magazine, and later became one of the *Times'* best City Hall reporters. She married Max Frankel, the *Times'* executive editor, in December 1988 (theirs was an autumn romance, after the death of Frankel's first wife of three decades). Frankel, acting as agent for the institutional *Times*, deemed it improper for Purnick to work under his jurisdiction, and she moved out of the news department to the editorial page. Her editorials concentrated on city politics; occasionally, she contributed to "Editorial Notebook," writing about herself as well as public policy. When "Mary Richards," the TV character played from 1970 to 1977 by the actress Mary Tyler Moore, was the subject of a CBS retrospective a few years ago, a Purnick "Notebook" observed: "Mary Richards made it all OK—OK to be a single woman, OK to be over thirty, OK to be independent . . . a gentle role model, someone for the shaky career woman to identify with in the transitional 1970s." Unfortunately, the career of the real-life woman, Purnick, suffered because of the *Times'* institutional position on her marriage; the fictional Mary Richards fared better.

Specialization was the journalistic future, in any case. "It's easier to bring writing style to a knowledgeable person than knowledge to a stylish writer," Jack Rosenthal argued. "So we find a former assistant secretary of state like Les Gelb, and bring him in. Then we get great clashes of the experts at our board meetings. The knowledgeable economist and the lawyer come at each other across the table. We get to be like a family. We're not afraid to appear stupid in our crosstalk. For example, someone can say, 'I missed that story, tell me about it. . . .' Or: 'I don't understand your use of that economics term, explain it. . . .' Or: 'Defend your position against the objection that . . .' The man who comments on the latest decision of the U.S. Supreme Court [John McKenzie, also trained in the law] has to take cognizance in his editorial of the points raised by the rest of the board in our discussions. The writer doesn't have to agree with the points, but he has to deal with them in the editorial."

The board tried to be part of the drive to be reader-friendly. Editorials were changing, just as news coverage was changing. To some extent, Rosenthal explained, "Editorials are the news of yesterday in review, with a point of view. But we don't want just a sterile recitation of what happened. There are other ways to process information. We can have fun. We can be the first to say 'Holy Cow!' on a topic. I expect the board to re-report everything." Quickly, he added: "Not that we don't trust our newsroom staff, they're the greatest in the world. But reporters are often on deadline, they are lied to, they are hurried. So our specialists have to do some work, too; we have to do our own reporting."

In fact, the 1990s *Times* broadened the scope of commentary to include new approaches to the editorial form. Rosenthal offered six examples from the editorial pages in the late summer and early fall of 1991 to illustrate how the old categories had expanded. Two were examples of Traditional Commentary—first, the *Times'* position on the big news of the day ("Anita Hill and the Senate's Duty," October 8, 1991, about Clarence Thomas's nomination to the Supreme Court) and, second, the *Times'* policy analyses of the major issues, or as Rosenthal explained it, "What should our intelligent readers think about family planning, D.C. statehood, the homeless, foreign affairs?" ("The President Is Right On Israel," September 17, 1991). Rosenthal's next three categories were less traditional. One, "Warren McCleskey Is Dead" (September 29, 1991) dealt with a convict who died in Georgia's electric chair. Rosenthal called this the Pure Outrage editorial form: "It did not have a policy point. It asked if McCleskey deserved to die. We didn't save his life but we did pound the table and rail at the Supreme Court." Another nontraditional category he called Music— "short commentary on what people are feeling and thinking, on what's in the air." "Still Crazy" (August 17, 1991) was a reflection on a Paul Simon concert ("Thursday night in Central Park turned into a milestone of mellowness. . . ."). The fourth editorial form, Social Comment, turned on even slighter subjects. "Sick Jokes" (August 6, 1991) speculated on how ad hoc jokes about the Dahmer multiple-murder case in Milwaukee and the Pee Wee Herman morals arrest in Sarasota moved by E-mail throughout the country. The casual assumption that readers of the editorial page were the kind of people who have desktop computers with modems and networking services—stock brokers, writers, high technologists—fitted neatly with the *Times'* image of itself.

The Social Comment form appeared regularly. Many dealt with "up" subjects. "The Busiest Day" recounted the demanding schedule of "one Manhattan socialite," whose appointments calendar for that day, October 24, started at 9:00 A.M. and listed five events ("She already has turned down two more"). Among the events, according to the *Times*: "the new Royalton Hotel for a *Vanity Fair* party, Mortimer's to celebrate the launch of a new jewelry firm, the Plaza for the Casita Maria fiesta and the Rainbow Room for a Duke Ellington memorial fund-raiser." Another woman was said to be so stressed by all the social demands that she was "looking forward to escape on a yacht in Antigua." There was no sign that the *Times* was being sarcastic; my dear! these are our readers.

Historically, the most venerable commentary on newspaper editorial pages has dealt with government and the political parties, rather than *Vanity Fair's* parties. Newspapers identified themselves as Federalist or Whig, later as Democratic or Republican. That changed, too, though the modern *Times* was hardly the only newspaper affected. The colonial press was partisan on the editorial pages and in the news columns. In the late nineteenth century, the doctrine of objectivity in the news began taking hold; general-interest dailies started restricting their political views more and more to the editorial pages, cleaning up their news acts in the interests of greater credibility and wider acceptance in the marketplace. By the midpoint of the twentieth century, the move toward "objectivity" had taken many newspapers' editorial pages away from party identification entirely. Since 1932, when the trade magazine *Editor & Publisher* began its quadrennial survey of editorial-page endorsements in U.S. dailies, the number of papers endorsing presidential candidates has steadily dropped. By 1988, and the George Bush–Michael Dukakis race, 436 daily newspapers, or 56.5 percent of the 772 responding to the *Editor & Publisher* mail and telephone survey, said they would not endorse either candidate—the largest number of abstentions recorded by the magazine over almost sixty years. Hundreds of big-city papers, including the *Washington Post* and the

Los Angeles Times, declined to recommend either candidate to their readers in 1988. The reasons varied: The *Post* said it didn't have confidence in Bush or Dukakis; the *Los Angeles Times* stopped making presidential endorsements in the early 1970s, as competing papers in the city disappeared and the *Times* "was no longer one voice among many." Other newspapers declined to make endorsements because they didn't think the paper's views made much difference to the voters. In 1992 the endorsement record marginally changed; the *Washington Post*, for example, endorsed the Democrat, Bill Clinton, but few analysts doubted any lasting reversal of the downward trend.

While there were fewer abstentions in 1992, not many publishers would say publicly what many in their ranks believed: Readers were hard enough to come by, the less materials that turned them off, the better. The Sulzbergers had no use for such behavior, regarding it as a dereliction of journalistic duty. "If a publisher is going to allow his editorial page to comment on what goes on in the world when it comes to every other issue," Punch Sulzberger declared, "he can't pretend that he can't make up his mind on who should run the country."

If there were readers who didn't care, the *Times* nevertheless shouldered its electoral responsibilities. Before making the paper's endorsements for the New York City Council in 1991, board members interviewed all 105 candidates for the council's fifty-one seats. "It was as if we were able to put a finger on the pulse of the city," Jack Rosenthal remembered. "It gave us a feeling that we knew what we were talking about." The candidates were happy to be interviewed. When the *Times* is on the line, almost everyone pays attention. "It's the joy of working at the *Times*," said Jack Rosenthal. "Leave a phone message that the *Times* has called, and they'll call you back right away."

Politicians and the Op-Ed brigade called on the *Times*, without waiting to be called. For decades, mayoral, congressional, and presidential candidates dutifully trooped to the tenth-floor conference room to meet with the board and the publisher, and make their cases for the *Times'* endorsement. These election-year encounters were usually low-key affairs, conducted with a minimum of publicity. In recent years, however, when the *Times* was deciding its choices for president of the United States in 1988 and for New York City mayor in 1989, the process got out of hand. The two high-profile episodes helped shatter the Oz-like institutional aura the *Times* liked to project.

*   *   *

The *Times'* editorial page has been the voice of the liberal establishment for half a century. As Karl E. Meyer explained, "liberal" traditionally meant "centrist" or "mainstream." The word "establishment" has murkier roots. The writer Richard Rovere helped popularize the idea of an American Establishment in the early 1960s; Rovere didn't actually believe that a single, unelected, unacknowledged elite "ran" America. He used the word "establishment" somewhat facetiously. By 1980, however, the economics writer (and *Times* Business Day columnist) Leonard Silk treated the American establishment as if it were a tangible entity. Silk, together with his son, Mark, at the time a Harvard teaching fellow, described the establishment as "a third force" that mediated between popular democracy and corporate capitalism. According to the Silks, the institutions that made the establishment the establishment were, in order: the establishment's leading university, Harvard; its "premiere newspaper," the *New York Times*—"disinterested, pure, apostle of moderation and business progress"; the Ford Foundation, the Brookings Institute, the Council on Foreign Relations; groups such as the Business Roundtable, the Eastern wing of the Republican Party, and the Trilateral Commission.

Today the Silks' list has mainly antiquarian value. Americans encounter Eastern Moderate Republicans as infrequently as the spotted owl; not even conspiracy theorists bother to mention trilateralism anymore. The *Times'* editorial page, however, perseveres. It still tries to act as honest broker on "the issues." It addresses both major matters—for example, mediating between the White House and Israel—and the more minor concerns of the moment (a socialite's "Busiest Day"). "What the *Times* said" on the editorial page became a shorthand for the midground consensus. It said what the thoughtful people thought. A few years back, Hedley Donovan, the former editor in chief of the Time Inc. magazines, despaired of the leadership qualities of Jason McManus, who became Time Inc. editor in chief in 1988. Donovan didn't think McManus had the necessary imagination or the new ideas to keep the magazines fresh and vital. "Jason," Donovan complained, looking for the right words to convey his disappointment, "never expressed an opinion at our meetings that couldn't be found on the editorial pages of *The New York Times*."

Donovan was perhaps too harsh on the *Times*, and on McManus. The editorial page was not always predictable. The *Times* endorsed

Franklin D. Roosevelt in 1932 and 1936, and broke with him in 1940 when he ran for a third term, spurning presidential tradition (read: moderation). But then Roosevelt, the wartime president leading the allied coalition, won the *Times'* endorsement for his *fourth* term in 1944. During the cold-war years, the *Times'* editorial choices swung back to moderate Republicans—Thomas E. Dewey and Dwight Eisenhower, twice (the voters also liked Ike). By the 1960s, the country, and the *Times* along with it, was ready for change again. A new liberal voice, John Oakes's, was heard on the editorial pages; the *Times* endorsed the cool centrist John Kennedy in 1960 against the hot Richard Nixon, Lyndon Johnson over New Right Republican Barry Goldwater in 1964, and Hubert Humphrey instead of Nixon in 1968—Oakes was still unable to stomach Nixon, while the Sulzbergers thought he was an anti-Semite.

During the 1970s and '80s, the editorial page's enthusiasm for moderate Democrats Jimmy Carter and Walter Mondale grew fainter and fainter. Then came the 1988 presidential elections. The Democrat Michael Dukakis was the board's favorite by a clear majority. Soon after the candidate came to lunch with the publisher and selected editors and board members, however, the word spread in the newsroom that Punch Sulzberger had been underwhelmed by Dukakis. He came across as narrow, a technocrat, programmed, "as if he were running mechanically, like a candidate for sanitary district engineer." There were reports that the *Times* would not endorse either man.

The Sunday before election day, October 30, 1988, Jack Rosenthal's lead editorial appeared; "Two Good Men," the headline read. The editorial complained about the "sour, superficial, misleading campaign." But then George Bush was described as informed and affable, and Michael Dukakis as disciplined and decent. Bush was serious. Dukakis was also serious. And so on, down the page. Readers couldn't discern the *Times'* choice for president that next Tuesday until the last paragraph. After 1,785 words of analysis, the *Times'* verdict came in the final thirty-six words: "Here, then, is the final test. Getting America out of hock is, by far, the next president's most urgent job. Who's likely to do it better? The answer tips a closely balanced scale—to Michael Dukakis."

Later, when Jack Rosenthal and Punch Sulzberger were asked, separately, about the genesis of "Two Good Men," they offered two different explanations. Rosenthal gave an intellectual's policy-oriented answer. "It turned on Bush's cockamamie proposals to cut the capital gains tax." Sulzberger gave a more personal account. "Did I find Dukakis 'underwhelming'? That's semi-true, like all such stories. I could very easily have gone for Bush until he nominated Dan Quayle. That just knocked me over, and I couldn't do it. But we didn't cop out as some as our friends in the industry did. We went to Dukakis." Both men also offered a peek at the "collegial" process. "We have a contractual relationship with the reader," Rosenthal said. "They look to us for informed commentary. We nominated ourselves to ruminate, to think. But then when the time came to draw the line, and add it all up, we couldn't say at that point, 'We're going to pull away.' That would have been patronizing. That would have been evading responsibility. It was a hard call. The *Washington Post* did not endorse that same week. We did, yes, sure, on the thinnest grounds. But we did it. We endorsed." Punch Sulzberger was more direct: "When the discussion is about who we choose, the editorial page editor and I really don't have any philosophic arguments. We don't get into fights at the end of the day, about who goes for Mr. Jones or Mr. Smith. We work together and it comes quite naturally and quite easily." Then he said something that sounded familiar: "I play a very active role in these things. They don't go the other way if I don't want them to."

He had said the same thing about the *Times* choice in the Abzug-Moynihan race of 1976.

A year after Bush-Dukakis the choice facing the board was between two other "good men"—New York City's three-term mayor Edward I. Koch and the African-American challenger, David Dinkins. Koch was in a close race with Dinkins in the September 1989 primary (two other candidates, Richard Ravitch and Harrison Goldin—like Koch, white, Jewish men—were also on the Democratic ballot, but were not given much chance of winning). The *Times* editorial page had endorsed Koch for a third term in 1985, though with a mild warning that he ought to work harder "in advancing harmony"—editorialese for saying that the city badly needed better relations among its contentious black, white, Hispanic, and Asian racial and ethnic groups. After four more years of Koch, such harmony seemed as elusive as ever. But the *Times'* endorsement of Koch for a fourth term did not appear to be in doubt, certainly as far as reporters seven floors below in the newsroom were concerned. Two of the *Times'* best political reporters privately pointed to the Sulzbergers' long-standing relationship with Koch. "If there is any way they could see to endorse, I knew they would," the first reporter said. The second reporter said he understood why outsiders thought the *Times* might back Dinkins, but they didn't really know the Sulzbergers: "Punch and Arthur think Dinkins is 'too liberal.' That's not to say they are racists. Actually, Dinkins never made a good case for himself, except to say 'I can heal the rift between the races.' While that's powerful, it's not complete."

Again, the way the *Times* made its Koch endorsement called as much attention to the process as to the result. The editorial ran on September 3, with the headline "The Case for Ed Koch—and His Duty." It made a case for genetic engineering. According to the *Times*, Dinkins was "measured, highly likable, dignified, decent." Koch, while provocative, "has proved his ability to run the city." Each man, said the *Times*, offered what the other most lacks. "The ideal outcome would be both." And so it went, as the *Times* laid out the pluses and minuses of both men, before recommending Koch. The choice was presented so diffidently that Dinkins supporters carved a primary-day flier out of it. As the flier put it: " 'The city might be well served by a Mayor Dinkins.'—*The New York Times*."

The *Times* derived benefits from its exquisite even-handedness. Dinkins won the primary race, and the editorial page endorsed him against the Republican Rudolph Giuliani in the general election. The *Times* had it both ways, casting its vote first for "moderation" (Koch) and then for "progress" (Dinkins): for past and present, for white and black. In the spring of 1992, halfway through the presidential primaries, readers began looking for signs of what the *Times* was thinking about the fall election. Richard Harwood, then the press critic for the *Washington Post*, wryly noted that the *Times* recommended that the Republicans renominate George Bush ("a prudent player") and that the Democrats choose Governor Bill Clinton (he has "sensible priorities"). The recommendations appeared weeks after the outcomes of the two campaigns were settled. "The daredevil *Times*," Harwood joked.

An editorial at the time of the founding of Op-Ed explained that the page was intended to provide a forum for social, personal and political expression by writers "with no institutional connection to the *Times*." The page itself, as well as the new prominence accorded columns and opinion journalism throughout the *Times*, was offered as evidence of the Sulzberger family's desire to promote the principle of free speech, to honor *Times* "traditions" and "better serve its readers by welcoming a variety of views." It takes nothing from "tradition" to point out that the *Times* borrowed the idea of an Op-Ed from elsewhere. A version of a page devoted to opinion appeared in the *Chicago Tribune* as early as 1912; in 1921, Herbert Bayard Swope, editor of the *New York World*, conceived of a full page of columns. Swope spelled it *Op. Ed.* and invited some of the best newspaper writers of the day, including Heywood Broun, Alexander Woollcott, Deems Taylor, Harry Hansen, and Franklin P. Adams, to contribute (Swope didn't publish unsolicited manuscripts). Thirty years later, the *Times* began talking about an Op-Ed page, as we saw; ten more years passed before Punch Sulzberger agreed to move the obituary notices—a major part of the old Paper of Record—from their prominent position on the page across from the editorial page. There was no journalistic loss in this shift; it is the nature of obits that their regular audience will find them, wherever they run in the paper.

Times purists, like Clifton Daniel, had made the rearguard case against Op-Ed, arguing that outsiders' opinions would "dilute" the *Times'* authority, and appear to give its imprimatur to who-knows-what views. But Punch Sulzberger had good practical reasons to do just that. He knew exactly what views he wanted, worried as he was about the "perception" that the *Times'* editorial page was "too liberal" for the country in the post-Vietnam years. The publisher signaled as much in 1973, with his first big Op-Ed column hire, William Safire. Talk about abandoning the old purity: Safire was an outsider, spectacularly so, by *Times* standards. He had never worked for the *Times*, and his newsroom experience was minimal—actually, he was not a journalist at all but a public relations man and a speechwriter for the enemy, Richard Nixon. Nor was Safire the *Times'* first choice to be its house conservative.

The opinion explosion at the *Times* brought immediate payoffs to the paper, too. From the start, the bottom right-hand space on the Op-Ed page was available to advertisers with messages of a public policy nature. Through the 1970s and 1980s, Fortune 500 corporations, labor unions, and lobbying groups paid premium prices to the *Times* for the privilege "of renting space on the inside of the paper's cranium," in the writer Robert Sherrill's words. The Mobil Corporation, for example, was a longtime advertiser and sole sponsor for the *Times'* special supplement commemorating the twentieth anniversary of the Op-Ed page. On September 30, 1990, Mobil paid $300,000 to run eight pages of ads in the twenty-page section. Representative Op-Ed articles from 1970 to 1990 appeared interspersed with Mobil's views on entrepreneurial capitalism and ad copy proclaiming the oil company's devotion to the environment.

The *Times* had other practical reasons for promoting "diversity." The Sulzbergers were not the first press proprietors to discover that the essay form—five hundred to one thousand words of opinion by one writer, whether staff person or contributor—could be cost effective. A column was less expensive to produce than an equivalent amount of hard news, which required the time, legwork, and processing talents of a team of reporters and editors. The column form was also attractive as a management tool. The columnist's chair could serve as a prize to reward the deserving: Anna Quindlen became an Op-Ed columnist at the age of forty, in 1990, when—her celebrity assured—she was about to quit the *Times* and become a writer of novels and magazine articles. The publisher talked her out of leaving by making her a columnist. A generation before, the publisher similarly arranged a column for a thirty-seven-year-old named Russell Baker, after he received an attractive offer from the *Baltimore Sun*. Columns also were used as consolation prizes for the losers of bureaucratic wars—Tom Wicker became a columnist after his removal as the *Times'* Washington bureau chief— and to provide a soft landing for superannuated editors (veterans that the publisher, for whatever his reasons, wanted to move out of their posts). A. M. Rosenthal left the news department at the age of sixty-five to become an Op-Ed columnist, and Leslie Gelb went from Op-Ed page editor to Op-Ed columnist. But perhaps most important of all from the perspective of the publisher's office, the new array of columns, "Notebooks," and first-person opinion helped make the *Times* a friendlier read. The daily run of hard news was, inevitably, depressing: war, riot, crime, recession, bank failures, crumbling roads and bridges, the constant fraying of the social fabric. Sometimes stories were so discouraging that the reader wanted to put the paper down, and absorb no more (including the advertisements). Such hard news couldn't be controlled; it happened, and a news organization reacted. On the other hand, opinion was manageable; editors had it in their power to create pages with an up feeling. Columns provided an antidote to grim news; they were good for business. The night before Arthur Sulzberger was named publisher of the *Times* on January 16,

1992, he was in Washington, inaugurating a series of lectures about the *Times*. According to Arthur, people should read the *Times*, "not only because it is the best newspaper in the world, but also for the fun of it." Arthur specifically mentioned the joy of reading Russell Baker and Anna Quindlen.

For a variety of reasons, then, the *Times* changed the balance of news and opinion in its pages during the decade of the 1980s. The earlier sectional revolution had been accomplished with wide publicity; the *Times* trumpeted Weekend, Home, and the other new specialized services—there was no reason to conceal what was going on. The *Times'* shift to opinion in the 1980s was engineered gradually, with little public comment. Before anyone noticed, the *Times'* venerable word factory underwent a top-to-bottom conversion; the old, heavy-industry assembly line gave way to a kind of automated, post-industrial facility: opinion manufacturing. Operationally, the production of opinion was more efficient than the old, cumbersome techniques of hard-news gathering. The "Campus Life" news section required a staff of editors and dozens of stringers (albeit hourly-wage workers); one talented professional operator smoothly turned out "The Arm Fetish" for the hipper-than-thou pages of the new "Styles" section.

The opinion product proved popular with consumers. The modern *Times* shrewdly understood its niche in the contemporary marketplace. *Times*people explained patiently to outsiders that "Op-Ed" meant no more than "opposite the editorial page"—and not, as Clifton Daniel had feared, "contrary to the editorial policies of the *Times*."

The purists never should have worried. While quantitatively more opinion appeared in the *Times*, the qualitative differences along the contributions grew less and less discernible. The overall voice was unmistakable: measured, safe, conventional wisdom. Readers could remove the columnists' bylines on top, or the line at the bottom identifying the contributor, and know that, whatever the specific topic, they were reading the *Times*. The market success of the new *Times* suggested that the core audience wanted, at most, the appearance of diversity, and not riotous, subversive diversity itself.

Bill Safire, of all the *Times'* house columnists, managed to remain contrarian and consistently interesting over the years. He had obvious blind spots and played favorites; but his collection of pets had an eclectic charm: Richard Nixon, Israel, White House speech writers,

Roy Cohn. Safire had an original turn of mind, and created a repertory of recurring themes for his column—fashioning a speech that he wanted the president of the United States to give, or peering into the thoughts of one or another foreign leader, stream-of-consciousness fashion. In part, too, Safire stayed fresh because he worked hard at the column form, and cultivated a wide range of contacts. But Safire's columns also looked good by default: He was the only Washington-based writer on the page. Russell Baker, nominally a member of the Washington bureau, rarely came into the office, or the city. He preferred to stay at home in suburban Virginia, spinning out twice-weekly columns remarkable for their detachment. Many of these light essays—Baker, thirty years before, named the column "Observer"—took off from what he read in the morning newspapers or saw the night before on television. There was no pretense of reporting or research. Still, Baker usually managed to slip a needle into the received wisdom of the day, occasionally deflating some of the *Times'* own more self-serving editorial stands. In a column on New York City redevelopers' plans for the West Side, for example, Baker chided megadevelopments in language reminiscent of the deposed Sydney Schanberg (the radical Schanbergian thoughts that had so offended the Sulzbergers were offered with Baker's signature ironic touch).

Safire and Baker weren't pompous. Neither man was totally consumed by newspaper work; their energies also went into their books—Baker's multivolume memoirs, Safire's novels and series on grammar usage and etymology. Neither man took his Op-Ed status too seriously, either. When Abe Rosenthal started his column, Safire advised the new Op-Ed man, "Don't be objective."

At the very start, there was some talk about making the Op-Ed page more provocative. "I had a rule of thumb," Harrison Salisbury, the first Op-Ed–page editor, remembered in an interview a few years before his death in 1993. "I wanted people to pick up the paper each day, shake their head, and ask, 'What's that horse's ass done this morning?' " In the interests of shock, he ran a contribution by a father who shot his son after discovering the young man was a drug abuser. But the measure of Op-Ed "provocation" could be judged by what Salisbury cited as the most quoted contribution during his time—a slight turn by the writer J. B. Priestley, who argued the superiority of British civilization because of the English preference for eating brown eggs. Not surprisingly, Salisbury was happy to move on from the page after three years: "An editor has a few ideas, he runs through them, and then begins recycling them. The shorter tenure, the better. I don't mean to be invidious," he added, "but after my regime I think the page lost its zip." His successor, Charlotte Curtis, struggled through a losing battle with cancer. Her successor, Robert Semple, reported to Max Frankel, at the time the editorial-page editor and, Salisbury said, "a too predictable journalist: Max was not given to controversy."

Semple acknowledged that he "took a more conservative tack than Harrison." Semple said his favorite Op-Ed article during his time was a short essay on women and the "tyranny" of high-heel shoes. The most talked-about Semple-era article was William Buckley, Jr.'s, un-ironic proposal to tattoo an identification mark on people carrying the AIDS virus. In 1989, when Semple was replaced by Leslie Gelb, the page benefited from Gelb's extensive diplomatic contacts, and his Washington "perspective." "He knew all the players," Semple said. "He was one himself." Much less was expected of Mitchel Levitas, the editor who replaced Gelb in October 1990. A *Times* lifer and third-floor loyalist, Levitas was only a few years from retirement when he came up to the tenth floor; supposedly, he would quietly serve out his time—the bland leading the bland. Instead Levitas livened up the page, sometimes breaking genuine news. In April 1991, for example, Levitas published an article by Gary Sick, the former Carter admin-istration national security analyst who accused Ronald Reagan's 1980 presidential campaign team of an "October Surprise" (briefly, a plot to delay the release of U.S. hostages in Iran in order to insure Reagan's election). In August 1991 James H. Billington, a leading historian and the Librarian of Congress, happened to be visiting Moscow during the hardliners' attempted coup; his Op-Ed page account presented a better eyewitness picture of events than could be found in the news pages.

For a while a few years ago, the *Times*' quest for Op-Ed diversity seemed to be answered, as if from demographic heaven. When the Sulzbergers announced Anna Quindlen's appointment as an Op-Ed columnist, she had a husband, three children, and more than twelve years' experience as a reporter, editor, and writer for the *Times*. Quindlen had contributed to the "Hers" feature in the *Times*, then wrote the "Life in the 30s" column. She began appearing on the Op-Ed page in January 1990: the *Times*' signal at the start of the new decade that a fresh voice—young, female, and personal—was going to be heard among the old, familiar public-policy pundits. Quindlen was at home, Newsweek said, "in the rocky emotional terrain of marriage, parenthood, secret desires, and self-doubts." According to the magazine, her columns were the kind that other thirtysomethings tacked to their refrigerator doors, to be read and reread. A profile of Quindlen in Elle noted she had been named "one of the outstanding mothers in America." The magazine added that her readers were the ones the Times was trying to attract: "young, well-to-do women."

Quindlen's columns made her admirers feel that they had been invited into her house, to look at her refrigerator door and everything else. Readers came to recognize her from television appearances, university lectures, and book tours. In her columns, she described herself for them: small, dark, "no longer a size eight." She wrote in intimate terms of growing up in suburban Philadelphia in a large Irish-Italian family; the father, a management consultant; her mother, a victim of cancer when Anna Quindlen was nineteen. Her fans knew she went to Barnard; knew how at the college baby-sitting service, she looked through the files to find Times reporters who needed sitters, and how after a few months, she could turn to them, the Habermans, the Van Gelders, for career guidance. Then up the journalism ladder: the Brunswick, New Jersey, Home News, the New York Post, the New York Times to be a general-assignment reporter. Marriage to criminal lawyer Jerry Krovatin. The birth of their sons Quin and Christopher, and then daughter Maria. The story of her job interviews at the Times were recounted by admirers. Asked what she wanted to do at the Times, she squared her shoulders and declared that she wished most of all to be a street reporter for the Metro section. The editor gave her a stricken look: "I realized that was not the 'correct' answer." Sent on to the metro editor, John Vinocur, for her next interview, she remembered that he was a former foreign correspondent; he had worked in the Times' Bonn bureau, not in Brooklyn or the Bronx. "I want to work abroad, I want to cover Germany," she told him brightly.

By 1981 Quindlen was writing "About New York," the column that Meyer Berger once did. At the age of thirty-three, in 1983, Quindlen was named deputy metro editor, and became the highest-ranking newswoman at the Times. "A group of us at the Times call ourselves the 'class of '78,' " she liked to say. "We directly benefited from the women's discrimination suit [settled in 1978]." Now she reached out to a new generation of women at the Times, to smooth their path. "Women hit the glass ceiling later," she said. "It used to be at nineteen, now it's thirty-two. A generation ago, I would have tried to blend in with the men at the *Times*. Now I speak up on women's issues." Quindlen, the storyteller, could turn the account of how she named her Op-Ed column into a bright anecdote for her audience. She and Jack Rosenthal considered such titles as "Out of Bounds" and "Persuasions"—"I'm an admirer of the novels of Jane Austin," she said—but a data-base search disclosed that "Persuasions" was already being used for a column in an S&M magazine. The pair agreed on "Public & Private."

In many ways "Public & Private" was a dream assignment. Quindlen had complete freedom to write about any topic she wanted, with no editor looking over her shoulder (the column was read before publication solely by a copy editor, who checked for grammar and for conformity to *Times* usage). Her relationship with the Sulzbergers was ideal. She counted herself among the friends of Arthur Sulzberger and his wife, Gail Gregg; Punch Sulzberger took a fatherly though more distant interest in her work.

Initially, "Public & Private" worked. Quindlen told wonderful stories, mixed the serious and the personal, reporting and opinion. She visited a city shelter rather than telephoning some expert to talk about "the homeless." Quindlen, a practicing Roman Catholic, announced she was pro-choice on abortion; her column, too, quirkily blended liberal and traditional attitudes. The Pulitzer Board awarded her its prize for newspaper commentary for 1991. Then, curiously, the storytelling qualities that made the early columns so successful disappeared; there were fewer visits to shelters, the phone calls seeking expert information dropped off as well. Weeks went by, then months, with Quindlen having little fresh to say. In the late spring of 1992, the columnist Nat Hentoff said in public what a number of Quindlen readers were thinking in private: "Anna Quindlen . . . writes as if she were giving a dinner speech at a fund-raiser for one of a number of very worthy causes. There is less reporting and much more proclaiming." An Op-Ed column is supposed to be the place for a point of view; but absent reporting, Quindlen's proclamations became predictable. Name the cause and the reader knew the Quindlen position: Anita Hill versus Clarence Thomas, Hillary Clinton's career and marriage, the family values of Dan Quayle and "Murphy Brown." At times she reduced her column to a recitation of positions; at the height of the H. Ross Perotmania in the spring and summer of 1992, Quindlen wrote: "Fact is that on many current issues I'm in agreement with Mr. Perot. Opposed Gulf war, favors legal abortion. Thinks Anita Hill was treated shabbily, hawks early childhood education. Too much lobbying, too little listening. Wrestle that deficit to the ground. Hear, hear!" Trite, trite!

If Quindlen no longer offered any surprises on the Op-Ed page, there was always the *Times'* other "personal" columnist, A. M. Rosenthal. After all his years as the fearsome hard-news man, Abe Rosenthal revealed a new persona. He called his column "On My Mind," to signal he would speak his thoughts directly to the reader. The topics on his mind had little to do with the city he lived in or the work of his professional life. Consider a random sample of ninety-five Rosenthal columns published from July 1988 to March 1990, a period that included the U.S. presidential elections, the New York City mayoral race and, abroad, the penultimate days of the Soviet Union. Some of the topics overlapped; a column on the collapse of communism was as much about Washington as Moscow. But on a scale of frequency, George Bush was the most popular single subject; 34 of the 95 columns focused on or mentioned Bush. Abe Rosenthal was the second most frequent subject: More than a third of the columns (32) were written in the first person. Approximately a third of the columns (31) dealt with Israel and/or American Jews (four were about anti-Semitism). The Soviet Union and Gorbachev were the next most frequent topic (29 columns). At the other end of the scale, only two columns focused on or mentioned the New York governor, Mario Cuomo. The two New York mayors, Edward Koch and David Dinkins, combined receive fewer mentions than either the Israeli leaders Shamir or Peres (Dinkins succeeded Koch in 1989).

Jewish matters did not weigh so heavily on Rosenthal's mind when he was running the news department in the 1970s and 1980s. The *Times* archives contain scores of letters written to Rosenthal over the years from the American Jewish Committee and other Jewish organizations; many of these letters complained of the *Times'* inattention to stories that the writers considered worthy of coverage. Editor Rosenthal invariably upheld the *Times'* news judgments on "Jewish stories," as he did when black- or gay- or Irish-activist groups complained about coverage. Columnist Rosenthal, however, became a defender of the faith. Over several weeks in early 1992, he engaged in an acrimonious dispute with the Washington columnists Roland Evans and Robert Novak about whether Israel shared classified U.S. missile technology

with China; earlier, Rosenthal took on the commentator and sometime Republican presidential candidate Pat Buchanan for his "pattern"
of remarks (among other things, Buchanan accused Israel and its
"amen corner" in the U.S. of "beating the drums" for war against Iraq
and Saddam Hussein). Abe Rosenthal's late-life embrace of his Jewish
roots became material for the gossip writers, especially when, in the
spring of 1992, Rosenthal decided to be bar-mitzvahed. The religious
Jew's passage to manhood, the bar mitzvah involves biblical study,
Hebrew lessons, and prayer; it is normally undertaken when a Jewish
boy nears his thirteenth birthday. But as Rosenthal explained to Deborah Mitchell of the weekly *New York Observer*, his father died a few
months before the usual bar mitzvah time, making any ceremony
impossible; moreover, the father, Harry, was a socialist-agnostic who
had lost his faith in organized religion and had stopped going to temple. Through the years, the son was angry and upset, and "as he
worked to free himself of those emotions, he realized he could finally
release them by partaking of the ritual he had missed decades ago."
The bar mitzvah took place at the time of Rosenthal's seventieth birthday, on a Saturday at the Central Synagogue on Lexington Avenue.
The celebratory party afterward was held in the L'Orangerie at Le
Cirque, the East Side restaurant. The guest list included Rosenthal's
wife, Shirley Lord, several *Times*people, Elie and Marion Wiesel, and
some of New Society's most indefatigable partygoers, such as Henry
Kissinger, Saul and Gayfryd Steinberg, and Robert and Georgette
Mosbacher. The monologuist Jackie Mason would be hard-pressed to
top this social comedy of "real life."

The Op-Ed page continued to evolve. Les Gelb said he aimed for
"more liveliness." Jack Rosenthal described the need for a "variety of
features." From time to time, an old rumor kept resurfacing; the *Times*
was said to be considering an Op-Ed page political cartoon, in the style
of Herblock of the *Washington Post* or Doug Marlette of *Newsday*.
Publicly, the Sulzbergers continued to resist proposals for a full-time
cartoonist. According to Robert Semple, "The official answer is 'an
in-house political cartoon would be read as reflecting the *Times*' point
of view' "—and the Sulzbergers were not yet prepared to accord any
one cartoonist that much "authority." That position began to evolve,
too, slowly. In the mid-1980s, the cartoonist Garry Trudeau—fearful
that the *News*, the New York City outlet for his "Doonesbury" comic
strip, might go out of business as a result of strikes and inept manage-

ment—made private inquiries about the possibility of switching the strip to the *Times*. He was told through intermediaries that the *Times* wasn't interested in "Doonesbury." But Trudeau had admirers at the paper, including Jack Rosenthal, and in the spring of 1990, Trudeau formally became an "occasional contributor" to the Op-Ed page. His Op-Ed work combined text and drawings, offering sardonic commentary on such topics as Richard Nixon's paranoid style (inspired by the publication of a new volume of Nixon memoirs), the Oliver Stone film *J.F.K.*, the prevalence of spin doctors in politics, and the marketing of the singer Madonna. By the time of the 1992 presidential campaign, Trudeau was appearing monthly, though always described with the bland ID, "occasional contributor."

Perhaps the greatest Op-Ed shift of all occurred about this time, with no public hint that anything on the page had changed. The retirement of the veteran Flora Lewis and, a year later, the departure of Tom Wicker after almost three decades on the page, marked more than the end of two long-running Op-Ed columnists. Lewis and Wicker had a lifetime assignment: It was understood that they would write their columns until the normal age-range for retirement (Punch Sulzberger's sacking of Syd Schanberg was the exception that proved the tenure rule). With Lewis and Wicker gone—and with Russell Baker, A. M. Rosenthal, and Anthony Lewis to follow, relatively soon—the old University-style tenure system was dead. Though very few of the newshounds on the third floor knew it, the Op-Ed rules seven floors above had been rewritten, in stealth fashion: the two newest columnists, Les Gelb and Anna Quindlen, received three-year appointments only, with a provision that the agreements were renewable, although not automatically.

The journalistic value of the shift from lifetime tenure to short-term contracts could be endlessly debated: On one side, there was the loss of the writer's independence, at least in the abstract, to be balanced, on the other side, against the editors' desire for "liveliness" and going with the market flow. Would Quindlen or Gelb, say, find themselves rotated off the page to make room for a hotter, younger writing talent?

As it turned out, Gelb never started his "second term." In the spring of 1993, he left the *Times* to join *Foreign Affairs* magazine—retrograde career movement, in even the best interpretation. His departure coincided with the arrival of Bob Herbert, then forty-eight, as an Op-Ed columnist. The product of area parochial schools and the Manhattan borough unit of the State University of New York, Herbert spent seventeen years at the *New York Daily News*, rising to columnist and editorial board member. In many ways, he was the ideal Op-Ed hire: Arthur Sulzberger at last had a writer with a strong background in city affairs to fill the long-vacant Schanberg chair. The new columnist was, in the bargain, a black American, who met the new publisher's standard of greater "diversity" . . . up to a point, of course: for Herbert, despite his raffish tabloid background, was as middle-class and mainstream as any of his new colleagues. His moderate views insured that Arthur Sulzberger was making the best possible P.C.—politically centrist—appointment.

While Herbert wasn't exactly a one-for-one replacement of the pale male Gelb, the presence (finally) of a black man on the Op-Ed page nevertheless cleared the way, diversity-wise, for another white woman columnist. In the *Times* Washington bureau, reporter Maureen Dowd had attracted attention with her sharp-eyed coverage of politics. A few traditionalists thought Dowd was already writing opinion pieces and belonged somewhere other than the news pages. Dowd herself had none of the old Paper of Record drive. A newsroom colleague remembered her reaction when, finishing her tour in the New York office, her ticket punched, she learned she was going back to Washington. She would write big-time features, and eventually cover the Reagan-Bush White House, Dowd told her coworker, in that way she had of leaning intimately into the conversation. "I know one thing," she said. "I'm not going to be covering any of those dreary regulatory agencies." Post–White House, Dowd was plainly destined for Bigger Things. Her "news analysis" pieces during the 1992 presidential campaign offered un-*Times*ian generational attitudes and pop culture references. Rather than write "traditionally" about politics and "the issues," she would typically spin out the conceit of the candidates as people we knew in high school—class president Clinton, greaser Jerry Brown, etc. Covering a U.S.-Russian summit in misty Vancouver, Dowd wrote of the "bad hair day" threatening the presidential coiffeurs of Bill Clinton and Boris Yeltsin.

A case could be made in favor of such flexibility at the modern *Times*. Perhaps the old column form had outlived its usefulness. The era when the generalists—a Reston in the *Times*, or a Walter Lippmann in the *Herald Tribune*, the other "thoughtful" morning paper—addressed the full sweep of national and international politics had long passed. The world was a more complicated place; the contemporary columnist had to be a specialist of a sort, less magisterial, more personal.

Some things, in truth, did not change. The *Times* was still "The *Times*" in one important sense. Throughout the paper, on the editorial page and Op-Ed page, in the Sports section and in Styles of the Times, the opinions were predictable. Readers knew what Anna Quindlen would say on Clarence Thomas, where A. M. Rosenthal would come out on foreign aid, and who the editorial board would endorse. Thus, the *Times'* 1992 presidential endorsements wrote themselves. The editorial as expected judiciously added up the pluses and minuses for right-moderate George Bush and left-moderate Bill Clinton, and mystery-moderate H. Ross Perot—as it did in 1988 when Bush faced Michael Dukakis. The *Times* then decided for Clinton, as it did for Dukakis. Readers grew to expect such (slightly) off-center positions every four years. But genuinely *new* news events produced expected responses as well. When the pro basketball superstar Ervin "Magic" Johnson announced that he was HIV-positive at a news conference in November 1991, the *Times'* initial editorial praised Johnson's courage in coming forward. Johnson's willingness to be a role model in the cause of AIDS research and prevention was another matter, and the *Times* had Second Thoughts. Over the next few days, *Times* sports columnists Dave Anderson and Robert Lipsyte both questioned Johnson's status as a spokesman for safe sex because of his own "irresponsible" behavior. Johnson had slept with scores of women in National Basketball Association cities around the country, Lipsyte scolded. What's more, he was a college dropout who was paying child support for a son born to a former girlfriend back in his home state of Michigan. "He has been hailed by many as a 'hero,' when hedonist might be a better word," Anderson wrote. "Magic Johnson is hardly a model or ideal to anyone with a sense of sexual morality." Five months later, the same *Times* sports columns were full of praise for Arthur Ashe, another HIV-positive athlete. Ashe contracted the virus asexually, from a blood transfusion. He was, moreover, well-spoken and well-mannered; he lived temperately (one wife, one legitimate child). There was no replay of the coverage this time. "The role model most on our minds these days is Arthur Ashe, quiet gentlemanly Arthur Ashe," wrote Heywood Hale Broun, a guest columnist on the *Times* sports pages. A few weeks later, Barry Lorge, another guest columnist, called Ashe "the gentleman who has been the conscience of tennis. . . ." The *Times* could well imagine the gentlemanly Ashe as a regular reader, as it could not the hedonistic Johnson.

* * *

For all the talk of diversity, the outpouring of opinion at the modern *Times* was actually well controlled. It stayed within the banks of the mainstream: the received wisdom, thoughtful, midbrow, safe. In the 1870s, a tumultuous time for America and for journalism, Wilbur Story, editor of the *Chicago Times*, announced that his paper intended "to print the news and raise hell." The traditional *New York Times* printed the news and occasionally raised . . . heck. The modern *Times* moved further away from the record and from heck raising. When the *Times'* opinion-page editors, columnists, and editorialists looked at the world, they saw their own mannerly reflection. The readers returned the compliment: They found their views of the world reinforced by the *Times*. And why not? The modern *Times* was designed to be friendly to a well-defined class of readers.

The leftist critique of American journalism usually looks at that friendliness and conspiratorily concludes that "the media" are the captives of the advertisers, toadies of Corporate America. The left misses the more intriguing story: Newspapers like the *Times* have captured a demographic segment of the population highly desired by the advertisers; Corporate America then pays the *Times*—and CBS, *Newsweek*, et al.—for the privilege of talking to that audience. In the decade of the 1990s, a million-plus people around the U.S. were willing to pay whatever the *Times* asked for a copy of the paper; while the newsstand sale price kept rising, the demand remained elastic. The user was happy. Consumer satisfaction helped explain the rise of opinion at the modern *Times* and equally significant, the content of that opinion.

The modern *Times'* audience and the *Times* had both changed. Jack Rosenthal concluded that the media were "de-aggregating into a range of special-interest services." The opinion columns and the downtown Styles pages were just the beginning. Secondary markets were opening up; beginning in 1991, fans of the *Times* crossword could call a 900 number and get three clues to that day's puzzle, 75 cents for the first minute, 50 cents for each additional minute. Within a few months, the pay service was bringing in revenues of $20,000 a week. Puzzle addicts were a strange breed but they weren't unique. In similar fashion, the *Times* turned its inability to distribute a paper with the final sports results into a money-making opportunity. Sports fans who received their copies of the paper without an account of their favorite team's night game were advised in a box on the sports page that they could dial another 900 number, and pay 50 cents per minute to get the late scores the *Times* didn't have.

The deaggregated, electronically wired paper of the future, it seems, won't actually have to carry news.

A DAY IN THE LIFE
6:00 P.M.—7:05 P.M.

6:00 P.M.

Al Scardino made notes on a story idea that, he thought, would create some media chatter—the demise of the "Joe Friday" reporter. No longer were journalists willing to say, "Just the facts, ma'am." Instead, Scardino explained, the new breed of opinionated reporters informed their interviewees, "I have my own opinions but I'll try to suppress them a little to hear you out for a moment or two." (The story never appeared; Scardino left the *Times* later in the year, to become press secretary for the mayor-elect of New York, David Dinkins.)

7:00 P.M.

Edited pages began to flow to the composing room in five-minute intervals.

7:05 P.M.

Paul Winfield, late-night desk man in the Sports section, held a quick meeting with his staff to go over expected changes in their four pages. Sports' dress front was set with features on the Yankees and Dallas Cowboys, plus one of the *Times'* columnists. Everything else was happening inside the section: the pro hockey scores, and the college basketball results, for both men's and women's teams. Winfield selected the Sports section's postage-stamp-size cartoon at the top of the fronting page—a ritual sweetened by the fact that no other *Times* cartoon of any size appeared in the news pages. An umpire had been voted into the baseball Hall of Fame, and the cartoon showed the busts of a catcher and an umpire, arguing with each other. The caption read: "You're in!" ("Our fans will get it," Winfield reassured his staff).

10

ROUGHING IT
IN CULTURE GULCH

BRYAN MILLER ate out at least eight times a week as the *Times'* chief restaurant critic for almost ten years. He started in the job in October 1984, at the age of thirty-two, and served until July 1993, when he moved on to do *Times Magazine* features. He treated his assignments as "a consumer beat." He had, he once explained, "the vital function of tipping off readers where they should spend their precious dining dollars." Like the other *Times* reviewers who covered America's cultural and leisure-time life, Miller's words often had a strong influence on the economic fate of the restaurants he wrote about. Or more precisely, the fact that Miller's words appeared in the *Times* could be critical to the fortunes of the restaurant he was reviewing. That power resided more in the *Times* itself than in the talent of any of its individual critics. Miller's immediate predecessors, Mimi Sheraton and Craig Claiborne, for example, wielded similar influence during their time at the paper. And Miller's successor, a former *Los Angeles Times* food writer named Ruth Reichl, whose work began appearing in the late summer of 1993, is sure to exert a powerful influence as well.

Ruth Reichl's roots were urban and middle class, again, much like most of the other *Times* critics. In one respect, though, Bryan Miller had been unusual; unlike most of his other colleagues who wrote about theater, music, sculpture, architecture, television, and the rest of the topics covered on the *Times'* arts and leisure pages, Miller had some direct, hands-on experience in the field he was assigned to review.

Miller was born in New York City, graduated from Columbia University, and worked for newspapers in the Northeast and for the Associated Press before joining the *Times.* Along the way, too, he took cooking classes and wine courses. In his words, "It was just as a diversion at first," but then he started thinking seriously about being a chef. In 1981 he quit his job as an editor at *Connecticut* magazine, and worked for twenty-three months in the kitchen of Restaurant du Village, a bistro in Chester, Connecticut. (Reichl also had experience as a chef, in Berkeley, California.) He also volunteered briefly for waiter service during his stay, an experience that "instilled in me respect for a professional waiter." Miller's combination of youth, magazine training, and kitchen experience made him attractive when the *Times* was looking for the right person to hire as chief restaurant reviewer—a high-profile job and something of a symbol of the paper's new interests. After Restaurant du Village, too, Miller was ready to put aside his ladle and whisks.

In the course of a normal year at the *Times*, he encountered a battalion of chefs and waiters; Miller estimated that he dined out at least four hundred times a year, either for lunch or dinner, in the interests of his readers. Before writing his review, he tried to visit the restaurant under scrutiny at least three times and in the company of a minimum of three people; a Miller group might sample thirty to forty dishes so he could get "the proper handle on the restaurant's style." His American Express and Visa bills came to $125,000 a year for New York restaurants alone, not counting out-of-town and out-of-country expenses; or, more accurately, the *Times* reimbursed him that amount, plus his taxis and other costs. The *Times'* tab for Miller's dining out exceeded his salary by almost 40 percent; in all, Miller's twice-weekly restaurant reviews cost the *Times* approximately as much as the paper spent to maintain a correspondent and bureau in Africa. Once Miller shared some feelings of guilt about his expenses with a senior editor. He was told to relax, and spend. Of course, the *Times* wants a bureau in Nairobi or Lagos, but "in terms of reader interest, we get a helluva lot more bang for the buck out of the food column."

Once, Miller resorted to an elaborate disguise, complete with a beard that took him two weeks to grow, in order to write about the food at Bellini, a New York restaurant whose owner had publicly announced that he did not want a Miller review.

The Affair Bellini illustrated one aspect of the *Times'* critical powers, as well as its self-image. It began in 1985, when Miller gave, in his own words, "a lackluster review" to Harry Cipriani, the eponymously named restaurant in the Sherry Netherlands hotel. When the owner, Italian restaurateur Harry Cipriani, opened a second high-end restaurant, called Bellini by Cipriani, on Seventh Avenue in 1987, he ran advertisements in the *Times* asking Bryan Miller *not* to come. Restaurant Bellini, Cipriani informed the dining world, could get along without a Miller review. "Of course, I marched right up there," Miller remembered; he also took two fellow *Times*men with him, Pierre Franey, the cook-author and at the time a contributing columnist for the Living section, and James Sterngold, at the time a business-news reporter. If the *Times* was going to pick up the $300-plus tab at Cipriani's elegant new establishment, then the editors had the comfort of knowing that their own staff people would be the beneficiaries.

There was no bill that night; not even a menu was offered to Miller. The three *Times*men sat unattended for fifteen minutes. Cipriani's son was running the dining room that day, and, says Miller, "we summoned" the younger Cipriani (the cachet of a *Times* expense account sometimes encourages upper-class styles even among the middle classes). "He told us that the kitchen refused to serve us." Miller thought that was "a silly way to shirk responsibility." The *Times*men left quietly. A few days later, Miller discussed his foodless night out with Max Frankel, the *Times* executive editor, and with the assistant managing editor, Allan Siegal. They instructed Miller to write a "dispassionate" "Diner's Journal" item about the episode. Casually, Frankel turned to Miller and asked: "Do you think you can get in?" Miller promised to try.

Miller is a clean-cut Irish-American, with a taste for preppie clothes. He began to grow a beard for an undercover operation aimed at Bellini. He called in a friend, Cris Evans, a theatrical makeup artist, who dyed the writer's brown hair and gave him a modish haircut. She went to SoHo with him to pick out a new set of downtown clothes—"the kind of getup John Travolta would have liked in *Saturday Night Fever*." A pair of shaded eyeglasses completed the make-over. Miller and Evans tested the disguise, successfully, at lunch at La Grenouille ("not exactly a Bryan Miller fan club," either, the writer noted). Then Miller went unannounced with four other *Times*people—"my dining team"—to Bellini; he sat facing the wall of the downstairs dining area, undetected. He completed two more Bellini missions before delivering his verdict. As Miller later summarized his review, "the food ranged from merely passable to dismal. Mr. Cipriani's charms notwithstanding, service was slipshod if not outright clownish." (Three and a half years later, Miller revisited Bellini and upgraded his opinion, advising his consumer-readers that the restaurant was "a reliable though pricy theater-district dining option.")

That was the *Times*, as it saw itself: dedicated critic, ready to go to extraordinary lengths to get the story; high-minded editors, demanding an extra effort of their reporters; the institutional *Times*, taking its role of consumer guide seriously, and willing to pay all the expenses necessary to do the job. The Affair Bellini demonstrated that the *Times* reporters, writers, critics, and editors—the people's surrogates—ought not be crossed. From the *Times*' perspective, the story proffered the face of incorruptible authority—the *Times*' power seen in the most flattering light, in the cause of dispassionate public service: a review, and then a re-review, all for the reader.

The face of the *Times* its critics presented to the world sometimes revealed a less attractive side. All power is said to corrupt, and the fact that pettiness and pique sometimes influenced the stances of the *Times*' powerful critics ought not be too surprising. What, after all, was Harry Cipriani's crime that the *Times* should pursue him so? If he was guilty of offering overpriced food, his beautiful-people clientele didn't seem to care, nor did the expense-account set; like Miller, corporate diners passed on the bill to their companies (the restaurants Cipriani *and* Bellini both stayed afloat despite the *Times*' equivocal judgments). The real surprise came in the form that the "corruption" took. The *Times* did not use its acknowledged powers over entertainment, culture, or the arts to advance personal careers, assuage swollen egos, push an ideological agenda or promote the *Times*' own reputation—although each of these elements did show up from time to time on the arts, leisure, and news pages. Deplorable as such ad hoc lapses were, the more pervasive fault was systemic. News and cultural coverage increasingly reflected the *Times*' newfound devotion to that self-deceiving banality of contemporary Big Media—audience research. More and more, the *Times* allowed calculations about what a desired readership might want to shape its news report. The critics, reporters, and editors of culture gulch, the warren of desks and cubicles where the arts and leisure department worked in the newsroom, began to pick up on the trite Newspeak of the audience researchers. The *Times*, they began hearing, was market-driven rather than news-driven.

Miller meant it when he said that the *Times* expected his restaurant reviews to be a service to consumers. Out of concern for its own operational comfort level, if not for reasons of flat-out financial gain, management turned to market researchers to plumb readers' cultural-news interests. Much like a modern political candidate, Arthur Sulzberger's *Times* polled target constituencies, found out what excited them, or *thought* might excite them, and shaped its cultural campaign accordingly. Many of the changes on the arts and leisure pages in the past decade, from the decline of space devoted to classical music reviews to the prominence given the "Critic's Notebook" pieces of the *Times'* star writers, were influenced by the findings of this market research. Perhaps high culture wasn't out, but it was certainly down for the count; consumerism, pop culture, and bright, smart—often, smartass—writing were in. Readers told the surveyors that's what they liked. "It's a generation thing," the *Times* cultural reporter Richard Shepard explained to me in the winter of 1991. "They want younger readers and what appeals to them. They got annoyed with me when I mentioned our 'traditional' readers."

Shepard joined the *Times* in 1946 as a copy boy; he did shipboard interviews with celebrities when sleek oceangoing ships still docked at the West Side terminals. In his forty-five years at the *Times* he wrote about everything from the Yiddish theater on Second Avenue to the story of an Iowa farm girl who was a pen-pal of Anne Frank. That was then. Now Shepard and Gerald Gold, a cultural news editor and classical record reviewer, arts reporter Grace Glueck, cultural reporter C. Gerald Fraser, and a dozen other *Times* editors and reporters all saw the market-research writing on the wall. They digested these findings, along with brisket and borscht at the "Polish Tea Room" of the Edison Hotel. The market research, the Tea Room crowd realized, indicated that the critics could set the "tone" and "pace" of the arts and leisure pages. And so the *Times* was giving greater emphasis to its stable of bright writers who, like Miller, were in their thirties and early forties.

The editors talked up the new thinking. The *Times* wanted to "read young," explained Warren Hoge, the assistant managing editor in charge of cultural coverage during the period of transition in the late 1980s. (The slim and elegantly outfitted Hoge wasn't the sort of *Times*-man who would be seen in the Edison's shabby booths; for his fiftieth birthday, he gave himself a party at the Russian Tea Room, the expense-account restaurant the old-timers were sending up when they "renamed" the Edison luncheonette.) Naturally, some stories had to give to make way for the snappier—read: "young"—*Times*; the pages are printed on paper, not stretch Lycra. Reviews of "small" recitals, cultural-news stories, and offbeat features of the kind that Shepard and Fraser had specialized in, were downgraded. The critic Peter Davis, who spent twelve years as a reviewer of concerts and classical music recordings for the *Times*, remembered when he wrote up three or four recitals a week for the paper, "and that was when there were eight of us covering serious music." Davis left the *Times* in 1986. Another reviewer of classical music, Donal Henahan, the winner of a Pulitzer Prize for music criticism, left in 1991. By then, the *Times* was sweeping together into a once-weekly package short, five-paragraph reviews of concert-recitals. Short reviews of independent dance companies, off- and off-off-Broadway and experimental theater, and art show openings at smaller galleries were similarly packaged. Performances of a select two or three of the scores of dance companies in the city, for example, were reviewed on Mondays, under the headline "Dance in Review"; smaller theatrical companies on Wednesdays ("Theater in Review"). The package of short classical-music reviews appeared on Saturdays, the day of the week when the *Times* has its lowest circulation.

The "new regime," as Gerald Gold called it, placed more emphasis on the big feature, and on the star-critics. "They don't want a lot of 'little reviews,' and so those three- or four-inch stories no longer appear." Gold thought the senior editors were trying to reinvent the wheel. He hoped that "they" would settle down, and remember what had made the *Times* important culturally over the years. But Gold wasn't too optimistic.

Neither was Grace Glueck, who joined the *Times* in 1951, when she was twenty-five years old. Glueck was born in Manhattan, the same year as Punch Sulzberger; she majored in English at NYU, and worked on a fashion magazine before the *Times* hired her. She began as a secretary-typist-receptionist and then spent ten years as an art researcher for the Sunday *Book Review*, during the period when the *Review* used paintings and museum graphics to illustrate its pages. She kept pressing her (male) editors, asking for writing assignments; one senior editor turned her down, advising her to go home and get married. Glueck managed to make her breakthrough in the early 1960s. "It was the time of the great pop art explosion," she said, "Jack the Dripper and all that. The Sunday editor Lester Markel wanted an art-news feature, something modeled on 'News of the Rialto,' the weekly theater-news column by Lewis Funt. The male art critics thought 'news' was beneath their dignity, and so I got the assignment. I had never been a reporter, and I was terrified, but a wonderful editor and human being, Seymour Peck, helped me." Her column was called "Art People." She did the column until 1972, singlehandedly creating the art-news beat at a time when New York had become the art capital of the world. When a group of *Times*women organized and challenged management with evidence of sex discrimination—as reflected, for example, in the minuscule number of women editors—Glueck was suddenly offered the title of cultural news editor. "I did it for eighteen months. I hated it; I wasn't the real cultural editor. Arthur Gelb was." (During this period she pronounced her memorable line, since widely quoted, "Who do I have to fuck to get *out* of this job?" Then she corrected herself: "Sorry. Whom . . . ?") In 1991 Glueck marked her sixty-fifth birthday. Although retirement was no longer mandatory for *Times* reporters, she counted herself smart enough to figure out what was going on. "Junior [Arthur O. Sulzberger, Jr.] wanted to see young faces around the newsroom. He was more comfortable with them."

The emphasis on hiring and promoting younger talent was not happenstance, nor was it confined to culture gulch or, for that matter, to the *Times*. The clouded business climate of the late 1980s and early 1990s impelled other newspapers, the television network news organizations, magazine groups, and book publishers to search for ways to control costs and reduce staff (to become "lean and mean"). Younger employees typically earned lower salaries than older ones, and nonstaff "contract workers" were cheaper than full-timers, who received pension, health, and insurance packages. But the *Times* was not thinking only of the size of its newsroom budgets. As Warren Hoge explained, the *Times* wanted to "appeal to a new generation, people whose attention spans were shorter." The market researchers, whose in-depth interviews and focus groups *Times* management was paying for, had a term for many members of the new generation: they were "aliterate"— they knew how to read but didn't read very much. According to Hoge, it was imperative that the modern *Times* "replenish the supply" of older readers, with new readers. "We have to grab younger readers by the lapels because they are less interested in reading," Hoge said.

"That's our challenge. We don't think it is the Gray Lady, and we don't want our language or our graphics to convey that impression, either. We monitor that." Hoge was particularly proud of the young, ambitious team of staff critics and contract writers covering popular music concerts and records. "Everyone assumes we have the best Latin American coverage," Hoge said. "They don't realize that we have the best coverage of rock and pop music, too." He had special praise for the work of Jon Pareles, Peter Watrous, and Stephen Holden.

A number of people, inside and outside the *Times*, singled out Pareles, et al. too, though not necessarily for praise. The Polish Tea Room crowd joked about the *Times'* newfound fixation on pop-culture stars such as Madonna. Gerry Gold cited one weighty, postmodernist decoding of the feminist sensibility in the singer's rock videos. "We do all these pieces on pop icons, as if they're important 'artistes,' " Gold said. "In fact, they are creations of the big record companies. Yet we try to intellectualize them; we treat this material as if it is coming out of university graduate departments." Gold's words were mild compared to the flame-thrower prose of the editor and art critic Hilton Kramer. Kramer was for seventeen years a member of the *Times'* cultural news staff, though never part of the Tea Room crowd. He left the *Times* in 1982, to nurture along *The New Criterion*, a high-culture periodical that regularly viewed with hyperbolic alarm the alleged decline of intellectual life in America. In the years immediately before he resigned as the chief art critic of the *Times*, Kramer said he had become increasingly appalled by the *Times'* strategy of "reaching down" in its cultural coverage: The editors, he claimed, "wanted a larger, less informed, lower-level readership." Since then, in Kramer's neo-con eyes, the *Times'* complicity in the debasement of culture has only worsened. He thundered against the views of Michael Brenson, one of the writers who succeeded Kramer as art critic for the *Times*. In the summer of 1990, Brenson stirred up the cozy world of cultural criticism with a major article in the *Times* suggesting that the idea of quality in art was elitist, divisive, and passé. Kramer took Brenson's rather mild maunderings to a parodic extreme; the former *Times*man dismissed the new *Times*man as just one more politically correct apparatchik railing against the "hegemony" of white European males.

Kramer reserved his sharpest scorn for Jon Pareles. Kramer called Pareles "the *Times'* most important critic . . . and that isn't meant as a compliment." Reading Pareles on rap music, he said, "always leaves me feeling the way that thoughtful people must have felt in the latter years of the Roman Empire, just before it all came down." (After some of Kramer's comments were published, Pareles sent him a postcard with a depiction of ancient ruins; on the back of the card Pareles wrote, "You don't know the half of it.")

Dick Shepard, Gerry Gold, Grace Glueck, and the rest of the Polish Tea Room crowd reacted more mildly; they found the paper's emphasis on rock and pop somewhat misplaced. Gold granted that the new publisher, Arthur Sulzberger and his editors, Frankel and Lelyveld, were "very devoted to finding a younger audience: They think that's where the action is." But: "In my own view, the people who buy rap records and listen to that music just don't read. They watch TV." Gold paused. "I suppose I'm an old fart, aren't I?"

Pareles's preeminence may not have signaled the decline of the West, but he did present *Times* editors with a challenge. Pareles championed rap in one after another of his daily reviews and Sunday critic's features. For example, explaining the appeal of 2 Live Crew and Public Enemy (both black male rap groups), Pareles noted approvingly that "rappers live by their ability to rhyme—the speed of their articulation—and by their ability to create outsized personas with words." He deflected some of the shock of these outsized personas, as well as the arguments that many rap groups were racist, misogynistic and obscene, by quoting the Harvard professor and post-structuralist Henry Louis Gates, Jr. According to Gates, "The rappers take the white Western culture's worst fear of black men and make a game of it."

The *Times* displayed these Pareles stories prominently on the culture pages. His two-thousand-word essay, "On Rap, Symbolism and Fear," appeared on page one of the Sunday Arts and Leisure section of February 2, 1992. In it Pareles described rap "as the epicenter of popular music and a significant influence on fashion, visual arts, and language" over the past decade. Rap, he acknowledged, has created a generation gap: While young people dance to it, their "otherwise well-informed" elders vilify and fear it as outlaw music—black "gangsta" rap. Pareles wondered how much of the American mainstream's opposition to "the rhetoric" of rap really had to do with "the larger tensions of race and class."

It was a finely attuned, modern *Times*ian analysis, locating as it did the larger "social issue" in the pop-culture particular. But there were two major omissions. Pareles left out the dirty little secret about outlaw rap: that its chief packagers were white-owned Fortune 500 companies and that its biggest customers at the record stores, where these things counted, were white, suburban male teenagers. This voyeuristic white audience, the record producer Hank Shocklee has explained (though not in Pareles's essay), basically sought "safe" terror: rap records gave listeners a sense of what "gangsta" life might be like on ghetto streets without having to go there. The rap record was similar to an amusement park's roller-coaster ride: Consumers can experience the thrill and turn it off when they want, something quite different from, say, taking the subway to 125th Street and actually getting off. Pareles's second omission was equally substantive. Nowhere in the Sunday article, or, for that matter, in any of Pareles's day-to-day rap reviews, did the critic or his editors permit themselves those quotes from the rappers' rhymes that would illuminate what had agitated square, elder America, and produced all the fear and loathing. As a result, the otherwise well-informed *Times* reader was deprived of such examples of articulation and metaphoric symbolism as "Forget the salad, just eat my meat," "Suck my dick, bitch, and make it puke," and "I can't be pussywhipped by a dick sucker." As the *New Republic* pointed out: "The chanting about (children, cover your parents' eyes and ears) 'cunts,' 'dicks,' 'pussy' and 'cocks' knows no end. The lyrics drip with contempt for women, especially black women." Pareles and the other *Times* rock critics not only endorsed this genital madness, the *New Republic* concluded, "They are regularly laughable in their polysyllabic prettifications of the primal and the obscene." Worse, the bowdlerizing was a measure of just how far the *Times'* pop critics were willing to bend reality in the course of wooing the target "hip" demographic cohort (an audience probably non-existent to start with).

The Polish Tea Room crowd heard another sort of complaint, from classical musicians, dancers, and other performers. These artists of the high culture believed that their work was being neglected by the *Times'* reviewers. "These changes are causing a lot of artistic pain out there," Gerry Gold reported. If the idea of quality was passé, as Michael Brenson had proposed, then many artists and performers were in trouble; without mention in the *Times*, they didn't exist. Aggrieved cultural organizations began remonstrating privately to the *Times*, and in some instances, made their cases in public. During the 1990–91 concert season, the staff of the 92nd Street Y, a vital center of music and recitals in New York, did an analysis of the *Times'* cultural coverage, and formally presented its findings to the *Times* during a meeting with managing editor, Joe Lelyveld. Of 120 concert dates in Merkin Hall, the Y staff reported, the *Times* had covered sixteen. The percentage of reviews of events held in the Y auditorium was slightly higher. One of the Y program directors, Omus Hershbein, an accomplished classical pianist in his own right, told Lelyveld—politely—that the *Times* apparently no longer cared about serious music. Barbara Rose, editor in chief of the *Journal of Art*, offered a similar analysis in a 1991 editorial decrying the "centralization" of American culture. Her general point involved the long-standing complaint that the major museums and institutions enjoyed special access to the *Times;* more immediately, though, less well-connected arts groups now were competing with the new constituencies for *Times* column space: "Suffice it to say that the paper's average of less than ten gallery reviews per week hardly gives a fair indication of what is happening in New York City alone."

Times editors had sat through such lectures before. Between 1971 and 1981, the Museum of Modern Art offered a "Projects" program of contemporary art, essentially one-person shows by unknowns or semi-knowns. According to Riva Castleman, then director of the Department of Prints and Illustrated Books at the museum, fifty-seven gallery exhibitions and thirty-eight video programs were sponsored by "Projects"; the *Times* ignored most of the ninety-five presentations. Beginning in 1982, "Projects" began publishing books by the artists; review copies of the first five Artists' Book Project volumes went to *Times* critics. "They too were ignored." Castleman blamed the victims to some extent: The artists hadn't made their reputations yet. She didn't fully grasp the bigger picture: Her "Projects" series was among the first casualties of the shifting ground in the *Times'* world of cultural coverage. The youthquake was only one manifestation of the underlying changes in the *Times'* approach to news.

The modern *Times* was not trying to encompass all that was happening. In part, it couldn't, given the dozens of cultural events every day. More important, the editors no longer wanted the *Times* to be the Paper of Record, whether for quality culture or anything else. The record was regarded as boring, Warren Hoge had declared. His successor, the architecture critic Paul Goldberger, who was appointed cultural news editor in 1990, at the age of forty, distanced his pages still more from "the boring news." Goldberger gathered an extraordinary amount of authority at the *Times*; he ran the daily arts and leisure pages, the Weekend section on Fridays and the Sunday Arts and Leisure section—in addition to retaining the title of chief architecture critic and continuing to write a monthly column. When Goldberger was interviewed a few months after he took control of the cultural news report, he spoke about his intentions to scrutinize arts institutions, and "to do bottom-up and not just top-down coverage." He said that he felt "no more obligation to turn out the 'standard' feature—the aimless PR piece, the slight feature, the feature tied to a show opening. We'll only do that when there's something new to say, or if the story is well written." The *Times* reader, he explained, "is an intelligent observer of society who cares about culture, and about what the *Times* has to say. The audience wants to be enlightened and it wants some consumer guidance."

Some seventy staff reporters, critics and editors—including a dozen contract writers—were under Goldberger's jurisdiction when he became cultural news editor. His initial priorities reflected the *Times*' broad, up-to-date definition of culture. Goldberger wanted to add a second cultural news reporter in Los Angeles, where there was, he said, enough work for three people. One reporter would cover the motion picture industry full-time; "the other reporter would be assigned to the more creative side—not just films, but all the visual arts. I'd add in Los Angeles before I'd add in New York City. For all my passion for New York"—Goldberger was born across the Hudson River, in Nutley, and his parents still lived in New Jersey—"I am not one of those New Yorkers who disdains L.A. It's central to American culture. We ignore it at our peril." Goldberger's biggest plans centered on the *Times*' critics: "We will play up their work. They are our calling cards. They'll always have pride of place."

The Polish Tea Room crowd understood the message. In the summer of 1991, Dick Shepard took up management's offer of a cash buyout. So did Gerald Gold, Gerald Fraser, and Grace Glueck. Fraser, who was among the first African-Americans to work at the *Times* as other than an elevator operator or production employee, unhesitatingly applied for the retirement package. "They were offering me a bundle of money, and I was quite clear and fast in accepting. . . . It's a chance to do other things." As for the *Times'* new approach to cultural coverage, "We're not doing what we did best: the paper of record. We're trying to be something different. Maybe we had to change," he said, sounding not at all convinced. None of the crowd stopped working. Shepard and Fraser continued to write free-lance articles for the *Times* and other publications. Shepard also became a columnist for the *Summit News Times*, an "instant newspaper" published in connection with a United Nations conference on the environment held in New York City during the winter of 1992 (at seventy-one, he at last had the column that the *Times* never offered him). Grace Glueck's "retirement" was the most unusual of all. The *Times* had been a kind of home to her—she never took her editor's dismissive advice to marry, and she never spent a lot of time fixing up her Manhattan apartment, either. A small, self-contained figure with an air of quiet distraction, she seemed most comfortable surrounded by the piles of clippings, folders, magazines, and books that covered the surface of her desk. Glueck continued to come to the *Times* each day. She moved her files to another desk, one space away from her old location in culture gulch, and used the *Times'* telephones, the *Times'* computers, and the *Times'* data base—"Nexis is so expensive!" she said with a wave of her hands—to work on free-lance articles. When she met an interviewer for tea and corn muffins one afternoon in mid-February, 1992, she was finishing up *Times* assignments for Arts and Leisure and for the Sunday *Book Review*. She was so busy that, for the second year in a row, she could not get the paperwork for her U.S. income taxes together. "I've talked to my accountant, but I still may have a lien attached," she said vaguely. Glueck smiled brightly: "Wouldn't that be just terrible?"

Another Tea Room regular, Gerry Gold, seldom came back to the old neighborhood, although he continued to be a faithful reader (the buyout package included free home delivery of the *Times*). At home in Queens, Gold skimmed his old pages and shook his head, sounding at times a bit like a Hilton Kramerian elitist. "All this emphasis on pop and rap and the rest," Gold said. "In a period of cultural decline, they're writing more and more about less and less."

Arthur Sulzberger, Frankel, Goldberger, and the senior editors may have convinced themselves that their keen journalistic instincts had led them to the *Times'* new attitudes about cultural coverage. Practically

speaking, however, the changes in the arts and leisure sections represented, yet again, the triumph of Mattsonism. The dour former production specialist Walt Mattson and his sales team from the business
departments had pushed Abe Rosenthal and the news editors to produce a daily report with wider popular appeal for the prototypical
"suburban housewife." Even then, Mattson wanted the arts and leisure
pages to devote more space to motion picture news and pop culture
reviews; he regularly asked Rosenthal for more features of "service to
Times readers planning their weekends." At a minimum the business
side thought the movie coverage should match the heavy volume of
movie ads in the Friday and Sunday papers. Once, during the planning of the proposed new Weekend section, Mattson bolstered his case
for more coverage of movies by circulating readership surveys showing
that "the affluent" liked to read movie news and reviews and were
frequent moviegoers. In contrast to the unsatisfactory amount of
movie-related materials in the paper, Mattson complained, the "intellectual" arts were getting ample space. The *Times'* cultural coverage, he said, needed to be "more human." In addition to coverage of
Hollywood, Mattson proposed that the editors "work in at least four
single-frame cartoons à la the old *Saturday Evening Post.*"

Rosenthal resisted, as he initially did all of Mattson's incursions into
the news department. Defending his independence and the editors'
responsibilities to decide what was newsworthy, Rosenthal circulated
his own memos, darkly referring to efforts to change "the character" of
the *Times*. Rosenthal argued, rather inconsistently, that there was not
much real movie news and that in any case the *Times* was already
doing a terrific job covering movies. As frequently happened during
the sectional revolution, Rosenthal eventually embraced the strategy of
added space for movies and the popular arts—making it appear to be
the editors' own idea—and later took the bows when the applause
began. (Mattson's cartoon proposal was a nonstarter; Punch Sulzberger
agreed with the editors that it *would* change the character of the paper.)
During an interview in February 1990, three years after he left the
newsroom, Rosenthal proudly claimed that the major studios now
opened their movies officially on Thursdays, in order to be reviewed
the next morning in the *Times'* Weekend section.

By the 1990s the desired new demographic was the young urbanite,
a thirtysomething white-collar worker or professional who knew how to
read (obviously) but didn't necessarily read a newspaper every day.

These men and women, said to be "into" film, pop music, and video, had to be grabbed by their Perry Ellis and Donna Karan lapels to get them to pay attention to old, demanding, linear print.

The modern *Times* adapted to cultural Mattsonism rather awkwardly at first; the Gray Lady image was hard to shed. "Reading the culture pages I think of a middle-aged woman learning to disco," said Howard Kissel, the theater critic of the *New York Daily News*. "She put on a miniskirt and her varicose veins are showing." It was a common, albeit nasty, metaphor. To create the new *Times* of the 1990s, Arthur Sulzberger, Frankel, Lelyveld, Goldberger, et al. had to shed a part of the cultural weight that had made the *Times* the *Times* over the decades. Some parts of this history were easier to lose than others.

The classic Gray Lady of the Adolph Ochs–Arthur Hays Sulzberger eras approached arts and leisure news almost as an afterthought. The city's entertainment life and its popular culture interested Ochs less than national, international, and business news. A *Book Review* section was judged worthwhile as long as the books under consideration were clearly "literary" or dealt with public policy. Ochs's son-in-law and successor Sulzberger assented more or less to the idea that hard news was the *Times*' one true "franchise." "Cultural affairs had for years been handled casually," Turner Catledge wrote in his memoirs of the *Times* during the post–World War II years. "We chose our critics often for the wrong reasons: seniority, or because a reporter had an interest in books or music, and no one else wanted the job." Catledge tried to improve the coverage beginning in the late 1950s, arguing that readers were more educated, that the arts and artists were a "cutting edge" for social and political change, and that postwar prosperity had created a new national interest in culture. But Catledge didn't think the *Times* should get too close to the edges of change. While he was interested in the high culture, he wanted a system of critical "checks and balances"; they suited his adroit style of office politics. He encouraged separate daily and Sunday book reviews—"the luxury of diversity," he called it. But it was one way of locating the safe cultural center. When former *Times*man Gay Talese's semiauthorized book on the *Times* appeared, Catledge was proud of the overlapping reviews; the daily staff reviewer was slightly negative while an outside reviewer for the Sunday *Book Review* enthusiastically praised it: the

Times had it both ways, preening itself in its own mirror while appearing to be judiciously neutral.

Clifton Daniel, in his turn, showed less Ochsian caution. He promoted Charlotte Curtis to women's page editor, just at the right social moment in the 1960s, and told her to cover that old standard, "society news," as if she were a sociologist among a tribal culture. Curtis was on hand, with notebook open, for Leonard and Felicia Bernstein's cocktail party for the Black Panther Defense Fund, held in the composer's thirteen-room Park Avenue duplex penthouse. Daniel also helped hire Ada Louise Huxtable as the *Times'* architecture critic, and encouraged her to treat New York's changing skyline with the same informed wit that Curtis brought to the New Society. Assessing "Black Rock," Eero Saarinen's CBS Headquarters on the Avenue of the Americas, Huxtable listed her reasons for praising the building: "It is not, like so much of today's large-scale construction, a handy commercial package, a shiny wraparound envelope, a packing case, a box of cards, a trick with mirrors. It does not look like a cigar lighter, a vending machine, a nutmeg grater." Daniel, however, continued the Catledge search for critical "balance." He was too politic to break wholly with tradition, and so he consulted "the experts in the field" when deciding on the hiring of a new critic (a practice that still continues at the *Times*). The consultations sometimes produced surprising information. When John Martin retired after four decades as the *Times'* dance critic, Daniel solicited the recommendations of the great American choreographer Agnes De Mille. She told Daniel to be sure to hire a heterosexual critic. According to De Mille, Martin "used to fall in love, now and then, with some of her dancers." Further, she had angered Martin, "because I wouldn't favor him in certain ways relating to certain young men that he was interested in. He simply ignored me for seven years . . . [using] his great weapon of *The New York Times* personally." De Mille remembered that Daniel expressed his wide-eyed surprise that the *Times* "ever had any homosexuality in our critical forces." When Daniel was asked about De Mille's story, he said he had not been aware that the choreographer's work was ignored for seven years; less wide-eyed, he added: "John Martin was certainly not the first critic to fall in love with dancers whose performances were being reviewed."

Catledge and Daniel never quite got a handle on the *Times'* cultural coverage, in large part because of the bifurcated organization of the paper in their day. The formidable Lester Markel ran the Sunday department, which included the Sunday Arts and Leisure section and the *Book Review*. While Markel's tastes were also traditional, he occupied himself through the war and the postwar years mostly with the great matters of public policy, spending a large part of his energies on the *Times Magazine* and the Week in Review section. When Punch Sulzberger finally forced Markel out, his immediate successors as Sunday editor kept much the same focus on the *Magazine* and the Review. The daily cultural coverage, meanwhile, came under the control of a new metropolitan editor, the energetic, manic Arthur Gelb. Beginning in 1967, and continuing over the next twenty years, Gelb was the boss of culture gulch. Other editors had formal responsibilities for the *Times'* arts and leisure sections; but no one doubted where the true cultural power lay, no more than anyone was neutral on the subject of the Gelb Years.

Gelb's supporters on the staff praised his ideas, curiosity, enthusiasm— "his spewing imagination and unmatched news sense," in the words of Alex Jones. Frank Rich, the theater critic, declared that Gelb approached journalism like a playwright or novelist; "he never lost the artists's sponge-like 'sense of wonder,' without which an artist cannot stay an artist." The metro desk reporter Maureen Dowd, later a star Washington correspondent, recounted how Gelb worked "on the presumption that every conversation contains the germ of a great newspaper story. I would make some pompous or inane remarks, just trying to make conversation, and I would suddenly find myself with a story assignment. 'Brian de Palma is so derivative,' I said. *'That's a story,'* Arthur screamed. 'Woody Allen is so secretive,' I said. *'That's a story,'* Arthur bellowed." Everyone had a Gelb story, including Gelb himself. He joined the *Times* in 1944, as a copy boy. By his own description, he was a tall, gangling kid from an immigrant family in the Bronx, and he was stagestruck. He traveled down to Broadway to spend Saturday matinees in the theater; second-balcony seats cost 50 cents then. Trying to figure out how to be part of The Theater, he decided to become a reporter. Gelb found his life's work as well as his wife at the *Times*; Barbara Stone was a fellow copy boy. They married in 1946. By the mid-1950s he had worked his way up from running copy to the metro desk and then to the heady assignment of combination drama critic and reporter—covering a developing beat called Off Broadway.

When Punch Sulzberger eased Daniel aside to make Abe Rosenthal the top editor, Rosenthal persuaded Gelb to be his deputy. Thus began the long-running Abe 'n' Artie Show of *Times* legend, and the successful start-ups of Business Day, SportsMonday, Home, Living, Weekend, and Science Times.

The Abe 'n' Artie Show had its share of bad scenes, as well. Post-Daniel, both the ascerbic Curtis and the independent Huxtable were "promoted" to new positions that effectively removed them from the news and cultural sections. Curtis traded in her reporter's notebook and became the editor of the Op-Ed page; Huxtable went to the *Times* editorial pages to become a member of the Board of Editors. Her criticisms of building projects by major real estate operators upset other pro-development board members, as well as publisher Sulzberger. As a critic Huxtable could make any aesthetic comments she wanted. On the editorial board, she had to be part of a "consensus." Huxtable resigned from the *Times* in 1981. She was at the peak of her intellectual powers, or so the MacArthur Foundation thought: It awarded her a $250,000 "genius" grant.

Complaints of cronyism and critical backscratching haunted both Rosenthal and Gelb throughout their careers. The *Times'* solicitous treatment of cultural figures as disparate as Jerzy Kosinski, Joseph Heller, and Betty Friedan became a running joke among the Polish Tea Room crowd. The sharpest lines were saved for the news department's role as keepers of the Eugene O'Neill flame. Because Barbara and Arthur Gelb were O'Neill experts, the scorekeepers noted not only the *Times'* legitimate attention to O'Neill revivals but also its continuing coverage of O'Neill minutiae (in perhaps the greatest reach, the Wallingford, Connecticut, hospital where O'Neill was treated for tuberculosis in 1912 was the object of a long story in the *Times*). The influence of the Gelbs on critical opinions supposedly descended unto their son, Peter Gelb. The younger Gelb was the business manager for both the pianist Vladimir Horowitz and the conductor Herbert von Karajan. The editors of the satirical magazine *Spy* jumped on this connection, and ran a data-base search of cultural-pages coverage of the two musicians. The computer turned up nineteen major *Times* stories of 750 words or more on Horowitz in the period from August 1981 to April 1988. The 1981 date was picked because it marked the beginning of Peter Gelb's management of Horowitz's career. The search also uncovered a thousand-word feature about Horowitz's new manager, Peter Gelb, without mentioning that he was the son of the editor of the section in which the article appeared. Independent of the *Spy* survey, critic Peter Davis recalls how an article of his was scaled back to make room for a story "ordered from on high"—another in the "seemingly endless series of articles that we ran about Horowitz."

Spy's accounting of the *Times'* von Karajan coverage was equally malicious; according to *Spy*, the *Times* struck a deal with manager Gelb for a friendly von Karajan profile in the culture pages: The *Times* would get access if it promised not to mention the conductor's Nazi past. The Polish Tea Room crowd turned all this into a long-running punch line; whenever a senior editor, Gelb or anyone else, pushed for a major cultural story, newsroom schmoozers would ask, with more humor than malice, "Who's got the contract?" When Gelb left the newsroom in 1989 to become head of the New York Times Foundation, he dismissed the stories with a wave of his hands, and derided the notion of an Abe 'n' Artie Show; "I don't know where anyone got that idea. We weren't linked together; I was my own man." But he didn't deny his high opinion of the *Times* when he was second in command: "We were *the* great paper, the showcase and model for the world. Other editors came to our newsroom to see what we were doing."

Enlisted men (and women) normally gripe about their officers, whether in the Army or in a similarly hierarchical institution such as the *Times*. One senior editor in culture gulch seemed exempt from the troops' complaints; indeed, he and the section he edited, Sunday Arts and Leisure, won their praise and admiration.

By all accounts, Seymour Peck stood out in the newsroom. He was a journalist with a rakish Popular Front past. He joined the *Times* in 1952 after working for the left-liberal newspaper *PM*, a short-lived experiment in daily journalism. *Times*people from his era remember Peck for his efforts to liven up the culture pages, not so much politically—he had by then blended into the centrist ethos—as journalistically. Peck collected around him a varied group, including editors Guy Flatley and Wayne Lawson, and Charles Higham, a "full-time freelance" critic. Higham was born in London in 1931, emigrated to Australia in his twenties, and then moved to California in 1969, to pursue a lifelong love affair with film. From 1970 to 1980 he wrote about the movies and movie people for the *Times* while publishing well-received biographies of figures from Hollywood's golden age, such as Orson Welles, Errol Flynn, and Bette Davis. When he was interviewed in the late fall of 1990, his book on the Duchess of Windsor had been on the *Times* best-seller list for nineteen weeks and he was well along on his next project, an unauthorized biography of Prince Philip and Queen Elizabeth.

To hear Higham tell it, the arts and leisure pages in the years when Peck was more or less left alone were the golden age of the *Times'* cultural coverage, unmatched before or since. Peck was a risk-taker by *Times* standards. When the film director Peter Bogdanovich criticized Higham's book on Orson Welles, Peck commissioned Higham to reply in an article in which he interviewed himself. It was the first of the hundred-odd articles Higham did as the *Times'* man in Hollywood. Higham remembers the day he entered culture gulch for the first time. "Sy Peck wore a striped shirt and a modish tie. He struck a note of color in a monochrome room, where everything was gray—the people, the suits, the air." Peck encouraged Higham as well as Chris Chase, an actress turned writer. The theater reviews of Clive Barnes and Walter Kerr appeared regularly. When Higham was assigned to do a standard piece on the actor Robert Young, Peck urged the writer to get Young to talk of his alcoholism. Peck also encouraged a more skeptical approach. He wanted the *Times* to be a sharp-eyed chronicler of culture, recording the shifting tastes of the post-Vietnam years without necessarily judging (and dismissing) them. Peck was a middleman: his mildly irreverent staff on one side, the top editors and the publisher on the other, wary and in shock of the new. Management wanted an "evenhanded" approach, remembered the critic John Leonard. There was an uneasiness in culture gulch around the time of the publication of a big new book, or the opening of a major play, Leonard recalled. "The editors worried about 'The *Times'* deciding what was praiseworthy: They wanted to wait for critical and public support to develop." Peck's skill lay in keeping both staff and editors happy. He was good at judging "the climate." When Higham suggested an article idea, Peck would say, "Let's wait for 'word.' " "Sy was always conscious of the need for consensus within the house," Higham said.

Sunday Arts and Leisure came under the control of Arthur Gelb in the great realignment of 1976. Because Gelb wanted his own choices in the top Sunday editing posts, Peck was moved off the culture pages and assigned to the Sunday *Magazine*. Visiting from California, Higham found Peck a changed, beaten man; his face had aged, he looked miserable. Construction was going on around him; carpenters were building his successor's office. Lawson and Flatley left the *Times* entirely; their careers flourished—Lawson's at *Vanity Fair*, Flatley's at *Cosmopolitan*. Chase became a television reporter-host. Higham continued to contribute features, though with less edge. The *Times* wanted "generalized pop pieces," for example, violence in the movies and previews of the Oscar awards. Peck was transferred a second time, to a dead-end editing job at the *Book Review*. He had been effectively emasculated; "the execution of Sy Peck," Higham called it. On New Year's Day, January 1, 1985, Seymour Peck died in an auto accident. The car he was driving was hit head on by another car traveling the wrong way on the Henry Hudson Parkway. Peck was sixty-seven years old.

When Paul Goldberger was appointed cultural news editor, he became the single most formidable cultural journalist in the country. Unlike Gelb, Goldberger kept his hand in as a working critic. In the *Times'* company of young eager-to-succeed talents, it was all but impossible to stand out. Goldberger managed the art of success; he was contributing free-lance articles to the *Times* while a Yale undergraduate. He joined the *Times Magazine* in 1972, after a brief stay at the *Wall Street Journal*. When Ada Louise Huxtable moved to the editorial board a year later, Goldberger became daily architectural critic. He won a Pulitzer Prize for criticism in 1984, as well as a reputation for being literate, industrious, and a fast writer—he was known for getting his copy in well ahead of deadline. Architecture and architectural criticism, however, are notoriously clique-ridden and vendetta-prone, perhaps because the field is small and everyone knows everyone else. The critics' language can turn personal and intemperate, as if in inverse ratio to the cool abstractions of design blueprints. Both Goldberger the man and the *Times'* aesthetic authority attracted ferocious attacks. Usually, such criticism of the critic could be discounted as the sour grapes peddled by lesser known writers envious of Goldberger's status, and the *Times'* reach. Pointedly, though, the criticism replicated the traditional complaints—that the *Times* promoted its personal favorites and played safe cultural politics—while adding a third charge. The establishment architects Philip Johnson, Robert Stern, and Robert Venturi, complained Michael Sorkin, himself an architect and an architectural critic, "are by actual count, Goldberger's most frequently recurring subjects." They are "the architectural clique who invented Goldberger"—Johnson was, in fact, an early mentor. "Never mind the one's a monstrosity, the next's a mediocrity, and the third, for all his merits, has built almost nothing in the city. . . ." Sorkin was withering in his treatment of the typical Goldbergerian appraisal, a style that Sorkin characterized as seeming to convey "the impression of measured consideration while at the same time camouflaging a lack of independent insight." At best, "Goldberger leaves the reader the impression of an opinion but no recall as to what it might actually be." Further: No point of view is offered at variance with the interests of Goldberger's *"Times* constituency." It all made sense, Sorkin concluded, because Goldberger is "the embodiment of the aesthetics of yuppiefication now ascendant" at the *Times.* Goldberger replied in kind: "Michael Sorkin's brand of writing is to thoughtful criticism what the Ayatollah Khomeini is to religious tolerance." Still, the yuppiefication line hit home. Goldberger's columns on megadevelopments around the city were kinder and gentler than the "difficult" Huxtable's (Sorkin's specific point of departure was Goldberger's initial support of the Times Square renewal project—a development of direct interest to the Times Company). And, in his early forties, culture news editor Goldberger was hardly older than most of the urbane young writers he supervised.

The *Times'* critical talents shared social and intellectual backgrounds as well as the generational tie signified by the "yuppie" label. They were university trained (usually, but not always, Ivy Leaguers) and they were, journalistically, generalists. One of Goldberger's classmates at Yale, Lawrie Mifflin, worked in the *Times'* sports department before becoming education editor of the national desk. Film critic Janet Maslin (University of Rochester '70) spent four years as a music columnist for *New Times* magazine. Maslin was born in 1949, the same year as chief theater critic Frank Rich (Harvard '70). Rich wrote film and TV criticism for *Time* magazine before joining the *Times.* Sunday theater reviewer David Richards was a professor of French and an actor before beginning his career as a theater critic. Michael Kimmelman became chief art critic in 1990 at the age of thirty-one, succeeding the sixtyish John Russell (another Harvard man). Kimmelman had degrees from Harvard *and* Yale; he wrote for the trade magazine *Industrial Design* before joining the *Times* in 1988 as a classical-music critic. In June 1992 Herbert Muschamp was named architecture critic, at the relatively advanced age of forty-five.

The new cultural team had one other distinguishing characteristic.

The *Times'* acknowledged influence was no longer confined to New York City's artistic and leisure life. The field of vision encompassed all of America. "When the *Times* turns its attention to a given story, parts of the world light up," Warren Hoge explained expansively. Hoge found little positive to say about anyone else's cultural and entertainment coverage. "There's not much check on our performance. Our business reporting competes with the *Wall Street Journal,* our foreign desk with the *Washington Post* and the *Los Angeles Times,* our metro desk with the tabloids. The cultural-news desk competes with some magazines and newspapers, and if the net is cast wide enough geographically, the *Los Angeles Times* provides competition in movies but not in other disciplines." As for coverage of high culture, such as the theater, "We are told by that community that we have undisputed power. They think we do. We dispute this. But since the appearance of power gives power, the perception exists and it carries weight."

Hoge was not far off the mark. In the "old days" of the 1950s and 1960s, the *Times'* cultural influence was confined to New York. The paper distributed no more than 35,000 to 40,000 copies around the country; of that, most were bought in Washington. By the early 1990s, the National edition of the *Times* had a circulation in excess of 240,000, and the paper was available to the cultural elites on a daily basis. In a study commissioned by the Twentieth Century Fund, John E. Booth, a member of the Fund as well as a former *Times*man, examined the critics' power over the performing arts in the late 1980s and early 1990s. He found that the *Times* was particularly important for classical musicians. When a young performer makes a concert debut, "its critical reception can frame an entire career. For pianists, violinists, indeed any instrumentalist or singer, a New York debut is essential." A business agent for classical music artists told Booth that a New York recital, along with a *Times* review, could make a non–New York artist as well. Booking agents and managers around the country read the *Times,* and planned their concert schedules accordingly. Booth, not so incidentally, emphasized the "extraordinary clout" of the paper, rather than the reviewer: "In those instances where a critic has left the *Times* to go elsewhere, he has usually discovered how much less power his voice then commands."

To paraphrase Gertrude Stein, there seems to be no elsewhere in American cultural journalism. The *Los Angeles Times* critic David Shaw systematically surveyed the state of cultural reporting across the country in 1988, and reached a conclusion much like Booth's—and Hoge's. Shaw found that the *Wall Street Journal* did a good but highly limited job—offering but one page of cultural coverage on the five days a week it published. The other national newspaper, *USA Today*, was far more interested in popular culture than high culture. The weekly newsmagazines *Time* and *Newsweek* "had too little space for cultural coverage, and the TV networks, except for CBS's 'Sunday Morning,' virtually ignored culture." Shaw omitted his own paper from his survey, though he discreetly observed that the city of Los Angeles, "despite recent efforts, has yet to win its battle for full respectability." In the years following Shaw's survey, the *Los Angeles Times* narrowed the gap, and became the only publication approaching the *New York Times* as measured by editorial resources devoted to arts, culture, and entertainment coverage. Nevertheless, an examination of the number of critics, reporters, editors, and staff of the two papers as of 1990 showed how great the disparity remained. For comparison's sake, the other elite daily newspaper, the *Washington Post*, is included:

	NYT	LAT	WPost
Full-time critics	21	11	10+
Part-time and free-lance critics	10	6	—
Reporters	16	10	*1+
Editors	**28	**14	6
Book review staff	25–28	4–5	7
Book editors	11	***2.5	***4.5

NOTES: *Post had 30 Style-section reporters who sometimes contributed to "cultural" coverage
**Estimates included copy editors
***Indicates editors shared with other departments
(Source: internal documents made available to present author)

The comparable figures for the two major newsmagazines, *Time* and *Newsweek*, amounted to half or less than half of the third-ranked *Post's* totals. Other publications' figures reflected still more modest resources. These more recent figures confirm David Shaw's earlier conclusion that the *New York Times*, "as even its detractors acknowledge, does a better job of covering culture than any other national general interest news organization. . . . [It] is really the only national news organ that even purports to thoroughly cover the entire country."

*   *   *

Shaw and Booth were more concerned with the high culture than with popular culture. Not all ventures lived or died on the word of the *Times*. The audiences for mass media entertainment—big studio motion pictures, television shows, rock, pop, rap, country and western, and other nonclassical music—are large and scattered. They consult many different sources, including their peers' and their own opinions. In the areas of high-end culture, art, entertainment, and leisure activities, though, the *Times'* powers in New York and throughout the country were unquestioned.

As a rough rule, the more expensive the entertainment or cultural fare, the more important the *Times'* opinions. Upper-end commercial culture was especially vulnerable to the question, "What did the *Times* say?" In some cultural worlds, there was *no* other verdict worth considering, a situation that caused much gnashing of capped teeth among elites. *Art & Auction*, for example, devoted a long, rancorous article to Rita Reif, a *Times'* auction reporter, in its issue of January 1991. The magazine noted Reif's "feared status" at those citadels of class consciousness, auction houses. According to the magazine, Reif set the tone for the *Times'* treatment of auction-house news and, by extension, of all auction coverage—no other paper has a reporter assigned full-time to the field. As a consequence of being the *Times'* lead reporter, the magazine explained, Reif was "treated with kid gloves" by Sotheby's and Christie's; the auction houses called her first when important consignment contracts cleared, spoon-fed her exclusive advance information on sales, and arranged private screenings and interviews for her. The velvet ropes used at auctions to separate the house staff from the public, including members of the press, always came down to make room for Reif. *Art & Auction* seemed most offended by Reif's alleged lack of knowledge about the business—compared, that is, to *Art & Auction*. The magazine claimed that, despite all the special attention showered on Reif, her work was still full of mistakes, that it lacked both balance and depth, and that it was badly written. The article was called "Educating Rita."

Variations of the "Educating Rita" story were repeated about Bryan Miller, John Rockwell, and any number of other *Times* reporters and critics. (The tales of favoritism and philistinism in the pages of the *Book Review* attained mythic status in the publishing world; they could fill a book—they are treated in the next chapter.) One *Times* critic above all others, however, inspired the greatest mixture of fear, admiration, respect, and loathing. Frank Rich's presumptive stranglehold on the American theater was analyzed and reanalyzed constantly, until both supporters and detractors had memorized one another's positions, like professional wrestlers on television. In the early spring of 1992, these predictable gruntings and posturings took an unexpected turn. Rich and his supervising editors were accused of regularly exercising arrogant power—and appearing to enjoy themselves. They had discovered a useful marketing tool. The diffident mask of "service to the consumer" had slipped a little.

Rich's accuser, Robert Brustein, could not be dismissed as easily as one of the chronic complainers-around-the-coffee-cart in culture gulch. Brustein was a producer, a professor at Harvard, and artistic director of the American Repertory Theater. He took the case against the *Times* public in an essay in the *New Republic*. Brustein didn't waste any time arguing about the *Times*' power; he assumed as a given "the causal link between Rich's dramatic opinions and the crisis in the American theater." Brustein said that Rich promoted the work of his friends and favorites in *Times* reviews while putting down the serious and the avant garde (including some of Brustein's favorites). The typical Rich review, Brustein wrote, was safe, centrist, and, in the bargain, slick: Rich's lively literary style had the effect of "exacerbating the problem, since it has helped enhance his position with his editors and his readers."

If Brustein had stopped at that, his essay would have been one more chunk of Broadway boilerplate. The power of the *Times*' man on the aisle has been a fact of life in the New York theater for five decades. In the 1950s, the *Times*' amiable critic Brooks Atkinson complained that he had more power than he wanted—and that was when reviewers from a dozen other dailies covered opening nights. In the years since, one after another of the New York dailies disappeared, and the *Times*' cultural power increased. Since the 1980s, Rich has practically stood alone as the chief arbiter of middlebrow theater. In the early winter of the 1989–90 New York theater season, to take one example, the musical *City of Angels* opened with at least four strikes against it, given the prevailing bleak Broadway climate: *Angels* had no name stars; it was experimental, a big-budget American original, not an established British import; there were no crashing chandeliers or ascending helicopters; and the book and lyrics were somewhat demanding (reminiscent of a Sondheim musical or a Pirandello play). Rich, however, liked *City of Angels*. "So potent was his rave," critic Thomas M. Disch wrote in *The Nation*, "that the next day the box office at the Virginia Theater raked in half a million dollars in ticket sales, thereby averting a threatened closing." One of Rich's smart pans, on the other hand, could stop a big-budget musical in mid-note. *Carrie*, a restaging of the movie cult classic, was done in the worst possible taste; "a wish fulfillment fantasy for very naughty ids," Disch called it. Sex and violence were its particular concerns, all played to excess with a catchy beat. Rich reacted in kind, excessively, with a devastating negative review. Charitably, Disch excused the *Times*man for his "sincere squeamishness," calling it a fair reflection of Rich's *Times* readership. *Carrie* quickly closed, having lost a staggering $7 million. Disch couldn't help wondering whether, in time, enough word-of-mouth to counter Rich's review might have spread to those adventurous theatergoers with an appetite for dirty dancing and glorious excess.

All that was background when Brustein widened "the Rich problem" to include an accomplice, Alex Witchel, the *Times*' theater reporter and Frank Rich's wife of eight months. They were, Brustein wrote, "a one-two punch, a husband and wife team on the same art beat." Both were talented but flawed writers, Brustein said, and they reinforced each other's judgments, or covered over each other's mistakes. They were, in short, "an embarrassment of Riches." Rich and Witchel declined to reply to Brustein. But colleagues did speak up on their behalf, privately and not for attribution. One senior *Times* editor described Brustein as an unceasing grinder of axes, with his own conflicts of interests (he produced plays at his Cambridge-based theater as well as reviewing plays). Brustein was supposedly embittered because Frank Rich, with his *Times*' megaphone, was a more prominent voice in the theater than Robert Brustein.

Rich-Witchel versus Brustein made for good gossip within a twenty-block radius of Times Square. The blood feuds in the theater have such long histories that few people remember anymore why they are at each other's throats, like Serbs and Bosnians. The *Times* considered Brustein for its chief reviewer's job in the mid-1960s; he turned the job down, he said, because he didn't want to pronounce judgment on a play within a two-hour deadline and "be responsible for people's unemployment." Rich, in his turn, declined a Brustein offer to be a visiting lecturer at Harvard.

But beyond the sideshow of dueling egos on the aisles, Brustein had reinvigorated the long-running argument about how the *Times* used its acknowledged powers over Broadway and the other arts and entertainments. In the past, *Times* critics would shift from one foot to another, and dissemble about their authority in an aw, shucks sort of way. "I don't close plays; producers and theater owners do," Rich said on more than one occasion. Brustein threw open for discussion the possibility that the *Times* had a chokehold on arts and culture and *didn't intend to let go*. It relished its leverage.

Brustein's case for "an embarrassment of Riches" required a labored reading between the lines. According to Brustein, shows that Rich liked out of town, for example, the musical *Falsettos*, received advance attention in Witchel's "On Stage and Off" column. The innovative director-producer Joanne Akalaitis, the late Joe Papp's successor at the Public Theater, was "regularly panned" by Rich and "regularly assailed" by Witchel. (Bereft of the *Times'* support, Akalaitis soon lost the support as well of the Public's board; in March 1993, she was fired.) A Sunday feature by Witchel, a 2,648-word personality interview with the actress Joan Collins, was followed by an exquisitely sandpapered Rich review (Noël Coward's *Private Lives*, "while not remotely a satisfying production . . . may well titillate Miss Collins' most ardent admirers"). To the fair-minded, these examples did not prove collusion. A Joan Collins interview had become a Sunday *Times* staple: big feature treatment for a popular star. If another of culture gulch's up-and-comers had done the Collins story, it would have turned out the same. Similarly, absent Witchel, Rich in his Collins review wouldn't have strayed very far from his middle-of-the-road sensibility.

Times editors' reactions to the more general point about abusive power was disingenuous. They chose to talk about Rich-Witchel narrowly, as a "problem of perceptions," in the same way that the Bush administration airily ignored the faltering American economy of the early 1990s as just a matter of how consumers "feel." While some people might think that a "husband and wife team might collude or influence each other, *Times*men and -women were too conscientious for that to happen. What's more, the *Times* had husband and wife teams reporting from all over the world, including China, where Nicholas Kristof and Sheryl WuDun won a Pulitzer Prize last year" (as if there were no difference between two people covering a country with a population of one billion and two people on Broadway assignment).

The institutional *Times*, acting in character, took no public notice of the Brustein brief; perhaps the editors hoped that, like George Bush facing the national recession, if they ignored it, it would go away. "The *Times* does not like to be told by the outside world how to run its affairs," the magazine *TheaterWeek* commented. But because the institutional *Times* also does not like to be embarrassed, or see its reputation for fairness undercut, *TheaterWeek* suggested that the *Times'* editors would wait a decent interval post-Brustein and then "do something to break or at least temper the couple's hammerlock on the theater." True to that scenario, the *Times* quietly resolved its "embarrassment of Riches" by moving Witchel off the theater beat. A year later, the *Times* announced that Rich himself was moving to the Op-Ed page to do a twice-weekly cultural column. There he could produce more opinion "product" with no need to await the opening of a new play.

Witchel's reassignment represented nothing more than the rearrangement of the deck chairs on the *Times*. The editors had no intention of changing the paper's new course. Indeed the *Times* welcomed the attention its critics received. Rich was bankable; the *Times* intended to feature him, as well as the reviews and "Critic's Notebook" of its other bright, snappy writers. They were stars, as big at the box office as a Joan Collins.

The ascendancy of the critic-star, a crowd-pleasing kind of guy, came at a bad moment culturally in New York. The three other dailies in the city that regularly covered the theater were struggling to make a profit. On television, Channel 5 dropped its reviewer Stewart Klein from the staff (he was paid for a time by the review) and Channel 11 dropped its reviewer, Jeffrey Lyons, completely. In March 1992, WINS radio dismissed its theater critic, Leida Snow, after thirteen years. Snow's old listeners could turn the dial to the *Times'* radio station, WQXR-FM, where *Times* critics regularly read from their reviews. Snow herself took an announcer's job at the same station.

When *City of Angels* opened to Rich's warm praise, other theater critics, including Thomas Disch of *The Nation*, liked the musical as well. But Disch understood the importance of the *Times'* word in keeping *City of Angels* alive. "There is a God," Disch concluded, adding pensively, "whether that God's name is Rich and whether he is a just God" were matters for more discussion.

The godlike authority of the *Times* over the fate of plays—on, off, and off-off-Broadway—as well as its effects on the economic health of new books, ballet, music, and other cultural and entertainment offerings was a fact of commercial life. Some plays survived a scathing review from Rich, just as some restaurants weathered a bad write-up from Bryan Miller—but not that many.

The *Times* is a general-interest newspaper and it has, as Miller said, a consumerist function. It conveys to readers how much a given experience is worth. That is, whether to see the show, or buy the book, or patronize the new restaurant, or make other cultural purchases. The *Times'* cultural report also offers quantitative information unequaled by any other news organization. Finally, though, the *Times'* cultural authority rests neither on the quality of its reviews, nor the amount of space devoted to the arts and entertainment. It is powerful by default.

To the extent that a *Times* review pumps up, or deflates, an individual's reputation among peers, then what the *Times* says matters. The *Times'* critical opinions also affect investors (in plays or restaurants), New York theater-party bookers, and concert managers in Chicago, Cleveland, Houston, Atlanta, and other points west and south. They all believe the wider audience consults no other sources—in part because the audience thinks that the *Times* is good, or good enough, in part because of laziness or inertia. Harry Cipriani was remarkable for being the condemned man who faced the firing squad disdaining both blindfold and last cigarette. He survived in spite of the attack by Bryan Miller, but then developed a wonderful case of protective amnesia afterward ("Really, the *Times* trashed me?"). Most targets of the *Times*—restaurateurs, producers, writers, artists, promoters of the arts and leisure—are not so bold, or so foolish to risk the musketry in the first place.

A DAY IN THE LIFE
8:00 P.M.—9:45 P.M.

8:00 P.M.

The late-desk staff arrived for work on the 8:00 P.M. to 3:00 A.M. shift.

The news pages took shape. Columns of type spewed out of computers; they were pasted up on the makeup boards, and the sheets of headlines, photos, and line rules trimmed and dropped in.

8:30 P.M.

The main shift of pressmen reported to work. In the pressroom, finished plates—the pages on photographic sheets—began to arrive from the platemaking department. John O'Keefe, a junior pressman, carried one of the plates to the designated press. The first sheets of newsprint paper were webbed, led through the presses.

9:03 P.M.

Final first edition pages left the composing room. A ten- to twenty-minute cheat factor was built in, allowing for late closings and still enabling the pressroom to "make the trucks."

9:15 P.M.

Pressman Tom O'Brien plated up—attached the plate to the rollers in one of the presses. Flashing green lights and clanging bells signaled a "Safe" on the presses, stopping any mechanical movement while pressmen worked inside on the rollers. In the press room, green lights meant Stop. The Safes stayed on almost continuously until 9:30, when plating was completed. The green Safe went off. Red lights signaled the start of the press run.

As usual, the first papers in the print run were all black; the ink and water had not yet mixed together correctly. The black paper, streaming up through the ceiling from each press, bypassed the main floor where the stacking machines were, and continued up to the mezzanine level. There, the stream was directed north toward the truck bays on 44th Street; the black paper spilled off into rag tops—open-top trailers—to be trucked away for recycling.

9:40 P.M.

Rudy Rella and Nick D'Andrea, the nightside plant managers at 43rd Street, checked and finally approved the quality of the ink-water mixture. The printed papers moved from the presses to the main floor and the stackers. The stackers and their machines counted the papers, bundled them in fifty-pound packages, and tied the bundles.

Outside, along the 43rd Street bays, mailers loaded the bundled papers into their delivery boxes—42-foot-long trailers. The trailers were hooked to the *Times'* fleet of Kenilworth trucks, twenty feet long and powered by 250-horsepower Cummins V-8 diesel engines. Paul Medina, a *Times* driver for twenty years, climbed into the cab of truck no. 70134. He pulled out, turned west on 43rd Street, right onto Eighth Avenue, right again onto West 44th, over to Madison Avenue, and uptown to the Major Deegan and on to the Albany-Troy area.

9:45 P.M.

The turnaround meeting. The late desk ran through the layouts it would update for the second edition, working from fresh photocopies of pages provided by the pressroom.

11

TWEEDY BACKWATER:
BEHIND THE LINES
AT THE BOOK REVIEW

GLORIA EMERSON, who covered the Vietnam war as a correspondent for the *New York Times*, was a ferociously determined reporter. Tall and rail thin, she stood over six feet tall in her combat boots, prompting a friend to describe her as "all arms, legs, and talent." Emerson left the *Times* in 1972 to do free-lance work and to write *Winners and Losers*, a memoir of the war and its effects on some Americans. The book received favorable reviews from, among others, David Halberstam in the *Los Angeles Times*, Walter Clemons in *Newsweek*, and Alden Whitman in the *Chicago Tribune*; it was not well received in the *New York Times*. One of the *Times'* daily book critics, Christopher Lehmann-Haupt—the three Germans, columnist Jimmy Breslin called him, not affectionately—wrote that Emerson's prose was "execrable." According to Emerson, Lehmann-Haupt was "clearly infuriated" at her because she had "mocked" him in the preface to *Winners and Losers*. "That he was allowed to review a book that scorned him," Emerson complained, "says much about the prevailing ethic of that newspaper."

Winners and Losers could very well be the title of a memoir about the *New York Times Book Review*. Every other author has a story about the crimes that *Times* reviewers committed, in the name of literature, on the author's book. For the author of a mainstream book—a book like Emerson's or a book such as the one you hold in your hands now—the *Book Review* is regarded as the preeminent sales tool in the trade-book business. New York is the center of the U.S. publishing industry, and New Yorkers purchase more books than the residents of any other metropolitan area in the country. But the influence of the *Times* is felt beyond the city as well; if the *Book Review* did not reach every book buyer in the country, it came closer than any other publication. Television was an increasingly important marketing force; a segment on the "Today" Show or an appearance on "Donahue" or "Oprah" could help the sales of any given book. So could good word-of-mouth: Every publishing season, two or three trade book titles defied the laws of gravity and publishing and managed, like magic water, to run uphill without a major *Times* review, and sometimes without any notice by the *Times* at all. These successes aside, trade publishers put their money where the market was: In 1991 advertisers spent over $16,000,000 to buy space in the *Book Review*.

Other newspapers and the weekly magazines—most notably, the *Los Angeles Times*, the *Washington Post*, the *Chicago Tribune*, the *Boston Globe*, *Newsday*, the *Chicago Sun-Times*, *Time*, *Newsweek*, *New York*, the *New Republic*, and *The Nation*—have excellent staff reviewers and smartly edited book pages or book sections. Only the *Times* has the *Book Review*. The *Times'* chief rival for influence, and a small percentage of the ad dollar, is the *New York Review of Books*. The *NYRB* is the more serious and admired publication, and it has the *Times* to thank for its existence. When the strike of 1962–63 shut down New York City's newspapers, three young editors, Robert Silvers, Barbara and Jason Epstein, started the *Review*. Great trees were crashing down in the publishing forests, and without the *Times* they made no sound. In the *Review* new books could be noted, reviewers could review, advertisers advertise. The *Review* was prepared from the first for the long haul, and didn't intend to go away after the strike was settled. It quickly established a kind of disdainful intellectual rivalry with the *Times*. "The disappearance of the *Times* Sunday book section at the time of the printers' strike," the critic Edmund Wilson noted in the third issue of the *Review*, "only made us realize it had never existed." But there was really no contest between the two publications. Or, rather, they compete in entirely different events: the *Review* academic, magisterial, relentlessly specialized; the *Times* journalistic, mainstream, and concerned about trade-book ads. In 1993, at the time of the *Review's* thirtieth anniversary, its circulation stood at 120,000; by then, 1.6 million copies of the *Book Review* were being printed; in addition, 60,000 stand-alone *Book Review* copies were being mailed out each week to subscribers who paid $39 a year for the privilege of getting their copies without having to wait until the weekend.

Many of these subscribers were in the business—bookstore owners, agents, editors, paperback houses, other publishers. A good part of the advertising in the pages of the *Book Review* is intended not so much for the individual reader as for these other players, and for motion picture and TV entertainment companies. A prominent ad in the *Times* was a way to let them all know of the existence of a "big book" or a "publishing event"; indeed, some authors insisted that their contracts be written to include the promise of advertisements in the *Times*. The same people who said they feared and resented the *Times'* authority over books thus contributed to the power of the *Book Review*. They were like the frontier-town gamblers who complained that the poker cards were marked, but kept playing anyway, dementedly reasoning: "It's the only game in town."

As in poker, too, when the politics of book reviewing played out in the pages of the *Times*, the winners smiled and the losers cried "Deal!" Ethical failures were alleged, vendettas uncovered, mutual admiration societies espied; log rolling and backscratching, paybacks and careerism, conflicts of interest, political correctness—you name it, someone already had, and attributed it to *Times'* book reviewers, though seldom on the record. The losers' complaints were both general and specific; they sometimes pointed a finger at Lehmann-Haupt, a daily reviewer since 1965, at the *Times'* other daily critics, or at one or another of the outside experts who were tapped by *Times* editors to write for the *Book Review* on Sundays. Recipients of a so-so *Times* review, or no notice at all, suffered from severely bruised egos, not to mention damage to their prospective earnings; they reacted by questioning the motives of the messenger, rather than the quality of their own production. Edmund Wilson's put-down to the contrary, the *Times'* existence was all too palpable for aggrieved authors. Sophisticates might slyly refer to the NYRB as the "New York Review of Each Other's Books," and enjoy the laugh. Few people were able to take the *Book Review* lightly. The *Times'* power was such that its critics watched it with colder eyes, held it perhaps to a higher standard than the competition, and were quicker to assume deals on the basis of circumstance and suspicion alone. A "conspiracy" in the pages of *The New York Review* involved "only" ideology, or reputation. At the *New York Times Book Review*, a good hand or a bad hand affected sales figures. A *Times* review was serious business.

Naturally, some of the people who wrote, edited, sold, or bought books were curious about how the place worked.

On one level, the *Book Review* runs much like any other clerical operation. The staff guards its prerogatives, worries about pay raises, vacation schedules, and working hours. Martin Levine, a Harvard man (class of '66) and a former editor and critic at the *Washington Post* and *Newsday*, joined the *Book Review* in 1982. While the *Times* paid more than the other papers, Levine was not a happy *Times*man. The promises made him by one senior editor were abrogated when that editor lost his authority in one of the periodic "politburo shake-ups" in the news department. The hierarchical organization of the *Book Review* was jarring after the looser attitudes at the *Post* and *Newsday*. During one of the *Times'* annual drives to hold down costs, Levine remembered, editors were informed that if they didn't finish all their work in the standard thirty-seven-hour week, they could work overtime—but not expect to be paid for it. Though Levine was chief editor of the *Book Review* copy desk, he was prohibited from talking to the reviewer whose copy was being edited. All queries for the reviewer had to be transmitted via the assigning editor. "The attitude was, 'This is the most prestigious place in the business,' " Levine said. "You should obey the ukases. 'Like it or leave, because plenty of others are lined up, waiting to work here.' " In Levine's mind, the prestige that outsiders attached to the *Book Review* was at odds with what actually happened inside. Decision making was increasingly centralized, and the *Book Review* became less independent. "We more and more became part of the 'mediaworld'—attuned to what the PR people were pushing, what the book clubs were doing, what the trendy magazines were saying." The public authority of the *Book Review* remained undiminished, however. "It saddened me to see how eagerly awaited *Times* reviews were," Levine said. Levine left in 1987, at the beginning of the Frankel era.

It was easy to dismiss complaints like his, and others', as those of disgruntled employees: How many *gruntled* employees are encountered in large organizations? More than a hint of the Postal Service wafts through the air at West 43rd Street. Like any bureaucracy, the *Book Review* has its paperwork procedures. Editors insert report forms, made out in quadruplicate, inside the books, noting whether they are recommending the title for review. Then there are the meetings; when one ended, another began. Because the *Book Review* is part of the news department, the book editor reports to the managing editor; in recent years, that means Rebecca Pepper Sinkler, the book editor since 1989, meets formally with Joe Lelyveld once a week. Sinkler apprises Lelyveld of what will be appearing on page one of the *Book Review* in the issue going to press, and discusses more general book news and publishing trends. Sinkler and her deputy also meet regularly to talk about what books to consider for reviewing, and to get these prospects into the hands of the previewing editors. The editor and the deputy then meet with the previewing editors, to get their recommendations. At midweek, editors meet to decide which reviews to run and when— the scheduling meeting. "We are all part of a collegial process," Sinkler said.

The core staff of eight previewing editors do the scut work of reading the books—or, minimally, riffling through the pages—to form a judgment. Levine took with him an enduring memory of the *Book Review*, an image composed of three elements: a previewing editor, with a pad of report forms and a desktop piled with books, the stacks so high they threatened to topple and bury the editor alive in review copies. "They claim to read them all, but they just can't," he said. Before the quadruplicate slips are made out, before the books reach the previewing editors' desks, the major screening takes place as each day's mail and messengers' deliveries arrive—"elimination at the point of entry," in Sinkler's phrase. Out of the 70,000 to 80,000 books published annually in the United States in recent years, the *Book Review* reviewed or mentioned forty-five to fifty books on an average Sunday. Each year, then, Sinkler and her staff turned away thousands and thousands of books in the process of deciding which 2,500, give or take a hundred or so, to tell the public about. This elimination work is vastly simplified by the organizing principles of the *Book Review*. There were whole categories of books that the *New York Times* did not review, period. The overwhelming majority of books could be judged literally by their covers.

The annual book crop includes some obvious candidates for elimination, such as airline schedule guides, medical and scientific texts, reference books, and vanity-press books. In addition, according to Sinkler, "We don't review certain genres—romance fiction, he-man adventure, manuals, self-help and how-to books, the very academic or the Ph.D. dissertation packaged as book. We can tell very quickly that a given book is not worth our previewing editors' time." The *Times* is interested in mainstream books. While Silhouette Harlequin fiction, for example, was not a *Times* kind of genre, and is automatically passed over, the *Book Review* under Becky Sinkler looks at every first novel published by a reputable house. The editors wanted to be able to alert readers to the existence of a new talent. There is also a desire to avoid the embarrassment of failing to spot that talent. When the Pulitzer Prizes for best novel and the other big awards were announced each year, *Book Review* editors tended to greet the news with two questions: Did we review it? What did we say?

By restricting the world of the *Book Review* to mainstream trade titles, Sinkler estimated, the actual selection process came down to choosing from a pool of about seven thousand books a year. That still left it up to the editors to eliminate almost two thirds of the pool, as well as to decide who should do the review, at what length, and when in the publishing cycle it should run.

The formal system distributes this authority throughout the *Book Review* hierarchy, so that in theory several hands determine the outcome of any one review. The editor or the deputy editor approves the selection of books to be noted, supervises the assignments of the reviewers, determines the length and placement of individual reviews, and reads the major reviews before publication. The previewing editors recommend books for review and, once the book is assigned, work with the reviewer, doing the initial editing when the copy is submitted. After the select 2,500 titles make the editors' first cut, they are sorted out into further selective categories. Each week, the editors designate six or eight books for major attention in reviews of up to 2,500 words; these reviews either begin on the front page or take up a full inside page. Another dozen or so books receive more modest display in a half-page review. Six or seven others warrant only "In Short" mention in reviews of about 250 words each (together, these brief reviews fill one page, usually divided between two or three novels and four or five non-fiction titles). The editors' selective power works retroactively as well: a "New & Noteworthy" page for paperback reprints repeats in a paragraph what the *Times* review said when the original hardcover edition came out, as if no other judgment counted. Finally, in an end piece in the back, a previewing editor with the time and inclination was able to mention five or six books he liked, offering short excerpts from them under the heading "Noted with Pleasure." In August 1992, Sinkler dropped the feature. She explained that "the *Review* could use the space better, for more reviews."

The end product, of course, carries the byline of the reviewer, theoretically leaving no doubt whose views are being expressed. Again, however, the theory could be at odds with the practical outcome. Several people, both from inside the *Times* and outsider reviewers, described the "nudging power" of the editors. Their examples came from the period of the last ten years, and involved past as well as present editors.

First, the *Book Review* editor, on the basis of a call from a well-connected friend or a publishing-world source, "might become excited about a new book." The editor could convey that excitement to the previewing editor, "who has a certain status, but is open to suggestion and nuance. . . ." The previewing editor grasps the subtext when the editor says, "Why don't we take a good look at . . . ?" The previewing editor then can make the assignment with a strong positive spin— telling the reviewer, for example, "We're hearing great things about . . ." The top editor can also call a reviewer directly and assign the review, without anyone in the system previewing the book. The next nudge can come in the choice of the reviewer. "We tend to assign books to a limited group of reviewers," a former *Times*person explained. "We look for reviewers who were trusted, literate, on time with their copy"—like most bureaucracies, the staff tries to lower its stress levels—"and have a track record." Another informant said: "If we get a book by a friend of a friend, say a first novel, we wouldn't assign it to someone known to be ruthless to first novelists. You know, someone who hasn't liked anything since 1975. Instead, we'd give that book to another first novelist." A third form of nudging can accompany the assignment. If the editor asks for fifteen hundred or two thousand words, it signals that the *Times* expects the reviewer to deliver "a big review."

All this could happen before the reviewer wrote one word. After the copy is delivered, the previewing editors do what editors everywhere are paid to do: ask for inserts and rewrites, or change words or phrases (the *Book Review* copy desk worried about commas and *Times* style). How much of this fiddling was "normal"—aiming for clarity, for example—and how much had the effect of altering meaning or tone, depended on the editor and reviewer and their relationship. The anecdotal evidence was just that—anecdotes. Some reviewers have said that the editing toned down parts of their reviews; others said the editing made reviews sharper, more ascerbic. A few mentioned that they went along with most of the editing requests because they liked reviewing for the *Times*, and wanted to be asked back again; friends and coworkers saw their byline, TV news-show bookers were reminded of their "expertise," other publications called with assignments, their deans, or their mothers, were pleased. The money was incidental; very few reviewers receive more than $750 for a big review; the more typical payment is $300 to $450, depending on the length of the review. Mostly, "Your name is just out there, part of the media buzz." "Believe me," one reviewer said, "you can be Justin Kaplan, published and tenured for life, and you still want the *Times* to call." Even with impeccable writers like Kaplan, this informant added, "The tendency when writing a review was to think, 'Why stir up too much trouble? I have my own book coming out . . . not that the *Times* would exact retribution. . . . They wouldn't, would they?' "

The *Book Review* could decide not to run a problematic review at all—the ultimate controlling mechanism. That, however, would run the risk of an item for the *Village Voice* or *Spy* magazine. More subtly, the editors may simply hold the review, and plead a space squeeze when the reviewer calls to inquire what was happening. After several weeks pass—during which the book is reviewed elsewhere, or makes its brief appearance on a best-seller list, or comes and goes from the stores—the editor explains that, "as the book is no longer new," it makes no sense to review it. This decision is delivered in a tone of regret, with as much sincerity as the system can generate. But these are rare cases; the entire assignment process is intended to eliminate surprises, and produce publishable reviews.

The process is different for the daily reviews by the *Times'* staff critics. Their reviews appear in the news columns of the Monday-through-Saturday paper. Almost by definition, these pieces are less literary, brisker, and more informative and newsier than the Sunday reviews. The daily reviews are, after all, a part of the hard-news report. Daily critics are their own men, and women; their judgments came through as individual assessments rather than outcomes of the *Book Review* editing system. True, authors wounded in the daily reviews, such as Gloria Emerson, saw dark deals going down. One aggrieved party, Gore Vidal, felt the *Times'* lash in his youth; for the subsequent half a century, he never let anyone forget his animosity, which he turned on and off like a faucet. Vidal was a one-man band of horror tunes about *Times'* reviewers, daily and Sunday. In 1946, when he was twenty-one years old, his first novel, *Williwaw*, was published to acclaim from Orville Prescott, the *Times'* daily book critic. "I was made," Vidal later wrote. Then, in 1948, E. P. Dutton published Vidal's novel *The City and the Pillar*, with its story of a homosexual love affair between "two ordinary American youths." According to Vidal, an editor at Dutton was told by Prescott that he would never read, much less review, a book by Vidal again. "True to Prescott's word," said Vidal, "my next five novels were not reviewed in the daily *Times*. . . . I was unmade." Vidal claimed that the curse of the *Times* continued to follow him when he took up, successively, playwriting (he said that the *Times* tried to "bloody" his play *The Best Man*) and electoral politics (a *Times* writer was "assigned to 'bloody' my campaign for Congress in New York's 29th District"). Five decades later, Vidal still was turning out catchy one-liners about the *Times*—the Typhoid Mary of American journalism, he called it—and about its book pages, where "the air is alive with the sound of axes grinding."

As a rule, *Times* staff reviewers don't go around expressing their intentions or their homophobia, as Prescott did (if Vidal's comments are to be believed). The *Times* has been more discreet and private, although there was one spectacular public exception. The episode involved a review by the book critic John Leonard. Given the circumstances of the Leonard review, there was no way that the *Times* could avoid public notice of the story. Leonard, then a book critic for the daily paper, reviewed two books on the assassination of John F. Kennedy. One was written by the New Orleans district attorney Jim Garrison (played by Kevin Costner in the Oliver Stone motion picture *J.F.K.*), the other book was by a friend of Clay Shaw (the Tommy Lee Jones character in the film). Leonard didn't particularly care for either book. He devoted the last third of the review, in his words, "to a sermon which began, 'Frankly, I prefer to believe that the Warren Commission did a poor job rather than a sloppy one. . . .' " According to Leonard, "What followed then was a list of questions about the two autopsies, the washed-out limousine, 'grassy knoll' witnesses, Oswald's marksmanship, Jack Ruby's strange connections. . . ." The review ended: "Something stinks about this whole affair." Leonard's review ran in the first edition of the *Times* of December 1, 1970, with the headline: "Who Killed John F. Kennedy?" In the next and subsequent editions of that day's *Times*, the review ended abruptly right after the observation about the sloppy job and before the list of questions. A new headline read: "The Shaw-Garrison Affair." According to Leonard, "Nobody from the executive editor to the culture desk to the bullpen to the composing room, would admit to this cosmetic surgery." The mystery remained as the microfilms of the *Times'* first edition and final edition for December 1 found their way into reference libraries across the country. Over the next six months, Leonard remembered, he received some four hundred letters asking about the two reviews and expressing dark thoughts about various conspiracies in Dallas, New Orleans, Washington, and at the *New York Times*. In the years since, Leonard continued to receive similar letters, especially when a new book on the Kennedy assassination was published or when "another paranoid apostrophizes on another television talk-show." For years, too, Leonard told his correspondents to direct their questions to A. M. Rosenthal, his top editor at the time.

The tale of the amputated review stirred vile thoughts about the politics of book reviewing at the *Times*. The *Book Review* machinery could pump up interest in any given book, or shunt attention away. Its power existed; but it did not necessarily follow that the juice moved in a certain conspiratorial direction or supported a specific agenda. Many of the alleged plots, upon inspection, are more bureaucratic than cablistic: they appear to be aimed at putting out a newspaper every day and a *Book Review* on Sundays, while trying to keep mistakes to a minimum—all without overtime. Leonard's editors, he recalled, thought he should keep his "leftist views" out of the paper; but they also valued his writing and kept giving him good display. He thought they were tilting rightward, and calling it centrism. In fact, the editors could live with Leonard's political attitude—up to the point where it implied some criticism of the *Times'* news-gathering abilities. Any attack on the Warren Commission's investigation of the Kennedy assassination by extension meant an attack as well on the news department's coverage of both the assassination and investigation. That's what brought on the Kennedy amputation. The operation over, the surgeons moved on. A few months later, the same people who cut Leonard's Kennedy review promoted him to editor of the *Book Review*, a powerful pulpit to give someone suspected of too much leftist sermonizing. Leonard repaid their confidence by devoting most of one issue of the *Book Review* to a critical essay on Vietnam by Neil Sheehan (the article wore the light camouflage cloth of a roundup review of a half-dozen books on the war). Leonard's tenure at the *Book Review* was relatively short; by 1975 he was back as a daily reviewer—bounced from the editor's job for his politics, in some accounts. In Leonard's version, however, he hated being a boss and hated not writing; in addition, his marriage was falling apart and he had what was euphemistically referred to as "a drinking problem." Leonard said that he tried to quit for the better part of a year before his editors could agree on a replacement. Again, they valued his talent; "They will love us just as much, or as little, as it serves their interests," he later wrote.

Leonard told the tale of the Garrison-Shaw review on several occasions, to me and to others. Not until the fall of 1992, however, did I learn from him the story of what I came to think of as (in the manner of Kennedy conspiracy theorists) The Second Amputation. Leonard reviewed *My Story*, Judith Exner's memoir of her years as the mistress of Sam Giancana, the Chicago mob boss, *and* John F. Kennedy, the president of the United States. The singer Frank Sinatra was the go-between in each case, according to Exner. Critic Leonard found Exner's story wholly believable; he discerned unsettling similarities in the behavior of the outwardly dissimilar characters of Giancana and Kennedy. The review was killed. "The editors had a thing about the Kennedys, they loved them," Leonard recalled. More accurately, the editors had "a thing" about the *Times*. Leonard said he asked for and received permission to publish the Exner review elsewhere, and it eventually appeared in the *SoHo News*, a now-defunct downtown New York weekly. Leonard could say whatever he wanted about the compulsive sexual adventurism of J.F.K.; he just couldn't say it in the pages of the *Times*.

In 1982 Leonard resigned from the *Times*. Self-interest was a two-way street; he had written for the *Times* because he wanted to, and the paper ran his reviews because they fit its marketing plans: "They did not publish me out of the kindness of their hearts. We were even every day."

         *   *   *

If there was not a unified conspiracy theory that explained every publishing decision at the *Times*, the notion that the *Book Review* was apolitical also belonged in the fiction genre, as improbable as any Harlequin romance. The fantasy had its origins in the Adolph Ochs years. Then as now, the *Book Review* carried no masthead or any other indication of the men or women involved in the selection and editing of its materials. "To list any names of the editors would be to imply that a personal point of view might be involved," a previewing editor of the *Book Review* explained not long ago. But the individual editors themselves—the ones no longer at the *Book Review*, at any rate—acknowledged that they brought just such a point of view to their work. John Leonard was cast as the bright, young California hipster, imported from Berkeley, to bring the *Book Review* into the twentieth century. "I was hired in the late 1960s as part of a general loosening up at the *Times*," he says now. "They wanted younger, more stylish writing." (A quarter of a century later, Max Frankel was still seeking the same fountain of youth for the *Times*' news columns.) When Leonard arrived, "the place was full of good old AFL-CIO anti-Communists. I had worked at Pacifica radio." Leonard had an agenda for the *Book Review*: "I wanted something eye-catching on the front page each week, something that would make people think and talk about it."

Leonard's successor, Harvey Shapiro, promoted a different agenda. Shapiro represented another tradition at the *Times*; a second-generation American Jew, he grew up in an apartment building near the LIRR tracks in the Five Towns area just across the Nassau County line from New York City. He served with distinction in the Air Corps during World War II, attended Yale on the GI Bill, and worked at the *Times* for over thirty years in a variety of editing jobs. Shapiro was among the last of a breed of journalists who regarded the *Times* as a day job that enabled them to pursue their muses. "The *Times* paid the rent so that you could write your novel at night, or, in my case, poetry. Now it's a full-time, demanding occupation." Shapiro edited the *Book Review* from 1975 to 1983. "I looked for the consumer element in our reviews. I wanted to tell people whether to buy and read the book; I didn't think that we could engage in a pure literary exercise." As an example of his approach, he cited his reasoning when Norman Mailer's novel *Ancient Evenings* was published. "I first thought about assigning the Mailer to Harold Bloom. Then I realized that Bloom wouldn't review the book, but would launch into some other disquisition. I asked Ben DeMott, and Bloom did it for the *New York Review* . . . Leonard wanted to stir things up. With me, there was more celebration of the writer." As for reviewers, "I invited the usual suspects, like Irving Howe." After Leonard, the Vietnam-era provocateur-editor, Shapiro wanted to be recognized as a more literary editor. "My proudest moment came when I put an anthology of Chinese poetry on the front page of the *Book Review*." Later Shapiro amended the record slightly. He said a prouder moment came back in July 1962, before he joined the *Book Review*. The Reverend Martin Luther King was serving a jail sentence in Albany, Georgia; Shapiro telephoned the Southern Christian Leadership Council offices in Atlanta and said the *Times Magazine* would be interested in publishing a "letter from prison" written by King. The SCLC people decided it was best for King to hold off for a while; a year later, in April 1963, King was arrested again. The Shapiro idea reappeared in the form of King's "Letter from Birmingham Jail." That August, the *Atlantic Monthly* published it.

Shapiro was moved off the *Book Review* in 1983. "They"—Abe Rosenthal and Arthur Gelb—"wanted their own man in." Did that mean "they" were unhappy with his editing? Did he fail to carry out management's wishes? No, he never felt any pressure from his superiors. Shapiro is a small man, still slender as he approached his seventieth birthday. His half-closed eyes, wispy beard, and thinning white hair, worn long in back, gave him the aspect of a Mandarin of the Middle Kingdom court. Why then would "they" want him out? There must have been some conflict? Assignments refused? Requests ignored? In the manner of a careful witness on the stand, he repeated, several times, "No, I can't recall anything like that." His Mandarin eyes, now almost shut, suggested otherwise. Shapiro took his demotion from the *Book Review* with equanimity. Rosenthal wanted to know what Shapiro would like to do next: "He said, 'Ask for anything.' So I asked for a trip to Japan and got it. Then I went back to the *Magazine*. I made my peace." During an interview in January 1992, he said he just sent his ninth book off to his publisher. Shapiro smiled a Mandarin smile. The *Times* was still a day job.

The editors' "own man" was Mitchel Levitas. Levitas was a native New Yorker and a graduate of Brooklyn College. He joined the *Times* in 1965, as an editor for the *Times Magazine*. Unlike Shapiro, Levitas never regarded the *Times* as a way to help with the rent; he put his full-time energies into his *Times* career. Rebecca Sinkler became Levitas's deputy in 1985 and succeeded him in 1989, the first woman editor of the *Book Review*. Levitas returned to the news department as Max Frankel's weekend editor, in charge of the Sunday–Monday front pages. Twenty months later he became Op-Ed page editor. During the Levitas-Sinkler years the *Book Review* paid more attention to politics and current events; it was, at once, less literary and more predictable. Levitas introduced an essay feature that started at the bottom of page one and often filled one or two inside pages. The essays, usually by big-name authors and academics, were intended to discuss books in ways other than the review form. "I wanted to make the *Book Review* more journalistic," Levitas remembered. "I wanted it to carry news as well as reviews." In pursuit of a newsy *Book Review*, Levitas introduced boxed interviews with authors to accompany the reviews. He also consolidated all the shorter reviews on their own page in the center of the *Book Review*. As Levitas explained, authors might not receive full-length treatment, but they were still entitled to some "dignity" in a 250–300-word review.

The Levitas-inspired page-one essays were, in effect, lengthy columns; they contributed to the explosion of opinion pieces throughout the Frankel *Times*. "We wanted to expand our role, range about, take a broader look at ideas and trends," Sinkler explained. As with the news pages during the Frankel years, the *Book Review* tried to be lively. Levitas and, later, Sinkler, wanted the *Book Review* to serve, in part, as a consumer guide, recommending titles for the buying public. But they placed a high value on the quality of writing, in the book being reviewed and in the reviewer's review. "We don't care how expert an expert may be," Sinkler said. "A book is entirely useless if it is dry or dense, or doesn't communicate. The same is true for the reviewer. We try out authorities in their fields, and often they are not good writers. No matter how much the reviewer knows, if the judgment isn't expressed in a lively way, readers will not read the review."

Along with the rest of the Frankel *Times*, then, the *Book Review* worried about distracted readers, and the need to entice them into the newspaper habit. Sinkler wanted the *Book Review* to provoke news on the Rialto. It wasn't enough that heads didn't droop; the *Book Review* tried to make heads turn as well. In the fall of 1991, the publication of the Norman Mailer novel *Harlot's Ghost* achieved precisely that effect.

Harlot's Ghost came with a kind of warning, "long awaited." The label signified that the celebrated author had not produced anything significant for at least a decade, and that there was a suspicion he had run dry. It also signaled that the author's publishing house had paid a huge advance for the work and was nervously waiting, hoping to get some of its investment back. The advance word had been mixed to negative, and Random House didn't seem likely to recoup its $1 million advance. The *Times'* Sunday review, written by the theater and film critic John Simon, was published on the front page of the *Book Review*. Simon referred to Mailer's windy metaphysics and the novel's "lumpy, lopsided narrative that outstays its welcome." But Simon's mild judgments were less important than the marketing window of opportunity opened for Mailer. Mailer accused Simon of conflict of interest and, because he was Norman Mailer, he demanded—and got—what injured authors fantasize about: a meeting with Sinkler and Lelyveld to discuss the treatment of his book. Mailer thereupon produced some supposed examples of Simon's malice, including a mildly negative review Simon had given one of Mailer's daughters, an actress named Kate Mailer. No matter the dubiousness of Mailer's evidence. The *Times* gave him a full page in the *Book Review* to "answer" the review, further advertisements for himself. The letters to the editor that followed became another billboard for Mailer, while changing the subject from the worth of the book to a celebrity feud.

Such celebrity reviews succeeded in getting the *Book Review* talked about. Less than a year later, in the August 30, 1992, *Book Review*, Sinkler gave front-page display to Gore Vidal's *Screening History*, a slim Harvard University Press book based on lectures Vidal delivered at Harvard the year before. The university setting was deceptive; Vidal had lost none of his venom. "He has poisonous words in particular for academic historians and the *New York Times*," the academic historian Michael Kammen of Cornell noted in his review. Alongside Kammen's review was a half-page interview with Vidal, conducted by telephone from his Italian villa in Ravello. Sinkler said she never hesitated about assigning the book and playing it prominently. "Vidal told many people of his undisguised enmity for the *Book Review*, but we read these books with an open mind," she said. "We ask, Are our readers interested in this? Is this book important? I knew we'd be accused of trying to appease him. But a Vidal book is a newsworthy moment, and the book was good."

*   *   *

There was a category of book-news chatter that the *Times* absolutely did not seek. In the mid-1980s, the press critic David Shaw of the *Los Angeles Times* compiled a list of forty episodes where, he was told, "the fix was in" at the *New York Times*. Supposedly, in each case a book and a reviewer had been brought together by the *Times'* editors, to reward a friend or punish an enemy. Some of Shaw's sources telephoned him with their "leads" in the middle of the night; these tipsters, as well as other informants, asked for anonymity, explaining that, as they were writers or editors whose books would someday come up for scrutiny, they couldn't afford to offend the *Times*. Shaw checked through the list. He concluded that there was evidence of impropriety in about a half-dozen cases at most. And even then, the *Times'* assigning editors seemed less at fault than individual reviewers. Typically, the outside reviewers concealed their intentions to use the review to settle old scores or to provide a boost to a friend (or to someone who was a friend of a friend, or who shared the same publishing house). Two of Shaw's examples conveyed a sense of how that part of the game was played. The veteran author and journalist Roger Kahn gave a bad review to Daniel Okrent's baseball book, *Nine Innings*. Less than two years before, Okrent had panned Kahn's baseball book, *The Seventh Game*, also in the *Book Review*. According to Levitas, no one on the staff remembered the earlier review. Kahn's explanation put a much greater strain on credulity: Kahn said he didn't disqualify himself from reviewing *Nine Innings* because he didn't know Okrent had reviewed *The Seventh Game*. If true, Kahn belonged in the *Guinness Book of World Records*: first author *not* to read the *Times* review of his book. In the same period, too, the British author Margaret Drabble reviewed Mary Gordon's novel *Men and Angels* on the front page of the *Book Review*. Gordon and Drabble were friends, and Drabble had earlier written a jacket blurb for the paperback edition of Gordon's novel *Final Payments* ("Original, perceptive, highly intelligent and remarkably honest," the blurb read). Again, the reviewer, the previewing editor, and the supervising editors all suffered from another spell of collective amnesia: "No one noticed."

In at least one case, Levitas and the *Times* could hardly plead innocence. In 1985 Simon & Schuster published *Mayor*, the autobiography of the then New York City mayor, Edward I. Koch. Ed Koch received the *Times'* endorsement when he initially ran as well as for each of the three times he was up for reelection. To review *Mayor* for the *Book Review*, Levitas chose Gay Talese. Although he was a former *Times*man and a celebrated writer, Talese was not known for any particular knowledge of City Hall or local New York politics. Talese was known, however, as the author of a history of the *New York Times*. In one passage, Talese described how the *Book Review*, when choosing reviewers, relied on "friends of the *Times*"—academics, authors, intellectuals, journalists, and people in public life who "greatly admired the paper, stood by its principles, and shared its traditional respect for the established order and solid middle-class values." This passage came to mind when Talese's page-one appreciation of *Mayor* appeared in the *Book Review* of February 12, 1984. A Simon & Schuster publicity woman told Shaw that the pairing of Koch and Talese was "a match made in heaven," explaining that both men were "great friends of the *New York Times*." She added: "we knew it would be a wonderful review, and it was even better than we'd hoped." By contrast, in 1985, Arthur Browne of the *New York Daily News*, Michael Goodwin of the *Times*, and Dan Collins of the Associated Press—three journalists who covered the mayor and city politics, day to day, tribe by tribe, finagle by finagle—published a critical study of the mayor called *I, Koch*. The *Book Review* buried *I, Koch* on the "In Short" page.

The *Times* reemphasized its policy on conflict-of-interest reviews in the years since Shaw's survey. Editors were formally prohibited from assigning books to reviewers with "close ties to anyone who is prominently mentioned in the book under consideration." Unofficially, some assigning editors used a "names test"—checking the index of the book to determine whether a prospective reviewer was or was not mentioned. But the checking process sometimes broke down. The *Book Review* staff, like other desks in the news department, was under deadline pressures. Wrong assignments were made; friends got a chance to take care of friends, enemies to tuck it to enemies. An immaculately conceived *Book Review*, free of politics and intrigue, would have been a miracle of publishing. As the author and book editor Gordon Lish told Shaw: "There's no way for even the *New York Times* to have an up-to-date registry of all the alliances and misalliances in the literary world. They proliferate almost hourly."

Nevertheless, the *Book Review* did try. "We bend over backward, we pool our communal knowledge," Sinkler said. She was book editor of the *Philadelphia Inquirer* for five years and then served as a previewing editor and deputy editor of the *Book Review* from 1985 to 1989, before becoming its editor. When Sinkler, her deputy, and her previewing editors met to chose books for review and decide on the reviewers, she said, "We share a body of experience and history. We remember a lot, we try to be aware of what the reviewer has done in the past. But we are human." Sinkler wanted reviewers without conflicting interests; but she also wanted more stylish writing in the *Book Review* pages. Although hired during the A. M. Rosenthal era, she was promoted to *Book Review* editor by Max Frankel, the advocate of the livelier, brighter *Times*. Sinkler tried to navigate a middle course through the treacherous book territory of authors, editors, reviewers, and publishing houses. On one side, Sinkler explained, "If we pick someone with no connection at all to the book topic, then people will ask 'Why pick him?' There has to be some intuitive or imaginative connection." On the other side: "We don't want a predictable review. We look for a fair, interesting, informed, well written *and* entertaining review." The ideal *Times* reviewer, Sinkler suggested, "was someone not altogether predictable, but not off the wall, either." Pressed for a specific example of what she would try to avoid, Sinkler paused for a moment and then replied: "Where a public record exists, we try to avoid that reviewer as well. . . . We wouldn't give the Steinem to Friedan."

It was easy to understand why Sinkler did not ask Betty Friedan to review Gloria Steinem's 1992 book, *Revolution From Within: A Book for Self-Esteem*. The most casual newspaper reader had heard of the barely civil relationship between two of the founding mothers of the modern feminist movement. A previewing editor's check of the *Revolution from Within* index would have produced evidence of a remarkable omission: Steinem recommended some 140 books for further reading in her two appendixes—and managed to skip any mention of *The Feminine Mystique*, the book by Friedan that helped start the women's revolution from without. The harder calls for the previewing editors involve less well known figures. "We can't read every page of every single book," Sinkler acknowledged. "And so we are vulnerable. We have to rely on the reviewer to make the process credible. We ask the reviewer, 'Will the author have any grounds for objecting to you as a reviewer?' "

These procedures didn't dissuade the conspiracy theorists. David Shaw concluded that "paranoia" about the motives of the *Book Review* was the most common affliction among the congenitally jittery natives of the New York publishing world. The *Los Angeles Times* survey had minimal impact; it wasn't hard for me to collect a fresh batch of "fix stories." Three cases in particular offered rich details.

The first involved Joan Mellen, a professor at Temple University in Philadelphia. Mellen complained that the *Book Review* assigned her 1988 biography of Bobby Knight, the Indiana University basketball coach, to a reviewer on the staff of *Sports Illustrated*—despite the fact that the magazine had conducted an "unrelenting vendetta" against Knight. Moreover, the *Book Review*'s identification box at the bottom of the review did not mention reviewer Rick Telander's connection to the magazine. The review itself, which appeared in the *Book Review* of October 30, 1988, was hostile and gratuitously nasty. Mellen, who knew Sinkler from her days at the *Philadelphia Inquirer*, wrote to protest the way the book was treated. Three weeks later, on November 20, the *Times* ran both a formal letter from Mellen in the *Book Review* and an "Editors' Note" in the main news section stating that Telander should not have been chosen to review Mellen's book. But Mellen believed that by then all the damage had been done: "My book was on the *Times* best-seller list the week before," she remembered. "After the review appeared, it did not get on again. It's hard to prove that the review made the difference, but it sure had to hurt sales in the East. Indiana fans would laugh off such a review, of course."

A second case involved Dan Moldea, an independent journalist based in Washington. Since 1974 Moldea has concentrated on investigating organized-crime influences on putatively legitimate enterprises. In his 1986 book *Dark Victory: Ronald Reagan, MCA and the Mob*, Moldea explored Reagan's Hollywood years and his relationship to the communications giant Music Corporation of America when he was president of the Screen Actors Guild. In 1989 Moldea's book *Interference: How Organized Crime Influences Professional Football* alleged endemic corruption and gambling throughout the National Football League. The book was well received in regional publications such as the *Dallas Morning News* and the *Boston Herald*, and Moldea was interviewed by Larry King on CNN. But in the *Book Review* of September 3, 1989, *Times* sportswriter Gerald Eskenazi dismissed *Interference* as "sloppy journalism." Moldea complained to the *Book Review*, arguing that Eskenazi was not a neutral observer; rather, Eskenazi had covered the NFL for more than thirty years and "was determined to protect his friends and sources in the League." The

Times refused Moldea's request for a retraction or correction, telling him it was "standing by the review." Meanwhile, according to Moldea, his publisher, Morrow, "withdrew support for the book, more than twelve thousand copies were returned from bookstores, reviews and articles in other newspapers virtually ceased, and there was no paper-back book contract." A year later, Moldea sued the *Times* for defamatory libel, asking $10 million in damages. In February 1992, Judge John Garrett Penn in the Federal District Court in Washington granted the *Times'* motion for summary judgment. According to Penn, "A book review is . . . the type of article which the reasonable reader knows is comprised of the reviewer's opinion. . . . The statement at issue 'too much sloppy journalism' . . . is an unverifiable opinion and is thus not actionable under libel law." The law, narrowly interpreted, was on the *Times'* side; but the editors' decision to ignore Moldea meant that the antennas of the *Book Review* were attuned mostly to Big Noises like Mailer, and not to scuffling free-lancers or to small publishing houses on the fringes of mediaworld.

In a third case, however, a mainstream publisher stood together with its author against the *Book Review*—and won modest redress. In 1991 Sinkler and her editors assigned Stephen Ambrose, the historian and biographer of Richard M. Nixon, to review *Silent Coup*, an eccentric, revisionist retelling of the Watergate scandals. *Silent Coup's* coauthors were two free-lancers, Len Colodny and Robert Gettlin. Their book portrayed Nixon as the victim of Watergate rather than its villain. In the *Book Review* of June 23, 1991, Ambrose criticized Colodny-Gettlin for their research techniques and dismissed their "radical findings." George Witte of St. Martin's Press, the publishers of *Silent Coup*, received his advance copy of the *Book Review* earlier in the week. He immediately sent Rebecca Sinkler a two-page, single-spaced letter, detailing why he thought Ambrose should have been disqualified from reviewing Colodny-Gettlin. Among Witte's assertions were the following: Ambrose shared a publisher (Simon & Schuster) and an editor (Alice Mayhew) with two principals in the book that Colodny-Gettlin had dealt with harshly; Ambrose had his own Nixon book coming out in three months; and perhaps most damning of all, Ambrose had written Colodny two years before and offered to trade "findings." According to Witte, when Colodny refused, Ambrose supposedly said: "A historian like myself could make or break this type of book." Witte asked Sinkler to run the complete text of his letter in the *Book Review* of June 30, "on the heels of the Ambrose review, when readers will still have it handy or in mind." A *Times'* note of regret appeared on July 7, acknowledging that, if the editors had known of the Ambrose-Colodny exchange, the book would have been assigned to a different reviewer. The "Editors' Note" did little to reverse the downward plunge of the sales of *Silent Coup* after the Ambrose review appeared.

In the Ambrose case, the *Book Review* assumed the role of injured party, ill-used by less-than-honest outside reviewers. But there was a special group of cases where the book editors could not plead victimization. These reviews involved *Times* people, as authors or as reviewers.

In the *Book Review* of March 20, 1988, writer Richard Rhodes reviewed *Claiming the Heavens*, an account of Ronald Reagan's Strategic Defense Initiative (the "Star Wars" program.) The book was written by five *Times* reporters, including William J. Broad. The year before, Broad reviewed Rhodes's *The Making of the Atomic Bomb*, describing it as "a major historical synthesis." Unsurprisingly, Rhodes liked *Claiming the Heavens*, calling it "instructive" and "trenchant." In 1991, for another example, when Alex Jones, then the *Times'* press reporter, and his wife, Susan E. Tifft, published *The Patriarch*, an account of the Bingham newspaper family, they garnered two reviews. The daily *Times* used almost a half page to praise *The Patriarch* on April 5, 1991, while the *Book Review* featured it on page one on April 14. Both daily and Sunday reviews were written by non-*Times* people, respected authors in their own right. Both reviewers made clear from the first sentence their high regard for the Jones-Tifft work. *The Patriarch* was a "spacious and richly embroidered chronicle," according to the daily reviewer Richard Lingeman, while the Sunday reviewer, Richard Kluger, called it "an engrossing social document."

That same Sunday, the *Book Review* also featured a photograph of *Times* columnist Anna Quindlen inset at the top of the front page, above the Jones-Tifft review. The photograph was a refer—a referral—to the review of Quindlen's novel *Object Lessons* on page seven. *Times* readers, reviewer Anne Tyler wrote, "will not be surprised to learn that [Quindlen's] first novel is intelligent, highly entertaining and laced with acute perceptions. . . ." Nor were readers surprised that the *Book Review* ran such a favorable review.

A Sunday as rewarding as that for *Times* authors would be hard to top. Less than a month later, however, the *Book Review* outdid itself in the interests of the *Times* family. Eric Lax's *Woody Allen: A Biography* was prominently played on the front page of the *Book Review* for May 12, 1991. An excerpt from the book had been featured on the cover of the *Times Magazine* a few weeks before the review appeared, and on subsequent Sundays the Lax book received the "Editors' Choice" recommendation in the *Book Review*. The Sunday reviewer and film critic, Molly Haskell, pointed out that six previous books had been written about Allen; while Lax, she wrote, was not the "authorized biographer, he is certainly the anointed one." Her judgments were carefully modulated and spoke to the reader as consumer: The biography, although not a work of scholarship, was "addressed to Woody Allen fans, and . . . should fascinate and delight them." Haskell's review provided just what a review editor attuned to the marketplace would want: a long, anecdote-rich read focused on Allen as a New York institution. (A year later, when Allen's affair with the young daughter of his lover Mia Farrow became public knowledge, the "funny Woody" stories turned sick and sour.) All in all, Haskell and the *Book Review* managed an excellent send-off for a pleasant coffee-table book by the well-mannered, young Lax—who was also the son-in-law of Punch Sulzberger, chairman of the board of the *Times*. "I felt very comfortable with my judgment when we put the book on page one," Sinkler said when asked about the Lax review. "Woody Allen was someone our readers cared for a lot. There was immense interest in him and his films. I would have put a biography of Allen on the cover *not* written by Lax."

Rhodes, Lingeman, Kluger, and Haskell were part of a rich tradition at the *Times*, although they may not have fully realized it. In the *Book Review* of August 18, 1946, the entire front page and two inside pages were devoted to a review of *An Honorable Titan: A Biographical Study* of Adolph S. Ochs, the modern *Times'* own patriarch. The author was Gerald Johnson, a well-known newspaperman and a biographer of Woodrow Wilson; the reviewer was Kent Cooper, executive director of the Associated Press; the occasion was the fiftieth anniversary of Ochs's purchase of the *Times*. Cooper began his review on a refreshingly direct note. He had been both a friend of Ochs's and a business associate: the AP was then—and remains today—a news-gathering cooperative financed by fees from member newspapers and broadcast outlets. "Lest there be any misunderstanding," Cooper wrote near the top of his review, in true, above-board AP style, "let me say on my own behalf that this is not a regular book review. It cannot be for a very honest reason: I treasure an honest bias in favor of Adolph Ochs. . . . I cannot write objectively about this objective biography." Cooper's honesty stopped short of full disclosure; the book and the review made only veiled references to Ochs's history of severe emotional illnesses.

In the *Book Review*'s defense, other non-*Times* reviews of the Jones-Tifft book and the Quindlen novel were mild to positive. Also, Jones and Quindlen were among the star journalists in their fields; they had earned the attention. Jones in particular steered a judicious course during the decade he reported on the American press for the *Times*, and on some of the *Times*' negotiations with its unions. It would have been wrong of the *Times* to penalize Jones or Quindlen for their *Times* connection by ignoring their books. By the same standard, however, did the *Times* connection require a reward so prominently placed?

Careful readers of the *Book Review* noted an exception to the care extended to family. *Times* reporter Richard Severo was coauthor of *The Wages of War*, a journalistic history covering two centuries of U.S. government neglect of veterans (Severo's coauthor, Lewis Milford, a lawyer, represented Vietnam veterans in the Agent Orange cases). *The Wages of War* came out in the spring of 1989. The reviewer for the *Washington Post* called the book "a vivid, factual picture" of the way veterans had been treated; the *Houston Chronicle* described it as "the definitive work" on the subject. The *New York Review of Books* judged it "powerful." Only the *Book Review* among major publications managed a negative note. The *Book Review* assigned *The Wages of War* to Michael S. Sherry, a professor of history at Northwestern, who criticized the authors' "overwrought style of storytelling" and their "shock value" approach. Severo, of course, was the *Times*' hard case, sentenced to duty on the obit desk after his well-publicized conflicts with senior management. He regarded the Sherry review as one more payback for his intransigence. One need not be a paranoid to suspect that when the assigning editors gave the Severo book to an academic historian, they could well have guessed he would turn up his doctoral nose at a journalistic effort to write history. Again, though, nothing can be proved in court.

Some outcomes are much easier to forecast. In September 1992, Alex Jones resigned from the *Times* in order to work with Susan Tifft on an authorized history of the Ochs-Sulzberger family for Little,

Brown & Company. A short article in the *Times* reported that Jones and Tifft had been granted "complete, exclusive, and unconditional access to family members and archives . . . the first time the family had granted such access." The book is scheduled for publication in the summer of 1996, to mark the one hundredth anniversary of Ochs's purchase of the *Times*. It takes no great powers of prediction to envision the *Book Review* of August 18, 1996: The front page and two inside pages are devoted to a review of the Jones-Tifft book; the photograph shows Punch and Arthur Sulzberger standing in the *Times* boardroom with the oil painting of Adolph Ochs behind them. The reviewer is a tenured professor of history whose name is familiar to *Times* readers; his own books have been well received by the *Times*. The reviewer thinks the Ochs-Sulzberger family book is an engrossing social document, and entertaining as well, a great American success story.

If one feature of the *Book Review* could be taken as representative of the *Times*' self-regard and incorruptible "standards," it is the *Times* Best Sellers list. Actually there are six such lists—for hardcover fiction, hardcover non-fiction, hardcover "advice, how to and miscellaneous," paperback fiction, paperback nonfiction, and paperback "advice, how to and miscellaneous." The best-seller lists stand at that dizzying freeway interchange of art and commerce, journalism and public opinion polling. The lists were checked out by readers—curious about how their tastes might match those of the vox populi—and they were avidly studied by people in the book business. A mention on the *Times* list, wrote the novelist William Peter Blatty, means "discounts and displays of your book and free hype." Blatty was the author of *The Exorcist*, a mega-seller of the 1970s (made into a motion picture). He also wrote a novel called *Legion*, which didn't make the *Times* Best Sellers list in the early summer of 1983, when Blatty first checked. He had expected to see it there because Michael Korda, his editor at Simon & Schuster, assured him that *Legion* was selling at the rate of fifteen thousand books a week. Indeed, it sold more books than another S&S book that *was* on the *Times* list. According to Blatty, Korda also told him that the *Times*' "computerized system" for determining its best-seller lists had some very human and self-fulfilling features.

First, the *Times* mailed report sheets to its sample of two thousand bookstores across the country. The sheets had an introduction that stated: "Below are listed 36 titles which, on the basis of our most recent information, are contenders for the Best Sellers list." The bookstores were then supposed to provide the sales figures for each title. The report forms allowed space at the bottom for "write-ins"—books that eventually could be contenders and then actual best-sellers. Blatty took this thirty-six title format to mean that the *Times* data collectors were prompting the stores. He was implying that the *Times* was tilting in the interests of one book, rather than just behaving as bureaucrats (the prompts, it would be argued, sped the preparation of the lists and made the paperwork more efficient). Second, and equally upsetting to Blatty and Korda, the *Book Review* pollers—members of the same *Times* desk that managed the paper's political surveys—"scientifically weighted" the raw figures to adjust for underrepresented parts of the survey "universe" (just as they did with various demographic groups when polling voters during presidential campaigns).

Blatty also disclosed that Korda and Richard Snyder, president of S&S at the time, took the extraordinary step of calling on the *Book Review* editors, and showing them the sales figures for *Legion*. According to Blatty, he was warned by Korda: "The *Times* can be very vindictive, don't tell anyone we have had this conversation." The S&S people had to deal with the *Book Review* regularly; Blatty had less interest in accommodation. He sued the *Times* in the Superior Court of California, County of Los Angeles (where he resided). The suit accused the *Book Review* of false and misleading advertising—calling its list "scientific." Blatty asked for $3 million in damages. The depositions and court documents still make engrossing reading today, a decade later. Blatty wanted the court to compel the *Times* to provide the raw sales figures that were the starting point for the weighing. The *Times* attorneys, Gibson, Dunn and Crutcher, argued that the procedures of the list makers constituted "a trade secret." Moreover, the *Times* lawyers called the suit "frivolous" and spoke of its chilling effect on the first amendment (in the Pentagon Papers case, the *Times* lawyers had argued for publication of "trade secrets"). The lawyers suggested Blatty cooked up the suit to get publicity for *Legion*. Beyond the name-calling, some revealing information came out. The court depositions pointed to a process that gave more weight to sales at independent (privately owned) bookstores than to the big chains such as B. Dalton and Waldenbooks. And Blatty testified that Korda told him no one at Simon & Schuster would talk about their contacts with the

Times "on the subject of *Legion's* exclusion from the Best Sellers list unless they were subpoenaed."

In August 1984, the superior court judge in Santa Monica dismissed the suit. Blatty, however, savored a minor victory in the pages of the *Book Review*. The tiny type under the names of the best-sellers explained that the list was based on "computer-processed sales figures." After the Santa Monica case, the *Times* inserted the phrase "statistically adjusted" just in front of the word "sales."

There were other changes in the years since Blatty's lawsuit. By the summer of 1992, the best-seller universe had been increased to encompass 3,050 bookstores, as well as "representative wholesalers with more than 28,000 other retail outlets, including variety stores and supermarkets." The list of bookstores and wholesalers was still classified as a trade secret, as was the weighting process and the data collectors' method of "balancing" chains and independents. Inquiring reporters from time to time breached the wall of secrecy. The writer David Blum reported that some of his publishing sources "think they have a pretty good idea which independent bookstores the *Times* weights most heavily." Blum's list included Endicott Booksellers and the two Shakespeare & Co. stores in New York, the Harvard Co-op in Boston, Kramerbooks in Washington, D.C., The Tattered Cover in Denver, Cody's in Berkeley, Powell's in Portland, and Oxford Books in Atlanta. These would be the stores to start with "if you're thinking of outfoxing the *Times* best-seller system," Blum offered lightly. Blum's investigation was prompted in part by the best-sellerdom of Allan Bloom's gloomy 1988 tract, *The Closing of the American Mind*. The initial printing was only ten thousand books, and many of those books were not yet in bookstores when Christopher Lehmann-Haupt gave Bloom a good review in the daily *Times*. "The strangest thing happened: All of a sudden *The Closing of the American Mind* showed up on the *New York Times* best-seller list." Blum was mystified by Bloom. "The only logical explanation" Blum could find was that the book had done "incredibly well at a few bookstores that the *New York Times* weighs heavily in its survey."

One year after the publication of Blum's throwaway advice on how to tip the *Times'* weighting scales, the *Washington Post* published a page-one investigative report about precisely one such apparently successful tipping. Allen H. Neuharth, the high-profile former chairman of the Gannett newspaper chain, wrote his autobiography, *Confessions of an S.O.B.* (many of the "confessions" described how smart Neu-harth was). The book made the *Times* Best Sellers list for seven weeks. According to the *Post*, the Gannett Foundation, a nonprofit education fund headed by Neuharth since his retirement, spent $40,000 to pur-chase two thousand copies of the book when it was published in the fall of 1989. Rather than make the purchase from the publisher in bulk, as large organizations usually do, foundation officials approached the editors at some of Gannett's eighty-one daily newspapers throughout the country and asked them to buy copies of the book in the editors' cities. After the *Post* story appeared, a publishing source told reporter Clare McHugh of the *New York Observer* that, considering it costs $19,000 to buy a full-page ad in the *Book Review*—which may or may not help sales—"sending employees out with $19,000 to buy copies of the books makes sense."

Times editors could appreciate such a straight cost-benefit analysis, if not welcome it. The *Book Review* licenses the *Times* Best Sellers logo and reproductions and blowups of its lists throughout the country as part of the paper's advertising, display, and promotional efforts. "Such activities," Blatty declared in a sworn statement, "are undertaken to enhance the *Times*, to encourage advertising and subscriptions, and to otherwise increase the profits for the New York Times Company." So much for the *Book Review* as a "tweedy backwater."

A DAY IN THE LIFE
10:00 P.M.—7:30 A.M.

10:00 P.M.

Times reporter Michael Martinez, assigned to the Yankees in Florida, reached former Yankees manager Lou Piniella by phone at Piniella's restaurant in Woodbridge, New Jersey, a few miles across the Hudson from the *Times* offices. Piniella confirmed the story of players' drinking on airplane flights, but denied it had cost his old team the pennant: "I can give you ten reasons why we lost, and drinking wasn't one of them," he told Martinez. The reporter phoned in the quote and other details to the sports desk. Winfield deleted the fudge-phrase "a Yankee official" in Mar-tinez's first edition story, and substituted Piniella's name as the source of confirmation. Winfield was pleased that readers of the second edition would get a more *Times*-like account of the Yan-kee's troubles, one complete with attribution.

Winfield encountered, in his words, "the first glitch of the night." The *Times* photographer that sports thought was assigned to the Devils game at the Meadowlands in New Jersey had instead been sent by the photo department to cover a tribute to the actor Sidney Poitier at the Waldorf-Astoria. The department failed to tell the sports desk of the switch. The Associated Press promised Winfield it would cover for the *Times.*

10:20 P.M.

No Devils picture arrived from the AP, so Winfield instead picked an AP photo from the Islanders game. Because the two stories were both planned for the upper half of the second sports page, the Islanders photo fitted with no difficulty.

The National edition closed, unfortunately, before David Jones had the Chicago Democratic primary results in hand. Richard M. Daley, son of Richard J. "Boss" Daley, won over the black incumbent, Acting Mayor Eugene Sawyer. The account, by Chicago bureau correspondent Dirk Johnson, arrived in time for the late city edition sold in New York. It also made the National editions printed via satellite on the West Coast, thanks to the three-hour time difference. Perversely, the news came too late to make the satellite edition printed in Chicago. As a result, *Times* subscribers in Los Angeles and San Francisco read of Daley's victory in their editions while Chicago readers did not.

11:20 P.M.

The Sports Department neared deadline for the second edition. Final copy for the Islanders game was not yet in. Robin Finn, the *Times* sportswriter assigned to the team, completed her running story—the chronological account of the game filed in takes to the sports desk. She began to write a compete sub: a fresh story.

The desk processed wire-service results of the night's basketball games for the agate page—the page with all the sports scores. The agate page closed at 11:31, one minute after the nominal deadline. Two pages of the four-page section were left to close. The Sports Department would miss its deadline for the second edition, Winfield acknowledged, "by a regrettable but acceptable four minutes."

11:34 P.M.

The real deadline. The second edition closed, with the turnaround desk's changes, including Chicago primary results and some sports scores.

12:00 midnight

The nightly "postscript" for the National edition. Postscript was *Times* talk for a brief interruption of the press run—rather than stopping the presses to plate a fresh edition—in order to make corrections, or insert late sports news, or update page-one stories.

1:28 A.M.

All sports copy set, including the complete sub from Islanders' reporter Finn. The final, or Late City edition, sports pages closed, with seventeen minutes to spare. Winfield gave a "good night" in sports.

1:30 A.M.

Hold it. Winfield spotted the wrong score for the Devils game in the final page proofs. The sports desk killed the page, and placed the proper score in the proper place by 1:40 A.M., still with five minutes to spare.

1:45 A.M.

Deadline. The third, or Late City, edition closed, on time. Now, a real Good Night for the desk editors. The printers began the final press run, signaled by the alternating green- and red-flashing lights and clanging bells in the pressroom.

2:00 A.M.

The New York Area edition of the *Times* of March 1, 1989, began streaming off the presses.

6:00 A.M.

Early Wednesday morning, before catching the 10:00 A.M. flight from Boston to Washington, Anthony Lewis redid his column. He dropped the reference to the Suciu case, promising himself to take it up at some later date. On the flight down to National Airport, Lewis wrote in longhand, on a yellow legal pad. Later in the morning, he turned in his finished column at the Washington bureau.

7:30 A.M.

The digital electric clock above the entrance of the Times Building flashed the hour and minute. From a row of four metal poles flew the flags of the United States, New York State, New York City, and the *New York Times*. The *Times* flag was a crisp white banner with the blue letters *NYT* emblazoned on it. Spotlights were trained on all four flags. A security guard at the entrance explained the etiquette; if the flag of the United States is kept lighted, it can remain flying through the night. Albin Krebs, finishing his career at the *Times*, listened to the explanation and looked at the four flags a long moment. How appropriate, he said, as much to himself as to his companion, that the *Times* has a flag, and that it is treated like Old Glory, "because the *Times* is a country itself."

12

Old Times, New Times

In April 1991, Anna Quindlen did something that *New York Times* columnists never do. She used her "Public & Private" column on the Op-Ed page to attack directly the editors of the *Times*. Specifically, she criticized the editors' treatment of Patricia Bowman, the woman who had accused William Smith of sexual assault in the "Palm Beach rape case." Quindlen wrote that the *Times*' news coverage of the woman's story—which used Bowman's name and recounted her bad-driver's record and sexual history ("she had a little wild streak," the story noted)—was "beneath the traditions" of the paper. Quindlen also accused the editors, in their own paper, of sexism and snobbery and of being voyeurs in the bargain. The editors were not named; but everyone in the *Times* newsroom knew that Max Frankel had initiated the story and that Al Siegal had supervised the editing as the copy moved toward deadline. Quindlen's column appeared in the Sunday editions of April 21; as is the custom of the Op-Ed page, Quindlen wrote the headline over the column herself. "A Mistake," it read.

The next morning, Quindlen arrived at work to find the *Times* staff divided and hesitant about how to respond to "A Mistake." Half the newsroom, seemingly, agreed with her criticisms. "The other half," Quindlen recalls, "thought I made a big mistake to air the *Times*' business." Then Arthur Ochs Sulzberger, Jr., visited the newsroom and sent everyone a strong signal. He passed Quindlen in an aisleway and, in a voice loud enough for a dozen witnesses to hear, complimented her on the column. It was important that she had spoken out the way she did, he told her.

Arthur Sulzberger's message to the staff went beyond the specifics of the column, and the broader feminist issues that Quindlen said she wanted to raise. At the time the column appeared, Arthur was listed as deputy publisher on the *Times'* masthead. His father, Arthur O. Sulzberger, Sr., held the title of publisher. In fact, Arthur had been running the *Times* day to day since late 1988, and eight months after the Palm Beach rape story roiled the newsroom, Arthur was formally designated publisher by the *Times'* board of directors, which included his father and his three aunts. Punch Sulzberger kept the title of chairman and CEO of the Times Company. To emphasize the *Times'* continuity along with the passing of authority, father and son invited a small group of reporters from other publications (and one official *Times* photographer), to the boardroom for a brief news conference on January 16, 1992. The Sulzbergers posed together under the oil portrait of Adolph Ochs, Arthur's great-grandfather. The son stood four inches taller than the father, his attractive, unlined face and full head of dark, curly hair contrasting with the pale, balding older man.

Whether Arthur Sulzberger's *Times* will be better or worse than the one his father supervised over the last quarter of a century is unclear. Certainly, it will be a different *Times*. The personalities and generational attitudes of the two men were different, as was the marketplace in which each found himself operating. The father left the affairs of the paper in order; the Adolph Ochs family, owners of the *Times* since the last years of the nineteenth century, would continue in control well into the twenty-first century. But the father's prudence could extend only so far. For all the forward planning, no one foresaw the severe economic downturn in the *Times'* business fortunes and the major internal effort to restructure the institutional *Times* in response to changes in the media landscape.

Punch Sulzberger began as the accidental publisher, elevated only because of the illness of his father and the death of his brother-in-law. Punch Sulzberger learned the business on the job, and exercised his authority ad hoc. "I read stories like any other *Times* subscriber, when the paper came out," he said. "Then if I wanted to, I'd pick up the phone and discuss the directions we're going in with the editor." He believed in the *Times* hierarchy, and dealt mostly with his executive editors—successively, Turner Catledge, A. M. Rosenthal, and Max Frankel. There are *Times* writers who in twenty-five years never heard from Punch Sulzberger, pre- or post-publication. By contrast, young Arthur Sulzberger quickly demonstrated, through highly visible episodes such as the one involving Quindlen, that he intended to be a hands-on, involved proprietor.

Unlike his father's, Arthur's ambitions became focused at a truly tender age. His succession was never considered inevitable, even though he was the sole Sulzberger son. For one, after his parents' divorce in 1956, when he was five years old, he lived with his mother, Barbara Grant Sulzberger. He was brought up as an Episcopalian, the religion of his mother, and was confirmed at that Upper East Side redoubt of proper churchmanship, St. James. At the age of fourteen, in an act of adult resolve, the boy decided to leave his mother's house and move in with his father. He left his religion as well as part of his past behind. In a conversation with Ari L. Goldman, the religion correspondent for the *Times*, Arthur Sulzberger explained his "betwixt and between state"—that is, a member of a Jewish family raised as an Episcoplian, who now, as an adult, observes neither religion. Arthur told Goldman, "ninety-nine out of one hundred people consider me Jewish. How could a Sulzberger not be Jewish?"

At the beginning of the long process of preparation to succeed his father, Arthur Sulzberger took his service as heir apparent seriously. There were no make-work assignments, or time spent inspecting building steam pipes. His first job was as a reporter for the *Times* . . . of Raleigh, North Carolina. From there, he went to the Associated Press in London and then to the *New York Times* Washington bureau. In the early 1980s, he went to New York to join the metro desk as a reporter. He got a ground-level view of the city. One of his more memorable pieces was an on-scene report of an abandoned brownstone in the Park Slope neighborhood of Brooklyn. The floorboards were ripped out and a bathtub pillaged and its cast-iron pipes broken "so the lead joints"—worth pennies each—"could be taken." As publisher, Arthur sometimes acted as if he were still in the newsroom. He had a core of reporter-pals from his days in the Washington bureau and on the metro desk. While he was still deputy publisher, he arranged a series of social dinners with small groups of *Times*people, typically, the younger reporters who were his contemporaries, men and women in their thirties and early forties. He impressed an acquaintance at the time as "a take-charge command guy; if possible, he wanted to get to know all one thousand people in the news department." Obviously, the acquaintance added, "as a Sulzberger and as the publisher, he can no longer be just one of the boys and girls."

When friends and associates described Arthur Sulzberger, certain adjectives kept coming up. He was called caring and ruthless, by the same former metro reporter in the same sentence. In private conversation, he could be very funny and fast on his feet. If his self-confident manner sometimes shaded into arrogance, there was a good reason: He was extraordinarily well prepared for the publisher's job, which he sensed was due him before late middle age. After his tours as a reporter, he crossed over to the business side in New York, working in advertising—making sales calls to corporate customers—and then in the circulation and production departments. People who claim to know say he is smarter than his father, or any of the Sulzberger cousins who, in theory, had a claim on the succession. Most of all, Arthur Sulzberger was a man of his generation. He wore his hair long as an undergraduate at Tufts, and owned a black leather jacket and a motorcycle. Like so many other children of the era, he trimmed the hair, married, and settled down. He and his wife, Gail Gregg, now live in an apartment building on Central Park West. Arthur helps out in the raising of their two young children, and was supportive of Gregg's decision to undertake a new career as an artist and painter. Anna Quindlen, who counted both Gregg and Arthur Sulzberger as friends, describes him as "a feminist." As she explained it, "He comes to feminism by virtue of his age. He belongs to that generation of men, like my husband, who willingly pitch in at home."

The responsibilities of running a newspaper with annual revenues of over $1 billion inhibited Arthur Sulzberger from being too openly New Age. Still, though he operated within the institutional imperatives of the *Times*, he showed that he could be sensitive to his surroundings, and to other people. "The Oldthink at this place tends not to worry about morale, or about how the staff feels," Quindlen explained. "Miserable was best." When Quindlen was thinking about leaving the *Times* after the birth of her third child, Arthur Sulzberger worked out the arrangements for the Op-Ed column. According to Quindlen, "His attitude was, 'Let's find arrangements that are mutually beneficial for the individual and the company.' " At the same time, however,

Arthur Sulzberger showed his reverence for the tools of market re-search—also a generational characteristic—and the other currently fashionable mechanistic approaches to modern journalism. His absorption with profit margins demonstrated that he could count beans as well as any MBA. "Arthur wanted those earnings-to-revenues margins of 17 and 18 percent annually for the *Times*," says Albert Scardino, who left the *Times* in late 1989 to become press secretary to New York City mayor David Dinkins.

During Arthur Sulzberger's tenure as deputy publisher, the news-room—and careful readers of the paper—were alert for clues to how he would run the *Times* of the twenty-first century. His public alliance with Quindlen carried the unmistakable message that he intended to be an activist publisher. Granted, the Palm Beach rape story was a monumentally obvious lapse in editorial judgment; it created a huge outcry, outside and inside the *Times*. It didn't require extraordinary courage to take a high-profile stand against such smarmy journalism. Upper management couldn't ignore the angry, closed-door confer-ences among some of the *Times'* top women editors, or the staff peti-tions of protest (which culminated in a tumultuous lunchtime meeting that filled the tenth-floor auditorium). The senior editors, principally Max Frankel, apologized for the rape story twice, once to the staff and then to the readers in an "Editors' Note."

But there were other clear signals that Arthur Sulzberger intended to put his own, activist mark on the *Times'* news pages and its business operations. He publicly announced his commitment to "diversity in the newsroom," and instructed his editors to follow a policy of affir-mative action, hiring women, African-Americans, Hispanics, and Asians whenever possible. Quietly, he extended his idea of diversity to include homosexual men and women, a minority that in the past felt the need to remain closeted at the *Times*. "We can no longer offer our readers a predominantly white, straight, male vision of events and say we're doing our job," he declared in the early summer of 1992. He also put his money quite literally where his mouth was, promising that he would provide *Times* health insurance and other benefits to employees living in "gay partnerships." In the first months after Arthur became publisher, several *Times*people, among them the reporter David Dun-lap, the photographer Sara Krulwich, and the advertising columnist Stuart Elliott, identified themselves with the newly formed organiza-tion, the National Lesbian and Gay Journalists Association. The gay-oriented magazine QW devoted a two-part series to what it called "The Lavender Revolution" at the *Times*.

Arthur Sulzberger's affirmative-action policies were sometimes mocked by the *Times'* more traditional hires, whether the old CCNY crowd or the newer Ivy League recruits. The most common complaint was that women and minorities were being promoted to midlevel and senior editing positions while they were a few years away from such leadership roles. One reporter lowered his voice and said of a Style section editor: "By talent, she's still just at the copy editor level." Each promotion contributed to the epidemic of title-itis throughout the paper. Arthur Sulzberger and his editor Frankel created two dozen sections, subsections, desks, subject "clusters" (media, fashion, law, education, etc.), and new administrative functions—each with an editor and deputy editor and, sometimes, an assistant to the editor *and* an assistant to the deputy editor. One of the cluster editors, Martin Arnold of the media desk, was credited for telling a joke on himself: the *Times* was creating so many new managerial positions that the newsroom would eventually resemble an inverse pyramid—one lone reporter working for 999 editors.

Arthur Sulzberger showed no inclination of retreating from his social agenda. "The old guard kept saying, 'It's a passing thing. He's young. He'll get over all this diversity talk the longer he's publisher,' " said Lena Williams, a black reporter on the metro desk. "But he's serious and committed about affirmative action. He's not 'getting over it.' " In July 1991, less than three months after Arthur Sulzberger praised the Quindlen column, he sent another strong public signal to the staff. In Kansas City, at the annual meeting of the National Association of Black Journalists, Arthur Sulzberger was the host at an elegant luncheon for two thousand NABJ delegates and their guests. He spoke of the current hard climate for racial change, and of the economic and political roadblocks to "our cause" of creating more jobs for minorities in the newsroom. "Keep pushing," he told the NABJ, "keep pushing to turn your vision of diversity into our reality." Racist practices in journalism did not normally occupy the attention of members of the 99.44 percent white-male American Newspaper Publishers Association. Newspaper publishers' energies, in the best of circumstances, tended to go into gentrified campaigns such as new convention centers, local airport expansion, and similar good works of the business classes. When Arthur made "our cause" of diversity his principal

ANPA activity, his out-front activism was a break with the ANPA's past as well as the *Times'*. The principal beneficiary of Punch Sulzberger's civic service was the Metropolitan Museum of Art.

Despite the newsroom sniping, the *Times'* overall record for hiring and promoting minorities improved. Women in particular were moved forward. Some of the *Times'* life-style departments had been for a long time run by women editors, a tradition dating from the days when there was a segregated Women's Page in American newspapers. The putatively more serious international and national news pages were considered male preserves (a "news gender gap" still dates from these practices: market surveys conducted in 1991 showed that men were more likely to be daily newspaper readers than women, by about four percentage points). A dozen women moved into previously male-dominated senior positions in the news department. In 1988 Rebecca Sinkler, then fifty-four, became the first woman to edit the *Book Review*. Two years later, Carolyn Lee, forty-four, was named an assistant managing editor, sexually integrating the news department names carried in "the box," the list of *Times* senior editors that appeared daily on the editorial-page masthead. Both Lee and Sinkler came to the *Times* in mid-career, after experience at other newspapers—the institutional *Times* itself had no coherent policy of preparing women for senior editing posts. Under Arthur Sulzberger that began to change, too. In the past, assignments that generated page-one bylines were a fast track upward for ambitious male reporters; a run of good stories inevitably raised one's visibility. At the start of the 1992 presidential campaign, the *Times* named twelve people to high-profile assignments covering the candidates and politics. Six were women; three were African-Americans.

At the same time, Arthur Sulzberger sent other, more ambiguous, signals about the direction he wanted to take the *Times*. In the mid-1980s, his father and Walter Mattson raised the *Times'* profits-to-revenues ratio to the newspaper industry's desired 15 to 20 percent annual figure. By 1991, with Arthur in day-to-day charge of the *Times*, the ratio had fallen back to around 5 percent. While annual revenues held fairly steady, operating expenses kept rising, and the Times Company's net income declined from $167,680,000 in 1988 to $44,709,000 in 1992. Arthur Sulzberger could not be held responsible for the national recession and the *Times'* consequent loss of advertising; the demise of important retailers like Alexander's and B. Altman's was not his fault. The *Times'* internal business affairs did come under his control. He let it be known that he wouldn't shrink from the management "efficiencies"—that is, staff cuts, salary caps, tougher work rules—the *Times* said it needed to hold down costs. "All around us we see once prosperous businesses failing or coming close to failing," he told the *Times* staff on April 7, 1992. "This newspaper will not be among them." He cast around for further efficiencies in the *Times'* business affairs, aided by the marketing theorist W. Edwards Deming. Deming, "the nation's preeminent quality pioneer."

The retreats of 1992 and 1993 were only the visible tip of the Deming iceberg at the *Times.* Arthur organized no fewer than seven employee-management committees to spread the teachings of Deming throughout the paper. *Times*people mastered a Demingistic vocabulary ("process-oriented management," "holistic vision") and learned the value of "the three virtues" of self-esteem, intrinsic motivation, and the curiosity to learn. They also picked up the rather unsettling news that when companies were Demingized they became "leaner and flatter." That is, they got along with fewer employees. Most important of all, Demingism meshed neatly with the strategy of a reader-friendly *Times.* Beneath the blather was a doctrine attuned to the marketplace, "a single holistic victim of anticipating and meeting the desires of the customer." When the in-house company newsletter, *Times Talk*, carried a report of the meetings, it used the Dylanesque heading "The Times, They Are A-changin'." The Deming lectures were not totally hot-air exercises; staff attendees at one all-day session received a catered lunch, and a briefing on the new Edison, New Jersey, printing plant. "The food was terrible," the cultural reporter Grace Glueck noted tartly, "but it was nice to hear of our future plans from the company rather than reading about them in the *Village Voice.*"

Arthur's faith in managerial bromides, like his father's before him, seemed harmless enough (except perhaps for employees like Glueck who were given retirement packages in the interests of a "leaner, flatter" *Times*). More unsettling were the long-range plans for the editorial content of the *Times.* The search for reader-friendly formulas at times sounded hostile to the physical existence of the newspaper itself. The fault was not entirely the *Times'.* Try as Arthur Sulzberger and his editors did to reach out and engage the reader, there were people who didn't return the compliment. The *Times'* market research kept coming upon the infamous aliterate American, twentysomething men and women who could read but didn't. Yes, the times were a-changin'. How much would the *Times* have to change as well?

Arthur Sulzberger and his lieutenants began talking up the importance of creating new "products." The Times Company needed to adopt "the thinking habits" of a larger corporation. Arthur's ongoing subcommittees on the future—in some respects, the son *was* like the father—began to act as if print were passé. If the newspaper of the future finally deaggregated into electronic data bases, then the *Times* had to be ready with its own array of marketable products. As Jack Rosenthal had asked, rhetorically, "Who said information must come in the format of a newspaper?" At one point, of course, the *Times* was involved with the new information media. In the 1980s it owned one of the premium cable-television systems in the country, NYT Cable in southern New Jersey. The securities analysts considered NYT Cable an attractive property; the system was equipped with the latest addressable-converter equipment, and it served a growing suburban audience. Yet in 1988 the *Times* sold NYT Cable, and walked away from its high-tech product line. Punch Sulzberger explained at the time that the company wanted "to focus our efforts on our core businesses." When Punch Sulzberger's father sold off the *Times*' facsimile business thirty years before, he cited that same intention to concentrate on the core paper. At the beginning of 1993, the Times Company owned thirty-one small- to modest-sized regional newspapers and published seventeen average-to-good-magazines, including *Family Circle* and *McCalls*; it also owned a group of television stations, mainly in smaller Southern markets. But the core of the core business was, obviously, the *New York Times* newspaper.

As Punch Sulzberger and Walt Mattson shifted company strategy away from the new media of cable, they put greater resources into the National edition of the *Times*. Although they were not exactly turning their backs on the "basic" *Times* newspaper distributed in New York City, the surrounding suburbs, and the Northeast region, Boston to Washington, the planning committees had concluded that further advertising and circulation gains in these areas were unlikely. The proposed acquisition of the *Boston Globe* in mid-1993 was further confirmation of the national strategy, and the belief that the "basic" *Times* was reaching its upper limits of growth. Consequently, if you can't lick 'em, join 'em.

The soft consumerist sections of the 1970s had attracted the upmarket New Yorkers and suburbanites needed to keep the *Times* financially and journalistically healthy. By the late 1980s, however, the city's population growth and its economic activity slowed. In the four decades since 1950 New York City lost 7 percent of its population, from 7.9 million to 7.3 million in 1990. While New York had to give up congressional seats, California, Texas, and Florida were gaining new seats. As New York appeared to stagnate, Sunbelt cities reached double digit growth rates; Los Angeles and San Francisco became, respectively, the nation's number-two and number-four metropolitan areas in population. Punch Sulzberger decided that the *Times* would reach out to its kind of readers no matter how far they lived from West 43rd Street. He was being prudent; but it still looked like the *Times* was joining an exodus from New York, along with Fortune 500 corporations relocating to low-tax states and a middle class in flight from an increasingly nonwhite city.

The new strategy became evident as early as 1988, when the *Times* began publishing three editions. The "basic" paper, the New York *New York Times*, was the four-section edition available in the city, the suburbs, and along the East Coast. It sold some 900,000 copies on weekdays. Even this paper was no longer city-specific; a majority of its readers lived outside the five boroughs. A second *Times*, the National edition, was the two-section paper beamed by satellite to five printing plants around the country. It sold 140,000 copies weekdays. The first section was composed of international and national news, plus one page of news of the New York metropolitan region, edited down from the basic paper. The second section led with material culled from the Business Day pages; a digest of the "basic" paper's coverage of culture, life-style, and sports followed. The third *Times* version was the California edition, a three-section daily also transmitted by satellite and printed at three West Coast plants. The added section, the Living Arts, offered a somewhat wider selection from the *Times*' cultural and consumer-service features. The California edition was introduced cautiously, like a swimmer testing the cold Pacific waters. Distribution began in the San Francisco Bay area in April, 1988, followed by expansion to Los Angeles, San Diego, Santa Barbara, and the Tacoma-Portland region. After more testing, the Living Arts idea was incorporated into the National edition and all eight satellite plants began distributing a three-section *Times*. The National edition staff learned how to think in "non–New York" terms. Copy editors were reminded by Al Siegal, the keeper of *Times* style, that a reference to "the mayor" could mean Tom Bradley to some readers while "upstate" might signify Northern Michigan for others. A story about a ballet company's plans could no longer refer to "a national five-city tour. . . ." The cities had to be specified. The play of page-one news often was different in the National edition; one typical morning, a major development involving the Shoreham nuclear plant on Long Island was the lead story in the "basic" New York paper, while the National edition editors consigned Shoreham to the bottom of their first page.

The *Times* invested $10 million in 1988 alone in the three-section California edition. Promotion efforts included an extensive television and billboard campaign in Los Angeles and San Francisco, and introductory subscriptions at half the newsstand price of 50 cents. The circulation department sponsored West Coast cultural events to give the paper visibility among potential readers and advertisers; a program note for the opening night of *Swan Lake* at the San Francisco Ballet called discreet attention to the *Times'* financial contribution. The *Times* also helped underwrite the fourth annual Moving Pictures Ball, honoring Steven Spielberg, in Los Angeles. The West Coast efforts produced modest results. Circulation in the San Francisco area increased from 18,000 to 31,000 the first year, while in the Los Angeles area, including Orange County, circulation went from 12,500 to 21,000. The numbers translated to about $454 in promotion and other expenditures for each new reader gained, a very high price to pay. On the other hand, these readers had the same desirable demographic profile found in readers of the "basic" New York edition.

The new strategy was correct in its assumption that thousands of professional men and women around the country wanted the *Times*. National advertisers were harder to find. The National edition was an aesthetic success: a smart, good-looking, fast-reading product, a compact version of the basic paper without—bluntly—too much of the crime, grime, and race tensions of the city. But it wasn't the engine for company growth that management initially envisioned. In fact, it wasn't making money at all. By 1991 some 250,000 upmarket people were reading the National edition; some special-interest advertisers, like book publishers, found the paper useful. The advertising-agency space buyers for such big-ticket products as automobiles, computers, and financial services were less impressed; they decided that a national *Times* didn't make good sense for them. From their point of view, they could reach almost two million readers for their clients in either of the other two national newspapers, the *Wall Street Journal* and *USA Today*; similarly, the newsweeklies, *U. S. News & World Report*, *Time*, and *Newsweek*, offered readerships ten to twenty times larger than that of the *Times*. As demographically desirable as the National edition audience was, the Sulzbergers' planning committees had to consider the strong possibility that it had a limited future; it might never be attractive for national advertisers until its circulation doubled.

The planning committees now reported to Arthur Sulzberger. They told him what he already knew: The expansionist 1980s were over. The *Times* newspaper "will probably never reclaim the dominance it had" in that gilded decade, suggested a *Times* internal document circulated in May 1992, four months after Arthur Sulzberger was named publisher. "We need to invest time and effort on the *Times*' other business. A considerable portion of our resources will be dedicated to pursuing other revenue opportunities." Arthur Sulzberger put the same conclusion in more direct terms: "The painful economic truth is that we can no longer do business the old way." If escape from New York was no longer possible, then perhaps the future lay in the escape from newsprint, into electronic publishing. The trouble was, when the *Times* ventured down that road with NYT Cable a few years earlier, it decided to turn back. Now it was taking yet another U-turn, slowly to be sure, gingerly exploring the on-line future with 900 numbers for crossword-puzzle clues, sports scores, and weather forecasts. It did not escape notice that the *Times*' business rivals were moving a bit faster. In 1991 the *Los Angeles Times* began testing two facsimile prototypes, one a six-page edition of late-news made available by fax to opinion makers in Moscow, the other, a "fast-fax" of the prices of the top fifteen stocks, sent out immediately after the 3:00 P.M. closing bells rang at the New York exchanges. In June 1992, Dow Jones & Company, publisher of the *Wall Street Journal*, announced that it was joining with Pacific Bell, the telephone company, to offer the *Daily Reporter*, a form of "voice mail news." For $2 a month, subscribers to the *Daily Reporter* could punch up the phone company's voice mailbox service and listen to three-minute news summaries—world news headlines, a financial report, and a sports update. The customer who wanted only one news service paid 75 cents a month; by contrast, a one-month subscription to the *Wall Street Journal* newspaper cost around $15. The two companies said that the service could be cus-

tomized to provide more specific kinds of news, depending on subscribers' suggestions. The *Daily Reporter* took reader-friendliness to the
next logical step, borrowing a slogan from the fast-food chains: Have it
your way.

Small and experimental as these projects were, from Arthur's perspective they meant that other media organizations were already testing
new "product." Facing slow-growth with the National *Times* and
uncertain-growth with blue-sky informational services, Arthur reversed
the marketing strategy of the previous decade. His *Times* would look
homeward. It would be a New York City newspaper, with a distinctly
popular appeal, to attract a broader, younger audience. As the 1990s
began, Arthur increased by 50 percent the size of the *Times'* sports
report, making room for more coverage of the local teams, and counting on more sports to bring in younger male readers. He started the
Styles of the *Times* section, with its features devoted to young, Downtown trendoids. And he hired new staff and invested major resources in
expanded coverage of the metropolitan region. These new beats of the
Times, like the people assigned to them, were intended to reflect
"diversity." New York at the time of Arthur's birth was essentially a
white city. In 1951 the population of blacks, Latinos, Asians, and
other non-whites numbered around one million, out of almost eight
million New Yorkers. By Arthur's fortieth birthday, the number of
whites in New York had declined by 50 percent while the non-white
population had increased fourfold. Whites were another one of the
racial minorities in Arthur's New York; the 1990 U.S. census showed
the city to be 43 percent Caucasian, 28 percent black, 24 percent
Latino, and 7 percent Asian (counting some white Hispanics twice).
The newest force in the city were foreign-born immigrants. According
to a city Planning Commission report released in February 1993, there
has been a 25 percent rise in New York's foreign-born population since
1980. As a result, 2.1 million of the city's 7.3 million residents were
born outside the United States—almost one in every three New Yorkers. At the City College of New York, an incubator for generations of
Times readers, as well as a recruiting ground for generations of *Times*
staff, fourteen thousand undergraduate students were registered for
classes in the spring of 1992; more than half of them were born outside
the United States. As Arthur explained to the meeting of black journalists in Kansas City, the *Times* had two good reasons for hiring the

children of the city and its new immigrants: first, the "moral impera-
tives" of affirmative action; second, with the end of "the fat, happy days
of the 1980s, diversity makes good business sense in these current
tough economic times."

The *Times* strategy during the Punch Sulzberger years was based on
an appeal to an affluent audience. The paper enterprisingly adapted to
the television age by developing consumer-oriented features. It transformed itself from a single-buy newsstand newspaper, in large part
dependent on that day's run of news and the local weather conditions,
to a subscription service that followed its readers to their suburban
homes, and in the case of the National edition, to their doorsteps in
Grosse Pointe and Palo Alto. Through those years the *Times* maintained its reputation for strong national and international reporting—
what Punch Sulzberger always referred to as "our franchise, what we
do best." On the day in January 1992 when Punch Sulzberger formally
turned over the title of publisher to his son, circulation was at an
all-time high, with 1.2 million copies sold daily and over 1.6 million
on Sundays. When the *Times* periodically raised its prices during the
Punch Sulzberger years, subscribers dutifully paid their higher bills.
The core audience wasn't put off by price. Explaining this demonstra-
tion of "demand elasticity," Donald Nizen, the former director of
circulation, asked: "When was the last time you heard anyone com-
plain at a dinner party that their copy of the *Times* costs too much?"
Note that in his example, the *Times*' readers weren't making small talk
at a subway station or corner coffee shop; they were not the sort of New
Yorker who fretted over spending a few pennies more a day.

Arthur's resolve to reposition the *Times* on a New York base broke
with the past: The readers he sought were not members of the dinner-
party set. The new populist strategy put one Sulzberger at odds with the
other Sulzberger. Punch Sulzberger had argued that the *Times* couldn't
be local, or too ethnic: "We're not New York's hometown paper.
We're read on Park Avenue but not in Chinatown or the east Bronx.
We have to approach journalism differently than, say, the *Sarasota
Herald Tribune*, where you try to blanket the community." Punch
Sulzberger believed that the *Times* should cover the city, but in its own
way and from the perspective of a class-based readership: "We should
deal with the overall important urban stories that are of interest to
Times readers wherever they live, Palo Alto or 82nd and Fifth."
Arthur's populist *Times* sounded like a violation of the tested form that

made the *Times* "the *Times*." There was an understanding inside the paper of his father that the *Times* was edited by elites for elites; the quality of the metro coverage or the space devoted to sports and the Downtown scene never seemed to matter much. Glory came through the international and national reporting; being read by the people who belonged to the Council of Foreign Relations—or who lived, as Punch Sulzberger did, at 82nd and Fifth—counted more than being read in Bay Ridge. "Our identity has not been primarily geographic, it has been demographic," Max Frankel acknowledged. A reconstituted geographic *Times* was undoubtedly a more attractive alternative for the traditionalists than the deaggregated, 900-number *Times*. Nevertheless, it represents a departure from the elitist past.

The traditional *Times* was a newspaper with a grand mission. In the postwar years of the late 1940s through the 1960s particularly, superpower America had global interests, and the *Times* saw itself as the paper of responsibility, covering the American era. The *Times'* self-importance would have been insufferable if it hadn't been accompanied by a certain sense of redeeming idealism. The lawyer James Goodale remembered that he joined the *Times* in the early 1960s just as the paper was preparing to remake itself. The older vision had not yet faded. Arthur Hays Sulzberger, Punch's father and Arthur's grandfather, wanted the *Times* to help shape American public policy. Arthur Hayes Sulzberger reasoned that no single newspaper, magazine, or radio broadcast between the two World Wars reached a significant number of the opinion elite. And so, in the absence of a nationally formed opinion, the Hitlers and Stalins of the world could rise to power, their manipulative propaganda unchallenged. Similarly, absent a consensus, isolationism and the America First movement thrived in the United States. "Arthur Hays Sulzberger wanted the *Times* to play the role of a great national forum," Goodale said. "Some of us saw that as the *Times'* unique contribution to the world."

By and large, the postwar *Times* delivered: In the earnest pages of the *Times'* Sunday Week in Review section and in the *Times Magazine*, public policy matters were explored for an audience of worldly readers. The *Magazine's* big-picture articles always seemed to be written by Dame Barbara Ward, the British economist; they always seemed to ponder the same grave "challenges" and "issues." But that was part of the point. By the 1990s, in Arthur's day, the big-picture article became . . . big color pictures with modest accompanying text. Warren Hoge, the *Magazine*'s editor in the first years of Arthur's tenure, sped the decline of the Dame Barbara form; the front of the *Magazine* (the letters columns, the ruminative introspection of "About Men") and the back (the outré high-fashion spreads) steadily encroached on the middle well of public policy. Even there, in the center space devoted to the longer articles, the *Magazine* regularly offered one soft feature, usually a personality profile, to provide "balance" for the substantive public-affairs analysis. And even then, the space for think pieces was given over to articles by *Times* staff writers; the number of contributions by policy makers declined.

The old wisdom held that the *Times*' news coverage couldn't be too "popular," and should not try to be. "We're not an easy paper to fall into—you've got to work at it," Punch Sulzberger declared without apologies, toward the end of his term as publisher. When it was suggested to him that one lesson of the uproar caused by "the Florida woman" story might be that *Times* senior editors were too high-minded and "intellectual" to do good tabloid journalism, he replied without missing a beat: "I certainly hope so."

The Newthink wisdom holds that the *Times* should be accessible to those who weren't falling into the paper. Every few months, the *Times* carried lengthy analyses detailing the decline of reading (a variant of the aliterate American form). On successive Sundays in June 1992, two such death-of-print stories appeared. The first, in the *Book Review*, was entitled "The End of Books." Its author, the novelist Robert Coover, said print was "doomed and outdated" and about to be replaced by hypertext, the humming, digitalized language of the new technology, written and read on a computer screen. If Coover intended to be ironic about the glories of hypertext, his irony was so arch that many readers missed it; he sounded serious, and approving. The second article, by the *Times* computer-news specialist John Markoff, appeared in the Business section. Markoff described technologist Roger Fidler's dream of a powerful, portable personal computer that would provide news and interactive information. According to Markoff, "Fidler envisions a row of commuters reaching into their briefcases on their ride to work. Instead of pulling out the morning paper, each grabs a thin tablet-sized computer." Fidler assured *Times* readers that the portable electronic newspaper was just five years away.

When the *Times* wasn't carrying the obituary for the written word, the American Newspaper Publishers Association was pointing its finger at those who killed reading. According to the ANPA, the perpetrators were members of the boomer gang, the generation of 77 million Americans born after World War II. These younger adults were in their peak spending years, raising families and buying homes, the kind of people an advertiser prizes. But they were intent on a life of aliteracy. They regarded reading a newspaper as a "complex and unrewarding activity." Worse, it was a single-dimensional activity; as the media consultant Christine Urban succinctly explained, "You have to sit down to read a newspaper." Busy, pressured boomer people considered it "more efficient" to be engaged in *multi*dimensional activities, simultaneously driving to work and listening to all-news radio, or doing aerobics while watching CNN. Thus, while media expenditures per family increased by 42 percent between 1982 and 1987, most of the money went for purchases of VCRs, cable services, fax machines, and personal computers. Newspaper readership was not keeping up with population growth: The same number of people read a daily paper in the 1990s as in the 1960s, when there were thirty million fewer Americans. Putting the figures another way, in 1967, three quarters of American adults said that they read a newspaper every day; by 1990, the figure had plummeted toward 50 percent. For young adults between the ages of eighteen and twenty-nine—the growing ranks of aliterate Americans—the numbers were even more sobering; roughly two thirds read a paper on a typical day in 1967 compared to 29 percent by 1988.

Younger *Times* reporters and midlevel editors serving on the publishers' planning committees didn't need any more studies to grasp the significance of these generational changes. They looked through the one-way windows at members of focus groups assembled by the *Times*. They listened with growing horror as one after another of the group—people who were their contemporaries, college graduates and professionals—said they had no interest in picking up a copy of the *Times*. Arthur was among the *Times*people who peered through the windows at the focus groups. He knew the survey data. If hypertext concerned him, it was still in the computer hackers' twilight zone. More immediately, he faced the everyday reality that the *Times* was going unattended in its home base, and that the *Times*' New York penetration—the percentage of metropolitan households that bought the paper regularly—was among the lowest of any big-city daily. The *Washington Post* had a penetration of 60 percent; the *Dallas Morning News*, 33 percent; the *Boston Globe*, the *Los Angeles Times*, and the *Chicago*

Tribune, around 23 to 25 percent. In the New York metro area, the *Times'* penetration was 10 percent: just one in ten households took the *Times*. These were upper-end households, and Arthur was glad to have them. But when he looked at New York in the 1990s, he saw a society "where the elites were redefining themselves," and where new elites, including younger New Yorkers and nonwhite arrivals to the city, were developing new interests. Or so the market research said. He feared that if the *Times* stood still, stayed "narrow," or talked only to an aging—and shrinking—elite, then it would no longer be relevant. "We would be serious and unread, like *The New Yorker*." He resolved to change the *Times'* mix of news and features.

Punch Sulzberger's response had been different. "They are scary," he replied, when asked about the aliterates. But he thought that the solution lay with a public and policymakers who "paid more attention to the kind of education young people received." He said nothing about a softer, featurized, friendlier *Times*. Some of the contrasting responses of the old *Times* and the new, the father and the son, were the consequence of generational emphasis; a young publisher's energetic resolve to do something about penetration in a changing market measured against an older man's practiced acceptance of the fact that New York isn't Sarasota, or even Washington. Sulzberger family members always tried to speak with one voice about their *Times* property, but the inevitable strains involved in any passing of institutional authority were intensified by the early 1990s business recession. In 1991 and again in 1992, *Times* advertising lineage continued to drop off in the key categories of retail (the department stores), help wanted, and real estate. The paper's profits fell by a third. The *Times* had hidden annual costs, computer-system upgrades, and replacement of delivery-truck fleets, among other recurring outlays. For a paper the size of the *Times*, these costs ran as high as $50 million a year. They had to be paid for out of earnings. The forecasters told the Sulzbergers that the city was coming out of the recession, "but so slowly that nobody knows it."

Arthur did what executives of most large corporations try to do in tough times. He looked for ways to reduce fixed operating costs. To cut the size of the staff, the *Times* in the summer of 1991 offered buyouts to employees age fifty-five or older and with more than fifteen years' service at the paper.

The buyouts were a civilized preview of the *Times'* bare-knuckle negotiations with its blue-collar unions the following year. Arthur and his chief associate, Lance Primus, concentrated on the three unions representing the pressmen, the mailers (the men who bundle and sort the papers), and the drivers. For years *Times* management sought to change work rules that encouraged featherbedding, routine overtime pay, and "lost" deliveries—bundles of papers that rogue drivers sold to dealers-accomplices and split the cash proceeds from, all at the expense of the *Times*. As usual, the dollar losses from what was "legal" far exceeded what was stolen under the table. For example, in the old days, work crews of ten or more were typically assigned to each printing-press unit at the New York newspapers. In the 1970s and 1980s, advances in technology drastically changed the need for such manning levels for the pressmen (there were no women, or for that matter, no nonwhites, in the union crews). In other cities, where papers operated in non-union shops, without the work rules built up over the years in New York, four- or five-person crews ran a press unit. The same disparities between New York and the rest of the country held for the mailers and drivers. To induce unions to surrender such prerogatives, the *Times* set aside a $30 million fund to buy out the contracts of hundreds of its workers and grant lifetime job security to those who remained.

The *Times'* negotiations with the Newspaper Mail and Deliverers' Union of New York and Vicinity (NMDU)—the truck-drivers union— were from the start complicated by one basic fact: The drivers had the only leverage remaining for the newspaper craft unions in the city. Union conflict was unpleasant and to be avoided by a prudent management. But it was no longer impossible for a strikebound daily to publish: A determined management could use its non-unionized staff and white-collar supervisors to collect some semblance of a news report, physically print the papers, and get them to plant delivery bays. It was something else entirely to truck the papers from the plant to subdistributors for home delivery or for drop-off at some 10,000 newsstands, convenience stores and street boxes in a three state area. The police authorities could not assure the safety of a "strike breaker" in a delivery truck on deserted roads between 3 A.M. and 6 A.M.—even if City Hall was of a mind to confront the unions.

If Arthur did not fully grasp this fact of New York street life, the lesson was brought home during the *Daily News* strike of 1990–91. Then, the *News* hired replacement workers—known, in an earlier day, as scabs—to drive its trucks. People were beaten up and trucks fire-bombed, and the replacement drivers were able to deliver no more than 400,000 copies of the *News* around New York (compared to the prestrike press run of just over one million). As the strike wore on, the police and City Hall felt pressure to maintain some law and order, and the *News'* delivery record improved. But the Tribune company of Chicago, the *News'* absentee owners, basically wanted to walk away from the paper; at the first plausible opportunity, Tribune gave the British press lord (and scoundrel) Robert Maxwell $60 million to take the paper off its hands. The *Times* observed the whole sorry mess and extracted a moral from the story: Someone with a strong enough stomach for conflict could defeat the drivers, eventually. Arthur Sulzberger was not that someone: He was a social progressive. The *Times'* solution, a model of simplicity, consisted of finding a stand-in unconcerned about public image.

Through the 1980s, the *Times* used four delivery services to distribute newspapers in the New York–New Jersey–Connecticut region. In early 1992, Arthur bought out the owners of two of the services. The remaining two services were purchased by a wealthy, tough New Jersey trucking magnate named Arthur Imperatore, who received a loan, with good terms, from the *Times*, in order to complete the deal. By federal law, existing labor contracts do not survive the sale of a property. Imperatore immediately imposed all the new work rules that the *Times*—if it was starting anew—would have most assuredly wanted. When three hundred drivers went out in protest, Imperatore hired replacement workers to do the union men's job, again a management "right" established by federal law (during the 1993–94 congressional session, Liberal Democrats in the House of Representatives tried again to amend the law, which dated from the 1930s). There was sporadic violence, but Imperatore more or less succeeded in making his trucks run on time. The NMDU had the choice: half a loaf (settle and get guaranteed lifetime jobs for some drivers) or nothing at all (stay out and be permanently replaced). The drivers capitulated to Imperatore, and then to the *Times*, giving the paper the money-saving "efficiencies" it sought on its routes. Arthur's liberal image stayed intact. He could claim, narrowly, that the *Times* did not engage in the union-busting tactic of using replacement workers. The other guy, Imperatore, did. The *Times* confidently proclaimed that it had achieved "labor peace through the year 2000."

*   *   *

Something more was on management's mind than a desire for new work contracts, important as they were. In the early 1990s, Arthur's *Times* faced its first real cross-town competition since the best days of the old *Herald Tribune* after World War II. The new competitor was *Newsday*, a daily in the process of transforming itself into a plausible alternative to the *Times*.

The newspaper heiress Alicia Patterson, with financial support from her husband, Captain Harry Guggenheim, started *Newsday* in a garage on Long Island in 1940. Her timing proved exquisite; *Newsday* was in place after World War II when the potato farms of Nassau County were plowed under to make room for the houses of suburbia. As the Levittowns grew, so did *Newsday*. The three million people who live in Nassau-Suffolk counties today make up one of the nation's top ten markets. Her idea of a handy tabloid-size newspaper executed tastefully suited a wide readership: big-city brass muted for the increasingly conservative mood of tract Long Island. Later, two brilliant editors, Bill Moyers and David Laventhol, perfected the form, creating a magazine-style daily journalism that the *Times* belatedly began to imitate. By then, both Guggenheim and Patterson were dead, and their heirs had sold the paper to the Times Mirror Company, publishers of the *Los Angeles Times*. As the 1980s began, *Newsday* was so firmly entrenched on Long Island that Times Mirror decided to expand to the west—it couldn't go any farther east for readers (the next doorstep after Montauk was in Portugal). Laventhol started *New York Newsday* in 1983. Twenty years after the *New York Times* had launched project Westward Ho, its National edition, in the *Los Angeles Times'* backyard, Times Mirror returned the thrust, sending *Newsday* westward into Queens and Brooklyn. The single-family-home owners on either side of the City–Nassau County line were more likely to be *News* readers, and when the *News'* fortunes sagged, *New York Newsday* benefited. The combined circulation for the New York and Long Island *Newsday* editions averaged 825,000 during the *News'* strike of 1990–91. Within a year, Maxwell was a suicide, and the *News* in bankruptcy court, fighting for its existence, until Mortimer Zuckerman, the real estate developer, breathed new life into it. By the summer of 1993, the *News* was holding on to a circulation of 780,000, while *Newsday* was selling 455,000 papers on Long Island and 270,000 in New York. Arthur naturally became solicitous about the fate of the

News. Should the News shut down for good, Newsday might gain enough circulation to achieve market parity with the Times. Readers might not notice, but advertisers would.

After all the worries about the challenges of television, the new technologies, aliteracy, and deaggregation, Arthur had to think about the old threat of newspaper competition. The Times' rediscovery of local news, sports, and Downtown styles was a direct response to the upstart Newsday. Senior Timesmen denied that they were chairbound intellectuals: Frankel played tennis, Joe Lelyveld and Arthur were runners. But they and their predecessors managed to shuffle off sports for decades, allowing the sports pages to wander around in the paper like a team forever on the road. When the Times' market surveyors discovered that young, affluent, male New Yorkers actually bought Newsday, or the News or the Post principally for their sports sections, Arthur resolved that if this desirable profile liked fun and games, the Times would supply them. He anchored sports in the same place in section B on Tuesday through Saturday so it could be more easily found. He intended to make the Times a one-stop paper: Readers could get all the sports coverage they wanted, including opinionated columnists and the agate fields of statistics that dedicated fans loved to graze on, without the need to pick up one of the tabloids.

The Metro section was also expanded with more than a glance at Newsday. Arthur implicitly acknowledged the Times' past disinterest in local news when he had to find "outsiders" to run the Metro pages. Gerald Boyd, a Midwesterner and a member of the Times' Washington bureau, became Metro editor; Michael Oreskes, a former Daily News political reporter, was named Boyd's chief deputy. Martin Gottlieb, an investigative reporter and former editor of the Village Voice, was another key addition. The Times also recruited Adam Moss, thirty-four, the founding editor of 7 Days, a self-consciously hip weekly aimed at young adults living on the Upper East and West sides of Manhattan (Moss was the closing editor as well, when the weekly was shut down after two years of losses in 1988). Moss informally joined the Times staff serving as "consultant to the managing editor," an unusual arrangement in the unbending hierarchy of the newsroom, and a measure of Arthur's commitment to shake up the Times. The experts around the office water coolers quickly passed word that Arthur brought Moss in to create a new "7 Days-type" section. The gossip was half-right. Moss, and Tom Botkin, the chief designer of the Times, transformed Sunday Main Part 2 into Styles of the Times. But Moss was not appointed the first editor of Styles. The title went to Stephen Drucker, another thirtysomething outsider who had previously worked at *Vogue*. Within a year, Drucker left and Moss went to the *Times Magazine*, while Styles of the *Times* continued to search for its "voice" under the editorship of Claudia Payne.

The expanded coverage of sports, metro, and Downtown represented the most visible alterations in the everyday façade of the institutional *Times*. Another fundamental restructuring took place in the subbasement where the paper was printed. In the mid-1980s, in those fat, happy boom years, Punch Sulzberger and Walter Mattson authorized the building of a new state-of-the-printing-arts plant across the Hudson River in Edison, New Jersey. Their long-range goal was to get all the *Times'* printing out of the antiquated facilities at West 43rd Street, and the marginally better presses at the Carlstadt plant, also in New Jersey. Edison had the capacity to handle more pages per edition, as well as color presses to match or surpass what *USA Today* and the newsmagazines could offer advertisers. Edison was completed in December 1990, at a cost of $450 to $500 million; it stood unused for over two years while the *Times* and its unions tried to come to accommodation on manning levels. The visitor to Edison doesn't require an engineering degree to realize that the number of employees needed is a tenth or twentieth the size of the work force at West 43rd Street: People were in the way of the robots at Edison. It hurt Arthur to see a half-billion-dollar plant lie idle. But the pain was unexpectedly eased by, of all things, the Bush-era recession: With the *Times'* advertising lineage down, the paper didn't need new press capacity to accommodate clamoring retailers.

Arthur Sulzberger has made clear what he wants his contribution to be in the succession of family publishers who have run the *Times* in this century. He plans to lead the return to New York, "our base and the energy that drives the *Times* machine." He hopes to hire a staff on both the business and news sides that reflects the city's diversity. He will try to engage new audiences with a relevant, reader-friendly *Times* of broad appeal. "We are a New York City paper," he emphasized the day he became publisher, his father at his side, the oil painting of Adolph Ochs on the wall behind him. "We have a role in the nation. But a majority of our advertisers are here. New York is the point from which we speak. I'm bullish on New York." He says that he will accomplish these new goals while honoring the old standards of the *Times*, "the values that make the place what it is." He will also nourish the international reporting "franchise." The Soviet Union may have collapsed and, with it, five decades of cold war journalism, but the new publisher says that these changes will not affect the *Times*' international commitments: "Foreign coverage is fundamental to what we are." And for the record, the *Times* National edition will continue to receive his support, to serve upper-end professional and business readers. "It's true no ads are out there right now," he said, "but there's still no limit to its potential for growth." Did the *Times*, then, aspire to be a national newspaper, a local New York newspaper, or a hybrid national and local paper? His answer is: "We are a little of all of the above."

While Arthur attempted this feat of balancing, he also tried to make the *Times* cost effective with profits once again equal to, or surpassing, the industry norm of 15 to 20 percent. Newsroom-staff cuts and union peace were supposed to contribute to a more efficient *Times*. Readers, too, were expected to do their part, and pay more for the paper. Quietly, without provoking any dinner-party conversation, Arthur's *Times* began shifting its revenue stream away from the usual formula of an 80–20 split—80 cents of each dollar coming from advertising and 20 cents from circulation—toward something closer to a 50-50 split. In the summer of 1992, the newsstand price of the *Sunday Times* sold around the country reached $3, and still the readers paid. Without sufficient national advertising, however, even robust national circulation could be harmful. Larger press runs meant more newsprint expenditures and delivery cost. The fate of *USA Today* was instructive: With over 1.8 million readers, it still lost an estimated $20 million in 1991 (*USA Today*'s total losses reached a staggering $800 million, from the paper's introduction in 1982 through January 1, 1992).

USA Today represented one print solution to aliteracy and the worries about readers' discretionary time. It was a TV-like newspaper: colorful, quick, high on human interest. Not too long ago, Arthur and a dinner guest were discussing the future of newspapers. The guest mourned the retreat from hard news. Arthur responded lightly, calling the guest "a child of the 1950s." The days when newspapers were riding high and didn't worry about readership or do audience surveys—those days were finished. Print was on a new wavelength now: shorter stories, enticing writing, gossip, sex, and service journalism (fitness, health, careers, and getting ahead). Arthur didn't mention it that night, but some newspapers were experimenting with features that a child of the 1990s might not recognize as news. In the name of reader-friendliness, papers were opening their pages to direct reader participation. Letters to the editors columns expanded; in California, the *Orange County Register* was inviting readers to send in their letters and postcards from vacation trips for publication; in Florida, the *West Palm Beach Post* covered shopping malls the way traditional newspapers used to cover the courts and City Hall.

The conventional wisdom, the assumption that drove Punch Sulzberger and his editors toward the new sections, held that television's ability to deliver hard-news headlines twelve to fourteen hours before the *Times* appeared on doorsteps had altered the role of newspapers. Print had to go toward consumer-oriented features. Arthur and his editors took the "news you can use" idea a step farther. Just as the definition of "news" was broadened, so too was the definition of "you" expanded to encompass potential new audiences. Possibly, though, both generations of *Times* managers misunderstood the new media landscape. When Tina Brown, the thirty-eight-year-old editor in chief of *Vanity Fair*, was invited to address the ANPA in May 1991, the assembled publishing executives expected some practical advice on how to be more popular and "with it." After all, *Vanity Fair* was an upscale *People* magazine. Brown had made it, the *Times* reported, "the hot book of the 1980s." Her magazine specialized in five thousand- to fifteen thousand-word personality pieces that matched first-rate writers with superstar subjects from movies and TV. Instead of offering her audience instructions in trendiness, Brown told the publishers that they were responding in the wrong way to the age of television. Their newspapers were too quiet, too bland, too user friendly, "too safe, safe, safe." She urged them to stop trying to be soft to attract readers. They should be shriller, harder edged: "Once in a while you have to bite the hand that reads you." (In June 1992, S. I. Newhouse, whose family owned both *Vanity Fair* and *The New Yorker*, decided that Brown was the editor needed to bring edge to *The New Yorker*.)

Critics have constantly told the *Times* how to run its business. Some suggestions were more helpful than others. The philosopher-catcher Yogi Berra observed, of life in general, "When you reach a crossroads, take it." Arthur's *Times* reached *several* crossroads in the early 1990s. It stood between the demands of its national ambitions and its rediscovered New York base; the interests of an older, elite readership and a new, less well-defined audience; the traditional desire to do one thing well and the attraction of creating new products; old-fashioned print versus new media technologies. If Tina Brown's views had merit, then Arthur needed also to stop and reconsider how far the *Times* ought to go down the road of reader friendliness.

He faced hard choices on a daunting journey. The obstacles that confronted Arthur Ochs Sulzberger, Jr., were arguably the greatest ever to face the publisher of the *New York Times*. All of his predecessors could at a minimum count on an intelligent audience that not only wanted to read the *Times* but felt that it *had* to read it. The paper's authority was unchallenged. These certitudes no longer exist. The *Times* is now one of a number of national agenda setters, whose ranks now include the *Washington Post*, the *Los Angeles Times*, the *Wall Street Journal*, the newsmagazines, and a half-dozen television and cable networks. The *Times* of the future, Arthur acknowledged, must share its old authority, as well as its primary market, with the present print competition, and with prospective electronic data-base rivals. But he insisted that the *Times'* kind of journalism will never be supplanted. "Twenty-five years from now, people will still need quality information, and that's the business were in," he said. "Given the way the human mind takes in knowledge, there will always be a *New York Times*."

Perhaps. Whether, as Arthur Sulzberger hopes, a new audience attracted to quality can be brought together from a polyglot city suffering deep economic and social strains is, at the least, debatable. His palpable energy and intelligence are important pluses. So are his progressive social views, and the people he has attracted around him. Many of the quickest and the brightest among the ranks of young journalists still respond to the lure of newspaper work, to the prospect of working at their trade in New York City, and to the opportunity of being a member of the news-gathering and writing staff of the *Times*. He will be able to count on good company as he moves the *Times* into the next century. It will take all the intelligence and enthusiasm that he and his associates of a New Age generation can muster to lead the *New York Times* successfully into its own new age.

Unfortunately, the high-profile objectives that Arthur Sulzberger has pursued in his first three years as publisher—the triad of skin-deep diversity, managerial Demingism, and Downtown chic (Styles of the *Times*)—seem limp banners for rallying the forces of sustained, serious journalism.

TIMES-LINE:
A SELECTED CHRONOLOGY
OF EVENTS

1851
New York Daily Times founded on September 18, a four-page paper produced by candlelight in downtown Manhattan loft.

1896
On August 18, Adolph S. Ochs buys near-bankrupt *Times* for $75,000. Later adopts a slogan "All the News That's Fit to Print."

1905
Times moves to Times Square. It is one of fourteen English-language dailies published in New York City.

1918
Times wins first Pulitzer Prize for accurate and complete wartime coverage.

1919
Illustrated Daily News started in New York; name later shortened to *Daily News*.

1923
Henry Luce and Britten Haddon create *Time*, the weekly magazine.

1935
Ochs dies, succeeded as publisher by Arthur Hays Sulzberger.

1938

Family of Max Frankel flees Hitler's Germany, emigrates to Washington Heights on the Upper West Side of New York City.

1940

Newsday started in former garage in Nassau County by Alicia Patterson, with support of husband Harry Guggenheim.

1941

Attack on Pearl Harbor, America enters war against Japan, Germany, Italy.

1942

First *Sunday Times* crossword puzzle.

1943

A. M. Rosenthal, a CCNY student, becomes $12 a week campus stringer for *Times*.

1945

World War II ends with unconditional surrender of Axis powers.

Times science writer William L. Laurence, allowed by U.S. government to be sole chronicler of the Manhattan Project, rides aboard B-29 that drops atom bomb on Nagasaki.

1948

State of Israel founded.

1950

North Korea invades South Korea. Thousands of U.S. reserve officers from World War II eventually recalled to active duty, including Marine Corps Lieutenant A. O. Sulzberger.

1956

Time's facsimile technology used to produce daily paper at Republican national convention in San Francisco (*Times* later sells off system on eve of "fax revolution").

Two ocean liners collide off northeastern U.S. coast; one, the *Andrea Doria*, sinks with heavy loss of life. Max Frankel on *Times* rewrite desk during rescue drama.

1957
Sputnik I, Soviet earth satellite, inaugurates Space Age.

1960
A. H. Sulzberger suffers stroke, Orvil Dryfoos named publisher. Punch Sulzberger serves as "vice president in charge of nothing."

1962–63
Bitter 114-day newspaper strike shuts down seven New York City papers. Times Company reports net loss of $1,831,000 for nine months ending September 30, 1963. (For comparable period the year before, the company reported net income of $1,552,000.) Strike settlement still leaves unresolved introduction of automation technology in city.

1963
New York Mirror, Hearst's morning tabloid, ceases publication.

Dryfoos dies after heart attack. Punch Sulzberger named publisher. A. M. Rosenthal returns to New York after duty as foreign correspondent, to become metropolitan editor.

John F. Kennedy assassinated in Dallas. Lyndon Johnson sworn in as president.

Critic Dwight Macdonald and others start *New York Review of Books* as alternative to *Book Review*.

CBS News and NBC News increase evening broadcasts from fifteen minutes to thirty minutes each week night. Walter Cronkite anchors CBS broadcast; Chet Huntley and David Brinkley together anchor NBC.

1964
Supreme Court rules in favor of *Times* in libel case, *New York Times vs. Sullivan*.

Johnson defeats Barry Goldwater.

1965
Malcolm X murdered in New York City.

Big Six printers' union authorizes new strike. New York newspaper publishers' "united front" crumbles. When Times is shut down and the morning Herald Tribune still publishes, latter's circulation rises to 900,000. When Times returns, Herald Trib drops again to around 300,000.

U.S. troop commitment to Vietnam at 500,000 mark.

1966

Times newspaper reports $100 million in advertising revenues. Total payroll reaches 5,300 employees, 700 of them working for news department.

Herald Tribune merges with two afternoon papers, Hearst's New York Journal-American and Scripps-Howard's New York World Telegram & Sun, to form World-Journal-Tribune, or "Widget." When Widget fails, only three papers remain in the city—the Times and two tabloids, the afternoon Post and the morning Daily News.

1967

Punch Sulzberger discontinues publication of Times international edition.

Times Company offers stock shares to public, begins series of acquisitions and expansions.

Israeli Defense Forces defeat combined Arab armies in "Six Day War." East and West Jerusalem united.

1968

Tet offensive by North Vietnamese main force troops and Viet Cong guerrilla units stuns U.S. public. Fighting reaches American Embassy grounds in Saigon.

Students occupy office of Columbia University president Grayson Kirk.

Reverend Martin Luther King, Jr., assassinated in Memphis.

Robert F. Kennedy assassinated in Los Angeles.

Lyndon Johnson announces he won't run again.

Richard M. Nixon elected president, says he has plan to end U.S. involvement in Vietnam war.

Times Washington columnist James Reston named executive editor and moves to New York.

Arthur Hays Sulzberger dies.

Clay S. Felker starts *New York*, weekly magazine offering service features and in-depth reports on life in the city (name and writers borrowed from Sunday supplement of old *Herald Tribune*).

1969

Thousands protest Vietnam war with march down Avenue of the Americas.

Census places New York City population at 7,964,200.

Mayor John V. Lindsay reelected to second term.

1970

Homosexuals march through Greenwich Village in show of "new militancy."

New York State's new abortion law goes into effect. In the city alone, 147 abortions are performed in first days after law takes effect.

Times Op-Ed page inaugurated.

Reston returns to Washington, relinquishing executive editor's job.

New York Governor Nelson A. Rockefeller reelected.

1971

Nine out of ten U.S. households own at least one television set.

U.S. Supreme Court rules in favor of *Times* in Pentagon Papers case. The *Times* and *Washington Post*, among others, print excerpts of archival documents tracing U.S. role in Vietnam.

Flag of People's Republic of China raised at UN.

1972

Bloomingdale's celebrates one hundredth anniversary.

Last issue of the weekly *Life* magazine.

Nixon reelected in landslide.

A group of eighty *Times*women present publisher Sulzberger with a list of their grievances, including lack of comparable pay.

1973

Watergate story reported extensively in *Washington Post*.

Max Frankel is *Times* D.C. bureau chief during unfolding scandals.

Abraham Beame elected mayor of New York.

Publisher Sulzberger adds titles Chairman and CEO of the New York Times Company.

1974

Watergate hearings—beginning of presidential impeachment process.

Nixon resigns, succeeded by Gerald Ford. Rockefeller later sworn in as vice president.

*Times*women file discrimination suit in U.S. Southern District Court. Case eventually settled out of court, with promises of faster promotion for women and a cash settlement to make up for past inequities.

1975

"Saturday Night Live" premiere on NBC. TV viewing by average American adult tops two hours and fifteen minutes a day.

Saigon falls, renamed Ho Chi Minh City.

Full impact of municipal fiscal crisis hits New York.

1976

New Jersey Weekly, first of four regional Sunday sections, is introduced by *Times*. Weeklies follow in Long Island, Connecticut, and Westchester.

Democratic-primary race matches front-runners Bella Abzug and Daniel Patrick Moynihan for U.S. Senate. *Times* endorsement choice divides Sulzberger and cousin John B. Oakes.

Title of *Times* Sunday editor abolished. Frankel to editorial page. All news operations consolidated under Rosenthal.

Times begins Weekend section.

Central Park smoke-in to promote legalization of marijuana.

Six-column format adopted by *Times* for news and advertising, except classifieds. Arts & Leisure section redesigned, with new guide to entertainment offerings. National classified ads begin in weekday paper.

Jimmy Carter elected president, Moynihan wins U.S. Senate race in general elections.

Living section started. *Times* Sunday circulation reaches 1.5 million.

1977

Cyrus R. Vance retires from *Times* board of directors to become secretary of state in Carter administration (Vance rejoins board in 1980).

Rupert Murdoch buys the *New York Post*, sole surviving afternoon paper in city. He also acquires *New York* magazine and the weekly *Village Voice*.

Home section appears.

First dancer steps on floor at Studio 54.

Edward I. Koch elected mayor of New York City.

1978

SportsMonday introduced, followed by Business Day.

Dow Jones down fifty-nine points, worst week in its history.

The eighty-eight-day pressman's strike. Murdoch breaks with publishers' association and *Post* resumes publishing.

Big Six printers union wins lifetime job security; in exchange, *Times* allowed to complete conversion to computerized newsroom.

Science Times started.

1979

Midtown rally for Soviet Jews draws 100,000.

Protests over Shoreham nuclear plant.

1980

Carter renominated at Democratic convention in Madison Square Garden.

Publication of the *Times'* National edition begins with satellite transmission to Chicago, the first of eight remote printing plants. Initial weekday circulation: 22,000.

John Lennon assassinated in front of his apartment building on Central Park West.

Black employees' suit settled at *Times*; plaintiffs win package worth $1.5 million.

Ronald Reagan elected president.

New York Daily News starts *Tonight*, an upmarket evening paper.

1981

Cable TV boxes and VCRs begin to appear in large numbers, bringing consumers more media choices in their homes.

News ceases publication of *Tonight* edition. *News'* owners try and fail to give paper away to a new publisher who would be willing to assume *News'* pension and job security obligations.

U.S. health officials report that forty-seven cases of Kaposi's sarcoma have been discovered among homosexual men.

1982

Times gains control of its home-delivery systems and begins major subscription drive in suburbs and exurbs.

Antinuclear protest in Central Park draws 800,000.

Mario Cuomo elected governor of New York.

Phil Donahue broadcasts show about AIDS.

1983

Conversion of *Times'* 43rd Street presses from letterpress to offset is completed after two years.

Metropolitan Opera celebrates its one hundredth birthday.

1984

Mondale wins Democratic presidential nomination, chooses a woman, Geraldine Ferraro of New York, as running mate.

Times' first use of national bar code on page two of National edition.

General Westmoreland, during his libel trial against CBS, admits he falsified estimates of enemy troop strength in Vietnam.

Bernard Goetz—the "subway vigilante"—shoots four black youths on a downtown IRT train.

1985

Circulation of *Newsday*, the Long Island daily, passes 500,000 mark. *Newsday*'s owner, Times-Mirror Corporation of Los Angeles, introduces morning edition in city, *New York Newsday*.

Edward I. Koch easily wins third term as mayor.

Law enforcement officials hold news conference to discuss rapid spread of new, smokable cocaine distillate, known on the street as *crack*.

Dow Jones jumps to record 1500.

1986

New York's City Council passes gay rights bill.

Statue of Liberty's one hundredth anniversary celebration.

Mets beat Red Sox in seventh game and win World Series.

Jennifer Levin found slain in Central Park in what becomes known as the "Preppy Murder" case.

Wall Street operator Ivan Boesky pleads guilty in insider trading scandal.

Michael Griffith, a black youth, chased to his death by gang of whites in Howard Beach, Queens.

Max Frankel named to succeed A. M. Rosenthal as executive editor of *Times*.

1987

Bess Meyerson resigns as New York City Cultural Affairs Commissioner amid growing scandals in Koch administration.

Lieutenant Colonel Oliver North begins testimony before House and Senate about his involvement in Iran-contra scandal.

Reverend Al Sharpton leads hundreds of demonstrators in "Days of Outrage." Sharpton denounces "white power structure" for handling of Tawana Brawley case (black teenager who reported that she was raped by white policemen).

October 19 "Black Monday" stock market crash.

1988

A weekly guide, *Television*, introduced by *Times*. Daily *Times* circulation goes over 1 million.

Expanded three-section National edition of *Times* available in San Francisco.

Jimmy Breslin starts column for *New York Newsday*, at reported salary of $350,000 a year.

George Bush elected forty-first president; Dan Quayle his vice president.

Pan Am jet flying from London to New York explodes in midair over Lockerbie, Scotland. All 244 passengers killed.

Real estate developer Peter Kalikow acquires *New York Post* from Rupert Murdoch.

New York area beaches closed as sewage, blood vials, syringes, and other waste products wash up on shore.

1989

Central Park jogger beaten and raped by gang of "wilding" youths.

Massacre of Chinese student protesters in Tiananmen Square, Beijing.

Black teenager Yusef Hawkins fatally shot in Bensonhurst, predominantly white section of Brooklyn.

David Dinkins becomes New York's first African-American mayor.

Berlin Wall falls; beginning of reunification of East and West Germany. Cold war over after forty-five years and, says Max Frankel, "the winner is Japan."

1990

U.S. troops land in Panama. Manuel Noriega taken into custody.

Expanded three-section *Times* National edition introduced across U.S. *Times* claims circulation of 240,000.

Iphigene Ochs Sulzberger, daughter of Adolph Ochs, dies. Ochs Trust dissolved and equal shares distributed to her children: Marian S. Heiskell, Ruth S. Holmberg, Judith P. Sulzberger, and Punch Sulzberger.

New York Post's unions agree to pay cuts.

Arthur Ochs Sulzberger, Jr., earns $275,000 and bonus of $47,500 as deputy publisher of *Times*.

1991

U.S.-led coalition goes to war against Iraq after UN deadline for withdrawal from Kuwait passes.

Iraq accepts UN ceasefire terms, ending Gulf war.

Tribune Company of Chicago pays British media mogul Robert Maxwell $60 million to take *News* off its hands.

New York Post owner Peter Kalikow files for personal bankruptcy; paper's future in doubt.

Times runs story of Kitty Kelley's bedroom biography of Nancy Reagan on page one. Paper names Florida woman in William Kennedy Smith rape case, describes her wild drinking and driving habits—prompting stories about *Times*' own "wild streak."

Times raises daily newsstand price to 50 cents in city, and to 75 cents for National edition. Circulation tops 1.1 million daily, 1.6 million Sunday—both new highs despite price increases.

Robert Maxwell dies at sea, as his empire collapses. *News* in Chapter 11.

Gorbachev survives hardliners' coup, and begins endgame for Soviet Union.

1992

USSR formally dissolved on first day of New Year. Boris Yeltsin vows to introduce free-market economy.

Arthur O. Sulzberger, Jr., succeeds father as *Times* publisher.

Museum of Modern Art opens "blockbuster" Matisse exhibit.

Times endorses Clinton-Gore ticket; Democrats win presidency; for first time since Jimmy Carter in 1976, *Times* on winning side.

Mortimer Zuckerman buys the *News*.

Howell Raines moved from *Times'* Washington bureau chief job to editorial-page editor, putting him in place to succeed Joe Lelyveld if Lelyveld moves up to take Frankel's place.

1993

Kim Foltz, *New York Times* reporter, dead at forty-four. *Times* obituary lists his cause of death as AIDS and also runs name of Foltz's male companion in obit.

New York Post reacquired by Rupert Murdoch, pending FCC waiver.

Times opens state-of-the-art production plant in Edison, New Jersey, after three years of delays. Costs spiral to $500 million.

First color pages appear in *Times*, in *Book Review* section.

Acknowledgments

The formal reporting for this study started in 1987 when several of the changes described here were getting under way. But my work as a *Times*-watcher goes back three decades. As a wire-service reporter in Washington during the mid-1950s, I first competed against the *Times*. During the 1960s, when I was an editor at *Newsweek*, the competition between daily paper and weekly newsmagazine was less direct, and so my work at *Newsweek* didn't prevent me from receiving regular assignments from the *Times Magazine*. These *Magazine* assignments stopped in 1970, when I became a contributing editor at *New York* magazine, writing about the press, including the *Times*. In the late 1960s and early 1970s, a right-wing bumper sticker challenged critics of the Vietnam war: "U.S.A.—Love It or Leave It." The slogan comes to mind whenever I read the *Times*, as subscriber and as critic; it remains a paper too smug to love, yet too important to leave.

Most of the materials in this book come from my own reporting over the past five years, including some two dozen tape-recorded interviews with *Times* people, present and past, as well as three times that number of non-taped interviews with other *Times*men and -women. I acknowledge their cooperation and interest. In addition, the *Times* allowed me access to its archives, or at least those portions open to outsiders. In general, the rule was that "inactive" files—that is, materials about

Times executives who were retired or dead—could be studied. Nevertheless, one or two exceptions involving still "active" executives were made. I thank the staff of the archives, and particularly its former director, Dr. John Rothman, for allowing me fair use of selected materials.

Several memoirs and studies of the *Times* have been published over the years, and I've tried to digest them all, even when they fell outside the time frame of this book. For example, I read Ruth Adler's *A Day in the Life of The New York Times* (Lippincott/NY Times, 1971) and used it as a model for reconstructing my own twenty-four-hour day in the life of the modern *Times*. (Adler was an Ochs family member, and her project had official status, unlike my "Day.") Several analyses of the American press that treated the *Times* in passing were helpful, particularly Deborah Lipstadt's study of how the press covered Hitler's persecution of European Jews. Some excellent studies of New York City and its media also exist. Richard Kluger's *The Paper: The Life and Death of the New York Herald Tribune* was especially helpful. Over the years, too, I've done content analyses and criticism of the *Times* for *New York* magazine, for various journalism reviews, and for a series of my own studies published by the MIT Press.

I've drawn on these interviews, reporting, analyses, and books. I would also like to acknowledge the research and administrative assistance of Mariah Bear, Eileen Clarke, Dale Fuchs, Gregg Geller, Kate O'Hara, Rebecca Mead, Lori Robinson, Whitney Scott, Stacy Shatkin, Robert Silverman, Christal Smith, Martha Bula Torres, David White, and Matthew Fenton. I am also grateful for the advice and support of Lois and Tom Wallace. I wish to thank Adelina Diamond, my best friend, and Edward Kosner, the best editor I know (and the editor and president of *New York* at the time I worked on this project), for their support and counsel. Finally, I owe a special debt to Diane Reverand and Emily Bestler, my infinitely patient and skilled editors at Villard Books.

All the opinions and conclusions here are my own, and I bear sole responsibility for them.

Edwin Diamond
New York, September 1993

Sources and Notes

INTRODUCTION: A LITTLE WILD STREAK

4 ". . . supermarket of news . . .": author interview, Max Frankel, 11.8.88 and 7.8.92.

4 ". . . is to experience awe . . .": *Winners & Sinners*, 2.28.91. My comment after reading this was, "Aw, shucks."

6 George Bush joke: *Washington Post*, 4.48.91 p. A17.

7 "a more with-it image": *Time* magazine, 5.6.91. p. 44.

7 Dowd's Reagan story: *New York Times*, 4.7.91. p. A1.

7 ". . . on its merits . . .": author interview, Josh Mills 4.20.91.

7 ". . . going to be screwups . . .": author interview, Alan Finder, 4.22.91.

8 ". . . liven up this story . . .": author interview, E. R. Shipp, 4.22.92. Shipp, a black woman reporter, resigned from the *Times* in January 1993, after thirteen years.

8 "ideas" and "execution": author interview, Arthur O. Sulzberger, Jr., 7.9.92.

9 "Staff meeting and protests . . ." See various accounts, Diamond, *New York* magazine, 5.1.91. Howard Kurtz, *Washington Post*, 5.1.91, *Time*, 5.6.91, *Newsweek*, 4.29.91. James Ledbetter, *Village Voice*, 4.30.91. See also "Editors' Note," *New York Times*, 5.26.91, and William Glaberson, in same edition of the *Times*.

10 ". . . never going to be the *Daily News*": author interview, Arthur O. Sulzberger, Jr., 7.8.92.

10 "to entice readers": *presstime*, May 1991.

11 "Teddy's Sexy Romp": author interview, Jerry Nachman, at the time the editor of the *New York Post*. 4.19.91. See also *Washington Post*, 4.18.91.

11–12 Brawley and Ritter stories: Diamond, *New York*, "The Brawley Fiasco" 7.18.88, also Edwin Diamond, *Columbia Journalism Review*, "The Priest, the Prostitute and the New York Press," May/June 1990.

12 "all the reporting was the *Times*": author interview, Nancy Nielsen, vice president of corporate communications, *Times*. Other quotes and materials from author interviews with Fox Butterfield, David Jones, and others involved in coverage.

13 Naming rape victims: The policy was explained in the *Times* editions of 4.17.91. Allan Siegal later elaborated on the episode at New York University, 10.14.92.

14 ". . . in a vacuum": Allan Siegal quoted by David Kaplan, *Newsweek* 4.2.90.

14 women who have prestigious jobs: Anna Quindlen, "A Mistake," *New York Times*, 4.21.91.

15 "I go places . . .": quoted by James Ledbetter, *Village Voice*, 4.30.92.

16 ". . . whole thing . . . out of control . . .": author interview, Max Frankel, 7.8.92.

20 "The *Times* is an elitist paper . . .": author interview, not for attribution. 4.18.92.

21 "We sensed the flexibility . . ." author interview, Janet Maslin, 7.24.87.

21 Richard Berke bylines: See *New York Times*, page A-12. 8.4.92.

21 "There is a single woman . . .": Jane Gross, *New York Times*, 4.28.87.

22 Candidates' questionnaire: Craig Whitney, letter dated 5.5.87. See also reply by Senator Paul Simon, dated 6.3.87, and Diamond, "Sexual Hysteria," *New York* magazine, 6.22.87.

22–23 Relevant sexual conduct: Max Frankel, memo to staff, 6.18.87.

24 "If the *Times* was . . . slow to react . . .": Robert McFadden, et al. *Outrage: The Story Behind the Tawana Brawley Hoax*," (Bantam, 1990) pp. 148–9.

25 Appeal of Murphy Brown: See *Washington Journalism Review*, July–August 1992.

1: PUNCH AND HIS TIMES

34 "The Marines woke me . . .": quoted in *"Iphigene: My Life and the New York Times"* (Dodd, Mead & Co. 1979), p. 152.

36 ". . . executive in charge of nothing . . .": See Ellis Cose, "The Press," (William Morrow, 1989), p. 197, and Turner Catledge, *My Life and the Times* (Harper & Row, 1971), p. 281.

36 Reston as Punch advocate: author interview, Tom Wicker, 10.16.89.

37 Oakes on the environment, abortion: author interview, John B. Oakes, 11.1.91.

38 Punch a gamble: *Iphigene*, p. 274.

38–39 Dedication and reopening of cornerstone: *Times Talk*, in-house newsletter, March 1964.

40 "Where do I sign?": See *Iphigene*. Also Gay Talese, *The Kingdom and the Power*, (World NAL 1969), and Harrison Salisbury, *Without Fear or Favor* (Times Books, 1980).

41 Ochs as target of criticism: Barbara Tuchman, introduction, *Iphigene*, p. xviii.

42 ". . . crème de la crème of Jewish culture . . ." quoted by Salisbury, p. 29.

42 Too much space for Jews: quoted by Talese, p. 168. See also *Iphigene* p. 11.

42 *Times* opposed to Jewish undesirables: *Hadassah*, January 1981.

43 Not a "Jewish paper": quoted by Catledge, p. 214. See also Leonard and Mark Silk, *The American Establishment*, (Basic Books 1980), p. 79.

43 "Jew-Arab count": author interview, Ben Franklin, 2.14.89.

43 Israel forced changes: author interview, E. Clifton Daniel, 8.1.89.

45 Account of massacre and *Times'* reactions: Thomas Friedman, *From Beirut to Jerusalem* (Farrar, Straus, & Giroux, 1989), p. 166.

46 The Reids' genteel anti-Semitism: Richard Kluger, *The Paper: The Life and Death of the New York Herald Tribune*, (Knopf, 1986), p. 388.

50 "Move up the Columbia bust. . . " Salisbury, p. 393.

51 "comically overstaffed": Russell Baker, *The Good Times* (William Morrow, 1989), pp. 267 et seq.

52 Popham and the civil rights story: author interview, John Herbers, 1.19.90.

53 penurious *Magazine* pay: As a steady contributor in the 1960s, I still have my check stubs, and the memories of some mild rewrites.

53 General MacArthur six-part interview: Catledge, pp. 192 et seq.

54 No-frills paper: Catledge, p. 198–99.

54 Disorganized *Times*: author interview, James Goodale, 2.17.89.

55–56 *Times* and facsimile technology: memoranda from *Times* Archives.

57 Sagan-Sulzberger exchange: author interview, Bruce Sagan 7.17.91, and original correspondence.

58 *Times* obligation to be profitable: quoted by Leonard and Mark Silk, p. 66.

2: OUR CROWD, OUR PAPER

64 "professional . . . stress": Barbara Tuchman, *Iphigene*, p. xviii.

64–65 Punch Sulzberger's medical problems: author interview, A. O. Sulzberger, 9.10.91.

65 The heady *Times*: Warren Hoge interview, National Public Radio; the interviewer was Frank Darcy. I was interviewed by Darcy for the same series on the *Times'* cultural coverage. 7.11.90.

66 "Iphigene memoir rejected . . ." author interview with two different *Times* editors, on background.

67 "Ochs trust . . . and a dirty Jewish trick": Salisbury, p. 110–11.

68 "They copied us . . .": author interview, A. O. Sulzberger 12.6.90.

68–69 The Binghams as cautionary tale: author interviews, A. O. Sulzberger and A. O. Sulzberger, Jr. For the full Bingham story, see Susan E. Tifft and Alex S. Jones, *The Patriarch: The Rise and Fall of the Bingham Dynasty*, (Summit Books, 1991).

70 *Times* in family control "until way out there": author interview, A. O. Sulzberger. See also *Times* news accounts 9.19.86 and 2.27.90.

71 Jackson chided the Sulzbergers: Edward Klein, "The Kingdom and the Prince", *Manhattan Inc.*, August 1988.

72 ". . . time for a change": author interview, A. O. Sulzberger, 12.6.90.

73 "a sense of dispossession": author interview, Edward Klein, 9.15.88.

74 "I'm a journalist . . .": author interview, Arthur O. Sulzberger, Jr. 12.7.87.

74 Franklin "embalmed": author interview, Ben Franklin. See also Klein, *Manhattan Inc.*

76 ". . . call me that, once": author interview Arthur O. Sulzberger, Jr.

76 Odds on the Adler-Sulzberger competition: Talese, p. 174–5.

77 Punch Sulzberger's beavers: author interview, A. O. Sulzberger, 9.10.91.

77 "Give it, or get it": author interview, museum board member, not for attribution.

78 " 'Charlie, give me a couple of million . . .' ": author interview, A. O. Sulzberger, 12.6.90.

79 "Why not open it up?" quoted in John Taylor, "Party Palace," *New York* magazine, 1.9.89, pp. 20–30.

79 "The record is boring . . .": Warren Hoge, NPR interview.

3: THE CHANGES: 1. SOFT TIMES

85 Home not "pertinent": memo, A. M. Rosenthal to Nancy Newhouse, 7.6.78.

85 "Area rugs . . . coming back": memo, 7.10.78.

86 Teddy White as reader: author interview, A. M. Rosenthal, 2.3.90.

86 ". . . I have no problem expressing myself . . .": author interview, A. O. Sulzberger, 12.6.90.

87 ". . . Can't we think of other names": memo 2.11.71.

88 "There are rules . . .": author interview, A. O. Sulzberger.

88 Ruth Golden's profile: Ruth Golden, *Times Talk*, July-August 1963.

92 ". . . new sections reinvigorated the *Times* . . .": author interview, A. O. Sulzberger, 9.10.91.

94 "absolutely way-out crazy furniture": Catledge, p. 223.

94 "I am not an expert on singing . . .": memo, 10.12.81.

94 "Just once . . . I wished he had asked . . .": author interview, John Leonard, 5.31.89.

94 ". . . incredible goobledegook . . .": memo, 7.13.81.

95 "You put this bosom . . .": memo, 11.23.77.

95 "So far this morning . . .": memo, 3.5.71.

96 Influence exercised discreetly: author interview, A. O. Sulzberger, 12.8.90.

97 "When the new rooms open . . .": memos, 7.6.78 and 12.6.76.

97 Employing Larry Lachman: memo exchange, 4.4.78, and 4.6.78.

98 "I gave my blood . . .": author interview, James Goodale, 10.7.88.

99 "You know you've become . . ." Chris Argyris, *Behind the Front Page: Organizational Self-Renewal in a Metropolitan Paper* (Jossey Bass, 1974), p. 37.

100 Oakes wanted to accommodate: author interview, John B. Oakes, 11.1.91.

101 "Don't reopen old wounds": author interview, *Times* senior editor, not for attribution.

104 ". . . I cast my vote . . .": memo, 12.19.74.

105 ". . . happy to play Solomon . . .": memo. 11.21.75. Also, author interview, A. O. Sulzberger 12.6.90.

4 THE CHANGES: 2. SAFE TIMES

114 Not every subject captured . . .: author interview, *Times* cultural reporter, not for attribution.

116 Oakes resolved to abolish: author interview, John B. Oakes, 11.1.91. See also John Oakes–Michael Straight exchange, letters to the editor, *New York Times*, 11.9.89 and 11.14.89.

117 Most news organizations . . . ignored: Edwin Diamond, "How the Press Played the Pentagon Papers," *New York* magazine 8.16.71.

118 Mitchell had no idea: Griswold quoted in the *Washington Post*, 2.15.91. See also Stephen Bates, *If No News Send Rumors* (St. Martin's Press, 1985), p. 157.

118 "It was a very scary thing . . .": author interview, A. O. Sulzberger.

118–19 Nixon later explained: Richard Nixon, *RN: The Memoirs of Richard Nixon* (Crosset & Dunlap, 1978), p. 509.

119 Leftist, Jewish *Times*: memo 6.6.78.

119 The *Times* antagonized "The Club": author interview, John B. Oakes.

120 A good story but wrong: author interview, William Safire, 11.17.92.

121–24 Sulzberger's two-part quiz: memo and replies, A. M. Rosenthal 12.9.74. Max Frankel 12.11.74.

124 "I don't believe in telling . . .": author interview, A. O. Sulzberger.

125 "Punch heard from . . .": author interview, on background.

125–26 "Stephen Birmingham suggested": The article appeared in *MORE*, July-August 1976, as did Oakes's reply, October 1976.

135 ". . . most malign events . . .": author interview, A. H. Raskin, 1.26.89.

137 Serrin told to cover "work in America": author interview, William Serrin, 10.16.89.

138 ". . . Johnny Oakes to blow the whistle": author interview, on background. The Oakes article appeared on 6.19.88.

138 "Punch was making the transition . . .": author interview, John Oakes.

138 ". . . a savaging of the board . . .": author interview, A. H. Raskin.

139 ". . . there was a rightward shift . . .": author interview, Tom Wicker, 10.16.89.

5 THE CHANGES: 3. MONEY TIMES

146 "I used to have a nightmare . . .": author interview, A. M. Rosenthal, 2.13.91.

147 "soup speech": author interview, A. M. Rosenthal.

148 "Once, the best people . . .": author interview, Albert Scardino, 7.11.91.

149 Quindlen and the copy editor: Anna Quindlen told the story at the New School, New York, 12.8.90

150 "The . . . *Times* hired real . . .": author interview, Tom Rosensteil, 7.14.91.

150–51 Adler memo: *Times* archives.

152 "Some of us had ideas for 'modernizing' . . .": author interview, E. Clifton Daniel 8.1.89.

154 "the highlight of the careers . . .": Walter Mattson quoted by Mitch Stephens and Jerry Lanson, *Washington Journalism Review*, July/August, 1983.

154 "there was no real debate": author interview, Walter Mattson, 5.31.91.

155 Rosenthal's contrary recollection: author interview, A. M. Rosenthal.

155 "Our first major effort . . .": memo, 7.12.76.

155 "If we continue to grow . . .": memo, 12.16.76.

155 Research department study: memo, 4.2.76.

155–56 Rosenthal liked the pages: memo to staff, 4.30.76.

156 "I was terrified . . .": author interview, A. M. Rosenthal.

156–57 Joan Whitman's dissent: memo 7.22.76.

157 "I am . . . not contemplating a heavy section . . .": memo, 7.13.76.

157 "Mr. Revson strongly urged . . .": memo 9.17.70.

158 "break new journalistic ground": memo, 1.11.78.

158–59 Sullivan's proposal: memo, 11.4.77.

159 Sulzberger's "serious reservations . . .": memo, 1.16.78.

159 Rosenthal a sore loser: author interview, Donald Nizen, 4.20.89.

159–60 How Rosenthal started Science Times: author interview, A. M. Rosenthal.

160–61 Mutual sniping by news and business: memos 11.27.78 and 12.12.78.

161 "Pushing ad sales people . . .": memo, 3.31.77.

161 Computer ads dribble in: memos 1.26.82 and 2.2.82.

165 The private Donovan: Jonathan Van Meter, "Fashions of the Times," *Vogue,* September 1990.

6: LAST OF THE RED HOT MAMAS

170 "Salisbury's Rosenthal . . ." Harrison Salisbury, A *Time for Change,* pp. 85–86, 287–302. See also Salisbury, *"Without Fear or Favor,"* p. 395–410.

171 "I've heard it several times . . .": author interview, Robert Schiffer, 6.6.91.

172–73 MacLeish on the open phone: His contribution was not strictly a poem. The *Times* called it a "reflection" in the headline over the copy. MacLeish ended with the observation: "To see the earth as it truly is, small, and blue and beautiful in that eternal silence where it floats, is to see ourselves as riders on the earth together, brothers on that bright loveliness in the eternal cold—brothers who know now they are truly brothers."

173 "a grain of reality": Joseph Goulden, *"Fit to Print: A. M. Rosenthal and the Times,"* (Lyle Stuart, Inc., 1988).

174–75 Reagan and Bitburg: Lou Cannon, *President Reagan: The Role of a Lifetime,* (Simon & Schuster, 1991).

175 Aquino too soft: Raymond Bonner, *Waltzing with a Dictator,* (Random House, 1987), pp. 394–95. George Schultz, the former secretary of state under Ronald Reagan, tells a similar story in his memoir *Turmoil and Triumph,* (Scribners, 1993), p. 617. According to Schultz, Rosenthal told him that Aquino was "an empty headed housewife" with "no positions." Schultz also wrote that Rosenthal passed on the same opinion to Ronald and Nancy Reagan during a White House dinner, and that "his words made a deep and lasting impact on them." In his Op-Ed column, Rosenthal denounced the Schultz account as a fabrication.

176 "It didn't do me any good . . .": author interview, A. M. Rosenthal, 2.13.90.

177 "Solid new information": A. H. Raskin, review, *Silurian News,* November, 1988.

178 "We live in a time of commitment . . .": staff memo, A. M. Rosenthal.

179 ". . . decent quotes from Betty Friedan . . .": memo, A. M. Rosenthal.

180 "Kosinski was raped . . .": author interview, A. M. Rosenthal.

181 "Harrison . . . grinds axes . . .": author interview, A. M. Rosenthal.

183 "No detail . . . too small . . .": excerpts from staff memos, A. M. Rosenthal, over the period 1971–82.

184 A "silly and destructive" request . . .: memo, Max Frankel, 3.5.76.

186 ". . . a lot of head shaking . . .": author interview, David Sanger, 6.20.89, Tokyo.

187 " 'Why not do a new column? . . .' ": Anna Quindlen, New School.

190 The meeting of "the cabal": Edwin Diamond, "The Cabal at the Times," *New York* magazine, 5.18.70.

192–94 The Severo case: author interviews, Richard Severo, 11.15.89, and A. M. Rosenthal.

196–97 Schanberg-Rosenthal exchange on homosexuals: memos of 10.12.77, 10.13.77.

197–99 Kinsella's findings: James Kinsella, *Covering the Plague: AIDS and the American Media* (Rutgers University Press, 1989).

199–200 Larry Kramer's examples: author interview, Larry Kramer, 1.15.91. Also see *Tikkun*, July-August 1990.

201 "Expect a surge in AIDS . . ." memo, 11.9.84.

202 Daniel . . . chided Rosenthal: author interview, E. Clifton Daniel, and Rosenthal-Daniel correspondence, May-June 1986.

203 A reporter with AIDS covering AIDS: Jeffrey Schmalz spoke about his *Times* work and his illness at NYU, 2.24.93. See also Schmalz "Covering AIDS and Living It: A Reporter's Testimony," *Times*, 12.20.92.

206 worst year of his life: quoted in Gay Talese, *The Kingdom and the Power*, p. 515.

206 He succeeded because of his tenacity: author interview, Tom Wicker.

7: CHOOSING MAX (AND JOE)

213 The lunch with Punch: author interview, Max Frankel, 11.8.88.

215 Gene Roberts as better man: author interview, Tom Wicker.

216–17 Catledge's hardest decisions: Catledge, p. xii.

217 Frankel's personal style: author interview, Max Frankel.

217–18 Frankel's short-lived resignation: The story is told in Catledge, p. 302.

220 "Editor for life" story a joke: author interview, A. M. Rosenthal.

222 ". . . I identify with the underdog": author interview, Sydney Schanberg, 6.22.88.

225 Kovach's direction was not Sulzberger's: author interview, Bill Kovach, 7.17.88, Atlanta.

229 Rosenthal's MBO list: memo 1.1.83.

230 ". . . 'no list of "ins" or "outs" . . .' " memo, 9.15.83.

231 ". . . Did I want to go at the stroke of sixty-five? . . .": author interview, A. M. Rosenthal.

232 Frankel not there "to make radical changes": author interview, Max Frankel.

8: THE NEWSROOM: THE TIMES THAT TRIES MEN'S SOULS

240 "Some people just aren't . . .": author interview, John Rothman, 7.7.89.

241 ". . . always a sinking feeling . . .": quoted by David Shaw, *Los Angeles Times*, 1.1.89.

241 The content of news: Robert Darnton, *The Kiss of Lamourette* (Norton, 1989), p. 93.

242 Introspection a waste: Chris Argyris, p. 18.

244–45 Ray Bonner's unhappy career: The story is told best by Michael Massing "About-face in El Salvador," *Columbia Journalism Review*, Nov./ Dec. 1983. See also *AIM Report*, Feb. 1982, July 1982.

245 Stock not ready to retire: author interview, Robert Stock, 9.12.91.

246 Guarding against vulgarity: *New York Times Manual of Style and Usage*, p. 148.

247 Affirmative action produces more homogeneity: author interview, on background.

247 Halberstam and rewrites: letter to author, David Halberstam, 3.10.93.

248 "Get them to like me . . .": Catledge, p. 16.

248 "No one takes a pay cut . . .": author interview, Martin Levine 6.23.89, Tokyo.

249 Paternalistic *Times*: various memos, e.g. 1.24.83, and 1.6.89.

249 "This is a special place . . .": author interview, Margo Jefferson, 5.3.89. Similar stories were repeated to me by others.

250 "They wanted me . . .": author interview, John Crudele, 1.8.92.

251 Women tried to blend in: Anna Quindlen, NYU seminar, 11.6.91.

254 "I read in Liz Smith's gossip column . . .": author interview, Michael Gross, 5.16.88.

256 Like Filene's basement: author correspondence, Michael Norman, 3.14.93.

256 Like an insurance office: Russell Baker, p. 275.

256 "Subgroups clustered . . .": Darnton, p. 70.

256 Always low morale: author interview, John Corry, 1.24.89.

257 "We simply cannot run a newspaper . . .": memo, 11.15.78.

257 Whole groups gone until 3 P.M.: memo, 12.2.83.

257 ". . . no one ever talked . . .": author interview, Terri Brooks, 10.15.91.

258 "I wouldn't recognize . . . them": Dave Anderson, New School seminar, 12.10.90.

258 Frankel's Germanic penchant: author interview, 7.12.90; not for attribution.

259 ". . . hired to be a star . . .": author interviews William Serrin, 10.16.89 and 10.23.89. Also correspondence, 3.15.93.

260–61 "Serrin on Homestead . . .": Serrin, *Times*, 7.26.86. See also William Serrin, *Homestead: The Rise and Fall of an American Town* (Times Books, 1992).

262 "My writing . . . considered too soft . . .": author interview. Steven R. Weisman, 6.28.89, Tokyo.

262–63 Life and death of Fay Joyce: David Blum, *New York* magazine, 1.13.86, p. 32.

264 "The drift of Darnton's conversation . . . ": author interview, Fred Friendly, 11.29.88.

264–65 *Winners & Sinners*: The newsletter was discontinued in its public form in 1992.

265 The challenge to survive: author interview, Josh Mills, 1.30.89 and 8.5.90.

266 "Three things have dominated . . .": James Reston, *Deadline: Our Times and The New York Times* (Random House, 1991), p. xi.

267 ". . . a kick in the balls . . .": Baker, pp. 338–42.

268 ". . . she fell between the cracks": author interview, Robert Semple, 3.8.89.

268 "I got to do . . . big stuff . . .": author interview, Pam Hollie, 9.29.88.

268 ". . . a check for $400 . . .": Nan Robertson in *The Girls in the Balcony* (Random House, 1992), described how the lawsuit brought by a group of *Times*women was settled out of court; Robertson reports that 550 *Times*women got a onetime check of $454.54.

270–71 Paul Delaney's Resignation: Robert Sam Anson, "The Best of Times, the Worst of Times," *Esquire*, March 1993, p. 105.

271 "It was the substance . . .": Richard Shepard, *New York Times*, 9.28.88.

271 Dougherty always arrived early: George Lois, *7 Days*, 10.12.88.

9: OPINION TIMES: ANNA AND ABE AND BILL AND MAUREEN AND GARRY

274 "official" *Times* of the 1960s: author interview, Joseph Lelyveld, 7.26.91.

277 " 'Styles' isn't intended for you . . .": author interview, A. O. Sulzberger, Jr., 5.7.92.

277 "Downtown isn't going to read . . . ": author interview, Enid Nemy, 5.20.92.

278 "How Op-Ed works . .": author interview, Mitchel Levitas, 11.10.92.

278 "It was as if the Gray Lady . . .": Robert Semple, *New York Times*, 9.30.90.

278 "I developed a fantasy . . .": Robert Semple, speaking at a Center for Communications seminar, New York City, 3.8.89.

279–80 six rules of the "Op-Ed page game": Susan Lee, *Journal of Financial Reporting*, 1989, unnumbered.

280 The Op-Ed culling process: two Op-Ed editors described the system to me in background interviews in mid-1991 and late 1992.

280 the *Times* like *The Wizard of Oz*: Anna Quindlen, NYU seminar, 11.6.91.

281 "It is a great forum . . .": author interview, Karl Meyer, 4.19.90.

281 "The . . . board used to be . . . white males . . .": author interview, Jack Rosenthal, 8.1.91.

282 "It wasn't a status occupation . . .": author interview, Jack Rosenthal. Four months later, Rosenthal elaborated on the shift away from general interest newspapers at a NYU seminar, 12.4.91.

285 "Mary Richards made it all OK . . .": Joyce Purnick, "The Legacy of Mary Richards," *New York Times*, 2.20.91.

287 "The Busiest Day": *New York Times*, 10.24.88. Tom Wolfe named this journalistic form "plutography"—writing about the rich.

287–88 Newspaper endorsements: Albert Scardino, *New York Times*, 11.4.88.

289 The Establishment and the *Times*: Leonard and Mark Silk, *The American Establishment*, (Basic Books, 1980).

289 ". . . never expressed an opinion . . .": the story is told by Richard Clurman, *To the End of Time* (Simon & Schuster, 1992), p. 101.

290 "Two Good Men": editorial, *New York Times*, 10.30.88.

290–91 The genesis of "Two Good Men": author interview, Jack Rosenthal, 11.12.88. This account was reconfirmed, author interview, A. O. Sulzberger, 9.10.91.

291–92 Koch vs. Dinkins: author interviews. Two reporters spoke on condition of anonymity. They were interviewed on 9.7.89.

292 The daredevil *Times*: Richard Harwood, *Washington Post*, 5.3.92.

292–93 Op-Ed founding: Robert Semple, "Op-Ed at 20," *New York Times*, 9.30.90.

293 Op-Ed idea borrowed: See, for example, E. J. Kahn, *The World of Swope*, (now out of print); and Karl E. Meyer, *Pundits, Poets & Wits* (Oxford, 1990).

293 Op-Ed for rent: Robert Sherrill, *The Nation*, 10.22.90.

295 The "fun" *Times*: Arthur O. Sulzberger, Jr., Smithsonian Institution seminar, Washington, D.C., 1.15.92.

295–96 Safire, Roy Cohn, and the *Times*: The journalist Nick von Hoffman, a biographer of Roy Cohn, argues that part of Cohn's appeal to the *Times* related to Cohn's connections to certain unions important to the *Times*, such as the drivers and handlers. Nicholas von Hoffman, *Citizen Cohn* (Doubleday, 1988).

296 "I had a rule of thumb . . . ": author interview, Harrison Salisbury, 3.2.89.

297 "Semple took a more conservative tack . . . ": Robert Semple, Center of Communications seminar, New York, 3.8.89.

298 Quindlen at home: Melinda Beck, *Newsweek*, 4.4.89.

298–99 The glass ceiling: Quindlen retold her story at the New School and at NYU.

299 Anna Quindlen proclaims too much: Nat Hentoff, *Village Voice*, 6.2.92.

299–300 ". . . in agreement with Mr. Perot . . . ": Quindlen, "Waiting for Perot," *New York Times*, 6.3.92.

300 Rosenthal's most popular subject: The content analysis was done by my associate Robert Silverman, a graduate student in American studies at NYU.

304 Magic Johnson's "irresponsible" behavior: Dave Anderson, "Sorry, But Magic Isn't a Hero," *New York Times*, 11.14.91.

304 Praise for Arthur Ashe: see Haywood Hale Broun, *New York Times*, 5.3.92, and Barry Lorge, 4.12.92.

10: ROUGHING IT IN CULTURE GULCH

308 African bureau vs. a food column: Jim Quinn, *Town & Country*, April 1992, p. 118.

309–10 The Cipriani episode: Bryan Miller tells the story himself in "Confessions," Times Company Report, Fall 1991. The second Cipriani restaurant review appeared in the *New York Times* editions of 9.21.90.

311 ". . . a generation thing . . .": author interview, Richard Shepard, 1.7.91.

311–12 The new orthodoxy: author interviews with the "Polish Tea Room" crowd at the Edison Hotel during three lunches in 1991 and 1992.

312 ". . . eight of us covering serious music . . .": author interview, Peter Davis, 9.21.91.

313 Grace Glueck and the art beat: author interview, Grace Glueck, 2.10.92. The who-whom story is told by Nan Robertson in *The Girls in the Balcony*, p. 168.

313 "We have to grab younger readers . . .": Warren Hoge, National Public Radio interview 7.11.90.

314 *Times* strategy of "reaching down": author interview, Hilton Kramer, 2.11.92. See also Kramer, *New York Observer*, 2.23.92.

316 The white audience for black rap: David Samuels, *New Republic*, 11.11.91, pp. 24–29. See also "Too Cruel, Live," *New Republic*, 7.9–16.90.

316 ". . . a lot of artistic pain . . .": author interview, Gerald Gold, 1.8.91.

317 "centralization" of American culture: Barbara Rose, *Journal of Art*, March 1991. Two years later, little had changed; in the summer of 1993, a group of small-gallery owners, led by Simon Watson, circulated petitions protesting the *Times'* treatment of "contemporary visual culture." The petition chided the paper for focusing on the commercial dealings of a few big names in the art world while ignoring the "thousands of other artists, critics, curators, dealers and patrons" not directly tied to the mainstream or to the art market. At the same time the artists' group Guerrilla Girls published an angry analysis of the *Times'* cultural coverage from a feminist point of view in its bulletin "Hot Flashes."

318 Covering culture in a new way: author interview, Paul Goldberger, 1.9.91.

320 "Too much intellectual arts . . .": memo, 1.6.76.

320 Not a lot of movie news: memo, 3.31.77.

320 Major studios open movies: author interview, A. M. Rosenthal.

321 The Gray Lady goes disco: author interview, Howard Kissel, 8.12.91.

321 Critics chosen for wrong reason: Catledge, p. 238.

322 Agnes De Mille's complaint: the story is told by John E. Booth in *The Critic, Power, and the Performing Arts* (Columbia University Press, 1991), pp. 17–18. It was confirmed by Daniel, author interview, 9.20.91.

323 The Gelb touch: recollections from Times Company Report, Spring, 1990.

324 O'Neill mania: see, for example, *Times* editions of 6.25.88 and 7.30.88.

324–25 The Horowitz count: *Spy*, April 1988, pp. 35–36.

325 Gelb's new job: In the interests of full disclosure, let the record show that after Gelb went to the Times Foundation I wrote a letter to him on behalf of an NYU training program for minority journalists; Gelb agreed to continue the *Times'* support.

325 No Abe 'n' Artie show: author interview, Arthur Gelb, 4.8.91.

326 The Sy Peck years: author interview, Charles Higham, 1.12.90.

326 Waiting for a consensus: author interview, John Leonard, 5.16.89.

327 Playing architectural favorites: Michael Sorkin, *The Exquisite Corpse* (Verso, 1991), p. 102.

329 The *Times'* extraordinary clout: John Booth, pp. 9–10, 17.

329–30 Comparing cultural coverage: David Shaw, *Los Angeles Times*, 11.22.88.

330 Chart comparing three newspapers: I based the chart on internal documents made available to me.

331 "Educating Rita": Charles A. Riley II, *Arts & Antiques*, January 1991, p. 111.

332 Brustein's complaint: Robert Brustein, *New Republic*, 3.16.92. Also author interview, Brustein, 3.17.92.

332 Brooks Atkinson's power: Catledge, p. 238.

333 Rich's potent rave: Thomas Disch, *The Nation*, 1.29.909, pp. 140–41.

333 The *Carrie* story: Thomas Disch, *The Nation*, 6.4.88, p. 804.

335 "The *Times* does not like . . .": Michael Reidel, *TheaterWeek*, 3.23–29.92, pp. 13–14. Reidel was correct: Witchel left the theater-news beat a few months later.

11: TWEEDY BACKWATER: BEHIND THE LINES AT THE BOOK REVIEW

339 Gloria Emerson's complaint: Paul Hendrickson, *Washington Post*, 6.15.91.

342 ". . . the most prestigious place . . .": author interview, Martin Levine, 6.29.89. Tokyo.

343 ". . . a collegial process": author interview, Rebecca Sinkler, 8.26.92.

345 The "nudging" system: I had some firsthand experience several years ago when the *Book Review* asked me to review a book on media coverage of the Vietnam war. The length requested and the leisurely deadline effectively meant that the review would run no more than a half page, and then only when it could be fitted in the schedule. I concluded that the *Times* did not regard it as a "big book." For some books, the *Book Review* wanted to toe the starting line and spring right out ahead of the pack with its review the first week of publication. There was no such pressure for the book I was assigned; like many of the books reviewed in the inside pages of the *Book Review*, it was being noted for "the record," and not as a Publishing Event. The review ran as I wrote it, except for one change the editor requested. A paragraph in my review discussed the author's criticisms of press performance during a specific period of the war; I was asked if the criticism applied to the *Times'* Vietnam correspondents, and if it did not, to make that clear. The evidence was mixed; the editor and I agreed, over the telephone, on some new wording. I didn't think that the change helped the review much; it didn't hurt it, either, and did nothing to alter the positive tone of my review. Still, I felt the active collaboration of the *Book Review* in the final outcome under my name.

347 Made and unmade by the *Times*: Gore Vidal, *New York Review of Books*, 8.18.88, p. 67.

347–48 "Censoring" the assassination books: author interview, John Leonard. 10.29.92.

349 Killing the Exner review: author interview, John Leonard.

350–51 The Shapiro era: author interview, Harvey Shapiro, 1.7.92.

352 Making the *Review* "newsier": author interview, Mitchel Levitas.

352 Sinkler wanted to provoke news: author interview, Rebecca Sinkler, 3.21.86.

354 "the fix was in": David Shaw, *Los Angeles Times*. The three-part Shaw series appeared in the fall of 1985. It was reprinted in the *National Book Critics Circle Journal*, 2.1.86.

355 "We bend over backward. . . ": author interview, Rebecca Sinkler.

357 The Bobby Knight case: author interview, Joan Mellen, 8.15.89, plus correspondence, Mellen to Sinkler, Oct.-Nov. 1988.

357–58 The NFL case: *Moldea v. New York Times Co.*, Case No. 902053. U.S. District Court for the District of Columbia (1990).

358–59 The Ambrose case: correspondence and documents made available to author by George Witte.

360 The Woody Allen case: author interview, Rebecca Sinkler.

361 The Severo case: author interview, Richard Severo, 11.18.89.

362–64 The Blatty Case: see Blatty's account in *Saturday Review*, Jan.-Feb. 1985, p. 29. Also court documents and discovery proceedings, *Blatty v. New York Times Co.* Case No. 82071, California (1984).

364 Blum's weighting advice: David Blum, *New York* magazine, 10.24.88.
365 Al Neuharth and bulk purchases: Paul Farhi, *Washington Post*, 9.6.90.

12: OLD TIMES, NEW TIMES

369 Half agreed, half "thought I made a big mistake. . . ": author interview, Anna Quindlen. Arthur O. Sulzberger, Jr., confirmed the episode, author interview 7.9.92.
371 "How could a Sulzberger not be Jewish?" quoted by Ari Goldman, *The Search for God at Harvard*, (Times Books 1991).
372 Arthur "a feminist": author interview, Anna Quindlen.
373 Arthur and diversity: author interview, Arthur O. Sulzberger, Jr. See also *New York Times*, 6.29.92.
374 "The old guard's attitude:" author interview, Lena Williams, 7.1.92.
375 "news gender gap": Simmons Market Research Bureau, quoted in *Wall Street Journal*, 5.4.92.
375 The 1992 campaign assignments: figures cited by Howell Raines, then *Times* Washington bureau chief, Smithsonian seminar, Washington, D.C., 2.15.92.
375 Decline in net income: *New York Times*, 1991 Annual Report, p. 1.
376 Demingism here to stay: see *Times Talk*, July/August 1991, p. 8.
376 "The food was terrible. . . ": author interview, Grace Glueck.
377 "Who said information . . .": author interview, Jack Rosenthal.
377 Selling off cable: A. O. Sulzberger quoted in *Wall Street Journal*, 10.31.88.
380 Dominant days over: The new thinking was summarized by John O'Brien, deputy general manager of the *Times*, in *Times Talk*, May 1992.
380 "The painful economic truth. . . ": Arthur O. Sulzberger, Jr., staff letter, 4.7.92.
380 Customized electronic news: Anthony Ramirez, *New York Times*, 6.17.92.
381 Changing face of New York: see, for example, Samuel H. Ehrenhalt, regional commissioner, U.S. Bureau of Labor Statistics, quoted in *New York* magazine, 11.17.91, p. 68.
382 Diversity as good business: Author O. Sulzberger, Jr., speech, National Association of Black Journalists, Kansas City, 7.25.91.
382 *Times'* "demand elasticity": author interview, Donald Nizen.
382 "We're not New York's hometown paper. . . ": author interview, A. O. Sulzberger.
383 The demographic *Times*: author interview, Max Frankel, 7.8.92. See also Tom Rosensteil, *Los Angeles Times*, 6.11.91.
383 *Times* postwar vision: author interview, James Goodale.
384 "We're not an easy paper. . . ": author interview, A. O. Sulzberger, 9.10.91.

384 Print is doomed: Robert Coover, *New York Times Book Review*, 6.21.92. See also John Markoff, *New York Times*, 6.28.92.

385 Aliterate Americans: see, for example, Nieman Reports, Autumn 1990, pp. 9–10. Also Knight-Ridder surveys, Christine Urban Associates reports, and the data of the National Opinion Research Center at the University of Chicago.

386 Education needed: Arthur O. Sulzberger, news conference, *Times* boardroom, 1.16.92.

386 Region's slow recovery: author interview, Arthur O. Sulzberger.

387 "*Times*' 1990s labor strategy. . . ": author interviews, Lance Primus, 5.7.92 and 6.23.92.

391 New York our base. . . : Arthur Sulzberger, Jr., news conference, 1.16.92.

392 *USA Today*'s losses. . . : *Newsweek*, 4.27.92, p. 58.

393 Covering the malls: author interview, Dale Fuchs, a reporter in the Boca Raton, Fla., *News*, 1.15.93.

393 Tina Brown's speech: 5.13.91. Brown provided a copy to me.

394 ". . . people will still need. . . ": Arthur O. Sulzberger, Jr., news conference, 1.16.92.

INDEX

Edwin Diamond writes on media for *New York* magazine, where his column has appeared since 1985. He is also a professor in the Department of Journalism at New York University. Throughout his career he has worked for newspapers, wire services, and television stations in Chicago, Washington, Boston, and New York, has been a senior editor at *Newsweek* magazine, and has written ten books on media and politics. He lives in New York.